Freeway

Ausgabe Wirtschaft

Englisch für berufliche Schulen

von
Catherine Küpper
Susanne Neyer
Wolfgang Rosenkranz (Hrsg.)
Graham Tucker

Ernst Klett Verlag
Stuttgart · Leipzig

Freeway Ausgabe Wirtschaft
Englisch für berufliche Schulen

Herausgeber: Wolfgang Rosenkranz

Autoren: Catherine Küpper, Susanne Neyer, Wolfgang Rosenkranz, Graham Tucker

Berater: Veit Kibele, Christian Rode, Dagmar Wagner

Werkübersicht:
Schülerbuch, 978-3-12-800031-2
Lehrerhandbuch, mit Lehrer-Service-DVD-ROM und 2 Audio-CDs, 978-3-12-800032-9
Workbook mit 1 Audio-CD-ROM, 978-3-12-800033-6
Vokabellernheft 978-3-12-800045-9
Schülerpaket: Workbook und Vokabellernheft, 978-3-12-800049-7
Freeway Online-Ergänzungen unter www.klett.de/online

1. Auflage 1   5 4 3 2 1 | 15 14 13 12 11

Alle Drucke dieser Auflage sind unverändert und können im Unterricht nebeneinander verwendet werden. Die letzte Zahl bezeichnet das Jahr des Druckes.

Das Werk und seine Teile sind urheberrechtlich geschützt. Jede Nutzung in anderen als den gesetzlich zugelassenen Fällen bedarf der vorherigen schriftlichen Einwilligung des Verlages. Hinweis §52 a UrhG: Weder das Werk noch seine Teile dürfen ohne eine solche Einwilligung eingescannt und in ein Netzwerk eingestellt werden. Dies gilt auch für Intranets von Schulen und sonstigen Bildungseinrichtungen. Fotomechanische oder andere Wiedergabeverfahren nur mit Genehmigung des Verlages.

Auf verschiedenen Seiten dieses Heftes befinden sich Verweise (Links) auf Internet-Adressen. Haftungshinweis: Trotz sorgfältiger inhaltlicher Kontrolle wird die Haftung für die Inhalte der externen Seiten ausgeschlossen. Für den Inhalt dieser externen Seiten sind ausschließlich die Betreiber verantwortlich. Sollten Sie daher auf kostenpflichtige, illegale oder anstößige Inhalte treffen, so bedauern wir dies ausdrücklich und bitten Sie, uns umgehend per E-Mail davon in Kenntnis zu setzen, damit beim Nachdruck der Verweis gelöscht wird.

© Ernst Klett Verlag GmbH, Stuttgart 2011. Alle Rechte vorbehalten. www.klett.de

Projektleitung: Matthias Rupp
Redaktion: Volker Wendland
Herstellung: Angelika Lindner

Gestaltung: B2 Büro für Gestaltung, Andreas Staiger, Stuttgart
Umschlaggestaltung: ya:design, Roman Triebelhorn, Stuttgart
Illustrationen: Jeonsook Lee, Köln; Andreas Staiger, Susanne Kunz, Stuttgart
Satz: Satzkiste, Stuttgart; B2 Büro für Gestaltung, Andreas Staiger, Susanne Kunz, Stuttgart
Reproduktion: Meyle + Müller Medien-Management, Pforzheim
Druck: Druckhaus Götz GmbH, Ludwigsburg

Printed in Germany
ISBN 978-3-12-800031-2

Vorwort

Das neue *Freeway – Ausgabe Wirtschaft* deckt die neuesten Lehrpläne und die neuen Prüfungsformate aller Bundesländer ab und führt zielsicher zur Fachhochschulreife-Prüfung an Fach- und Berufsoberschulen, Höheren Berufsfachschulen und Fachschulen. Es orientiert sich an den fremdsprachlichen Kompetenzen des Europäischen Referenzrahmens (Niveau B1/B2).

Die wichtigsten Neuerungen auf einen Blick:
- durchgehend neue Texte und neue Aufgaben
- erweiterter „Practice"-Teil mit interaktiven und produktiven Aufgaben, insbesondere im Bereich Wirtschaft
- durchgehend verstärkte Förderung der kommunikativen Kompetenzen – auch in den Übungen zur Grammatik
- systematische Schulung der verschiedenen Kompetenzen von der ersten Unit an („Training skills – How to …")
- Einbindung abwechslungsreicher Mediationsaufgaben
- Förderung des eigenverantwortlichen Lernens durch ausführliche deutschsprachige Anleitungen und Übersichten zur Schulung der Kompetenzen im Anhang („Skills files") mit durchgehenden Verweisen im Lehrbuch
- verstärktes interkulturelles Lernen sowie Einbindung der Berufswelt am Beispiel eines Auslandspraktikums
- „Video lounge", u. a. mit Filmen der **BBC Motion Gallery** zur Förderung des Seh-Hör-Verstehens

Bewährtes bleibt erhalten:
- systematischer Aufbau der Units nach dem bewährten Doppelseitenprinzip

Unitteil	Überschrift	Inhalte
A	Getting started	nach einem bildgesteuerten Einstieg erste inhaltliche Auseinandersetzung mit dem Thema
B	Language	systematische Übung der Grammatikschwerpunkte – im *Basic course* die Wiederholung der grundlegenden *tenses*, im *Advanced course* komplexere Formen, wie z. B. *passive voice*, *conditional* oder *reported speech*
C	Reading	intensive Textarbeit zur gezielten Vorbereitung auf die schriftliche Abschlussprüfung
D	Practice	handlungsorientierte interaktive und produktive Aufgaben (u. a. Rollenspiele); Förderung des Hörverständnisses

- flexible Handhabung: Einzelne Unitteile (z. B. „Language") können entfallen oder in die individuelle (häusliche) Arbeit verlagert werden.
- klare grammatikalische Strukturierung und bewährte Grammatik-Progression
- benutzerfreundliche Grammatikübersicht im Anhang
- viele interaktive und produktive Aufgaben zur Bürokommunikation
- umfangreiche Einführung in die englische Handelskorrespondenz
- systematische und intensive Prüfungsvorbereitung durch „Training skills" und eine große Anzahl von „Exam preparation units"

Weitere Bestandteile des Lehrwerks:

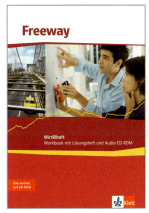 

- Workbook mit Audio-CD-ROM und Prüfungsvorbereitung
- Vocabulary notebook: Übungen zum thematischen Aufbauwortschatz
- Lehrerhandbuch mit den Audio-CDs und einer Lehrer-Service-DVD-ROM: u. a. mit Hinweisen zur Differenzierung

Wir wünschen Ihnen viel Spaß und Erfolg bei der Arbeit mit *Freeway – Ausgabe Wirtschaft*.

Inhaltsverzeichnis

Basic course

1 Preparing for the world of work   8

TOPICS: blogs of young Europeans, colleges and jobs, work placements
GRAMMAR: Present simple, Present continuous 10
TRAINING SKILLS: How to describe pictures . 14

2 Getting a job   16

TOPICS: a company success story, applications, job interviews
TRAINING SKILLS: How to describe statistics   17
GRAMMAR: Past simple, Present perfect simple, Present perfect continuous 18
VIDEO LOUNGE 1:
Applying for a job placement 23

3 Marketing and advertising   24

TOPICS: young people's attitudes to branded products, protecting young consumers, radio and TV commercials, analyzing advertisements
GRAMMAR: Past simple, Past perfect, Past continuous 26
TRAINING SKILLS: How to do a role play .. 29

4 Media in our lives   32

TOPICS: young people and media consumption, advantages and dangers of computers and the Internet, Big Brother is watching you
GRAMMAR: Will-future, Future with 'going to'; Adjectives, Adverbs 34
TRAINING SKILLS: How to write a composition/comment (I) 36
TRAINING SKILLS: How to describe a cartoon   39

5 Social and economic changes   40

TOPICS: social and economic problems of young people, the Internet generation, industrial revolutions
GRAMMAR: Relative clauses, Modal auxiliaries 42
TRAINING SKILLS: How to anticipate, skim and scan 44
VIDEO LOUNGE 2: Manufacturing 46

Inhaltsverzeichnis

Advanced course

6 Ecology and economy 48

TOPICS: climate change, food miles, consuming the world, sustainable schools
GRAMMAR: Reported speech 50
TRAINING SKILLS: How to work with a dictionary 53

7 Man and technology 56

TOPICS: wind energy and other sources of energy, green technology and economic growth, office technology
VIDEO LOUNGE 3: Ecology and/or economy? 56
GRAMMAR: Passive voice 58
TRAINING SKILLS: How to write a composition/comment (II) 61

8 The tourist industry 64

TOPICS: developments in the tourist industry, mass tourism and sustainable tourism, developing an area in the Third World
VIDEO LOUNGE 4: Travel and tourism 64
GRAMMAR: Conditionals/If-clauses 66
TRAINING SKILLS: How to answer questions on a text 69

9 Globalisation and multiculturalism 72

TOPICS: young people and globalisation, multicultural Britain, keeping trade fair
GRAMMAR: Infinitive, Gerund 74
TRAINING SKILLS: How to do multiple choice exercises 77

10 International politics 80

TOPICS: the United Nations, a poor country in the Third World (Zimbabwe), the political systems of the USA, Britain and the European Union
GRAMMAR: Present participle, Past participle 82
VIDEO LOUNGE 5: American immigration .. 84
TRAINING SKILLS: How to do mediation exercises 85

Inhaltsverzeichnis

Cross-cultural business communication

11 Living and working in Britain — 88
   VIDEO LOUNGE 6: A job placement at reception 90

12 Meeting people — 92

13 Working in an office — 96

14 Different countries, different cultures — 100

International business correspondence

15 Enquiries — 104

16 Offers — 112

17 Orders — 120

18 Complaints — 128

19 Reminders — 136

Exam Preparation

20 Youth unemployment — 144
   TOPICS: Difficulties in finding jobs, job advertisements, writing a letter of application

21 New Jobs — 148
   TOPICS: Development of a rundown area, the future of jobs, writing an enquiry

22 Modern technology — 152
   TOPICS: Development of Google, robots, writing an offer

23 Plastic money for young people — 156
   TOPICS: Credit cards, Internet shopping, writing an order

24 Transport and ecology — 160
   TOPICS: Online supermarket, planning a business trip, writing a complaint

25 Globalisation and fair trade — 164
   TOPICS: Ecological and social developments in trade, advertisements and sales figures, writing a reminder

Anhang

Video lounge 168
Role cards 172
Skills files 176
Grammar files 229
Unit vocabulary 248
Alphabetical vocabulary 292
Basic vocabulary 303
Incoterms 2010 311

Online-Links unter www.klett.de

800031-0030: der alphabetische Wortschatz zum Schülerbuch (deutsch-englisch) einschließlich Grundwortschatz

800031-0040: die berufsspezifischen Vokabeln zu den Bereichen Wirtschaft, Technik und Sozialwesen

Der jeweilige **Unit Online-Link**: die thematischen Wortfelder im MP3-Format

Symbole

Verwendete Symbole

⊙ A1.1	Hörtexte auf der Schüler-CD im Workbook und den Lehrer-Audio-CDs, inkl. Tracknummer (A1.1 = Audio-CD 1, Track 1)
‹R›	Verweis auf eine Kompetenz, die in der Aufgabe besonders geübt wird: P = Produktion; R = Rezeption; I = Interaktion; M = Mediation.
📖	Wortschatz-Aufgabe
👥	Partnerarbeit
👥👥	Gruppenarbeit
💻	weiterführende Aufgabe im Internet bzw. Verweis auf nützliche Stichwörter für eine Internetrecherche
►SF9	Verweis auf die entsprechenden Fertigkeiten im Anhang; SF = Skills file
►GF3	Verweis auf die entsprechende Grammatik-Information im Anhang; GF = Grammar file
Video lounge ▶ 1	Videos, u.a. der **BBC Motion Gallery** auf der Lehrer-Service-DVD-ROM; Aufgaben zur Video lounge im Anhang
Online-Link 800031-0001	Unter www.klett.de/online stehen Zusatzmaterialien zum Download bereit.
Training skills	Lern- und Arbeitstechniken
Facts	Hintergrundinformationen
Language	nützliche Redewendungen
Grammar	Zusammenfassung der wichtigsten Grammatik-Themen

Textquellenverzeichnis   **S. 32** people-press.org, Dezember 2008, © (date and title) by The Pew Research Center For the People & the Press; **S. 41** Two Caravans by Marina Lewycka, London: Penguin / Fig Tree, 2007, page 242; **S. 41** Slam by Nick Hornby, London: Penguin, 2008, page 92; **S. 41** Bend it like Beckham by Narinder Dhami, Stuttgart: Ernst Klett Verlag, 2003, page 25; **S. 52** www.climatechoices.org.uk; **S. 70** www.statistik.at, Statistik Austria: Urlaubs- und Geschäftsreisen, Erstellt am 12.2.2009; **S. 150** www.wko.at, EU Commission, EUROSTAT, OECD, Februar 2010; **S. 157** www.marketingcharts.com, ©2010 Experian Information Solutions, Inc. All rights reserved; **S. 166** www.fairtrade.org.uk

Unit 1
Preparing for the world of work

A Getting started: www.thisisme.uk

‹P› **Before reading**

a) Look at the photos above. What is your first impression of the young people? What do you think they are interested in?

‹R› **Understanding the text**

b) Read the personal blogs of these young people on page 9. Then match the photos to the blogs.

c) Which of the following statements about the young people are true and which are false? Correct the false statements.

1. The young people are all college students.
2. Julie's hobby is going out with friends.
3. Julie earns money at a supermarket to pay for her own flat.
4. Derek is studying Information and Communication Technology.
5. Derek often meets his friends.
6. Luca is currently living in Switzerland.
7. Luca wants to work in marketing.
8. Linda wants to get into contact with people from other countries.
9. Linda teaches languages at college.

d) Copy the table below into your exercise book. Write down what the young people usually do and what they are currently doing.

What he/she usually does	What he/she is currently doing
Example: Julie usually …	She is currently …
…	…

8 | Basic course　　　　　　Advanced course　　　　　　Cross-cultural communication

A Getting started | Preparing for the world of work 1

A1.1

A Hello! I'm Julie from Birmingham in England. I'm 17 years old and I live at home with my mum and my younger brother. At the moment I'm doing a National Diploma in business studies at Birmingham
5 College. When I'm not studying at college I have a part-time job at a clothes shop. I work there twice a week because I need the money to buy things and to go to clubs with my friends.

B Hello there! I'm Derek. I'm 18 years old and I
10 live in a small flat in Cork in Ireland. I want to become an ICT shop assistant. That's why I'm attending an ICT course at Cork College at the moment. It's a two-year course. I have a really interesting part-time job in a computer store just a few minutes from where I live. I
15 work there every day after college so I don't have much time to see my friends.

C Hi there! My name is Luca from Geneva in Switzerland. I'm 19 and I'm currently living and working full-time in London where I hope to achieve my dream and find a job in marketing. I was happy to 20 get the chance of doing a placement with one of the leading advertising agencies in London. Most of the time I do interviews in the streets for our market research department. I really love my work!

D Hi! I'm Linda. I'm 19 and I'm from Bielefeld in 25 Germany. I go to college. At the moment I'm studying languages there. I want to become a foreign language assistant at a big international company in Germany. I often spend my holidays in Britain, France or Spain in order to improve my language skills. I'm interested in 30 finding friends all over the world.

(291 words)

e) Sie haben im Internet Julies Blog gelesen und erzählen Ihrer Freundin auf Deutsch, was Sie über Julie wissen.
► SF22 Mediation/translation

f) Match the words from the text on the left with their definitions.

1. part-time job (line 6)	a) a plan of study which usually ends with an exam
2. twice (line 6)	b) work which you do for only some of the day or the week
3. club (line 8)	c) a large shop where you can buy many different types of goods
4. course (line 12)	d) at the present time, at the moment, now
5. store (line 14)	e) two times
6. currently (line 18)	f) reach an aim, especially after a lot of work
7. achieve (line 19)	g) part of a company
8. department (line 24)	h) people meet there to do things together in their free time

After reading

g) Interview a partner. Find out the following information about him/her and write it down. Then present your partner to your class. You can use the expressions in the box for the presentation.

Interview
- name • age • family • home town • interests • likes and dislikes
- personality • favourite music • future plans

h) Write your own personal blog for the social networking website, www.thisisme.uk.

Language
- I would like to introduce …
- He/She is …
- He/She has …
- He/She comes from …
- He/She lives in …
- In his/her free time …
- He/She likes/enjoys/loves/can't stand …
- He/She plans to …

International business correspondence | Exam preparation | 9

1 Preparing for the world of work

B Language

1 College and work ▶ GF16 Present simple

http://www.newcastle-college.uk/international

Newcastle College

Home | School leavers | Adults and Part-time | **International**

What you must study on the International Diploma Course:
1. English
2. second language (French or German)
3. History or Geography
4. Science (Biology and Physics)
5. Mathematics
6. Information technology

How we test you: four projects, class presentations, essays (at the end of term), work placements (office, hospital or factory), tests (every 3 months) and six final examinations (at the end of the second year).

After the course: go to university, start a job training programme, get a good job – anywhere in Europe

a) Work in pairs. One of you is a student at Newcastle College who is on the International Diploma course. The other person uses the prompts below to ask questions. The answers are given in the website.

Example: Which second language – learn?
Student A: Which second language do you learn on the course?
Student B: I learn French on the course.

1. Which science subjects – study?
2. How many projects – carry out?
3. How often – take – tests?
4. When – hand in – essays?
5. Where – do – your work placement?
6. When – sit – final exams?
7. How many exams – do?
8. What – plan to do after the course?
9. What kind of job – want to have later?

Grammar

Present simple
Example: Polly goes to college by bus.
Bei regelmäßigen oder wiederholten Handlungen

Present continuous
Example: Now Polly is talking to her teacher.
Bei Handlungen, die im Augenblick oder vorübergehend stattfinden

▶ GF16 Present simple
▶ GF17 Present continuous

b) Now find another partner. He/she uses the prompts in exercise a) to ask questions about the student from Newcastle.

2 In the college

Describe what the students are doing in the photos.
▶ GF17 Present continuous

Example: Tom is reading a newspaper.

1 Tom

2 Sue and Dave

3 Alice and Karen

4 Sarah

5 Lisa

Basic course | Advanced course | Cross-cultural communication

3 A work placement

- Wayne is a student at Newcastle College. At the moment he is doing a work placement at Carrick's, a local factory.

Compare Wayne's normal day at college with what he is doing today. Make complete sentences and use as many of the tense markers in the box below as possible.

Example: Wayne usually goes to college by bus, but today he's driving his mum's car to work.

A normal day at college	Today
1. go to college by bus	– drive his mum's car to work
2. start college at half past nine	– begin work in the factory
3. have English till half past eleven	– work on a machine
4. have an hour's break at lunchtime	– have half an hour for his lunch
5. eat lunch in college with his classmates	– have lunch with the other workers
6. work in the library till three o'clock	– help one worker with a project
7. have a Mathematics course till five o'clock	– clean a machine for another worker
8. go home by bus	– drive home
9. do homework at eight o'clock	– go to bed early

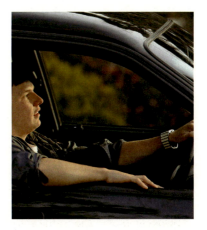

Tense markers

Present simple		Present continuous	
usually	every day	at the moment	this evening
normally	in the evenings	this morning	right now
every morning	every afternoon	currently	today

‹M/I› ## 4 A phone call

- Work in pairs. ▶ SF 22 Mediation/translation

Sie interessieren sich für einen International Diploma Course und wollen mehr über die Praktika wissen, die man dabei ableisten muss. Sie telefonieren mit einer englischen Studentin und stellen ihr Fragen zum Praktikum.

Sie wollen wissen:
1. wo sie das Praktikum jetzt durchführt
2. wie viele Stunden sie normalerweise pro Woche arbeitet
3. was sie in ihrem Praktikum im Augenblick macht
4. wie viel Geld sie normalerweise bekommt
5. ob sie dieses Praktikum genießt.

‹P› ## 5 An e-mail to a friend

- You are a student at Newcastle College and are currently doing an International Diploma Course. You want to tell an English-speaking friend about it. Write an e-mail to him/her in about 100 words.
  ▶ SF 25 Personal letters and e-mails

1 Preparing for the world of work

C Reading: Why we are here

A1.2 http://www.thisisme.uk

HOME **PHOTOS**

"For me life in England is wonderful because you meet so many people of different nationalities here. Where I come from it is completely different. My home town in Germany is very small and it certainly doesn't have a cosmopolitan atmosphere like London. I go to a college of further education here in London where I am currently doing a course in business studies. I'm staying at my aunt's house in Croydon, so life is not too expensive here. On Saturdays and Sundays I work in a supermarket. It's a very good way to meet many different people. My English is much better now, so I can communicate more easily. In my free time I also like to go out with my English friends and practise my English. I don't really know what to do after the course at college. After my exams maybe I can start a job training programme in Germany."

Catherine, 20, from Germany, lives in London (Croydon).

A1.2 http://www.thisisme.uk

HOME **PHOTOS**

"I come from a village near Prague but currently I am living and working in Edinburgh in Scotland. It is a big change for me. I like the multicultural feeling of Edinburgh and I have friends from many different countries. But I want to save as much money as I can during my stay here in Britain and so I have two jobs. Every day I work as a waiter in a restaurant at lunchtime and in the evening, and as a paperboy early in the morning. This gives me enough money to live on and to save, but it also means I am at work most of the time. I have a nice boss at the restaurant and the chef there makes very good meals. The rest of the staff is friendly, too, but I don't have much time to socialize. I think after about two years in Edinburgh I want to go home. I think it is hard to settle here in Scotland. Although my English is much better now than at the beginning I still find it difficult to understand the Scots. I want to start a better life in the Czech Republic. Maybe I can train to be a hotel or restaurant manager."

(360 words)

Jakub, 19, from the Czech Republic, lives in Edinburgh.

12 | Basic course | Advanced course | Cross-cultural communication

C Reading | **Preparing for the world of work** **1**

Understanding the text

a) Find the most suitable option. Only one option is true.

▶ **SF12 Multiple choice exercises**

1. Both of the young people come from …
   a) Eastern Europe.
   b) small towns in Europe.
   c) large towns in Europe.
   d) European capital cities.

2. They both like to live in Britain because they …
   a) can go to a good college there.
   b) are with people from their own countries.
   c) meet people from all over the world.
   d) like English food.

3. To earn money they both …
   a) have two part-time jobs.
   b) have more than one job.
   c) work on Sundays.
   d) work in shops.

4. They both want to go back to their home countries because they …
   a) don't like the people in Britain.
   b) don't speak English well enough.
   c) want to start job training courses.
   d) want to study at university there.

b) Answer the following questions in complete sentences.

1. What is Catherine studying at the moment?
2. How does she get to meet interesting people?
3. How is Jakub's English?
4. Why doesn't he have much time to socialize?

After reading

c) Explain the jobs in the box using the words on the right.

Example: A salesperson is a person who sells goods in a shop.

salesperson		sell	buy	goods in a shop	help	in a doctor's practice

bank employee
doctor's assistant
industrial manager
import merchant
assistant tax consultant
IT management assistant
dental assistant

assist | people on their money | advise | in the computer business

in industrial companies | work | the dentist with their work

goods in foreign countries | people to save taxes

‹I› **d)** A British college's online magazine wants to do an article about young Europeans who live in Britain. The magazine sends its student journalists to interview some young people who have come to Britain.

Work in pairs. Prepare the interview and then act it out.
Student A is a student journalist. Use role card A to find out about the young European.
Student B is a young European who answers the journalist's questions. See role card B on page 172.

‹P› **e)** Write an article about young Europeans in Britain for the online magazine in about 100 words.

> **Role card A**
>
> **A student journalist**
>
> Find out about the young European.
> his/her name • country of origin • reasons for coming to Britain • workplace • free time • plans for the future

| International business correspondence | Exam preparation | 13 |

1 Preparing for the world of work

D Practice

Training skills – How to describe pictures

‹R› **1 A part-time job** ► SF 26 Describing illustrations and photographs

a) Look at photo number 1 and choose the most suitable option. Only one option is true.

1. What type of picture is it?
   a) cartoon
   b) black-and-white photo
   c) colour photo

2. What kind of situation can you see?
   a) serving a customer
   b) sales talk
   c) interview

3. What is the location?
   a) supermarket
   b) restaurant
   c) kitchen

4. Who do you see in the picture?
   a) a young woman, wearing a white T-shirt and blue jeans
   b) a young woman, wearing a red shirt and white trousers
   c) a young woman, wearing a blue top and a black skirt

5. What is the person doing?
   a) watching TV
   b) serving salad
   c) talking to a friend

6. Where exactly is the person in the picture?
   a) on the right-hand side in the background
   b) on the left-hand side in the background
   c) on the left-hand side in the foreground

7. How can you describe the atmosphere in the picture?
   a) awful
   b) friendly
   c) quiet

8. Why does it have this kind of atmosphere?
   a) because the people are smiling
   b) because the people are screaming
   c) because the people are watching TV

1

2

b) Describe the first photo using the answers from exercise a).

c) Describe the second photo on your own.

‹R› While listening

A1.3 d) Listen to Sarah Smith. She is talking about her part-time job. Then give short answers to the following questions. ► SF 14 Short answer questions

1. Where does Sarah work?
2. How much money does she earn?
3. What does she like best about the part-time job?

e) Listen to the CD again and complete the following sentences.

1. Sarah works on Fridays, Saturdays and …
2. Sarah has a part-time job because she wants to finance …
3. Sarah's work clothes consist of …
4. Most guests arrive at …
5. Sarah's favourite bands play …
6. Sarah does not like …

14 | Basic course | Advanced course | Cross-cultural communication

D Practice | **Preparing for the world of work 1**

‹P› **2 Working after college**

a) Look at the photos. Match them with the job activities in the box below.

• receive delivery • order goods • store goods • fill shelves in the shop • scan goods and receive money • advise customers

b) Put the activities in the correct order.

Example: 1. "order goods"

c) Describe the assistants' activities in complete sentences. The following words can help you.

• office • cash desk • storage room • incoming goods department

Example: When stocks are low one of the assistants orders new goods from their office. The next day …

| International business correspondence | Exam preparation | 15

Unit 2
Getting a job

A Getting started

1 MTC – A successful company

Before reading

a) Match the people in the photos with the statements below.

| A Hi. I'm Suzy Wong. I'm in the Sales Department at MTC. | B Hello. My name's Peter Turner. I work in the IT Department. | C I'm Jack O'Toole. I'm head of the Personnel Department. | D Hello, I'm Debbie, Debbie King. I'm in Manufacturing at MTC. | E I'm Ray Austen. I work in Research and Development. |

b) Match the activities with the statements. Two activities do not match.

1. look after the computer systems
2. operate machines
3. buy raw materials
4. manage the staff
5. manage the money that the company makes
6. find and test recipes for new products
7. sell the company's products

Understanding the text

‹R› c) Put the following events in the order they appear in the text on page 17.

1. find a successful recipe
2. sell drinks in cans
3. produce ready-to-eat meals
4. open their first factory
5. begin with the production of pet food
6. earn a million pounds for the first time
7. go to the USA
8. make cakes and sweets at home

‹P› d) Use the phrases in c) to give a summary of the development of MTC.

16 | Basic course | Advanced course | Cross-cultural communication

A Getting started | Getting a job **2**

A1.4

http://www.mtc.com/our_story

NEWS | BRANDS | CAREERS | **OUR STORY** | CONTACT

A MTC is one of the largest family-owned companies producing food, drinks, sweets and pet food in the world with more than 100 manufacturing units. Its headquarters is in England but it operates in about 120 countries.

5 **B** It all started in 1905 when Martha Trick sold her home-made cakes and sweets in York, England. She was so
10 successful that her husband George and all the family had to help her. A few years later Martha developed the
15 recipe for 'Trix', a new brand of sweets.

George and Martha Trick (1905)

This was a huge success and Martha and George soon opened their first factory, which still exists today. Many other products followed.

C In the 1920s they made their first million and the company, MTC (short for Martha Trick's Confectionery) has been growing ever since. In 1935 Martha's son Terence bought the Caddogg pet food company and started to sell pet food in cans. A year later Martha's other son Woody went to America with £50,000 in his pocket and opened a factory in Chicago.

D After World War II MTC began to produce canned drinks and frozen food. In the last few years new MTC boss and Martha's great-granddaughter, Sally Trick, has developed other business fields: MTC is now one of the biggest producers of convenience food worldwide. (215 words)

After reading

e) Which of the words below are used with 'make', which are used with 'do'?

Example: to make millions

- **millions** • products • business • money • test • a difference
- a choice • a job • friends • a favour • good • a speech
- a mistake • wrong

f) Make meaningful sentences with the expressions from exercise e).

Example: MTC <u>has made millions</u> by selling food and drinks.

Training skills – How to describe statistics

‹P› **2 The development at MTC**

a) Complete the description of chart 1 using the words below.
▶ SF 28 Describing diagrams

- sharply • slowly • rose
- fell • remained

b) Describe the development of profits at MTC (see chart 2) in the same way.

Chart 1 shows the changes in the number of employees at MTC from 1905 until 2010. In the beginning the number of employees was very small. It grew [**1**] but steadily until 1926. In the following years the number [**2**] at about the same level. However, from 1947 to 1989 the number of employees [**3**] [**4**] to about 20,000. From 1989 to 2010 the number [**5**] slowly for the first time.

Chart 1: MTC employees (1905–2010)
Number of employees

Chart 2: Profits at MTC (1905–2010)
Profits in millions of pounds

International business correspondence | Exam preparation | 17

2 Getting a job

B Language

1 The rise of Britain's biggest supermarket

a) Complete the information about Tesco using the past tense.

In 1919 Jack Cohen started to sell food at a market in the East End of London. He made a profit of £1 on his first day! The name Tesco [**1. come**] to life five years later when Mr Cohen [**2. buy**] tea from Mr T. E. Stockwell and Mr Cohen [**3. use**] the first letters of their names. In 1929 he [**4. open**] the first store in North London. More and more stores [**5. follow**]. The company [**6. continue**] to grow in the 1930s when Mr Cohen [**7. build**] large office buildings and a warehouse. In the 1950s Tesco [**8. expand**] quickly by buying other stores, and selling more and more products. Tesco Leicester [**9. enter**] the *Guinness Book of Records* in 1961 as the largest store in Europe. Seven years later Tesco [**10. develop**] its first 'superstore'. At that time supermarkets [**11. change**] the way in which people [**12. shop**]. In 1974 Tesco [**13. begin**] to sell petrol and [**14. become**] the UK's largest independent petrol dealer. In 1995 the company [**15. manage**] to become the largest food retailer in the UK. A year later Tesco [**16. introduce**] its first 24-hour store. In 2000 Tesco.com [**17. enter**] the online shopping market.

b) Complete the following information about Tesco in the same way as in the example. Use negative forms.

Example: On his first day Mr Cohen made a <u>small</u> profit. He did not make a <u>big</u> profit.

1. Mr Cohen bought tea from Mr Stockwell. He did not …
2. He used the first letters of their names. He …
3. In 1929 Mr Cohen opened his first store in North London.
4. Tesco built large office buildings in the 1930s.
5. In the 1950s the company expanded quickly.
6. In 1961 Tesco Leicester became the largest store in Europe.
7. In 1995 the company became the largest food retailer in the UK.

c) Make up questions about the words below. Ask a classmate to answer them. The answers are in the text in a).

Example:
Student A: How much profit did Jack Cohen make on his first day?
Student B: He made a profit of £1.

- **£1** • tea • North London • in 1961 • the first 'superstore'
- petrol • in 2000

Grammar

Past simple
Example: Sue lived in Glasgow from 2002 to 2008.
Bei Handlungen zu einem bestimmten Zeitpunkt oder in einem abgeschlossenen Zeitraum in der Vergangenheit

Present perfect simple
Example: Sue has lived in Leeds since 2008.
Mit einem Zeitraum, der noch andauert und mit bestimmten Zeitbestimmungen und Adverbien

▶ GF 18 Past simple
▶ GF 20 Present perfect simple

2 Big supermarkets, small supermarkets

Describe what has happened to Tesco and Royce & Sons in the last few years. ▶ GF 20 Present perfect simple

Example: Tesco has been in North London for many years. Royce & Sons have been in North London since 2005.

		Tesco	Royce & Sons
1.	be in North London	for many years	since 2005
2.	open	a lot of supermarkets up to now	only two little shops so far
3.	make a profit	always	only once
4.	start business in the USA	just	not yet
5.	break a record	already	never

18 | Basic course | Advanced course | Cross-cultural communication

B Language | Getting a job **2**

‹I› **3 A job for you?**

a) Linda Smith has applied for a job in a big supermarket. In an interview she has to talk about her life and career. In pairs, take her role, using the card on page 172 and the role of the interviewer and prepare the interview.

> **Role card A**
>
> **Interviewer**
> 1. When / born?
>   **Example:** When were you born, Ms Smith?
> 2. When / live / in Exeter?
> 3. How long / live / in London?
> 4. When / go to college?
> 5. What / do / then?
> 6. How long / be / a shop assistant at Morrisey's?
> 7. What / do / in your free time / when / young?
> 8. When / start / learning German?
> 9. How long / be interested / working with people?
> 10. When / hear / about the job advertisement?

b) Work in pairs and prepare a talk about yourselves. Work with a classmate and ask and answer questions about the following:

- date of birth • school • college • exams • address
- trips abroad • fluency in English • work experience • hobbies

‹I› **4 How long or how many?**

■ Work in pairs. Use the verbs in brackets to ask and answer questions.
▶ **GF 21 Present perfect continuous**

1. Daniel Jones got a job with a big supermarket chain a year ago. His job has been to work on two projects so far. [**work**]
   Example:
   Questions: How long <u>has</u> Daniel <u>been working</u> for the supermarket?
        – How many projects <u>has</u> he <u>worked</u> on?
   Answers: He has been working for the supermarket for a year.
        – He has worked on two projects.
2. Daniel's secretary Jane began to type letters an hour ago. Six letters are complete now. [**type**]
3. At the moment Larry, one of the shop assistants, is serving his 45th customer. He started work three hours ago. [**serve**]
4. Trudy's job is to look after the customers' children. Today she started at eight o'clock in the morning. She has just said hello to the 20th child. [**look after**]
5. The baker in the supermarket began work eight hours ago. Now there are five hundred fresh loaves of bread. [**make**]
6. Lucy is just finishing the third and last page of her homework. She sat down at her desk two hours ago. [**do**]

‹P› **5 The story of ???**

a) Find information about the development of an interesting company or organization on the Internet. Take notes. Use your notes to write about the company in about 100 words.

b) Read the text to the class but do not mention the name of the company or organization. The rest of the class have to find out the name.

> **Grammar**
>
> **Present perfect simple**
> **Example:** John has repaired the car.
> *Bei Handlungen in der Vergangenheit ohne Zeitangabe, das Ergebnis ist wichtig*
>
> **Present perfect continuous**
> **Example:** Alex has been repairing his car for two hours.
> *Bei Handlungen, die in der Vergangenheit begonnen haben und noch andauern*
>
> ▶ **GF 20 Present perfect simple**
> ▶ **GF 21 Present perfect continuous**

> **Key Words**
>
> - company • development
> - history • organization
> Or just use the name of the company that you are interested in.

| International business correspondence | Exam preparation | **19**

2 Getting a job

C Reading: Applications

Before reading

a) You need three things for a written job application. Find their names using the following words.

- application • certificates • copies • curriculum • letter • of
- of • vitae

Understanding the texts

b) Match the terms *job advertisement*, *curriculum vitae* and *letter of application* to the texts A, B and C.

c) Complete the sentences using the most suitable option according to the texts. Only one option is true.

1. The company is looking for somebody who …
   a) likes being with people.
   b) likes working alone.
   c) wants to work there permanently.
   d) likes working with computers.

2. One essential qualification is to …
   a) be able to deal with other people.
   b) speak Russian fluently.
   c) be a quick worker.
   d) be a smoker.

3. Sarah wants to study in …
   a) New Zealand.
   b) Mexico.
   c) Britain.
   d) Australia.

4. Sarah is …
   a) a tolerant person.
   b) an ignorant person.
   c) an arrogant person.
   d) a difficult person.

5. Sarah likes playing …
   a) football.
   b) table tennis.
   c) tennis.
   d) golf.

6. Sarah already has some experience …
   a) working in another country.
   b) leading people.
   c) working in a bar.
   d) working in England.

After reading

d) Would you invite Sarah for an interview? Why or why not?

e) Would you apply for a placement in an international company? Why or why not?

f) Describe your present and future qualifications, and say what kind of job or work placement you would like to apply for.

A **Looking for a WORK PLACEMENT in an international company?**

You like working with people from different countries? You speak different languages? Then we look forward to receiving your application.
During your placement you will get to know different departments
5 such as manufacturing, accountancy, export, and marketing.

Essential requirements:
– You must speak English and German fluently.
– You must be able to work in a team.
– You must have basic computer skills.

10 We offer work placements for one year. If you are interested, please send your letter of application and CV to:
MTC, Ms Joanne Kingsley, Hallfield Road, York YO31 7XG

(116 words)

---

20 | Basic course | Advanced course | Cross-cultural communication

C Reading | Getting a job 2

B

Sarah Fischer
Hilgenberg 28
46045 Oberhausen
Mobile: 0171 17149378
sarah.fischer@mynewjob.de

20 September 20…

MTC
Ms. Joanne Kingsley
Hallfield Road
York YO31 7XG
Great Britain

Dear Ms Kingsley

With reference to the online advert on your homepage, I would like to apply for a work placement at your company. I am German and 18 years old.

I am an open-minded person and am very interested in working in new areas. I have already gathered some experience in working in the retail trade. I have had a part-time job at Super 2000 in Oberhausen for two years now. I work in shelf control and at the checkout.

My present aim is to get to know as much as possible about work in an international company as my long-term aim is to work in the management of such a firm. In order to achieve this aim I want to study at the International Business School (IBS) in Sunderland (GB).

Your company is my first choice because of its size and its reputation. I believe the work placement would be a very interesting and rewarding experience for me.

I enclose my CV and copies of certificates.

I look forward to hearing from you.

Yours sincerely

Sarah Fischer

Encls.

(199 words)

C

Sarah Fischer
Hilgenberg 28
46045 Oberhausen
Mobile: 0171 17149378
sarah.fischer@mynewjob.de

Personal Statement
I am a German student at a college of further education who is looking for a work placement in an international company with a good reputation. I enjoy working with people and I am interested in getting work experience. I am also looking for a challenge where I can use and improve my skills.

EDUCATION
2008 – 2011
Berufskolleg (college of further education)
Abitur (A-Levels) in 2011
Business studies   sehr gut (A)
English   sehr gut (A)
Spanish   gut (B)

2003 – 2008
Realschule (intermediate secondary school)
Mittlere Reife (GCSE) in 2008

WORK EXPERIENCE
Part-time job at Super 2000
Shelf control and checkout

INTERESTS
Sports: I am an active volleyball and tennis player, and I also enjoy watching football.
Leadership: I train a 9 – 12-year-old volleyball team at a sports club in Oberhausen.

SKILLS
Languages: I speak English fluently (B2) and have a good working knowledge of Spanish (A2)
Computing: I have good computer skills, especially in Word, Excel, Access, and PowerPoint.
Driving: driving licence

(174 words)

International business correspondence | Exam preparation

2 Getting a job

D Practice

1 Finding the right candidate

Before listening

a) Look at the photos and match the interview candidates with suitable jobs in the list below.

- chef • salesperson • motor mechanic • nursery school teacher
- nurse • computer technician • bank clerk • electrician

b) Give reasons why their clothes suit these jobs.

‹R› While listening

A1.5 c) Listen to the two interviews and find out the following information about each interview.

1. the name of the manager
2. the kind of job or work placement on offer
3. the applicant's name
4. the applicant's skills

After listening

d) Which applicant would you give the work placement to? Give reasons for your choice.

2 Word web: Applying for a job ▶ SF 21 Word webs

a) Copy the word web into your exercise book and write down words from Unit 2 and other words that you know. If necessary use a dictionary.
▶ SF 11 Using a dictionary

b) Work with a partner. Compare your word webs and then add more words to them.

22 | Basic course | Advanced course | Cross-cultural communication

D Practice | Getting a job **2**

‹P› **3 Writing an application**
▶ SF 23 Formal letters and e-mails

Sports Works

We are a leading British sports equipment
manufacturer. We are looking for young reliable
students from Europe to do work placements in
our plants in Hamburg, Rome and Budapest.
5 You can get experience in:

- Purchasing
- Administration
- Sales

If you are interested in one of these areas and are
10 aged 16–25, then send a letter of application and a
full CV to our personnel manager, Mr Jack Jones.
Please note that our company language is English.

Sports Works
Attn Mr Jack Jones
15 430 Bath Road
Bristol BS4 3HQ
England
http://www.sportsworks.co.uk

a) The above advertisement appeared in the German magazine *Sporty* last week. Apply for one of the job placements offered.

b) Use the word web on page 22 to make notes for your application.

c) Write your letter of application and CV.

‹I› **4 Role play: Having an interview** Video lounge ▷ 1

a) You have been invited for an interview for one of the work placements in the advertisement above.
Work in groups. Get together with students who have chosen to apply for the same work placement as you. Half of your group play the applicants (see role card A "applicant" on the right) and the other half play the employers (see role card B "employer" on page 172). Prepare the interview and act it out.

b) Decide in class which applicants you would give the work placement to.

Role card A
Applicant
Think about:
• education
• work experience
• skills and qualifications
• personality and character
• interests and hobbies
• possible questions.

International business correspondence | Exam preparation | **23**

Unit 3
Marketing and advertising

A Getting started

‹P› **1 Buy it!** ▶ SF 26 Describing illustrations and photographs

a) Describe the photos and say what products you could advertise with them.

b) Who could the target groups of these adverts be?

‹R› **2 Young people as consumers**

Before reading

a) Read the heading of the text on page 25. What do you think it is about?

‹R› **Understanding the text**

b) Complete the sentences with words or expressions from the text.

1. Andy did not know anybody on the first days in the ... ...
2. Like the other students Andy was interested in ... and ...
3. Andy's answers to the other students' questions were not ...
4. The group noticed that Andy did not have the right ...
5. Andy saw that the group's clothes had well-known ... on them.

c) What do you think? What did Andy do after he had met the group?

After reading

‹P› d) Write an ending to Andy's story in about 50 words.

| Basic course | Advanced course | Cross-cultural communication |

A Getting started | Marketing and advertising **3**

You're nothing – without the right brands
A1.6

by Cilla Brown

After Andy Burns had moved to a new town with his family he felt quite lonely. On his first day at college he decided to go to the cafeteria. He hoped to meet some new people there. While he was
5 eating his lunch he saw a group of students from one of his classes at the next table. They were talking about music and sport so Andy decided to join them. While they were getting to know each other one boy asked Andy: "Do you support
10 Manchester United?" A girl asked him: "Do you like Justin Timberlake?" Another boy in the group wanted to know if he had the new "Mega Racer" computer game. Andy answered "yes" to all the questions although the truthful answers were "no".
15 Things seemed to be going fine until one of the students saw his trainers. At once the student started to laugh: "Where did you get those shoes from?" Andy had not thought much about them before. They were just blue sport shoes that his
20 parents had bought him for Christmas.

Looking at the group Andy noticed that they all had similar logos on their trainers – ticks and stripes like the ones on footballers' boots on television. And it was not only their shoes: their T-shirts all had similar logos, and everyone in 25 the group seemed to have the same college bag with a puma in silver on the side.

Andy was very confused but from that day on he decided to be like the rest of the group.

(261 words)

3 Are you a well-informed consumer?
▶ SF32 Giving a talk or presentation

■ Think about the following questions and prepare a short presentation to give in class.

1. What is the best thing you have bought in the last few months?
2. Is it a branded or a no-name product?
3. Who made it?
4. Where did they produce it?
5. What is it made of?
6. What type of packaging did it come in?

4 Consumer goods – what do we really need?

a) Make a list of the three consumer goods and services that are most important to you. You can use the items below and/or your own ideas. Put the most important thing first, etc.

- television • mobile phone • MP3 player • car • pen and paper
- bicycle • books • telephone • PC • cosmetics • digital camera
- CDs • computer games • DVDs • running shoes • Internet

b) Work in pairs. Tell your partner what your three most important things are, and why. Then try to agree on a common order of the three most important things.

International business correspondence | Exam preparation | 25

3 Marketing and advertising

B Language

1 Manchester Shopping Centre ▶ GF 18 Past simple

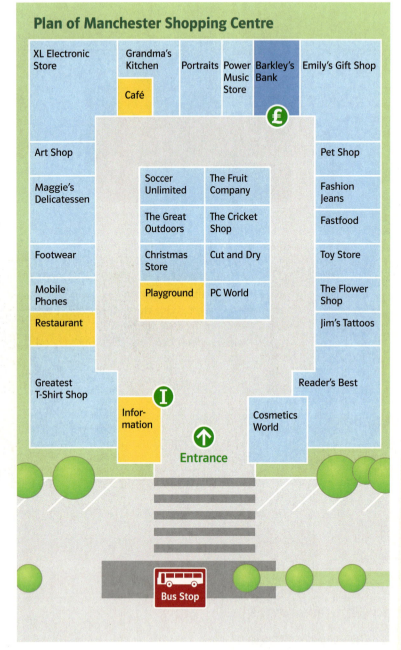

Grammar

Past simple
Example: Sue lived in Glasgow from 2002 to 2008.
Bei Handlungen zu einem bestimmten Zeitpunkt oder in einem abgeschlossenen Zeitraum in der Vergangenheit

Past perfect simple
Example: After Sam had bought a CD he went home.
Für Handlungen oder Zustände, die vor einem Zeitpunkt in der Vergangenheit abgeschlossen waren

Past continuous
Example: While Sam was waiting at the bus stop it started to rain.
Bei Handlungen, die in der Vergangenheit schon im Gange waren, als eine neue Handlung eintrat

▶ GF 18 Past simple
▶ GF 22 Past perfect simple
▶ GF 19 Past continuous

Things to do
1. test the new Manchester United football (Andy)
2. try on some new jeans (Mary)
3. buy a birthday present for Andy's mum (Andy)
4. exchange a red T-shirt for a smaller size (Mary)
5. find tennis shoes (Andy)
6. put on the new season's make-up (Mary)
7. listen to a new pop CD (Mary and Andy)
8. get a haircut (Mary)
9. look for a new book by Ann Summer (Mary)
10. have a look at the latest MP3 players (Andy)

a) Last Sunday Andy went shopping at Manchester Shopping Centre with his new girlfriend, Mary. Look at the list of what they had to do and find out where they did the different things on the plan of the centre.
Example: Andy tested the new Manchester United football at Soccer Unlimited.

b) Andy and Mary wanted to do their shopping as quickly as possible. Find the shortest way through the shopping centre and put the list on the right in the correct order. They started at the bus stop.

| Basic course | Advanced course | Cross-cultural communication |

c) Now describe Andy and Mary's shopping trip in the following way:
Example: After Andy and Mary had arrived at the shopping centre Mary exchanged the red T-shirt for a smaller size. After Mary had exchanged the red T-shirt …

2 What did you do after…?

a) Read the dialogue below in pairs. Replace the underlined parts and act out the new dialogue.

> Student A: What did you do <u>last weekend</u> (yesterday / last week / last Friday…)?
> Student B: I <u>went shopping</u>.
> Student A: What did you do after you <u>had been shopping</u>?
> Student B: After I <u>had been shopping</u> I <u>drank a coffee at the coffee bar</u>.

b) Find another partner and act out a similar dialogue.

3 A bad day for shopping   ▶ GF19 Past continuous

- While Andy and Mary were going home they met one of Andy's new classmates, Mark. He had been shopping, too. But some things had gone wrong. Say what happened to him.

    1. get dressed / telephone – ring
       Example: While Mark was getting dressed the telephone rang.
    2. run to – bus stop / bus – leave
    3. walk to – shopping centre / start – to rain
    4. listen to – new CD / meet – his ex-girlfriend
    5. look at – book / mobile phone – ring
    6. drink – cup of coffee / drop – cup
    7. test – MP3 player on offer / somebody – buy last one
    8. try on – new pair of jeans / fire-alarm – go off
    9. sit on – bus / bus – break down

4 Back from the shopping trip

- Put the verbs in brackets into the correct form of the past tense (past simple, past perfect or past continuous).

> After Andy and Mary [**1. arrive**] at Andy's house they [**2. unpack**] all the things they [**3. buy**]. After they [**4. put**] the things away, they [**5. turn on**] the TV. While they [**6. watch**] a commercial about tennis shoes, Andy [**7. notice**] that he [**8. buy**] the wrong shoes. After they [**9. discuss**] going back to the shop to change the tennis shoes, they [**10. decide**] to get the new shoes on their next shopping trip.

5 Your last shopping trip   ▶ SF25 Personal letters and e-mails

- You have a friend in the USA. Write him/her an e-mail. Describe your last shopping trip in about 100 words. Use each of the words 'after' and 'while' at least twice in your e-mail.

3 Marketing and advertising

C Reading

1 Protecting young consumers

Before reading

a) What does the photo on the right show us?

b) Have you ever bought something on the Internet or by phone? Talk about your experiences.

Every day we see adverts and commercials that say "buy this", "try it" or "do this". The advertisers try to tell us how to behave and what to buy. Young people in particular are at risk when shopping, especially on the Internet because they often believe more easily what the advertisers tell them.
Cheshire County Council in north-west England has created a page on its website that gives young people tips about shopping on the Internet and on the phone. You can read an extract from it below.

http://www.shopping-advice/

Home > Business > Young Consumer > **Shopping Advice**   **Cheshire County Council**

Shopping Advice for Young People

A Do you use the Internet to buy CDs, DVDs, and clothes? When you do this you have the same rights as when you buy in a shop, but the trader must give you some additional information. This must include details about the goods or services and confirmation of the sale. If you change your mind and want to cancel your order, the consumer protection regulations give you a cooling-off period of fourteen days after the day on which you receive the goods. In this period you can cancel your order. For services, this period is the same after the day you agreed to go ahead with the service.

B Have you ever bought or sold anything on eBay or on any other auction platform? These sites are very popular and you can buy anything from toys, books, clothes, DVDs, to concert tickets. But there are a few things to remember when buying things from Internet auctions:
– Check out the sellers. Can you trust them? Have they sold goods before? Is there any feedback on them? Can you get your money back if there is a problem with the goods? Where are the sellers based?
– Compare prices before you place a bid.
– Check to see how much postage you have to pay.
– Check how you have to pay and if your payment is safe.

C Do you use your mobile phone to read about goods or services? If you have a mobile phone you must be careful about scams. Sometimes you may receive a text message which says that you have won a cash prize. When you ring the number it is a premium rate number and the cost of the call can be very high. It is best to delete such messages immediately. Other messages offer ringtones, wallpapers or news alerts. Such services are generally expensive because you receive them at a premium rate. Such a text message can cost you as much as £2 per message. If you want to stop these expensive texts, all you must do is send the word "STOP" to the short code.

(351 words)

Understanding the text

c) Match the following headings with a suitable paragraph in the text. Two of the headings do not fit.

1. Dangers when using your mobile phone
2. Consumer protection
3. Shopping at home
4. Internet auctions
5. Buying a mobile phone

C Reading | Marketing and advertising 3

d) Answer the following questions about the text in complete sentences.

1. What can you do if you order something on the Internet and then you change your mind?
2. What other rights do you have as a buyer on the Internet?
3. What information can you find about a seller on the Internet?
4. What kind of messages is it best to delete on your mobile phone?
5. Why is it best to do this?

e) Use words and expressions from the text to complete the summary.

However, there are certain dangers when you buy [1] on the Internet. It is very important to know that you as a consumer have certain [2]. The [3] must give you detailed information about the product he is selling. Moreover, after you have bought something you can always [4] your order. You have fourteen days to do this. This is called the [5]. When buying something from an Internet [6] such as eBay you should also be careful before placing a [7]. Check out all the relevant details such as the cost of [8] you have to pay. When you use a mobile phone be careful of [9]. For example, when you read a [10] telling you that you have won something. This can often be very [11] for you. You should [12] such messages right away.

f) Find words in the text which have the same meaning as the following words and phrases and give line numbers.

1. purchase
2. further
3. products
4. to say 'yes' to
5. information about someone's experiences
6. cost of stamps and packaging
7. right away
8. money

‹M› **After reading** ▶ SF 22 Mediation/translation

g) You work for your local council and your head of department, who doesn't understand a lot of English, has asked you to give him a summary of section B of the Cheshire County's "Shopping Advice for Young People" in German. Complete this task.

‹P› h) Write some tips for young consumers about shopping in town. Use about 150 words.

Training skills – How to do a role play

‹I› ## 2 A sales talk

a) Work in pairs. Choose a product.
Possible products for sale: a mobile phone plus contract; the latest designer jeans; the latest MP3 player

b) Choose a role. Student A is a salesperson in a German department store. See role card A "salesperson".
Student B is an English-speaking customer. See role card B "customer" on page 172.

c) Prepare the role play and act it out.

Language

- Excuse me…
- Can you tell me…?
- Would you be interested in…?
- May I give you some information about…?
- That sounds interesting.
- I'm (not) interested in…
- What about…?

Role card A

Salesperson

You have a part-time job in a German department store. Your job is to persuade customers to buy.

Think about the advantages of the product, how it compares with other products on the market, its price, etc.

| International business correspondence | Exam preparation | 29

3 Marketing and advertising

D Practice

1 Radio commercials

‹R› **Before listening** ▶ SF 26 Describing illustrations and photographs

a) Describe the photos.

‹R› **While listening**

A1.8 b) Listen to the radio commercials and match them with the photos. Two of the pictures do not match.

c) Copy the chart below into your exercise book. Then listen to the commercials again and answer the questions.

	Commercial 1	Commercial 2	Commercial 3
1. Who are the advertisers?	…	…	…
2. What are they advertising?	…	…	…
3. What are the slogans?	…	…	…

After listening

d) Outline the message of each commercial.

e) Describe the target groups. Think about age, gender and interests.

‹M› f) Fassen Sie die Argumentation der „Friends of the Planet"-Radiowerbung auf Deutsch zusammen. ▶ SF 22 Mediation/translation

‹P› g) Create a flyer which will get people to support the "No Car Day" campaign.

‹P› 2 Creating a TV commercial

a) You have applied for a job at the advertising agency "Mad for Marketing". The agency wants to test you. Work in teams. Decide on a product or service and plan a TV commercial. Think about the following:

- name for the product/service • company • price • target group
- slogan • jingle • storyline • roles • sound • location • script
- logo

b) Act out your TV commercial and then present it to the other teams.

c) Write a short text for the agency in which you describe and explain the decisions that you made. Also give other ways to market your product.

Facts

The four important keywords of marketing are product, pricing, promotion, placement.

Product: The company needs to think about the quality of the product, its uniqueness, its packaging and the branding.

Pricing: The company needs to set a price for the product, including a discount.

Promotion: The company needs to think of various forms of advertising, e.g. newspaper advertisements, billboard, merchandising, sponsoring, online advertising.

Placement: The company needs to think about the distribution of the product, e.g. retailing.

D Practice | Marketing and advertising 3

3 An advertisement for a non-profit organization

Facts

The AIDA formula is a theory used in marketing. It describes how to sell products to possible target groups and it gets people to buy products.

Attention	**I**nterest	**D**esire	**A**ction
attract the target group	make the target group look more closely	convince the target group that they want the product or service	make the target group do something

a) Describe what you can see in the advertisement.
   ▶ SF 26 Describing illustrations and photographs

‹R› b) Match the parts of the AIDA formula in the Facts box with the numbers in the above advertisement.

c) What is the advert for?

d) Who do you think the target group is?

e) What effect does the advert have on you?

f) Do you think the advert is successful? Why? Why not?

‹P› g) Find an advert on the Internet and analyze it. Present it to the class.

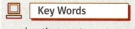

Key Words
- advertisement • commercial

‹I› 4 Should advertising be banned?

‹I› a) Discuss the topic below. Work in groups.

Topic: "Advertising should be banned from magazines and TV programmes for young people."

Group A: Take the position of a college student. See role card A.
Group B: Take the position of a company representative. See role card B "company representative" on page 172.
Group C: Take the position of a parent. See role card C "parent" on page 172.

Role card A

Student

You are not sure about the ban.
Possible arguments:
- information
- entertainment
- waste of time
- spend too much money

b) Choose one person in your team to take part in the discussion. This person introduces himself/herself and states his/her position.
   ▶ SF 3 Having a discussion

c) Discuss the pros and cons of the ban. The other students take notes.
   ▶ SF 33 Taking notes

d) After the discussion the other students vote for or against the ban.

| International business correspondence | Exam preparation | 31 |

Unit 4
Media in our lives

A Getting started

1 Who needs newspapers?

a) Describe the cartoon. ▶ SF 27 Describing cartoons

b) In your opinion, what is the message of the cartoon?

c) Describe how the numbers of people in the US getting news online, on TV and in the newspaper has changed. ▶ SF 28 Describing diagrams

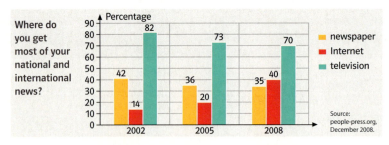

d) Analyse the bar chart and think of reasons for the changes.

e) Explain the link between the cartoon and the bar chart.

f) Work in groups. Do a survey to find out how many hours you and the other members of your group watch TV, do work or play games on the computer, and read newspapers or magazines during one week.

g) Produce a bar chart showing the results of your survey. Present your chart to the class and compare your results with the other groups.

2 Watching TV

Before reading

a) Look at the headline of the article. What do you think it is about?

Do you know what your children are doing right now?
by Jessy Clarkson

A Today more and more parents tend to use a screen – either a TV screen or a computer monitor – as an electronic babysitter. However, the reasons which parents often give for their decision are surprising. Firstly, they think watching TV and using the computer is educational. Secondly, they think that their children relax better in front of the screen.

B If you look at surveys you can see that the number of hours children spend sitting in front of the TV screen is constantly rising. Very young children already spend an average of two hours a day in front of the screen. Scientists say, however, that children of that age shouldn't watch any TV, because their brains are not able to understand so much information, and it can confuse them. Children aged between 2 and 8 years spend an average of 3 hours a day in front of the TV screen. By the age of 8 they can spend as much as 4 hours in front of the TV and an additional 2 hours in front of the computer.

C What effect does this have on children? Long-term surveys have found that children are more likely to be overweight and aggressive. They also have serious problems paying attention for a longer period of time and they often become slow learners at school. This means that their chances of going on to higher education fall dramatically.

D Another aspect is that because more and more commercials are shown on TV children can watch up to 40,000 commercials each year. The problem is that children between 6 and 8 are not able to understand that the aim of commercials is to sell products.

E The conclusion that scientists come to is that children should spend less time in front of the screen and spend more time reading books, or they should do more sport and meet friends.

(320 words)

Understanding the text

b) Now that you have read the text, summarize the writer's main ideas.

c) Answer the following questions about the text.
1. Why do parents let their children watch so much TV?
2. Why shouldn't children under the age of two watch TV?
3. Watching too much TV can have serious consequences for young children. What can happen?
4. Why shouldn't children watch so many commercials?
5. What should children do instead of watching TV?

After reading

d) Copy the chart on the right into your exercise book. Find further reasons in the text why children sit in front of the TV and the ways it affects them.

e) Add ideas of your own to the chart.

f) Prepare a talk about the uses of TV using the ideas in your chart.
   ▶ SF 32 Giving a talk or presentation

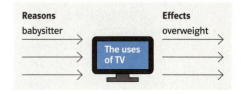

4 Media in our lives

B Language

1 The media in future ▶ GF 24 Will-future

a) Ask your classmates the following questions about the use of media in the future. The words in the language box below can help them to answer the questions.

1. people / use / Internet more often
   Example:
   Student A: What do you expect? Will people use the Internet more often in the future?
   Student B: I suppose people will use the Internet more often in the future.
2. people / write / more e-mails
3. young people / watch / less TV
4. we / buy / more newspapers
5. students / use / laptops in class
6. use of mobile phones / increase
7. the media / influence people / more

> **Grammar**
>
> **Will-future**
> *Bei unsicheren Vorhersagen*
> **Example:** I think the mobile phone will help us in many ways.
>
> *Bei Entscheidungen, die im Moment des Sprechens getroffen werden*
> **Example:** Just a minute, I'll help you!
>
> **Future with 'going to'**
> *Bei Absichten und geplanten Vorhaben*
> **Example:** I am going to stay in New York for a week.
>
> ▶ GF 23 Future with 'going to'
> ▶ GF 24 Will-future

Language
probably • I expect • I suppose

b) Now answer the questions using the short form and give reasons.

Example:
Student A: What do you expect? Will people use the Internet more often in the future?
Student B: Yes, they will because you can easily find important information on the Internet.

2 Doing homework on the PC ▶ GF 23 Future with 'going to'

Make sentences using 'going to' as shown in the example.

1. Jason is sitting in front of his laptop and has turned it on.
   Example: Jason is going to do some work on his laptop.
2. Jason cannot remember what homework he has to do. He opens his ICQ messaging service to talk to a classmate.
3. The homework is to find some information on the Internet. Jason starts his browser.
4. Jason has opened his e-mail program and clicks on the "Create mail" icon.
5. Jason has finished his homework and wants to relax. He clicks on his favourite game on the desktop.
6. It is seven o'clock in the evening. Jason's parents have prepared dinner.
7. Jason is tired. He switches off the laptop.

34 | Basic course | Advanced course | Cross-cultural communication

3 The development of a telecommunications company

◘ Put the verbs in brackets into the correct future form.

**Jim Dawson is managing director of a telecommunications company.
He is talking to his staff about the future development of the company.**

"Ladies and gentlemen, I would like to talk to you about the future development of our company. Management has already decided to go ahead with plans for the new office building. We **are going to open** it next March. We hope that it **will secure** the success of our company in the future.
   We all expect that Internet use [**1. increase**] in the next few years and that we [**2. have**] thousands of new customers. Management has plans to invest more in Internet technology, especially in the mobile web. That is why we [**3. buy**] new servers and we [**4. update**] our network. Since mobile phones have become more important and the number of users of the mobile web has also increased, the mobile web [**5. grow**] in the future. This [**6. probably help**] us to be more profitable. We have also had good news from our bank: They [**7. lend**] us £1 million. We expect that this [**8. make**] it easier for us to make innovations in a difficult market."

4 Comparing different kinds of media
▶ GF7 Adjective and adverb

◘ Complete the text with the suitable form of the words in brackets.

It is **easy** to find information on the Internet. You just press a button and a new page opens **quickly**. Usually the Internet works [**1. good**] and you can download your files [**2. accurate**], but sometimes it breaks down.
What about newspapers? They show [**3. interesting**] news and are [**4. educational**]. What are the [**5. real**] advantages of reading a newspaper or magazine compared to using the [**6. fast**] Internet? First of all, you can read a newspaper wherever you go. You do not need electricity or a wireless connection. If your newspaper is stolen, you can replace it [**7. easy**], because it is [**8. cheap**]. Another advantage is that a newspaper is [**9. good**] for the environment because it is [**10. recyclable**] and it is not made of [**11. harmful**] toxic material. In addition, if a newspaper prints something which is not correct, you can read the correction the following day. Finding out that something is wrong on the Internet is [**12. complicated**], if not [**13. impossible**]. Moreover, you can [**14. quick**] find the latest news in a newspaper, whereas on the Internet you have to look for the publishing date, which you cannot always find so [**15. easy**].

5 Managing situations – A new PC
▶ SF 22 Mediation/translation

‹M› ◘ Sie chatten mit einem englischen Freund und berichten ihm von Ihrem neuen PC. Übertragen Sie die folgenden Sätze sinngemäß ins Englische.

1. Sie haben Geld gespart und werden einen neuen PC kaufen.
2. Sie werden wahrscheinlich einen neuen PC mit einem großen Bildschirm kaufen.
3. Sie nehmen an, dass der neue Computer einen Blu-ray Player haben wird.
4. Ihr Lehrer hat Ihnen die Aufgabe gegeben, im Internet Informationen zu suchen. Sie werden das heute Abend tun.
5. Sie können im Augenblick Podcasts nicht schnell herunterladen.
6. Sie erwarten, dass auf Ihrem neuen, schnellen PC alle Programme besser laufen werden.

4 | Media in our lives

‹R› # C Reading: You can't escape it!

Before reading

a) Look at the pictures that go with the articles on page 37. What do you think the articles are about?

Understanding the texts

b) Match the four articles on the opposite page with suitable headings. Two headings do not match.

| 1 | **Net piracy may send parents to prison** |

| 2 | **The Internet stops your children reading** |

| 3 | **The history of the World Wide Web** |

| 4 | **Internet fraud on the rise** |

| 5 | **The Internet saves the world** |

| 6 | **Home Internet access for all pupils** |

c) Match the verbs in box A with the words in box B according to the text.

A
a) to download
b) to book
c) to exchange
d) to invent
e) to send
f) to provide
g) to prepare
h) to break
i) to record
j) to use
k) to take

B
1. the payment
2. ideas
3. music
4. interviews
5. the law
6. a programming language
7. pictures
8. Internet access
9. presentations
10. a trip
11. the Internet

Training skills – How to write a composition/comment

‹P› **d)** Find advantages and dangers of computers and the Internet in the texts on page 37. Make two lists.

Advantages of computers and the Internet	Dangers of computers and the Internet
...	...

e) Work in pairs. Add your own ideas to the list of advantages and dangers.

f) Comment on this statement: "Teenagers should not have their own computers because it is too dangerous." Write at least three arguments for and three against this statement using complete sentences.
► SF16 **Writing a composition/comment**

‹M› **g)** In Ihrem Politikunterricht sprechen Sie über die Chancen und Gefahren des Internets. Sie erhalten die Aufgabe, ein kurzes Referat über die Risiken des Internets auf Deutsch zu halten. Bereiten Sie dieses Referat mit Hilfe der Zeitungsartikel auf Seite 37 vor.
► SF22 **Mediation/translation**

36 | Basic course   Advanced course   Cross-cultural communication

C Reading | Media in our lives 4

A

Where would we be without it? We could not sell our old CDs on eBay, download music or book a cheap holiday trip to Majorca. All of these things are made possible by the World Wide Web and most of us cannot imagine life without it.

The Internet started as a service for the American Army which needed its own communication network. Soon universities found that they could use the Internet to exchange ideas over long distances. Then computer expert Tim Berners-Lee invented the new programming language HTML and in 1991 he put his software onto the Internet and people could use it for free. Two years later anyone could use the Web and suddenly, businesses and people worldwide could communicate with one another.

Now we can say that the Internet has really changed our lives!

(135 words)

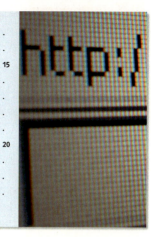

B

According to police reports, Internet crime is still rising sharply in Britain and criminal fantasy seems to be unlimited. In London, for example, online fraudsters are targeting students and holidaymakers by offering cheap rooms and flats. People who are interested have to pay deposits in cash before they even see their new homes, which only exist on the Internet.

"Phishing" of data is also on the rise. Fraudsters try to get people's credit card or account details by sending them e-mails that seem to come from their bank or the government. Many other Internet crimes are connected with the buying and selling of goods. The buyer sends the payment, but no goods arrive. Sometimes the seller agrees to payment after delivery or the buyer uses a stolen credit card. The police warn all internet users to be very careful about their personal data and to use the service of internet auction sites which guarantee safe payment up to a certain amount.

(161 words)

C

The government is planning to provide laptops and Internet access for the homes of 300,000 poor pupils. In this way these school children and their parents should be able to participate in school life. As one official says: "This step will help them to prepare their essays, calculations or presentations on the computer, surf the Internet for important information and hand in their homework online. It also makes interactive learning from home possible. Our government feels the need to support young people so that they can be prepared for life and work in a digital world. As more and more workplaces in all areas are linked to computers, the chances of school leavers without computer and Internet skills will decrease dramatically."

The government also supports the project of WI-FI access points in schools in order to make learning more flexible. So in the future laptops, netbooks or other portable devices can be used all over the school grounds. Some schools have even allowed pupils to bring mobile phones and other private devices that can be used for recording interviews or taking pictures of experiments.

(184 words)

D

Many parents do not know that their children download music and films illegally from the Internet. About 6.5 million Britons – most of them teenagers – downloaded music illegally last year. This costs the music industry alone £200 million a year.

Britain's biggest providers have now agreed on measures to stop Internet piracy. They will send thousands of letters to homes in the UK where they have found illegal downloading. In this way they want to inform parents that their children are breaking the law and warn them to keep an eye on them. If this does not help, these cases may go to court and parents may end up in prison.

After all – parents are responsible for their children!

(118 words)

| International business correspondence | Exam preparation | 37 |

4 Media in our lives

D Practice

1 It's all in the news

Before listening

a) Choose two of the following items which you are especially interested in when you listen to the news on the radio. Give reasons.

- weather • politics • local news • crimes • sports • accidents
- television • traffic news • famous people

‹R› While listening

A1.11 b) Listen to the news reports. Find out which items in the box above are mentioned and in which order.

c) Match the news reports with the following places. Two places do not match.

- Exeter • Delhi • Liverpool
- Chicago • London • California

d) Listen to the reports again. Find the most suitable options according to the news reports. More than one answer can be true.

Report 1
1. A small passenger plane crashed.
2. The plane went up in flames.
3. Fourteen children were killed.
4. A couple saw the crash.

Report 3
1. The weather report announces the weather for Monday and Tuesday.
2. In the afternoon there will be some showers and thunderstorms in London.
3. The temperature will go up to nearly 20 degrees Celsius on Monday.
4. The weather will be bright and sunny on Monday.

Report 2
1. Children watch thousands of killings on TV.
2. When they are 16, children watch 16,000 murders.
3. Children who watch too much TV can get fat.
4. Children should not have televisions and computers in their bedrooms.

Report 4
1. Steven McNeill reports on motorway No. 26.
2. A lane on the motorway near Exeter is closed.
3. The radio station asks its listeners to report details.
4. Steven McNeill will come on air again within the next half an hour.

‹P› After listening

e) You are a reporter for a local radio station. Prepare a short piece of news and present it in class.

D Practice | Media in our lives **4**

Training skills – How to describe a cartoon

2 Someone to watch over you …

▶ SF 27 **Describing cartoons**

a) Describe and analyze cartoon 1. Use the following phrases:

Description:
"The illustration shows …"

Analysis:
"The cartoonist wants to point out that …"

Your opinion:
"I think this cartoon is …"

desert island • palm tree • surveillance camera • to observe

b) Describe cartoon 2 in a similar way.

3 Big brother at school?

- Many schools in Britain have installed
- cameras in the yards and corridors to
- protect the children and the teachers.
- Now there is a discussion going on if
5 schools should also introduce CCTV
- (closed circuit television) cameras in
- classrooms. Head teachers believe that
- this will help to stop students breaking
- the rules. Students, however, …

■ Next week a discussion is going to take place in your college about the introduction of CCTV.

Student A is a student at the college. You are going to speak for the students. See role card A on the right.
Student B is a head teacher. Student C is a teacher. Student D is a police officer. See role cards on page 173.
Introduce yourselves and present your arguments. Discuss the pros and cons of the introduction of CCTV into the college and try to reach an agreement.

Role card A

Student

You and your classmates do not like the idea of cameras in the classroom. Try to find arguments against this idea and suggest other ways of making students behave better.

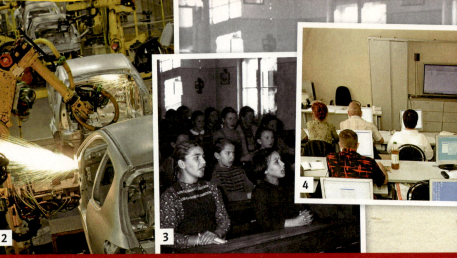

Unit 5
Social and economic changes

A Getting started: Times change

⟨P⟩ **Before reading**

a) Describe the above photos.
   ▶ SF 26 Describing illustrations and photographs

b) Describe how society and economy in western countries has changed over the past 100 years. Refer to the photos in your answer.

c) How is your lifestyle different to that of your parents and grandparents when they were your age?

⟨R⟩ **Understanding the texts**

d) You are in the English section of a German bookshop. You read the comments on the back of three books as well as an extract from each one. Match the comments (1–3) with the extracts (A–C) on page 41.

Comments on the backs of the books

1 He is sixteen and a skater. Life is going on nicely – he is thinking about college and he has met a nice girl. Then a little accident happens.

2 She lives in Southall, London, a part of the city where many families of Indian origin live. Her parents want her to be a nice conventional Indian girl. But she has other plans.

3 An idyll of the English countryside: a beautiful evening in a field, and a group of workers are having a birthday party. But who picks the strawberries these days?

40 | Basic course | Advanced course | Cross-cultural communication

A Getting started | Social and economic changes 5

Book extracts

A Yaketa said, "my [...] job pays only the minimum wage, not
a proper nurse's salary. Then they make deductions. Tax.
Food. Accommodation. Uniform. Training fee. Agency fee.
At the end of the week I have nothing left."
5 "I know about these deductions," I said. "We are strawberry
pickers. Accommodation, food, transport; everything comes
out of our wages. You know I had not expected such
meanness in England."

From Two Caravans by Marina Lewycka, London: Penguin/Fig Tree, 2007, page 242.

B There was a little chemist's next door to the Starbucks,
so we went in there, but we got out quick* when Alicia saw a
friend of her mum's in there. She saw us, too, this woman,
and you could tell she thought we'd gone in to buy condoms.
5 Ha! Condoms! We were way beyond condoms, missus!
Anyway, we realized that we could never go into a chemist's
that size – not just because we might have been spotted,
but because neither of us would be able to ask for what we
wanted. Condoms were bad enough, but pregnancy tests
10 were in a different class of trouble and embarrassment.
We walked on to the Superdrug around the corner.

From Slam by Nick Hornby, London: Penguin, 2008, page 92.

* colloquial form of quickly

C I was sitting on the sofa, still wearing
my Harriers kit. "You're not a young girl
anymore, Jesminder [...] now your
sister's engaged, it's different," said Dad.
5 He was at the bar in the corner, getting
himself a whisky. I didn't drink, but right
now I could have done with one myself.
"You know how our people talk."
"She's the one getting married, not
10 me!" I said resentfully.
"I was married at your age," Mum
snapped. "You don't even want to learn
how to cook Indian food!" I didn't see
what that had to do with it.
15 "Anyway I'm not playing with boys any
more." Maybe that would shut them up.
"Good." Mum headed off towards the
kitchen.
"I'm joining a girls' team," I went on.
20 "They want me to play in proper
matches."

*From Bend it like Beckham by Narinder Dhami,
Stuttgart: Ernst Klett Verlag, 2003, page 25.*

(317 words)

e) Choose the correct options. More than one answer can be true.

1. Alicia and her boyfriend go into a shop to buy …
   a) cosmetics.
   b) superdrugs.
   c) condoms.
   d) a pregnancy test.

2. They go to a drugstore because …
   a) they want to talk to the manager.
   b) it's cheaper than the chemist's.
   c) nobody knows them there.
   d) they couldn't get what they wanted.

3. In Yaketa's job she …
   a) gets free accommodation.
   b) receives a poor wage.
   c) has to buy her own food and uniform.
   d) earns a lot of money each week.

4. The strawberry pickers in England …
   a) are satisfied with their jobs.
   b) expected this treatment in England.
   c) don't have to pay for transport.
   d) are unhappy with their pay.

5. Jesminder is not happy because …
   a) her father drinks.
   b) she doesn't want to get married.
   c) she doesn't want to play football with girls.
   d) her parents don't really understand her.

6. Her mother isn't happy with Jesminder because …
   a) she is a typical Indian girl.
   b) she isn't interested in cooking Indian food.
   c) she doesn't want to eat Indian food.
   d) she isn't good enough for a football team.

f) Find the words in the above texts that match the definitions.

1. money which working people have to pay to the government
2. person who cares for ill people, especially in hospital
3. room or building in which you stay or live
4. amount of money which is paid regularly to a worker
5. shop in which you can buy medicine or cosmetics
6. a lot of problems
7. become part of a group

| International business correspondence | Exam preparation | 41

5 Social and economic changes

B Language

1 Guessing game ▶ GF14 Defining relative clauses

a) Explain the following words using 'who' or 'which'.
Example: A feminist is a person who fights for women's rights.

1. **feminist**	tool	(accommodate) ill people
2. drugstore	place	(explain) words
3. dictionary	film	**(fight) women's rights**
4. hospitals	shop	(hand out) credit cards
5. drill	**person**	(sell) beauty products
6. island	worker	(give) information about a special topic
7. documentaries	book	(lie) in the sea
8. bank clerk	building	(make) holes in walls

b) Now describe other people/things in the same way but don't mention their names. The rest of the class has to say who/what they are.
Example: It is a shop which sells food. Answer: It's a supermarket.

2 Women then and now ▶ GF15 Non-defining relative clauses

a) Complete the following text. Fill in 'who' or 'which' to make non-defining relative clauses.

Mary Wollstonecraft, [1] was born in London in 1759, was a British writer and feminist. One of her books, [2] is about the rights of women, became very important in the women's rights movement in Europe (see Facts). Wollstonecraft, [3] had various love affairs, got a bad name because of her lifestyle. One day she helped her sister Eliza, [4] wanted to leave her husband and her child for a better life. But social norms, [5] existed at that time, forced her sister to live in poverty, because she wasn't allowed to marry again. Wollstonecraft, [6] found out that women could not have a career, started to write. At about the same time she met William Godwin, [7] later became her husband. Godwin and Wollstonecraft, [8] married in 1797, had a daughter, [9] was also called Mary. She later became Mary Shelley and wrote the book "Frankenstein", [10] is very popular even today.

Mary Wollstonecraft

Grammar

Defining relative clauses
Example: The man who/that is getting on the bus is on his way home.
Bei Personen werden die Relativpronomen who *oder* that *verwendet.*
Example: The bus which/that is at the bus stop is going to Bristol.
Bei Sachen werden which *oder* that *verwendet.*
Example: The man (–) I saw was a good football player.
Ist das Relativpronomen Objekt des Satzes, kann es weggelassen werden.

Non-defining relative clauses
Example: His wife, who is 26, works in an office.
Nicht notwendige Relativsätze werden in Kommas eingeschlossen.
Example: The bus, which was a double-decker, was waiting.
That *wird hier nicht verwendet.*
Example: Henry, who I saw yesterday, is going to hospital next week.
Ist das Relativpronomen Objekt des Relativsatzes, darf es nicht weggelassen werden.

Modal auxiliaries
Example: Cars must/have to stop at red lights.
Für modale Hilfsverben können auch entsprechende Ersatzformen verwendet werden.
Examples: He was not allowed to park his car there.
You will have to leave at 8 o' clock.
Die Ersatzformen werden insbesondere für die Vergangenheit und die Zukunft eingesetzt.

▶ GF14 Defining relative clauses
▶ GF15 Non-defining relative clauses
▶ GF13 Modal auxiliaries

Facts

The women's rights movement refers to the fight for freedom and equality for women, e.g. the right to vote and to equal pay. The movement started in Europe in the late 18th century. Today the women's rights movement is called 'feminism'.

B Language | Social and economic changes **5**

b) Complete the text about British comedian, Shazia Mirza using the information about her life. Decide if a relative clause is necessary or not, or if you can leave out the relative pronoun.

Shazia Mirza [**1**], **who was born in England in 1975**, is a woman [**2**] **nearly everybody in Britain knows**. Shazia is the first British Muslim [**3**] **who has her own comedy show**. When she started doing her first comedy shows her parents [**4**] did not know about the new profession [**5**]. They thought that their daughter [**6**] was a teacher at a comprehensive school [**7**]. Shazia was so successful with her shows [**8**] that she gave up her job as a teacher. In her shows she makes fun of topics [**9**]. Her favourite topics are Muslim traditions and the new roles [**10**]. Shazia also writes articles for a current affairs magazine in Britain and in 2008 she won the Columnist of the Year Award [**11**].

Some information about Shazia Mirza's life

a) She had studied science at university.
b) The Columnist of the Year Award is one of the most important awards for British journalists.
c) **She has her own comedy show.**
d) The comprehensive school is in Tower Hamlets, London.
e) **She was born in England in 1975.**
f) Her parents are very religious Muslims.
g) Shazia had taken up a new profession.
h) Her shows were even broadcast on TV.
i) Her topics are of public interest.
j) **Nearly everybody in Britain knows her.**
k) Women have new roles in society.

3 Women's roles have changed

a) Talk about women's roles today. Make sentences using the verbs in brackets. ▶ GF13 Modal auxiliaries

1. take part in government [**can**]
   Example: Today women can take part in government.
2. go to school [**must**]
3. study at university [**can**]
4. wear what they like [**can**]
5. ask their husbands for their okay when they want to go out with friends [**needn't**]
6. marry the man their parents choose [**needn't**]
7. read [**can**]
8. give up their new roles [**needn't**]

b) Talk about women's roles in the past. Make sentences as in the example.

1. vote in elections [**not be allowed to**]
   Example: 200 years ago women were not allowed to vote in political elections.
2. work at home and in the fields [**have to**]
3. attend university [**not be allowed to**]
4. stay at home [**have to**]
5. marry the man their parents chose [**have to**]
6. wear trousers [**not be allowed to**]
7. read in most cases [**not be able to**]
8. take on new roles [**not be allowed to**]

c) Now compare women's roles today with women's roles 200 years ago.
Example: Today women can take part in government but 200 years ago they were not allowed to vote in elections.

4 Men's roles have changed, too

‹P› ▪ Compare men's roles 200 years ago, today and in future. Use modal auxiliaries and their substitutes.

Example: 200 years ago boys had to go to work when they were 14. Today they must go to school until they are 16. I suppose that in 200 years' time they will have to go to school until they are 18.

International business correspondence | Exam preparation | 43

5 Social and economic changes

C Reading: The Internet generation

Training skills – How to anticipate, skim and scan

<P> **Before reading**   ▶ SF 9 Anticipating, skimming, scanning

a) Where does the text come from?
   Example: This text comes from the "America …

b) Read the heading and guess what the text is about.
   Example: The heading "Internet generation" could refer to the generation of young people who …

c) Describe the photos and guess what further information they can give you about the text.   ▶ SF 26 Describing illustrations and photographs
   Example: The first photo shows us a young man using a mobile phone. This could mean that the text is about …

<R> d) Skim through the text without reading it in detail, i.e. run your eye over the subheadings quickly. Say in one or two sentences what the text is about.
   Example: This text is about young people who have grown up with new technology and who …

Understanding the text

d) Read the text in detail and match the key points below with the headings in the text.

   1. the first generation having grown up with computers and the Internet
      Example: This key point matches the heading: "Growing up with new technology".
   2. giving up the old job for an interesting new one
   3. many young people work after school – online social networks
   4. open-minded young generation – study and work abroad
   5. time management and multi-tasking skills

e) Answer the following questions in your own words. Your results from exercise d) can help you.

   1. Why does "Jimmy" give up his old job so quickly?
   2. Why is the "Generation Y" so qualified in the use of new technology?
   3. What may be an advantage and a disadvantage of the ability to do multi-tasking?
   4. How do young people very often meet other people?
   5. In which way have many young people become global citizens?

After reading

<P> f) You are also a member of the Internet generation. Which of the statements in the text on page 45 match your attitudes and experiences, which of them don't? Write about yourself.

44 | Basic course | Advanced course | Cross-cultural communication

C Reading | Social and economic changes 5

http://www.america-online-magazine.com

A1.12 **The Internet generation**

Switching jobs quickly
Let's call him Jimmy. He's just buying designer jeans in a new superstore in San Francisco when he meets his old school friend Derek who is desperately looking for a computer professional. Jimmy has just finished his work on some PC applications in his present job and has only got some dull work to do in the next few weeks. Derek hires him spontaneously. Still in the superstore Jimmy sends an e-mail to his old employer: "Sorry. Won't come back. Please send me the rest of my pay by check."

Growing up with new technology
Born in the 1980s or 1990s Jimmy is in the so-called "Internet generation" or "Generation Y" which is the first generation that has grown up surrounded by new technology. Armed with cell phones and laptops they are online twenty-four hours a day, seven days a week. They rely on new technology to do their jobs better. They prefer to communicate by e-mail or text messaging rather than face to face. Online communication with its automatic spell checks and instant messaging (where it takes too long to write "You made me laugh out loud") means that this generation doesn't need to know how to spell, or even speak English properly. Young people LOL and confess ILY.

On the move to better jobs
Nevertheless, members of generation Y are self-confident, creative and optimistic, independent and goal-oriented. Having grown up in play groups and doing team sports they appreciate team work. They belong to a generation whose free time was carefully planned by their parents when they were kids. That is why they are used to time management and multi-tasking. The flipside of the coin is that multi-tasking talents are unable to concentrate on a single task for a long period of time. A recent survey found out that nearly 50% of graduates are planning to stay with their first employer for less than two years. They want to learn as much as possible in a short time and then move on to a bigger and better position.

Online networks replace road networks
Young people today are willing to work and to earn money. About 50 per cent of the students in the 12th grade work more than twenty hours a week, most of them in the retail trade and in the service industry. On the other hand young employees are not only interested in money but also in flexible working hours and a better work/life balance. It is interesting to know that in Germany the percentage of car buyers under thirty has decreased from seventeen to seven per cent within twenty years. Some experts believe that young people today do not need cars any more because they see the world through the eyes of their computers. Internet connections have replaced road networks and so young people can stay at home and make their experiences online – in social networks.

Going global
Having grown up with people from other nationalities and cultures and connected to all continents through the Internet, members of generation Y are open-minded – they think globally and see everything connected. They can be called global citizens now. They are ready to do placements or to study abroad, their jobs may demand employment abroad in a more and more global world and they are ready to fit in – as long as it meets their requirements.
Young people today have to face new challenges but they also have new skills. Let us rely upon them as they rely on themselves. (585 words)

International business correspondence | Exam preparation 45

5 Social and economic changes

D Practice

1 Balancing work and family life

Before listening ▶ SF 27 Describing cartoons

a) Describe the cartoon.

b) After looking at the cartoon, what do you think the person who you are going to hear is talking about?

‹R› **While listening**

A1.13 c) Listen to the young woman and answer these questions.

1. What is the woman's name?
2. Where does she work?
3. Why is life sometimes difficult for her?
4. Who helps her?

d) Listen to the young woman again. Then correct these statements if necessary.

1. Her grandmother was a teacher.
2. Being a mother today is different from what her grandmother experienced.
3. In her job she works on her own.
4. She works part-time and does not do any work at the weekends.
5. Her job is the most important thing in her life so it has to come first.

‹P› **After listening**

e) In Britain, as in many other countries, single parents often have problems combining work and family life. Make a list of the problems they might have to face. Then find a solution to each problem.

f) Imagine you are a single parent and you have a full-time job. Describe your daily routine.

2 Economic changes   Video lounge ▶ 2

Before reading

a) Match the following inventions with the three periods shown on the next page.

- CNC production
- Assembly line
- Electric light bulb
- Steam ship

46 | Basic course | Advanced course | Cross-cultural communication

D Practice | Social and economic changes 5

around 1800

around 1900

around 2000

◉ A1.14

The rise of information and communication technologies (ICT) has had a large impact on the development of our economy and society. This new era is often called "The third industrial revolution", "The information age" or "New economy".

The first industrial revolution dates back to around 1800 when the steam engine was developed and industrial production in factories started. Steam ships and locomotives began to make transport faster and easier.

The second industrial revolution refers to the time around 1900 when for example the electric light bulb or the motor car started to change the world. Mass production on the assembly line made a lot of products available for the masses.

The third industrial revolution started with the introduction of personal computers and the rise of the World Wide Web. By 2000 the PC had reached about 50 per cent of American homes. Right now, nearly every company and every individual is linked to the Internet. New products include the computer, the internet or mobile phones; new processes include internet shopping, CNC-production and automated planning and control systems in every large company.

Technological changes have always had influence on the organisation of work and production processes and have increased productivity. Moreover they have changed our working and living conditions. **(208 words)**

‹R› **Understanding the text**

b) Scan the text to find out if your results in task a) were correct.

c) Find other inventions and innovations mentioned in the text.

‹P› **After reading**

d) Put the inventions in the box in a chronological order.

- mobile phone • wheel • motor car • steam engine • aeroplane • computer • assembly line

e) Choose one of the products in d) and describe in what way it has changed working and/or living conditions.

f) Do the following quiz. Only one answer is correct.

1. The steam engine was developed by …
   a) James Watt
   b) Jim Volt
   c) John Ohm

2. The internal combustion engine was invented by …
   a) Rudolf Diesel
   b) Nikolaus Otto
   c) Henry Ford

3. The first working computer was built by …
   a) Bill Gates
   b) Henri Compu
   c) Konrad Zuse

4. If a group of workers produces 10,000 mobile phones in one month, and 12,000 in the next month, productivity increases by …
   a) 2 %
   b) 12 %
   c) 20 %

| International business correspondence | Exam preparation | 47 |

Unit 6
Ecology and economy

A Getting started

1 Our beautiful planet?

‹P› **Before reading**   ▶ SF 27 Describing cartoons

a) Describe the above cartoons and explain their messages.

b) What do the cartoons have to do with the topic of ecology?
Match the cartoons with the following headings (1–6). Three headings do not match.

1. environmental education
2. air pollution
3. recycling waste
4. healthy food
5. vandalism
6. global warming

Understanding the text   ▶ SF 9 Anticipating, skimming, scanning

‹R› c) Match the following headings (1–4) with the paragraphs (A–D) on page 49 and with the key points (i–iv).

Headings	Key points
1. tasks of the Environment Bureau	i. air pollution – water pollution
2. environmental worries	ii. burning fossil fuels – greater rainfall
3. climate change	iii. planning improvements
4. looking after the local environment	iv. responsible use of resources – recycling – transport

48 | Basic course | Advanced course | Cross-cultural communication

A Getting started | Ecology and economy **6**

A1.15 A BETTER ENVIRONMENT FOR US ALL

A Concerns about the environment are growing day by day. According to a recent survey people in the UK are becoming increasingly worried about environmental issues and global warming. Air pollution is top of the list, but aspects such as waste management and the pollution of our seas, lakes and rivers follow closely.

B However, perhaps the most important issue affecting our environment is climate change. The burning of fossil fuels in cars, power stations and industry emits gases such as carbon dioxide (CO_2) into the atmosphere. According to experts these gases contribute to long-term climate change. In the UK these changes can affect us in a complex way. Winters are likely to become wetter and summers drier.

C Solving global and national environmental problems means taking action locally. So, helping to look after your local environment is very important. You can do this in different ways. We can all use fewer resources at home and work.

We can all recycle waste and reduce the number of trips we make in the car by walking, cycling or taking public transport instead.

D The Environment Bureau has a wide range of duties and powers relating to the improvement of our environment. Part of our responsibility is to encourage the conservation of natural resources, animals and plants. We at the Environment Bureau encourage local governments and communities to identify their local environmental problems so that they can then try to solve them. Problems range from the use of natural resources such as oil, to pollution control and the improvement in the quality of life in our communities. We at the Environment Bureau can give your community a service. We aim to provide you with the latest information on the state of the local environment so that we can then help you in planning any environmental improvements. You can get more information on the Internet.

(313 words)

d) Find the most suitable options according to the text. More than one answer can be true.

1. People are especially worried about …
   a) climate change.
   b) pollution.
   c) animals and plants.
   d) the conservation of natural resources.

2. The main cause of climate change is …
   a) fewer resources.
   b) gases from burning fossil fuels.
   c) rainfall.
   d) waste.

3. People can be more environmentally friendly by …
   a) not using their cars so often.
   b) using a bike.
   c) recycling rubbish.
   d) saving water.

4. The Environment Bureau helps people by …
   a) building new power stations.
   b) cleaning the rivers.
   c) giving them information.
   d) recycling waste.

After reading ▶ SF31 Internet research

e) Check the web to find out more about environmental organizations in Britain. Present your results to your class.

2 Do people care about the environment?

‹P› ◼ Give your opinion on the statements using the phrases in the box.

1. Michael is of the opinion that they should punish people who damage the environment much harder.
2. Lena believes that people should buy more organically grown food.
3. Carol sometimes does not know what to do with the different types of rubbish.
4. In Ben and Tara's view we have to use less water and then more people in the world will be able to survive.

Language

• I think that …
• I believe that …
• I'm of the opinion that … because …
• In my view …
• As far as I am concerned …

International business correspondence | Exam preparation | **49**

6 Ecology and economy

B Language

1 Water for life

■ Dr Emma Roberts, a voluntary worker with Water for Life, gave an interview on Radio Bristol last month. This is part of the interview. Report what she said using the reporting verbs in the language box.

1. "Every 17 seconds a child in the developing world <u>dies</u> from water-related diseases."
   Example: In the interview Dr Roberts said that every 17 seconds a child in the developing world <u>died</u> from water-related diseases.
2. "Every day people in the world's poorest countries face this problem."
3. "They can drink dirty water that can kill them or die of thirst."
4. "It is a gamble that often carries a high price."
5. "It is heartbreaking to see children who are dying."
6. "For £2 a month everyone here in Bristol can help."
7. "Whole communities can benefit from this help."
8. "It doesn't really matter how much a person gives."
9. "Every gift helps someone to get clean water to survive."

> **Language**
> She …
> - said that …
> - went on to say that …
> - told us that …
> - informed us that …
> - stated that …
> - added that …
> - concluded that …

> **Grammar**
> **Reported speech**
> **Example:** She said, "<u>I want</u> to help children in Africa." wird zu: She said that <u>she wanted</u> to help children in Africa.
> In der indirekten Rede ändern sich die Zeitformen wie folgt:
> present → past
> past → past perfect
> present perfect → past perfect
> will → would
>
> Auch Pronomen, Orts- und Zeitbestimmungen werden angepasst.
>
> ► GF 26 Reported speech

2 How you can help

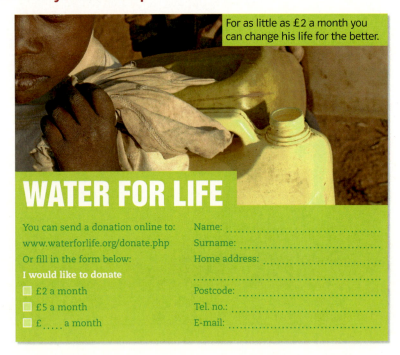

For as little as £2 a month you can change his life for the better.

WATER FOR LIFE

You can send a donation online to: www.waterforlife.org/donate.php
Or fill in the form below:
I would like to donate
☐ £2 a month
☐ £5 a month
☐ £ ….. a month

Name: ……………………
Surname: ……………………
Home address: ……………………
……………………
Postcode: ……………………
Tel. no.: ……………………
E-mail: ……………………

■ This is what some people said after reading the Water for Life advert. Report what they told you.

1. Ron: "I <u>saw this</u> advert in the newspaper, too."
   Example: Ron said/told me that he <u>had seen that</u> advert in the newspaper, too.
2. Julie: "My friend gave me the advert."
3. Sam: "I decided to give £2."
4. Tom and Mark: "We donated the money online."
5. Nick: "I filled in the form immediately."
6. Jack: "I didn't know much about this problem."
7. Lisa and Sarah: "We have made the decision to give £5 a month."
8. Jenny: "I haven't checked out this website yet."
9. Dan: "My friend has just read the advert, too."
10. Sandy and Darren: "We didn't realize how important it was to help."

3 A world without seafood

- After some people had seen this photo in a magazine, they started to talk about this environmental topic. Report what they said.

1. Sally: "Restaurants will soon have no fish on the menu."
   Example: Sally said that restaurants **would** soon **have** no fish on the menu.
2. Christian: "As I understand it, I will have to pay more for my fish and chips in the future."
3. Helen: "I like tuna, but as I see it I won't be able to get it so easily in the supermarket."
4. Alex and Jane: "We won't be able to buy so much seafood so cheaply."
5. Owen: "In my opinion, I won't have any fish protein to eat apart from algae."
6. Sharon: "As I see it, governments will have to act quickly to avoid a disaster."
7. Bill and Ben: "After reading this article we are sure the catastrophe will happen in our lifetime."
8. Donna: "I won't eat so much fish after reading this article."

4 World Nature Fund

- Sally Neville belongs to the World Nature Fund. Below you can find some questions that people have asked her.
  Work in pairs. One student reports the questions. The other student reports what Sally said.

1. "What do you do in the organization to protect the environment?" [**organize all kinds of activities**]
   Example:
   Student A: People often asked Sally what she did in the organization to protect the environment.
   Student B: Sally said that she organized all kinds of local activities.
2. "Where is the nearest branch of the organization?" [**have branches in all major cities**]
3. "How much do you have to pay to join the organization?" [**donate £10 a year**]
4. "Where can I get a membership form?" [**download online**]
5. "Have you sent leaflets about the organization to our college?" [**send some brochures some months ago**]
6. "When will you come to our college to give us more information?" [**come soon**]
7. "How long has the organization existed?" [**begin in 1961**]
8. "When did you join the organization?" [**become a member in 2007**]
9. "Why did you become a member of WNF?" [**read an interesting article about WNF's activities**]

5 "Water, water, everywhere, but not a drop to drink"

a) Work in groups of four. Discuss the problems relating to water in our world today. Use the role card on the right and the cards on page 173, and make meaningful statements. Make notes during the discussion.

b) Use your notes to write a report about what the members of your group said.

Example: Patrick thought that people had to …

Role card A

Talk about the following things:
- must help poor countries
- environmental organizations
- time is running out

6 Ecology and economy

C Reading: You are what you eat

‹P› Before reading

a) Describe the pie charts and the photos. ► SF 26 Describing illustrations and photographs
   ► SF 28 Describing diagrams

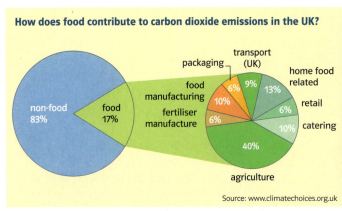

b) Look at the headline of the following article and guess what it is about.

ⓐ A1.16 How many air miles are there in your hamburger?
by Mary Brayshaw

A Have you ever asked yourself where the food you buy comes from? South African apples, Argentinian beef, Spanish strawberries, Brazilian pineapples, Indonesian king prawns, Indian bananas – they are all common on our supermarket shelves today.

B According to the latest research the average British basket of food has travelled over 50,000 miles from producer to consumer. Food miles, the transportation of food from the farm to your home, use enormous amounts of fossil fuels, which contribute to air pollution and global warming. For this reason food miles harm our environment.
This is why more than thirty food companies in Britain have signed a promise to reduce their food transport miles. They promise to reduce pollution by using rail and shipping instead of road and air transportation. Big food stores in Britain have promised to label products which come by air. These labels will have a logo of an aeroplane on them.

C But researchers have also found that agriculture, and manufacturing processes and packaging in the food industry have even greater negative effects on our environment than the so-called food miles. They say that the transport energy for hamburgers is only 20 per cent of the total energy needed in their production.

D In order to encourage its citizens to be more environmentally friendly, the City of Manchester has started an eco-food challenge. They picked out six families to take part in the six-month challenge. The families must cut their energy and water consumption as well as their waste, and they must pay attention to the food they buy. Rather than counting their food's calories they should try to calculate its environmental impact instead. When shopping they should choose organic food which has been grown locally. Also they should only buy fruit and vegetables which have been produced in season, for example strawberries in early summer. A "green advisor" helps the families. As a prize the winners will receive solar equipment for their house.

(331 words)

Understanding the text   ► SF 9 Anticipating, skimming, scanning

c) Without reading the text in detail skim through it and say what it is about in a few sentences.

C Reading | Ecology and economy 6

Training skills – How to work with a dictionary

d) The following words are taken from the text. Identify them as nouns, verbs or adjectives in the context of the text. ▶ **SF11 Using a dictionary**

1. average (l. 6)	3. harm (l. 12)	5. label (l. 17)
2. contribute (l. 11)	4. promise (l. 14)	6. challenge (l. 28)

e) Find the meaning of the above words using the following parts of an English-English dictionary. Words often have more than one meaning so make sure you find the meaning of the word in the text.

average (n.) – **1.** An **average** is what you get by adding two or more numbers and dividing the result by the amount of numbers you added. **2.** An amount or quality that is **average** is the standard or usual amount/quality of a group of things or people.
average (adj.) – **1.** You use **average** to say that a person or thing is typical or normal. **2.** Something that is **average** is ordinary: it is not so good, nor is it so bad.
challenge (n.) – A **challenge** is **1.** something new and difficult and you must make a big effort to do it. **2.** an invitation from a person to compete or argue with them.
challenge (v.) – If you **challenge** a person **1.** you ask them to compete or argue with you. **2.** You want to

know whether what they say is true or whether what they do is correct.
contribute (v.) – **1.** If you **contribute** to a thing **1.1.** you try to make it successful. **1.2.** you pay money or you give assistance to something, usually for charitable purposes. **2.** If something **contributes** to a situation it is one of the reasons for it. **3.** If you **contribute** to a newspaper or magazine, you write articles for them.
harm (v.) – **1.** To **harm** someone means to hurt them and cause them physical pain. **2.** To **harm** something means to damage it or make it less useful.
label (n.) – A **label** is a piece of paper or another material that is placed on an object. It gives information about the object, for example it tells what it is, who owns it, or how you can use it.

label (v.) – **1.** If you **label** something, you put a label on it to mark it. **2.** If you **label** people as something, you describe or think of them in a certain way, even though they do not agree with your opinion.
promise (n.) – **1.** A **promise** is a declaration which you make to a person saying that you will definitely do something or give them something. **2.** If someone or something shows **promise**, it looks as if they will be successful in future.
promise (v.) – **1.** If you **promise** that you will do a thing, you tell a person that you will certainly do it. **2.** If you **promise** someone a thing, you tell them that you will certainly give it to them. **3.** If a situation or event **promises** to have a special quality, you expect it to have that quality.

f) Identify the underlined words as nouns or verbs in the context of the sentences and find a suitable definition in the dictionary above.

1. The bottles got wet and all the labels came off.
2. The employees have long working hours – 50 hours a week is about the average.
3. The governments promise stricter laws on car emissions.
4. The elderly have much to contribute to the community.
5. The football team has challenged and beaten the best teams in the world.

g) Replace the words "average" (l. 6), "contribute" (l. 11), "harm" (l. 12) and "label" (l. 17) in the text on page 52 with words or phrases from the above dictionary.

h) Answer the following questions on the text using your own words.

1. Why are food miles a problem for the environment?
2. What have some companies done to reduce food miles?
3. What has the City of Manchester done to help the environment?
4. What kind of food should the families taking part in the Manchester challenge buy?

‹M› **i)** Als Mitglied einer Umweltorganisation wollen Sie Ihre Gruppe über diesen Zeitungsartikel informieren. Stellen Sie dazu die wichtigsten Aussagen des vorliegenden Textes auf Deutsch zusammen. Formulieren Sie ganze Sätze. ▶ **SF22 Mediation/translation**

| International business correspondence | Exam preparation | 53 |

6 Ecology and economy

D Practice

1 Consuming the world

Before listening

‹P› **a)** Describe and analyze the picture.
▶ SF 27 Describing cartoons

b) Read the newspaper headlines and guess what the following listening text is about.

1. **We are all over-consumers!**
2. **Can you teach an old society new tricks?**
3. **Ecology and economy go hand in hand**
4. **"Buy Nothing Day" is only the beginning**

‹R› **While listening**

🔊 A1.17 **c)** Listen to the radio commentary and find out if your ideas in exercise b) were mentioned in the commentary.

d) Listen again and find the most suitable options according to the text. More than one answer may be true.

1. According to the commentator, economy and ecology must …
   a) realize that they are opposites
   b) go hand in hand
   c) be the same
   d) not be opposites

2. At the moment people in the rich countries …
   a) consume too much.
   b) behave as if the world's resources are unlimited.
   c) consume more than nature can replace.
   d) consume 20 % of the world's resources.

3. A UK household …
   a) had 17 appliances 70 years ago.
   b) has a rising number of appliances.
   c) has around 50 appliances today.
   d) has around 15 appliances today.

4. Transport …
   a) by road is growing.
   b) is not always necessary.
   c) by plane can be less expensive than by train.
   d) will become cheaper.

5. Climate change …
   a) will not affect rich countries.
   b) will lead to conflicts between rich and poor.
   c) affects poor countries before rich countries.
   d) is caused by our demand for energy and resources.

6. We should …
   a) become different consumers.
   b) buy nothing any more.
   c) take part in the "Buy Nothing Day".
   d) count the adverts we see.

7. The commentator wants to point out that …
   a) we can do nothing about the problem.
   b) especially people in the rich part of the world should do something.
   c) we have to use the resources of our planet more carefully.
   d) we have no free will to change things.

‹P› **After listening**

e) Explain the relationship of the slogan on the right to the commentary "Consuming the world".

f) Think about the electrical appliances in your household.

1. Make a list of three items which you believe are necessary and three which are not.
2. Work in pairs. Compare your list with a classmate's list.
3. Make a common list with your partner. Present it to the class. Give reasons for your choice.

54 | Basic course | Advanced course | Cross-cultural communication

D Practice | Ecology and economy 6

2 Sustainable schools

Get the eco-label for your school

Hi! I'm Daniel and last year my college won the Green Flag because we took part in a world-wide challenge between schools to make them environmentally friendly. The programme is called "Eco-schools" and it is organized by the non-profit "Foundation for Environmental Education". Currently 43 countries around the world are taking part.

How did we win the Green Flag? We concentrated on four environmental topics: waste, school grounds and equipment, energy and healthy living. We used the future workshop to create an environmentally-friendly concept.

Now it's your turn. Get involved and win the Green Flag!

‹ P › ■ Read the personal statement above and use the future workshop (see Facts) to create an environmentally friendly concept for your college.

Critique phase I: Think of things that your college does to protect the environment. Structure them in a word web similar to the one below.

Critique phase II: Now think of things which are harmful to your college environment.

Fantasy phase I: Get together in small groups and collect ideas to turn your school into a sustainable college. Use the Internet for help.
Fantasy phase II: Prepare a presentation with your ideas. Suggestions for your presentation: posters, collages, market stalls, interviews, PowerPoint presentations.
▶ SF 32 Giving a talk or presentation
Fantasy phase III: Present your concept to your class.

Realisation phase I: Vote for the group that has got the best ideas.
‹ M › **Realisation phase II:** Verschriftlichen Sie die besten realisierbaren Ideen, indem Sie einen Brief auf Deutsch verfassen, der an die Schulleitung Ihrer Schule gerichtet ist. ▶ SF 22 Mediation/translation

Facts

A future workshop helps you to develop creative solutions to a problem. The future workshop has three phases:

1. In the critique phase you speak freely about the positive and negative aspects of your present situation.

2. In the fantasy phase you turn the results from the critique phase into positive ideas, visions and dreams. Be as creative as you can.

3. In the realisation phase you check your ideas regarding their practicability. When you have found a solution, write down an action plan.

Key Words

• eco-schools • environmental school programmes • environmental education • sustainability • sustainable schools

| International business correspondence | Exam preparation |

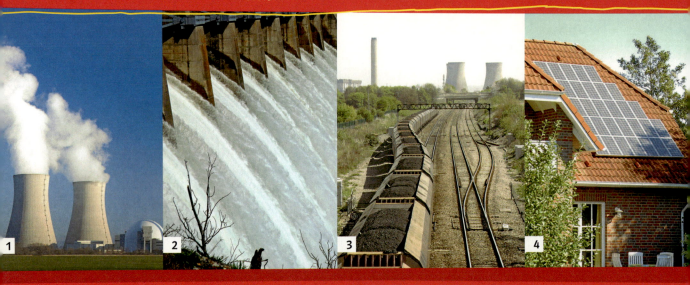

Unit 7
Man and technology

A Getting started: Your choice?

Before reading Video lounge ▶ 3

a) Look at the four photos above and describe the different ways in which electricity is produced.

Understanding the text

b) Find the most suitable options according to the text on page 57.
More than one answer can be true.

1. Ainsworth is a town in …
   a) Nebraska.
   b) Mexico.
   c) Canada.
   d) an area where not much really happens.

2. Today, visitors who go to Ainsworth can see …
   a) a big wind farm.
   b) a viewing platform.
   c) lots of horse thieves.
   d) wind turbines that are more than 100 metres high.

3. The area around Ainsworth is ideal for the installation of wind farms because …
   a) there are favourable winds from the north and south.
   b) there are favourable winds from the east and west.
   c) the winds are very strong.
   d) the winds are not too strong.

4. One of the big disadvantages of wind turbines is that …
   a) they can be seen against the sky.
   b) they are often built far away from the demand for energy.
   c) you can hear the sound of new technology.
   d) they need a lot of empty space.

A Getting started | Man and technology 7

The answer is blowing in the wind by Rick Martin

A Many people say that Ainsworth, Nebraska lies in the middle of nowhere. The town even has an annual Middle of Nowhere Festival. One of the big advantages of being in the middle of nowhere is the wind. Some years ago officials from the Nebraska Public Power District put up wind monitors at different places around the state. Soon they found out that Ainsworth has wonderful winds flowing down from Canada and up from Mexico. And the winds are just right, not too hard and not too soft.

B About ten years ago Nebraska Public built two small turbines just some miles north of Ainsworth in an area which was not known for its modern technology but for a long history of horse thieves. The first turbines generated power for nearly 400 homes. When you drive out of Ainsworth today, you can't miss the three dozen turbines – up to 350 feet high – in the hills beside grazing cattle. And you can hear the sound of a new era, the sound of energy that is created without burning coal, the sound of the future. Standing beneath the 8.5 ton blades of the turbines you can hear them go whoosh – whoosh – whoosh as they turn …

C "It was like a wonder when we were picked to be the first big wind farm in Nebraska," says the mayor of Ainsworth. When the project was finished, Nebraska Public even created a viewing platform near the main road where visitors can have an impressive view of the big flowers of steel standing out against the wide skies of Nebraska. "Nobody has complained about them," the mayor adds.

D Of course, wind energy can profit from high oil prices and the trend towards putting taxes on carbon dioxide emissions. However, smaller countries are running out of places where they can put wind turbines. Open land is not a problem in the United States, however, the main problems are that the wind does not blow all of the time and wind farms are often built far from the big cities where the demand for electricity is the greatest. So wind energy may be a wonder for Ainsworth, Nebraska, but it seems that it is not the answer to all of our energy problems.

(379 words)

c) You are preparing a presentation in German about wind energy in the USA. Find suitable information in the text to complete the chart in German.
▶ SF 22 Mediation/translation

Vorteile des Standorts	Beschreibung des Windparks	Reaktion der Bevölkerung	Vorteile der Windenergie	Nachteile der Windenergie
…	…	…	…	…

After reading

d) Make sentences about the advantages and disadvantages of wind power.

Example: On the one hand there is enough land for wind farms in the USA but on the other hand …

e) Talk about other ways of producing electricity, and their advantages and disadvantages in the same way. The words in the box may help you.

Forms of electricity production	Advantages and disadvantages
coal • oil • gas • biofuels • nuclear energy • solar energy • hydro power	enough land • relatively cheap • CO_2 • easy to produce • free • expensive technology • environmentally friendly • dangerous • renewable • exhaustible • problems with waste • emissions • dependent • climate changes • environmental problems • food production

International business correspondence | Exam preparation | 57

7 Man and technology

B Language

1 The future of energy

A lot of suggestions from different groups in society can be read in the newspapers or heard in the news. Complete the following suggestions in the passive voice. 'Must', 'should', 'can' or 'could' must be used at least once.

1. Use oil more carefully!
   Example: Oil should be used more carefully.
2. Save energy!
3. Promote solar power and other renewable forms of energy!
4. Reduce energy consumption!
5. Make nuclear energy safer!
6. Use more biogas!
7. Make wind turbines more efficient!
8. Find new deposits of gas and oil!
9. Make traditional power stations cleaner!

> **Grammar**
>
> **Passive voice**
> **Example:** New technologies were developed.
> *Das Passiv wird gebildet mit einer Form von* to be *in der jeweiligen Zeit und der 3. Form des Verbs (Partizip Perfekt).*
> **Example:** Coal is transported to power plants by ship.
> *Der Ausführende kann mit* by *angehängt werden.*
> **Example:** Energy consumption must (should, can) be reduced.
> *Das Passiv kann auch mit Hilfsverben gebildet werden.*
>
> ▶ GF 28 Passive voice

2 How electricity is produced

a) Describe how electricity is produced in a coal-fired power station.

1. coal / transport / to the coal-fired power plant / by ship
   Example: Coal is transported to the coal-fired power plant by ship.
2. it / store / near the power plant
3. coal / burn
4. water / heat
5. steam / produce
6. steam / lead / through turbines
7. the blades of the turbines / drive / by the steam
8. magnets inside the generators / move
9. electric energy / produce / in the generators
10. it / send / into power lines
11. steam / cool down
12. water / use again

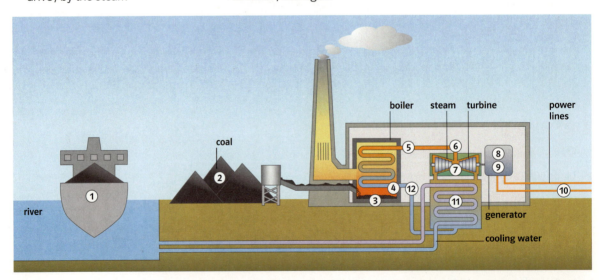

b) Write a description of the process in a complete text. Connect the sentences with words from the box.

> **Language**
>
> then • afterwards • later • finally • and so • in this way • next

58 | Basic course | Advanced course | Cross-cultural communication

B Language | Man and technology 7

3 Where were things made?

- Look around your classroom and you will see lots of different products like clothes, shoes and electronic goods. Where were they made? Ask and answer questions about products such as T-shirts, sweaters, caps, school bags, mobile phones, MP3 players, school books, glasses, earrings, pens, drinks, etc.

Example:

> Student A: Where were your trainers made?
> Student B: My trainers were made in Vietnam. – And where were your glasses produced?
> Student A: My glasses were produced in China. Or: I don't know where they were produced. Or: I think they were produced in Asia.

4 Ainsworth wind farm

- Complete the following text about Ainsworth wind farm using the passive voice in the right tense. The first example has been done for you.

> Some years ago wind monitors **were put up** [1. put up] in different places around Nebraska. Soon it [2. find out] that Ainsworth has wonderful winds. People in Ainsworth were surprised when their area [3. pick]. First two small turbines [4. build] north of Ainsworth in an area which [5. know] for its horse thieves a hundred years ago. Today there is a large wind farm which [6. cannot, miss] by visitors. When the project [7. finish] a year ago a viewing platform [8. create]. Power for nearly all of the homes in Ainsworth [9. can, generate] by the wind farm today. The sound of a new era [10. can, hear] and this is a sound that [11. create] without burning coal. "A disadvantage is that wind farms [12. often build] far from big cities in the last few years," says the mayor of Ainsworth. "Of course, not all questions [13. answer] by wind energy in the future but it is a big step forward."

5 The use of energy in transport/Production processes

- Do <u>one</u> of the following tasks, 1 or 2:

  1. Write a short report about the development of the use of energy in transport from the past to the future. Think about steam engines and other inventions, the transport situation today and ideas for the future. Use the passive voice at least five times. The words in the box can help you.

  2. Choose an interesting product and describe its production process. Information from the Internet can help you. Use the passive voice at least five times in your description. Connect your sentences using words from the language box in exercise 2b).

Language

engine • steam • diesel • petrol • electric motor • hybrid car • biodiesel • biofuels • solar power • hydrogen

| International business correspondence | Exam preparation | 59

7 Man and technology

C Reading

Green technology and economic growth

Before reading

a) What do you think? What does the term "green technology" refer to?

Commentary

The green-tech revolution in Britain
Commentary by Harold McLeod

About two centuries ago, when the first industrial revolution took place Britain led the world into a new industrial age. Our island was the centre of revolutionary engineering ideas and became the heart and the brains of the new economic development

Two hundred years on it could be Britain again that start the green-tech revolution. While green ideas were often things of the past years ago, today's green-technology revolution can lead Britain into the future.

Of course, it has to do with climate change that will affect every family, every business and every country. It is our moral duty to future generations and to poorer countries to turn into a low-carbon society. But this is only one side of the coin. Green technology will also mean new economic growth, new jobs, new industries and new opportunities.

Within a decade the global environmental sector will be worth £5 trillion and provide tens of millions of jobs. So the countries and the companies that develop the technologies fastest will be the most successful – as two hundred years ago. We already lead the world in many environmental technologies, as for example in offshore wind farms.

But we must take further steps in that direction. Energy-saving products must be developed, renewable energy systems erected, insulation in homes must be installed. Britain's future lies in digital, low-carbon and high-technology development – we must invest in a nationwide high-speed broadband network, build a first-class modern infrastructure and support future industries such as biotechnology. Onshore and offshore wind farms, wave and tidal energy systems will help us to increase the share of renewable energy sources. Our aim must be the environmentally-friendly community in which living and working is worthwhile.

Some people argue that in hard economic times we should reduce our efforts in this direction. They say that investing in green technology will raise the costs of production and services and make Britain less competitive. But the opposite is true. Being among the first developed countries that can offer a wide range of green products and services will lead to a rate of growth that the British economy has not experienced for a long time. ∎

(362 words)

C Reading | Man and technology **7**

‹R› ## Understanding the text

b) Say whether your ideas about "green technology" in exercise a) were right.

c) Do the following tasks.

1. Find a heading for each of the paragraphs.
2. Describe the two revolutions mentioned in the text and compare them.
3. Find examples of green technology in the text.
4. Explain why these technologies can be called green.

5. Is the author for or against green technology? Give reasons for your view.
6. Draw two word webs. As the central words choose "technology" and "economy". Find as many words and expressions as you can in the text that are related to them.

After reading

‹P› **f)** Describe possible effects of the climate change.

g) Explain how green technology can lead to economic growth and more jobs.

Training skills – How to write a composition/comment

‹P› **h)** Should we support green technology?
► **SF16 Writing a composition/comment**

■ There is a discussion going on in the media about the development of green technology. What do you think? Write a composition in about 150 words by following these steps:

1. Write an introduction to the topic.

   Example: Today there is a lot of discussion in the media about global warming. Politicians and scientists are arguing about the best way to deal with it. They want to …

2. Find arguments for and against green technology in the text "The green-tech revolution" and write them in a list.

   Example:

Green technology	
For	**Against**
climate change will affect everyone	higher costs of production

3. Find more arguments for and against green technology on your own and complete your list.

4. Write complete sentences and use suitable connectives from language box 1.

   Example: On the one hand climate change will affect everyone …

5. Draw conclusions from the arguments above and state your point of view. The words in language box 2 may help you.

   Example: In conclusion I would say that green technology can …

Language 1

firstly • secondly • in addition • moreover • on the one hand • on the other hand • in contrast • however • although • next • then • because • therefore • not only… but also • finally

Language 2

in conclusion • as a result • in my opinion • in my view • my opinion is • in short • on the whole

International business correspondence | Exam preparation | **61**

7 Man and technology

D Practice

1 A radio interview: The office of the future

Before listening

a) Read the heading and look at the photo. What do you think the radio interview will be about?

‹R› While listening

A1.20 b) Listen to the radio interview and find out if your ideas in exercise a) are mentioned in the report.

c) Listen again and correct the following statements.

1. Mike Turner meets Ron Silver for the first time.
2. Ron is in the studio.
3. Ron is an employee at WebApps Corporation.
4. Ron's headquarters is in Leeds.
5. The employees at WebApps Corporation work in their offices from nine to five.
6. They visit their clients on all continents.
7. Ron has offices in New York, London and Tokyo.
8. Ron thinks that only a few companies can use mobile offices in the future.

‹P› After listening

d) What activities can you do with the help of modern mobile or online communications without leaving your home that would not be possible without these tools?

‹P› 2 High-tech?

| 1 **Paperless office a dream?** |
| 2 **Net breaks down – no New Year's wishes** |
| 4 **1,000 friends – but not a single real one!** |
| 5 **No more cashiers at the cash desk?** |

3 **Just google it!**

a) Choose one of the headlines and say what you think the newspaper article could be about. Explain how modern technology could be used or has been used in the situation mentioned.

b) Make up headlines of your own.

---

62 | Basic course | Advanced course | Cross-cultural communication

D Practice | Man and technology 7

‹P› **3 Office technology**

▫ Describe and analyze the cartoon. ► SF 27 Describing cartoons

‹M› **4 Automation**

▫ Ein englischsprachiger Freund ist interessiert an der technologischen Entwicklung in Deutschland. Fassen Sie den folgenden Kommentar auf Englisch zusammen. Die Stichpunkte im Kästchen können Ihnen dabei helfen.

Language

automatic • fill up with petrol • petrol station • button • measure • labour costs • cash desk

Alles automatisch?
Kommentar von Angela Christina Müller

Immer mehr Unternehmen folgen dem Trend, Arbeitskräfte einzusparen und stattdessen den Kunden arbeiten zu lassen. Die Mitarbeiter werden durch Terminals ersetzt, an denen sich die Kunden
5 informieren, Fahrkarten kaufen oder neuerdings sogar bezahlen sollen. Es soll so einfach sein wie tanken oder Bargeld aus dem Automaten ziehen. Der Kunde nimmt den Scanner, der den Code auf dem Artikel liest, und zahlt mit der Karte durch Tastendruck. Dies soll Vorteile
10 für den Kunden bringen – insbesondere kürzere Wartezeiten an den Kassen. Aber durch diese Maßnahme können die Unternehmen natürlich ihre Arbeitskosten senken. Ob dadurch die Preise sinken, bleibt fraglich.

Aber der Trend scheint nicht aufzuhalten zu sein. 15
Längst haben wir uns daran gewöhnt, unsere Ware selbst auszuwählen, zur Kasse zu transportieren und danach einzupacken. Und unsere jungen Leute wissen sicherlich nicht mehr, was Bedienung an einer Tankstelle bedeutet. 20
Noch gibt es Angestellte bei der Bank, bei der Bahn oder der Post, da gerade ältere Menschen Probleme mit der Technik haben. Aber es wird wohl nicht mehr lange dauern, bis wir als Kunden alles selbst machen. Die Frage bleibt dann jedoch, woher wir das Geld zum 25
Bezahlen an der automatischen Kasse nehmen sollen, wenn es keine Arbeitsplätze mehr gibt. (202 Wörter)

Unit 8
The tourist industry

A Getting started: Holidays and leisure

Before reading Video lounge ▶ 4

a) Describe the above photos. ▶SF 26 Describing illustrations and photographs

b) Where would you like to spend your next holidays? Say why.

Trends in tourism

As part of our series of interviews with important members of the tourist industry this week we interviewed Sandra Peters, the manager of World Wide Tours.

5 **Travel Mag**   Ms Peters, the tourist industry has become one of the most profitable industries in society today. What kind of holiday do most of your customers want when they book with you?
S Peters   Well, traditionally, people like to spend
10 their holidays relaxing on the beach or doing some kind of sporting activity. And in the last few years people have increasingly liked to do these things abroad.

Travel Mag   But why do a lot of people decide to
15 go abroad for their holidays?
S Peters   That is easy to answer. People earn more money and have more days off work than in the past. So they have more time to spend their money and go away on holidays. And they
20 like to go abroad because of the sunshine. Do you remember the terrible summer we had in England last year? I can understand people wanting to get away for their holidays.
Travel Mag   And you have quite a lot of
25 inexpensive foreign holidays in your catalogue.
S Peters   That's right. Foreign travel is not as expensive as it was and that has made it even

64 | Basic course   Advanced course   Cross-cultural communication

A Getting started | The tourist industry **8**

    more attractive. The new technology in modern
    planes contributes to cheaper travel. It is also
30 easier to get to places as transport infrastructures
    are much better. New airports have been built
    all over the world. Consequently you can often
    travel directly to your holiday destination. In
    this way travelling times have been cut and more
35 exotic places have become more accessible to
    more tourists.
    Travel Mag So, mass tourism has arrived in
    faraway places, too?
    S Peters Yes, it has. Last year we had about
40 1 million bookings for Spain but we also had
    300,000 bookings to countries in the Far East.
    Travel Mag But not everybody wants to spend
    their holidays on a beach.
    S Peters No, of course not. We offer a whole
45 range of holidays, from adventure travel and
    cultural trips to ecotourism, extreme sports
    tourism, safaris, and even space tourism.

    Travel Mag So we can say that your business is
    still growing?
50 **S Peters** Yes, the tourist industry in general has
    expanded over the years and many companies
    have profited from this development. Just think
    about the number of new hotels, restaurants,
    airlines and taxi services that there are today.

(386 words)

‹R› **Understanding the text**

    c) Give examples of what most people do on holiday.

    d) List some reasons why British people go abroad on holiday.

    e) Give reasons why faraway destinations have become more attractive to tourists.

    f) Explain how the service sector has benefited from tourism (see Facts).

‹M› g) You tell a friend who wants to open a travel agency about the interview. Summarize the most important aspects in German.
     ▶ SF 22 Mediation/translation

‹P› **After reading** ▶ SF 21 Word webs

    h) Copy the word web into your exercise book. Write down words from the text and other words that you know. If necessary use a dictionary

    i) Work with a partner. Compare word webs and then add any new words your partner has found to your word web.

Facts

The economy is divided into three sectors.

Primary sector: extraction and production of raw materials.
Examples: agriculture and mining.

Secondary sector: production of goods.
Example: manufacturing of cars.

Tertiary sector (Service sector): services to consumers and businesses.
Examples: insurance companies, banks and shops.

| International business correspondence | Exam preparation | **65** |

8 The tourist industry

B Language

1 Sightseeing quiz

a) Match the following sights with the correct cities and countries.

Sights	Cities	Countries
Red Square	Paris	USA
Opera House	London	Australia
Ying Sin Koon Temple	Berlin	China
White House	New York City	France
Brandenburg Gate	Washington D.C.	Russia
Statue of Liberty	Sydney	Britain
Eiffel Tower	Moscow	Germany
Tower Bridge	Hong Kong	USA

b) Check if your partner's solutions are correct.

Example:
Student A: What will you see if you go to Paris?
Student B: If I go to Paris in France, I will see the Eiffel Tower.

2 Planning a trip

Jennifer and Carl, two Australians living in Ulm, have decided to get married. They want to get married at home because of their families and friends so they go to a travel agency to get some information about flights. Luckily, the travel agent speaks English, as they don't speak much German.

One student takes the role of Jennifer or Carl, and the other the role of the travel agent. Ask and answer questions.

Examples:
Jennifer/Carl: Which airline will we fly with if we depart at half past five?
Travel agent: If you depart at half past five, you will fly with British Airways.
Jennifer/Carl: Where will we leave from if we fly with Qantas?
Travel agent: If you fly with Qantas, you will leave from Stuttgart Airport.

> **Grammar**
>
> **Conditional Type 1**
> Example: If you travel to New York, you will see the Statue of Liberty.
> Present simple im if-Satz – Zukunft mit will im Hauptsatz
>
> **Conditional Type 2**
> Example: If I had the money, I would travel around the world.
> Past simple im if-Satz – Conditional mit would im Hauptsatz
>
> **Conditional Type 3**
> Example: If I had known better, I would have stayed at home.
> Past perfect im if-Satz – Conditional mit would have im Hauptsatz
>
> ▶ GF 27 Conditionals

Airline	Flight number	Departure	Destination	Departure time	Arrival time	Flight time	Price
British Airways	BA 955	Munich International Airport	London Heathrow	Sunday 17:30	Sunday 18:30	23 hours 50 minutes	€ 782.04
	Layover 3 hours 45 minutes						
	BA 7312	London Heathrow	Sydney Kingsford Smith Apt	Sunday 22:15	Tuesday 06:05		

Airline	Flight number	Departure	Destination	Departure time	Arrival time	Flight time	Price
Qantas	QF 3936	Stuttgart Airport	Frankfurt, International	Sunday 19:51	Sunday 20:30	20 hours 56 minutes	€ 805.50
	Layover 3 hours 25 minutes						
	QF 6	Frankfurt, International	Sydney Kingsford Smith Apt	Sunday 23:55	Tuesday 05:10		

| Basic course | Advanced course | Cross-cultural communication |

3 Tourism and the environment

■ What would happen if …? Complete the suggestions for a better environment using the correct forms of the verbs in brackets.

1. If people [**use**] public transport more, they [**save**] energy.
   Example: If people **used** public transport more, they **would save** energy.
2. If flights [**be**] more expensive, people [**fly**] less.
3. People [**not travel**] so far or so often if they [**think**] more about the environment.
4. If fuel [**be**] more expensive, people [**not use**] their cars so much.
5. Visitors [**do**] sightseeing by bike if cities [**have**] more bikes for hire.
6. If the transport of goods by ship [**be**] faster, more goods [**be delivered**] by ship.
7. If the beaches [**have**] some more bins, the tourists [**not drop**] so much litter.
8. If the guests [**not want**] fresh towels every day, the hotels [**save**] a lot of water.

4 What would you do if …?

■ Now use your imagination. Think about things you would do if …

Example: If I had my own plane, I would fly to the States whenever I liked.

1. If I were a travel agent …
2. If my parents owned a house on Hawaii …
3. If my friend asked me to go on holiday to Majorca …
4. If I spoke several languages …
5. If I won the lottery …

5 After the holidays

■ Jennifer and Carl have come back from their honeymoon in Ireland. They had some problems during the trip and now they are having an argument. Complete the dialogue with the highlighted verbs.

Jennifer: Before we can watch TV we must unpack all of our bags and put the washing machine on.
Carl: Well, if you **hadn't taken** so many clothes on holiday, we **wouldn't have needed** so many suitcases.
Jennifer: Oh come on, I needed those pretty dresses, otherwise we wouldn't have got into those trendy discos. If you [**1. not speak**] to that girl in the bar, I [**2. not be**] jealous and then we [**3. not have**] a big argument and we [**4. have**] a perfect trip.
Carl: You always blame me if anything goes wrong. If you [**5. book**] a holiday to Majorca instead of Ireland, we [**6. have**] a wonderful time in the sun and we [**7. relax**] more.
Jennifer: Well, I asked you and you didn't want me to change the flight. But it [**8. be**] more relaxing if you [**9. take**] your driving licence. Then I [**10. not drive**] the car and the accident [**11. not happen**].
Carl: Oh, never mind. If I [**12. not marry**] you, I [**13. not have**] so much fun.

C Reading: Tourism and conservation

🔊 A1.22 | http://www.ecotourism-foundation.com

About us | Our Initiatives | Learning centre | Support | Ecotourism – Blog

The Ecotourism Foundation

A Local communities and nature need to be preserved. The Ecotourism Foundation has made these two things their top priority. The Foundation is an organization which tries to
5 bring those people living in protected areas into the business of ecotourism. In this way the Foundation believes that nature can be preserved and at the same time the economic situation of the people in such areas can be improved.
10 So what the Foundation does is to help these people by establishing community businesses and providing tourism training and backup assistance.

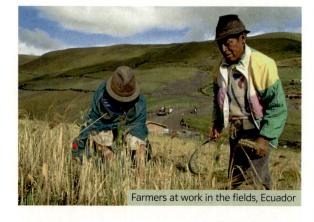
Farmers at work in the fields, Ecuador

B One perfect example can be found in Belize in
15 Central America: The second largest barrier reef in the world is located in southern Belize. Naturally this area needs to be protected. So the Foundation started a programme to train native fishermen to work as guides for the tourists. They are now able
20 to tell the tourists about the fascinating nature, legends and life in the Caribbean. The positive effect is that the native fishermen no longer need to go fishing. In this way the fish population is protected and the fishermen have a better and less
25 dangerous way of securing their incomes.

C Another example of ecotourism can be found in Ecuador's Condor Bioreserve. This area has a variety of attractions including thermal springs, forests, interesting animals and a tradition of
30 wood carving. Attractions like these are useful in several ways. Firstly, the money that the tourists spend contributes to the income of the communities in this area. Secondly, interesting traditions stay alive and thirdly, nature is
35 preserved because the communities no longer need to exploit their surroundings in a way that is harmful to the environment.

(279 words)

Fisherman in Belize

Facts

Ecotourism (also known as ecological tourism) means to travel to sensitive and untouched areas with the aim of educating the travellers, bringing money to local communities and most important, preserving nature and the different cultures there.

C Reading | The tourist industry **8**

Training skills – How to answer questions on a text

Before reading

a) Look at the photos on page 68 and the heading of the text. What do you think the text is about?

Example: I think the text is about tourism and the pictures show people who could be affected by tourism …

Understanding the text

b) Read the text carefully to get a general impression of it.

c) Summarize the text in a few sentences.

Example: The text is about ecotourism and deals with the functions of the Ecotourism Foundation …

d) Read the questions.

1. What has the Ecotourism Foundation made its top priority?
2. What positive effects does the work of the Foundation have for the people in a protected area?
3. How did the Foundation help people in the protected area in Belize?
4. How can attractions like the ones in Ecuador's Condor Bioreserve be useful?

e) Scan the text and note the lines where you can find the answers.

Example for question 1:
– Lines 1–3

Example for question 2:
– Lines 8–13

f) Look up all of the unknown words which are important for the answer.

Example: community (line 1)
community, n: 1. group of people living in an area of the same race or having the same job, religion or interests; 2. people sharing the same ideas; 3. a group of plants or animals interacting with one another in a place under similar conditions

Example: establish (line 11)
establish, v: 1. get people to believe in something; 2. start something such as a business; 3. show that something is correct

g) Decide which explanation is the most suitable according to the text.

– The first explanation is the most suitable.

– Here the second explanation is the most suitable.

h) Write down key words that you can use in your answers.

Example:
– help natives
– save nature

Example:
– earn money
– start businesses
– get training

i) Answer the questions using your own words.
  – You may use the question as an introduction in your answer.
  – Give and rephrase the main facts using your key words.
  – Always write full sentences.

Example: The Ecotourism Foundation has made nature and the people traditionally living in this area their top priority.

Example: People living in protected areas get help from the Foundation to start …

j) Check your answer.

| International business correspondence | Exam preparation | **69** |

8 The tourist industry

D Practice

1 Sustainable tourism meets mass tourism

Before listening

a) Which photo do you associate with sustainable tourism and which with mass tourism? Say why.

⟨R⟩ **While listening**

🎯 A1.23 b) Listen to Lisa and Matthew who have just come back from their holiday trips. Find the most suitable options according to the statements. More than one answer can be true.

1. What kind of holiday did Matthew go on?
   a) sustainable tourism
   b) mass tourism
   c) safari tourism
   d) medical tourism

2. What sporting activities did Matthew do during the day?
   a) jet-skiing
   b) paragliding
   c) free climbing
   d) swimming

3. How many young adults met in Calella?
   a) about 60 people
   b) about 560 people
   c) about 10 groups with 50 – 60 people per group
   d) about 800 young adults

4. How much did Lisa's hotel cost?
   a) £200
   b) £300 without breakfast
   c) £100
   d) £300 with breakfast

5. What did Lisa do during the day?
   a) hiked to the volcanoes
   b) slept
   c) swam
   d) watched birds and other animals

6. Where might Lisa go next summer?
   a) Costa Rica
   b) Spain
   c) Ireland
   d) Mali

⟨P⟩ ### 2 Reasons for travelling

a) Describe and compare the pie charts.   ▶ SF 28 Describing diagrams

b) Think of reasons for the main differences between the two charts.

c) Which European country could the charts refer to? Give reasons.

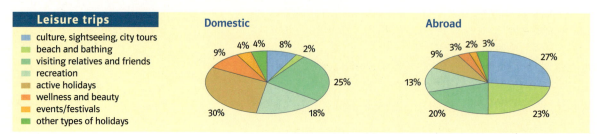

| Basic course | Advanced course | Cross-cultural communication |

D Practice | The tourist industry 8

3 Designing a brochure

- Choose a type of holiday that is possible in the area where you live and design a holiday brochure. You can find information on the Internet.

Key Words
• holiday brochure • holiday • ecotourism

4 Presentation and discussion: Developing an economy

▶ SF 32 Giving a talk or presentation ▶ SF 3 Having a discussion

a) The local government of a small area in South Africa (see map below) wants to expand its economy but cannot decide which sector to develop. Investors from different sectors have different ideas about how to use the area: one idea is to mine the gold there, another is to create a manufacturing area, and yet another idea is to develop tourism. The investors meet with the local government to present their ideas. Work in four groups. The first group represents the local government, the second group represents the mining company, the third group represents the manufacturers and the fourth group represents the travel organizations.

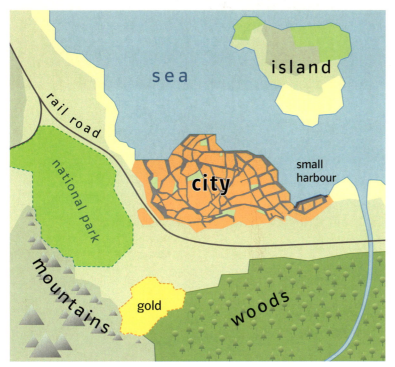

b) The local government group uses role card A "Local government" on the right. The other groups have to persuade the local government to use the area for their purpose. Prepare and give a presentation. You will find role card B "Mining company", role card C "Manufacturing company" and role card D "Travel organization" on page 173.

c) After the presentations the government asks questions about the effects of each type of development.

d) All of the groups discuss the pros and cons of the suggestions.

e) Decide in class which ideas are most suitable for the area.

Role card A

Local government

- Before the presentations you should think about the following:
  - what would be best for the area,
  - what would be best for the people living there.
- Ask about the possible effects of each development: jobs, pollution, traffic, tourism, income of people in the area, technical requirements, etc.
- Listen to the three groups carefully. Take notes during the presentation and discussion to help you make a decision later on.

Unit 9
Globalisation and multiculturalism

A Getting started: Globalisation – chance or risk?

‹P› **Before reading** ▶ SF 26 Describing illustrations and photographs

a) Describe the above photos.

b) Match the photos with the headings on the right. Two headings do not match.

c) Explain what the photos and headings could have to do with globalisation.

- sports • trade and transport
- communication
- education and training
- labour market • tourism

‹R› **Understanding the text**

d) Find the most suitable options according to the text. More than one answer can be true.

1. Bhanu works …
   a) in the cotton fields near Surat.
   b) for very little money.
   c) in a dyeing factory.
   d) in a T-shirt factory.

2. Marlene …
   a) wants to buy American labels.
   b) wants to buy Austrian clothes.
   c) lives a boring life.
   d) thinks American clothes are unfashionable.

3. Matthew can buy …
   a) over 160 different US-branded sneakers all over the world.
   b) US-branded trainers in 160 countries.
   c) fast food only in some countries.
   d) hamburgers all over the world.

4. Nicole's life will change, because …
   a) her company is going to close its factory in Germany.
   b) she must move to the Czech Republic for economic reasons.
   c) she will have to either work for less money in the Czech Republic or risk becoming unemployed.
   d) a manufacturer of MP3 players is moving to the Czech Republic.

| 72 | Basic course | Advanced course | Cross-cultural communication |

A Getting started | Globalisation and multiculturalism 9

What's globalisation to them?
◉ A1.24

A Bhanu, 15, from Surat, India: "Every day my work reminds me of how small the world is. Most of the people in our city work for the textile industry: they either collect cotton in the large cotton fields around Surat or they work in one of the dyeing factories. I'm a dyer and I dye the cotton which is used to make T-shirts that are sold all over the world. The pay is low and the chemicals we use are not good for us. So, some people risk their lives while others make money."

B Marlene, 18, from Vienna, Austria: "Well, what's globalisation to me? I don't know, I'm not very interested in things like that. Maybe it's about being able to buy whatever you like. I love to go shopping with my friends. We really like American labels, especially for T-shirts, jeans and all kinds of accessories. American clothes are so cool! Life would be very boring if we were only able to buy Austrian stuff."

C Matthew, 20, from Chicago, USA: "I'm very interested in other cultures and I love travelling to countries all over the world. Today it is possible to buy cheap flights to any destination. Also, international education standards are great because they help you to get into foreign colleges more easily. The world has changed in many ways, but not every change is for the better. You find the same coffee shops, fast food chains and clothing brands no matter where you go. I can eat a hamburger in more than 100 countries or buy US-branded trainers in 160 countries. So many cities are losing their identities."

D Nicole, 21, from Frankfurt, Germany: "Unfortunately globalisation is going to make life difficult for me in the future. I'm in the second year of my apprenticeship at a leading manufacturer of mobile phones and the company is going to move its factory to the Czech Republic for economic reasons. Should I go with them and make less money and leave my family and friends or should I stay and risk unemployment? Either way globalisation will change my life in a negative way."

(362 words)

e) Answer the following questions in complete sentences.
1. What does globalisation mean to the people in Surat?
2. What is Marlene interested in?
3. In which ways have many cities changed?
4. What kind of problem is Nicole facing?

f) Write down the pros and cons of globalisation according to the texts and discuss them in class. ▶ SF 3 Having a discussion

After reading

g) "The world is getting smaller." Use the information in the texts and your own ideas to write a comment of about 250 words.
▶ SF 16 Writing a composition/comment

| International business correspondence | Exam preparation | 73

9 Globalisation and multiculturalism

B Language: Welcome to Ohio!

a) Sam, a student in New Zealand, is spending a year in Ohio in the United States of America as part of his course. His tutor gives him a list of things to do before he leaves. Report what the tutor wants Sam to do as in the example. The verbs in the box may help you.

Example: Sam's tutor told him / advised him to send an e-mail to Mr Wilkins in Ohio.

Sam

Checklist
1. e-mail to Mr Wilkins, your tutor in Ohio
2. letter to your host family
3. courses at the college
4. flights to Ohio
5. company where students do their work placements in Ohio
6. more about the American way of life

read
find out
write
send
check
contact

Grammar

Infinitive with 'to'
Example: He told her to send an e-mail.
nach bestimmten Verben (ask, tell, advise, expect, etc.)

Infinitive without 'to'
Example: Please let me go.
als Objekt nach make und let ohne Präpositionen

Gerund
Example: Julie loves reading.
nach bestimmten Verben (enjoy, like, dislike, hate, prefer etc.)
Example: Julie is interested in reading love stories.
nach Verben, Adjektiven, Substantiven mit Präpositionen

▶ GF 29 Infinitive
▶ GF 30 Gerund

b) Sam has received an e-mail back from Ohio. Complete the e-mail using the correct form of the verbs in the box.

• let • expect • make • want • ask • expect

From: studentadvice@ohiouni.us
To: sam_80@wellingtoninstitute.nz
Subject: Student visit

Dear Sam,

We want to give you an idea of what we [1] expect you to do during your stay. Your tutors have [2] us to develop a work plan for you. They [3] you to do a work placement in a company two days a week.

You will spend the rest of the week at college. The college [4] you to give a presentation about life in New Zealand and how it differs from the American way of life. So you see, it's not a holiday! We [5] you work hard. But we will [6] you go early on Fridays so that you can see as much of Ohio as possible.

We look forward to meeting you soon.

Regards,
Cathy Jackson
Student Advisor Ohio University

B Language | Globalisation and multiculturalism **9**

c) Sam has arrived in Ohio and has already made two new friends, Julie and Marvin. You can see below what they like and don't like doing.

⊕⊕⊕ like	⊖⊖⊖ dislike
⊕⊕⊕ enjoy	⊖⊖⊖ not enjoy
⊕⊕⊕ love	⊖⊖⊖ hate

1. Work in pairs. Play the roles of Julie and Marvin. Tell each other about your likes and dislikes. Use the words in the box on the right.
   Example: Julie: I enjoy reading love stories.
2. What do they prefer doing?
   Example: Julie prefers reading love stories to fantasy novels.

Julie

Marvin

likes	doesn't like	likes	doesn't like
⊕⊕⊕ love stories	⊖⊖⊖ sport on TV	⊕⊕⊕ baseball	⊖⊖⊖ ice hockey
⊕⊕⊕ disco	⊖⊖⊖ fantasy novels	⊕⊕⊕ cinema	⊖⊖⊖ fast food
⊕⊕⊕ restaurant	⊖⊖⊖ tennis	⊕⊕⊕ pop music	⊖⊖⊖ TV

d) Match each phrase with the correct preposition. Then make sentences.
Example: I'm interested in playing … / in listening to … / in reading …

1. be **interested**   **in**
2. be good   to
3. be tired   in
4. be afraid   of
5. look forward   for
6. succeed   of
7. apologize   at

e) Sam's work placement is at a logistics company. When he arrives there, he is given a list of guidelines for new employees. Use the words in the box to complete the guidelines.

• persuade • have • ask • make • **help** • work • discuss • speak

- We are good at [1] **helping** customers with their logistic problems. A lot of our work is done on the phone, so remember to be polite. You must also be interested in [2] customers about their specific problems.
- Very often our phone lines are busy, so, first you should apologize to callers for [3] to wait before [4] to you.
- Remember we have to succeed in [5] them that we can solve their logistics problems. So, you have to be good at [6] their problems.
- At first the work can be difficult, but don't be afraid of [7] small mistakes. In this way you will learn. We look forward to [8] with you.

| International business correspondence | Exam preparation | 75 |

C Reading: Multicultural Britain in the global world

Before reading ▶ SF 26 Describing illustrations and photographs

a) Describe the photos.

b) Skim the text to find out what aspects of it the photos refer to.

Bradford – A global town

A Consumer habits have become more global: You can buy the same products in New York and New Delhi, and if you want an authentic Indian curry in Bradford, England, you only need
5 to go as far as the next takeaway. Companies are thinking more globally, too: In order to keep costs low, production is often moved from industrialized countries in the West to countries where labour is cheaper such as India, Pakistan and the Far East.
10 As a result those jeans you can buy in the high street, for example, are really cheap but they are produced thousands of miles away rather than in local factories. Finally, employees are forced to think globally: they must move to where the work
15 opportunities are. Such movements of companies and people can change the faces of cities radically and Bradford in the north of England is a good example of this.

B Bradford has a long history of immigration and
20 change. In the nineteenth century the city was a major producer of textiles in Europe. German merchants settled there and built warehouses to store their goods – Bradford's textiles – before selling them. We can still see many of these
25 buildings today in an area of Bradford known as "Little Germany". The German immigrants were soon followed by Italians and Eastern Europeans.

C In the 1950s the next wave of immigrants started to come from India and Pakistan. Most
30 of these immigrants came originally to work in the textile factories. Nowadays, most of the second and third generations work in other sectors. The reason is simple: nearly all of Bradford's textile factories have now closed. Ironically, much of the textile
35 production has moved to the immigrants' home countries. Nevertheless, Bradford still has a large Asian population and you can find a large range of Asian markets and stores which sell both modern and traditional Asian textiles. And so Bradford's
40 long history of the textile trade carries on into the 21st century.

D Bradford has become even more racially diverse following a more recent wave of immigration. Migrant workers from eastern
45 Europe have come to Britain to escape the poor economic situation in their own countries. If you visit one of Bradford's markets, you will hear a variety of languages, from Polish to Latvian to Russian. However, unlike the Asian immigrants,
50 this group of migrant workers will probably move on as soon as the economic situation changes.

(402 words)

C Reading | Globalisation and multiculturalism 9

Training skills – How to do multiple choice exercises

Understanding the text ▶ SF12 Multiple choice exercises

c) 1. Skim the text to get a general impression of it. Names, countries or places, numbers and dates can all be important key words.
   Example: Bradford, North of England, Germans, Italians, Eastern Europeans.

2. Read the options in the following exercise carefully.
   Example: Many Europeans came to Bradford in the 19th century because …
   a) it was a centre for Germans.
   b) it had become ethnically diverse.
   c) it offered work in the textile industry.
   d) it had become one of the leading textile centres in Europe.

3. Scan the text for the relevant information.
   Example: 19th century – German merchants – Italians and Eastern Europeans soon followed the German immigrants to the textile centre. (see lines 26 – 27).

4. Read the statements again and eliminate false statements. Is this information mentioned in the text? Is the opposite true?
   Example: Eliminate options a and b.

5. Decide which statement is true. Sometimes more than one option is correct.
   Example: This leads you to the options c and d.

6. To check your answer, find a reason or reasons why the statements are true.
   Example: Options c and d are true because it says in the text that Bradford was a major producer of textiles in Europe (lines 20 – 21).

7. If you are not sure, do not guess. You may lose credits if your answer is not correct.

d) Do the multiple choice exercise in the same way. Find the most suitable options according to the text. More than one answer can be true.

1. Many firms produce goods abroad because …
   a) the workers have left for other countries.
   b) they do not have to pay high wages there.
   c) they want to sell to tourists.
   d) they can then sell their products more cheaply.

2. The Pakistanis who first came to Bradford worked …
   a) in shops.
   b) in the textile mills.
   c) in engineering plants.
   d) in the digital media sector.

3. Almost all of the textile factories in Bradford have closed because …
   a) all of the immigrants have left Bradford.
   b) the immigrants sold them to companies in the Far East.
   c) textiles are now produced more cheaply in Asian countries.
   d) the second-generation immigrants do not want to work in Bradford.

4. You can say that Bradford is still very "Asian" because it has …
   a) many Thai restaurants.
   b) many Asian businesses.
   c) a lot of Chinese people.
   d) a lot of Asians who have remained there.

5. Bradford is truly multicultural because it has …
   a) people from all over the world.
   b) cheap markets.
   c) a mixture of people from Europe and Asia.
   d) textiles from all over the world.

6. The latest wave of migrants to Bradford has come from …
   a) India.
   b) Pakistan.
   c) Eastern Europe.
   d) China.

International business correspondence | Exam preparation | 77

9 Globalisation and multiculturalism

D Practice

1 People on the move

a) Describe the cartoon. ▶ SF 27 Describing cartoons

b) Explain the message of the cartoon.

2 Keeping trade fair

Before listening ▶ SF 26 Describing illustrations and photographs

a) Describe the photos. What aspects of global trade would you associate with them?

D Practice | Globalisation and multiculturalism **9**

‹R› **While listening**

A1.26 **b)** Listen to the podcast and note down the names of the people in the studio.

c) Match the photos on page 78 with the two people being interviewed.

d) Listen to the podcast again and find the most suitable options. More than one answer can be true.

1. The first studio guest has returned from …
   a) Dubai.
   b) India.
   c) Vietnam.
   d) the Far East.

2. He describes …
   a) the living conditions in Asia.
   b) the working conditions in some Vietnamese factories.
   c) some sights in Vietnam.
   d) some products which are made in Asia.

3. He tells us that many Vietnamese people are …
   a) working in Europe.
   b) working in India.
   c) unemployed.
   d) tourists abroad.

4. He works as a …
   a) teacher.
   b) journalist.
   c) disc jockey.
   d) foreign aid worker.

5. The second studio guest has just come back from …
   a) South East Asia.
   b) a Third World country.
   c) West Africa.
   d) abroad.

6. She tells us that Technoserve is an organization which …
   a) gives poor people food.
   b) produces machines.
   c) trains people to become politicians.
   d) helps to train people to run businesses.

7. She works for …
   a) Technoserve.
   b) Fairtrade.
   c) a local newspaper.
   d) an African restaurant in Bradford.

8. She describes how …
   a) the farmers in Ghana work.
   b) the aid workers help people.
   c) Fairtrade works.
   d) the newspaper works.

9. She wants the radio listeners to buy …
   a) the Bradford newspaper.
   b) Fairtrade products.
   c) some chocolate.
   d) the Fairtrade logo.

After listening

e) Describe what you can see in the photos. ▶ SF 26 Describing illustrations and photographs

1

2

3

f) Choose one of the products shown above. Find out the problems which producers of this product face. Then sum up the support that Fairtrade can offer producers.

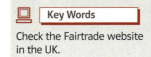

Key Words
Check the Fairtrade website in the UK.

| International business correspondence | Exam preparation | 79 |

Online-Link
800031-0010

Unit 10
International politics

A Getting started: The United Nations and the situation in Africa

Before reading

a) The photos show some of the tasks of the United Nations. Match the photos with the tasks. Two tasks do not fit.

Tasks
- economic development • humanitarian help
- peacekeeping • international law • human rights

‹P› b) Have a closer look at one of the photos. Say what the story behind it could be. Think about 'who', 'where', 'when', 'what' and 'why'.

Understanding the text

c) Do the following tasks in complete sentences.

1. Describe the situation of many people in Zimbabwe.
2. Give three reasons for the difficulties in Zimbabwe.
3. Describe the activities of the organizations which give aid in Zimbabwe.
4. Explain how not having enough to eat affects people who are infected with HIV.
5. Describe the effect the high rate of infections has on families and on children in particular.

Facts

The United Nations

Membership: 192 member states
Established: 24 October 1945
Staff: about 40,000
Peacekeeping operations: 16
Budget: USD 4.1 billion (excluding peacekeeping operations)
Official languages: Arabic, Chinese, English, French, Russian, Spanish

80 | Basic course | Advanced course | Cross-cultural communication

A Getting started | International politics 10

Help! by Jeremy Dalton | The Southern Sunday Magazine

A Thabita Moyo will probably die although she has got the drugs that can save her life. Each month her medicine arrives together with a delivery of Red Cross food aid. Thabita lives in a small village in Masvingo, Zimbabwe and her family's food always runs out after a week or two. After that, Thabita and her children have a small meal only once a day made from wild vegetables or maize that they get from their neighbours.

B Thabita suffers from an HIV infection and the pills help to prevent AIDS from breaking out. But she is not able to take the pills on an empty stomach because the pain is terrible. In this way her body is getting weaker and weaker, so at some point she will have AIDS.

C Thabita is not the only one who does not have enough to eat. As well as several non-governmental organizations, the United Nations' World Food Programme feeds about seven million people in Zimbabwe, more than two-thirds of the population. However, the rations only contain about 600 calories a day, which is less than a person needs to survive. That is why many Zimbabweans have fled across the border to South Africa in order to find work and food.

D Political problems, high inflation and bad harvests have caused the situation in Zimbabwe. Matt Coburn, a UN official, explains, "The soil looks healthy here but the problem is that there are not enough quality seeds and no fertilizers." The lack of food has led to an increase in cholera infections, which have already killed more than 3,000 people, and the number is rising. Moreover, one in four Zimbabweans is infected with HIV. AIDS has changed the traditional family model by killing thousands of fathers and mothers. Many children are now in the care of their grandparents or of older brothers and sisters. The number of adults in the working population is decreasing. 60-year-old Sylvia Nyakura had 13 children. Five have already died and they left her with twelve grandchildren who live with her. "There are days when we do not eat," she says. "There's nothing left."

E Furthermore there is no money for books or pens and as a result the children do not go to school. "I don't think I can send the children to school any more," says Shenghi Olomo, who looks after her own children and several grandchildren. "I've sold everything I have to keep them alive. I'm not so worried about school. I'm only worried about food."

(420 words)

Facts

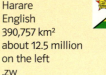

Zimbabwe
Capital: Harare
Official language: English
Area: 390,757 km²
Population: about 12.5 million
Drives: on the left
Internet TLD: .zw

---

d) Match the conditions in which a person can be with their needs.

Conditions	Needs
hungry • thirsty • ill • tired • illiterate • desperate • naked • homeless • cold • poor • barefoot • jobless • persecuted	medicine • hope • drink • food • sleep • clothes • refuge • place to live • heating • work • shoes • money • education

e) Compare your results in d) by making sentences as in the example.
Example: A person who is hungry needs food.

f) Sie wollen auf der Grundlage dieses Artikels an Ihrer Schule zu einer Hilfsaktion für die Menschen in Simbabwe aufrufen. Übernehmen Sie dazu die wesentlichen Argumente aus dem Text.

g) Find out what the following abbreviations stand for and describe their main tasks: UNHCR, UNICEF, WFP, UNCTAD, UNDP.

h) Find out what NGO stands for and give examples of different NGOs.

Key Words
- Zimbabwe • government • UN
- Red Cross • economy • food

International business correspondence | Exam preparation

10 International politics

B Language

1 A report about Senegal

- Replace the highlighted words with a present participle (ing-form) or past participle (third form of the verb).

Examples:
I belong to an ethnic group [1] **called** the Wolof.
A lot of the people [2] **living** in Senegal are very poor.

> **Grammar**
>
> **Present participle**
> Example: After speaking to the President she left New York.
> zur Verkürzung von Sätzen nach after, before, while, etc.
> Example: Every day you can see lots of people visiting the UN buildings statt … who are visiting the UN buildings.
> zur Verkürzung von Relativsätzen im Aktiv
>
> **Past participle**
> Example: There are lots of restaurants built for tourists statt … which were built for tourists.
> zur Verkürzung von Relativsätzen im Passiv
>
> ▶ GF 31 Participles

Hi, my name is Senghor Escale. I come from Senegal, but now I live in Britain. I belong to an
5 ethnic group [**1. which is called**] the Wolof. A lot of the people [**2. who live**] in Senegal are very poor. Most of the people [**3. who leave**]
10 my country come from the eastern part of Senegal. In these areas farmers [**4. who are trying**] to grow food fail to do so as conditions are too hot and dry, and rainfall is very low. For example, the rice [**5. which is grown**] there only amounts to 25% of all the rice [**6. which is needed**]
15 to feed the people.
   During the 17th and 18th centuries slaves and gold were the main items [**7. which were traded**] by the French and British. Nowadays the Senegalese want to organize the economy on their own and are trying to increase all kinds of industrial production
20 [**8. which includes**] the production of chemicals and clothes. I hope the situation in my home country will improve in the next few years. Maybe I will return there one day.

2 UNICEF

- Rewrite the statements about UNICEF, a well-known aid organization for children, using participles as in the examples.

1. Because the UN wanted to help children in need following World War II they founded UNICEF.
   Example: Wanting to help children in need following World War II the UN founded UNICEF.
2. After the UN had established the United Nations International Children's Emergency Fund in 1949 they could give food and clothes to children in need.
   Example: After establishing the United Nations International Children's Emergency Fund in 1949 the UN could give food and clothes to children in need.
3. Before UNICEF helped children with long-term projects they had only carried out short-term projects, like giving them clothes and food.
4. Because UNICEF wanted to help children to a better life they tried to improve their chances of a good education.
5. After they had organized projects to educate the children UNICEF then started to train the teachers.
6. Because the Nobel Prize committee knew that UNICEF had carried out so many successful projects to help children all over the world, they gave UNICEF the Nobel Peace Prize in 1965.
7. As UNICEF saw that many children in developing countries were dying they increased the aid given to them in the 1970s.
8. Because many children live in war zones nowadays they need help from organizations like UNICEF.

82 | Basic course | Advanced course | Cross-cultural communication

3 Food aid for Belarus

■ Work in pairs and complete the interview using the infinitive or -ing form of the verb in brackets. The first examples have been done for you.

Radio Livestation has created a series called "About your neighbour". Radio presenter Carla Cardoso is interviewing Luke Swanson.

Carla: Hello and welcome to our radio show "About your neighbour". Today we are going to talk **about helping** [**1. help**] our neighbours and for that reason I have invited Luke Swanson, who has organized an aid project called "Food aid for Belarus".

Luke: Thank you for **inviting** [**2. invite**] me. I really want **to tell** [**3. tell**] your listeners about our successful aid project for Belarus and I would like **to say** [**4. say**] thanks for the money we were able **to collect** [**5. collect**].

Carla: Before [**6. tell**] us about your trip I would first like [**7. know**] how you got the idea of [**8. help**] people in Belarus of all places?

Luke: Well, one of my friends comes from Belarus and some of her relatives still live there. One day while [**9. have**] lunch she told me about them and how the government has failed [**10. help**] them. So I decided [**11. collect**] money. I have always enjoyed [**12. help**] people.

Carla: How did you arrange [**13. get**] the food to Belarus?

Luke: After [**14. hear**] that it is very difficult to take food over the border we wanted [**15. avoid, drive**] there. So we decided [**16. take**] money there instead and [**17. buy**] the food in Belarus.

Carla: You made over £5,000. How did you succeed in [**18. get**] so much money?

Luke: Instead of just [**19. tell**] people about the project I also showed them photos of smiling children who had received food aid. That worked really well. And I hope [**20. be able, do**] this project again next year.

Carla: Thank you for [**21. tell**] us about your project, Luke, and good luck with it next year.

10 International politics

C Reading: The political system of the USA

Before reading | Video lounge ▶ 5

1   2   3

‹P› **a)** Describe the photos.
▶ SF 26 Describing illustrations and photographs

b) Match the photos with the headings in the text. Two headings do not match.

How the system works

A The federal government of the USA
The government of the United States of America is called a presidential federal government. That means both parliament and the president are elected by citizens.
5 A parliamentary federal government, as in Germany for example, works differently. Here the citizens vote for a parliamentary majority which makes up the government. The USA has a system of "separation of powers" with three branches: legislative, executive and judicial. Each
10 branch works independently of the others. A system of "checks and balances" prevents a concentration of power in only one branch.

B The legislative branch – Congress
The legislative branch is represented by Congress. The
15 primary task of Congress is to write, discuss and pass bills, which must be supported by the President. Other congressional tasks are to control the judiciary and the executive branch. Congress can impeach and get rid of the President. Congress can also reverse the President's
20 veto by a two-thirds majority, pass laws, and approve appointments made by the President. Congress can impeach and remove federal judges from office, and it establishes courts.

C The executive branch – The President
25 The President is Head of State, Head of the Executive and Commander-in-Chief of the armed forces. As Head of State the President meets the leaders of other countries and makes treaties with them if the treaty has been permitted by Congress. As the official head of the US military the
30 President can declare war, although he needs the permission of Congress to do so. The President also influences legislation although his power is limited here. The President passes bills, introduced by Congress, into laws, but he can also veto bills put forward by Congress.
35 Another presidential task is to nominate federal judges with the permission of Congress.

D The judicial branch – The Supreme Court
The Supreme Court was established by the Constitution of the United States of America as the highest court in
40 the country. One of its most important duties is to decide whether cases are constitutional or not. The Supreme Court can declare presidential and congressional actions or laws unconstitutional.

E Elections and voters
There are direct and indirect elections in the USA. Every
45 two years the voters elect the members of Congress by direct vote. The President of the United States of America is elected by indirect vote. Every four years voters elect 538 delegates, who then elect the President. Voters in the USA must be at least 18 years old, they must hold American
50 citizenship, they must have a registered residence and they must be registered in the register of voters.

(429 words)

| Basic course | Advanced course | Cross-cultural communication |

C Reading | International politics **10**

Training skills – How to do mediation exercises

Understanding the text

‹M› **c)** Als Experte des politischen Systems der USA werden Sie gebeten für das Schulportal „Schulen im Internet" eine tabellarische Darstellung des amerikanischen Regierungssystems auf Deutsch zu geben. Übernehmen Sie dazu die folgenden Stichwörter in Form einer Tabelle in Ihr Heft und vervollständigen diese mit den Informationen aus dem Text. Siehe Hilfestellung unten. ► **SF22 Mediation**

- Regierungsform • Verhinderung von Machtkonzentration
- Legislative • Hauptaufgabe der Legislative • Exekutive
- Funktionen des Präsidenten • Judikative
- Hauptaufgabe der Judikative • Wahlverfahren • Wahlrecht

1. Read the text to get a general impression.
   ► **SF9 Anticipating, skimming and scanning**
2. Read the task carefully and find out the text type you are supposed to produce and which language you must use.
   Example: Text type: chart   Language: German
3. Read the text again and either mark or note down the information you need to do the exercise.
   ► **SF9 Anticipating, skimming and scanning**
   Examples: "Regierungsform" only matches the headline of paragraph A, "The federal government of the USA".
4. Now scan paragraph A for words that are similar to or describe "Regierungsform". Select only the relevant points.
   Example: "Regierungsform": Do not describe the kind of "Regierungsform" but only name it: "presidential federal government".
5. A mediation exercise is not a translation! Do not translate words or sentences literally. If you do not know the exact German term, try to paraphrase the English expression.
   Example: "Presidential federal government" = bundesstaatliche Regierungsform mit starker Stellung des Präsidenten

‹M› **d)** Das Schulportal „Schulen im Internet" bittet Sie nun zusätzlich, ein Schaubild auf Deutsch zu beschreiben, in dem das System der Gewaltenteilung in den USA deutlich wird. Übernehmen Sie hierzu die Informationen aus dem Text.

Gewaltenteilung in den USA

| International business correspondence | Exam preparation | 85

10 International politics

D Practice

1 The future of the European Union

Before listening

⟨P⟩ **a)** Decide which of the countries belong to the EU.

- Italy • Slovenia • Norway • Latvia • Russia • Germany
- the Netherlands • Bulgaria • Luxembourg • Turkey • Belarus
- Spain • Greece • Switzerland

⟨R⟩ **While listening**

A2.2 **b)** Listen to four European college students who took part in a discussion in Brussels about "Europe's future". Find out which of the above countries they come from.

c) Listen again and find the most suitable options according to the text. More than one answer can be true.

1. Marika strongly identifies with Europe because …
    a) she has learned a lot about Europe on her travels.
    b) she wants to compete internationally.
    c) she is studying Irish literature.
    d) she has already lived in some European countries and speaks five languages.

2. When asked about the enlargement of the EU, Sanne says that …
    a) every country should be allowed to enter the EU.
    b) too many member states will cause problems.
    c) it is not easy to decide which countries can join.
    d) it will not stay a "Union" because the European continent does not have borders.

3. Marko hopes to see …
    a) more competition between EU member states.
    b) good job opportunities in the EU.
    c) a stable economy in the EU.
    d) German workers losing their jobs.

4. Ilana's country still has big problems as …
    a) EU standards make her countrymen reduce production costs.
    b) EU regulations and laws have not come into effect yet.
    c) there is much corruption and people break laws.
    d) small farmers are going bankrupt.

⟨P⟩ **After listening**

d) Get into five groups and pick one potential candidate for EU membership. Find at least five arguments for the accession of "your" country.

e) Have a discussion in class. At least one member of each group must take part. The rest of the students should support their group member and take notes. Then decide in class which country should be allowed access to the EU.

> **Key Words**
>
> • EU enlargement • Copenhagen criteria • future enlargement of the EU
> • potential EU candidates

2 Britain's role in the European Union

⟨P⟩ **a)** Describe the cartoon on the right. ▶ SF 27 Describing cartoons

b) Explain the attitude towards the EU expressed in the cartoon.

"He says we have to change our name to 'The Kilo Shop'."

D Practice | **International politics** **10**

‹M› **c)** Während Sie ein Praktikum beim Europäischen Parlament (siehe Facts) absolvieren, werden Sie gebeten, für zwei englischsprachige Mitarbeiter den folgenden Kommentar zur EU zusammenzufassen. Schreiben Sie ganze Sätze in englischer Sprache, übersetzen Sie dabei nicht Wort für Wort. ▶ **SF22 Mediation/translation**

Language
European Economic Community (EEC) • Continentals • hostile • to slow down • the Schengen agreement • Schengen II agreement • European Monetary Union • referendum • opponents • supporters

Kommentar

Wohin steuert Großbritannien?
Peer Hanken, Norddeutsche Post

Lange bevor die Briten der damaligen Europäischen Wirtschaftsgemeinschaft (EWG) beitraten, dachten viele Festland-Europäer, dass die Briten sich zu stark vom Rest der Europäer unterscheiden, um nützliche Mitglieder zu werden. Dennoch trat Großbritannien 1973 der EWG bei. Auch britische Regierungen haben ihren Einfluss immer wieder genutzt, um den Integrationsprozess in die EU zu verlangsamen. So hat Großbritannien beispielsweise weder das Schengener Abkommen (Verzicht auf Personenkontrollen an gemeinsamen Grenzen) noch den Prümer Vertrag (grenzüberschreitender Informationsaustausch zur Verfolgung von Straftaten) unterschrieben. Eines der zentralsten Projekte der Europäischen Union ist die Währungsunion. Bezüglich des Euros hat Großbritannien jedoch entschieden, die eigene Währung, das Pfund, so lange beizubehalten, bis sich die Briten in einem Referendum für den Euro aussprechen.

Auch heute noch wird in Großbritannien immer wieder diskutiert, ob das Land die Beziehungen zur EU intensivieren soll oder die Gesetzgebung der EU in einigen Bereichen im eigenen Land reduzieren. Die Gegner einer Intensivierung der politischen Beziehungen mit der EU werden in GB „*Eurosceptics*" genannt, die Befürworter „*Europhiles*". Wollen wir im Interesse einer starken Europäischen Union hoffen, dass am Ende das Pendel zugunsten der Befürworter ausschlägt. ∎

(180 Wörter)

Facts

The institutions of the EU

- European Commission:
  - consists of as many Commissioners as there are member states;
  - executive branch of the EU;
  - proposes legislation and implements EU decisions
- European Council:
  - consists of the heads of state / government of member states;
  - intergovernmental institution with great influence outside the European Community

- Council of the EU:
  - consists of varying representatives of the member states; countries have different voting weights;
  - the main decision-making institution
- European Parliament:
  - consists of 736 members;
  - with the council of the EU it forms the legislative branch of the EU
- European Court of Justice:
  - one judge per member state;
  - represents the judiciary branch;
  - is the highest court in the EU

The EU's main aims: to provide peace, safety, economic and political stability for its peoples.

International business correspondence | Exam preparation | 87

Unit 11
Living and working in Britain

1 Finding a work placement

Before reading

a) Describe the photos. ▶ SF 26 Describing illustrations and photographs

b) Nick Müller is a trainee at a company in Cologne. His company in partnership with the local college is sending some students to Britain on job placements. Look at the photos again and guess where the trainees are going to work.

Understanding the text ▶ SF 22 Mediation / translation

c) The teacher at college has just given the trainees a copy of an e-mail from the place where they are going to work. Sum up Cara Law's e-mail on page 89 in German.

From: cara.law@allthingsscottish.co.uk
To: info@partnerschaften_bw.de
Subject: Work placements

. Dear German trainees

. As part of our partnership with your company and your college we will be delighted to have you here
. at our company "All Things Scottish", based in Perth, Scotland.

. We would like to take this opportunity to introduce ourselves: We at All Things Scottish are wholesalers
5 and distributors for Scottish tourist articles. These articles have been designed for tourists in Scotland.

Living and working in Britain 11

. We also sell these articles to people abroad who are interested in
. things Scottish. Some of these articles are made in Great Britain,
. but a lot of them are produced abroad. This is one reason why we
. have invited you to work with us. We believe that by having
10 foreign students helping in our company that we, too, can learn.

. We are also sure that you will learn a lot from your time with us.
. You will be helping in different areas of the company. You will
. do your placement in the front office, in the general office and
. also in our warehouse and logistics department.

15 Moreover, we can recommend good and relatively cheap accom-
. modation nearby. We advise you to contact either Mrs Fletcher at
. the Belfort Guest House on Perth 30691 or the Scotsman's Hotel
. on Perth 62275.

. We are looking forward to meeting you next month.

20 Yours sincerely

. Cara Law

. Personnel manager

Facts

Formal e-mails
A formal e-mail should have a good structure. Always think about the following parts:
1. salutation
2. reason for the e-mail
3. news/information/requests (for help)/apologies
4. attachment(s)
5. final comment
6. complimentary close

After reading

d) The teacher at college has told the trainees to write a polite e-mail to the company in Scotland, thanking them for the chance of working there. Complete Nick's e-mail using the words in the box.

- meeting • course • appreciate
- allowing • sincerely • forward
- opportunity • experience

From: nick.mueller@gmx.net
To: cara.law@allthingsscottish.co.uk
Subject: My work placement

. Dear Ms Law

. Thank you very much for your e-mail of 15 October 20… .
. I would also like to thank you for [**a.**] me to work at your company.
. Firstly, I would like to take this [**b.**] to introduce myself. My name is Nick Müller and I am 18 years old.
5 At present I am doing a job training [**c.**] here in Germany
. I am really looking [**d.**] to working at your company. I am sure it will be a rewarding [**e.**] for me.
. Once again I would like to say that I really [**f.**] your offer and I look forward to [**g.**] you soon.
. Yours [**h.**]
. Nick Müller

---

e) Look at the fact file above and identify the different parts of the two e-mails above.

Example: "Dear German trainees" and "Dear Ms Law" are both salutations.

f) One of Nick's classmates has fallen ill and cannot do the placement. Write his/her e-mail, explaining what has happened. Show interest in doing a placement in the future.

International business correspondence | Exam preparation | 89

11 Living and working in Britain

2 Finding accommodation – Making phone calls Video lounge ▶ 6

While listening

A2.3 **a)** Nick, the German trainee, is trying to find accommodation for his stay in Scotland. First he phones Mrs Fletcher at the Belfort Guest House. Listen to the call and put the photos into the order they are mentioned.

1

2

3

4

b) Listen to the call again. Note down what Mrs Fletcher said when …

1. Nick told her when he wanted to stay with her.
2. Nick said "your hotel".
3. Nick asked her if she did evening meals.
4. she made Nick a special offer.
5. Nick asked how he could book.
6. Nick didn't quite understand what she said.

After listening

c) Nick phones the Scotsman's Hotel to compare prices, availability, the distance to All Things Scottish, and booking and deposit requirements. Student A plays the role of Nick. Student B plays the role of the receptionist at the Scotsman's Hotel. You can find the receptionist's role card on page 174. Use the phrases in the box.
▶ SF5 Making phone calls

d) Decide where you think Nick would rather stay, at Mrs Fletcher's or at the Scotsman's Guest House. Give reasons.

e) Write an e-mail to the place you chose for Nick to stay in exercise d). Mention the following:

- the phone call • the dates and prices • your personal details have been filled in on the reservation form (attachment) • you look forward to meeting the person you are writing to • a formal complimentary close

Facts

Telephone tips
- In the UK answer the phone by using the number of the connection.
- Try to speak as clearly as possible.
- Don't be afraid to say that you haven't quite understood what the other person has said.
- Try to be friendly and polite.

Role card: Nick

Phone the Scotsman's Hotel to find out the following information:
- availability of a room from the 2nd to the 30th of next month
- rates
- meals
- distance from the company
- booking requirements
- payment.

Language

- Excuse me, could you speak more slowly, please?
- I didn't quite catch that. Could you repeat what you just said?
- Could you spell that, please?
- Thanks a lot. I'll be in touch. Bye.

| Basic course | Advanced course | Cross-cultural business communication |

Living and working in Britain **11**

3 Writing an e-mail to a friend

Understanding the text

‹R› **a)** Nick and Andy met when Andy was in Germany two years ago. Find out why Nick has written to Andy.

> **From:** nick.mueller@gmx.net
> **To:** andy-white-gc@googlemail.com
> **Subject:** I'm coming!
>
> Hi Andy,
>
> Long time, no see. How are you?
>
> Life here in Germany is the same as always. I'm busy at work, you know how it is.
>
> 5 Anyway, to be honest, the reason I'm writing is that I've lost your mobile number and I'd like to get in contact again. And guess what! I'm coming over to Scotland next month. I'll be working at All Things Scottish, a company in Perth as part of my job training.
>
> 10 And to cut a long story short, maybe we could meet again. Are you still studying in Edinburgh?
>
> It would be great to see you. Anyway, just give me a buzz on 0049 171 6868251 or send me an e-mail.
>
> By the way, do you remember the great time we had on
> 15 New Year's Eve in Cologne? I think you call it Hogmanay in Scotland?
>
> Best wishes
>
> Nick
>
> Attachment: New_Year_Cologne.jpg

‹R/P› **b)** Find colloquial expressions Nick used in his e-mail.

c) Write Andy's e-mail to Nick using some of these expressions and giving the following points. ▶ SF 25 Personal letters and e-mails

- Andy now works in a garage
- He had also lost Nick' phone number.
- He could meet him next month.
- He remembers Hogmanay, too – good time.
- He wants to know if Nick remembers Sandy – now his girlfriend.
- He asks Nick to mail him back – cheaper than phoning.
- He ends the e-mail informally.

After reading

d) Use the Internet to find out more about Scotland and the Scottish. In particular find out what the following are:

Facts

Informal e-mails
When writing informal e-mails you can use some words and expressions to make the letters sound more friendly.
For example, you can use the following expressions when you want to
- go back to a topic – Well, ...
- summarize the topic – Anyway,...
- change the topic – By the way,...
- say something is obvious – Of course,...
- say show good or bad fortune – (Un)luckily,...
- say what you really mean – To be honest,...

Key Words

- Hogmanay • the Edinburgh festival
- Robert the Bruce's spider
- Burn's night

International business correspondence | Exam preparation | 91

Unit 12
Meeting people

1 Meeting people for the first time

Before reading

⟨P⟩ **a)** Describe the photos above. ▶ SF 26 Describing illustrations and photographs

Understanding the text

A2.4 **b)** Nick from Germany has arrived in Perth in Scotland for his work placement. He goes to All Things Scottish (ATS) and is met by the personnel manager, Cara Law.

Cara: Hello there, Nick. May I call you Nick? My name's Cara Law, but please call me Cara. I hope you had a nice flight over from Germany.
Nick: Yes.
Cara: And is everything all right with your accommodation?
Nick: Yes.
Cara: Well, would you like a tea or coffee before I introduce you to some of the colleagues you'll be working with?
Nick: Coffee.
Cara: OK. Yes, most young people seem to prefer coffee to tea these days – even here in Scotland. How do you like your coffee? Cappuccino, latte macchiato or just plain coffee? You see we've become very "European" here in Scotland.
Nick: Cappuccino.
Cara: Right. Well, let's go to my office and I'll give the colleagues a ring so that they can meet you and you can have your cappuccino.

A few minutes later.

Cara: Hello there. Good morning, Amy. Hi Ian. May I introduce you both to Nick Müller from Germany. Nick, this is Amy Andrews from the front office and Ian McGregor is our logistics manager.

They all shake hands.

Amy: Nice to meet you, Nick. As Cara said, I work on the front desk, so we'll be working together quite a lot in the next few weeks.

Meeting people 12

Nick: Yes, good.

Ian: And as Cara said, I'm Ian. Pleased to meet you. When you come to the stores, I can promise you, you'll experience Scottish organisation at its very best.

Cara: Amy, may I suggest that you take Nick on a tour of the buildings first? I'll get someone to cover for you in the front office.

⟨R⟩ b) Match the photos on page 92 with the people at All Things Scottish.

c) Read the dialogue again to find out what Nick did not do so well.

d) Change Nick's responses so that they are more polite. Use the expressions in the box.

> **Language**
> - That sounds great.
> - Yes, please.
> - It's fine, thank you.
> - I'll look forward to that.
> - Thank you.
> - I'd like …

2 Showing people around

⟨R⟩ **While listening**

A2.5 a) Amy takes Nick on a tour of the company's building. Listen to their conversation. Follow their way through the building. Find out which rooms they entered or passed

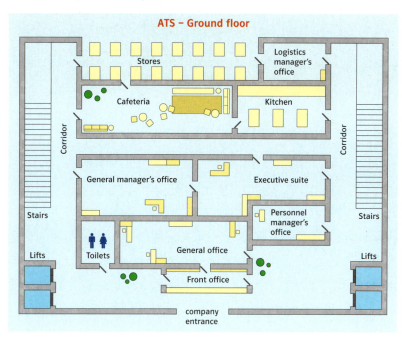

ATS – Ground floor

b) Listen to the conversation again and answer the following questions:

1. What is the name of the area in front of the front office?
2. Why does Nick know Joanne?
3. Why can they enter the manager's office without knocking?
4. What is the executive suite used for?
5. Why is Amy happy when they arrive at the cafeteria?

After listening

⟨I⟩ c) Work with a partner. Student A is a friend of Ian's, the logistics manager. He/she is at the front office desk and wants to talk to Ian. Student B is the member of staff on duty and gives Ian's friend directions to the logistics manager's office using the plan.

| International business correspondence | Exam preparation | 93 |

12 Meeting people

3 Finding the way

■ An ATS customer wants to walk into town. Explain how to get to the following places using the map below and the phrases in the box.

1. the Glen Theatre
2. the town hall
3. the Highlands Shopping Centre
4. the nearest cash point

Language
- turn right (into)
- turn left (into)
- take the first / second street on the right / left
- go straight on
- cross
- go along… until you come to
- at the traffic lights you turn …
- at the roundabout
- at / around the corner

4 Eating out

Before listening

a) It is lunch time. Amy, Cara and Nick are sitting in a restaurant. The waitress brings the menu. Look at this list of words and match them with the correct definition.

1. chicken tikka	a)	a fish often caught in the rivers of Scotland
2. rainbow trout	b)	a popular, Scottish soft drink
3. haggis	c)	seafood like a shrimp
4. prawn	d)	a type of beer, best served cold
5. Irn-Bru	e)	an Indian dish, which is spicy but not too hot
6. lager	f)	a traditional Scottish dish

b) Nick cannot understand the menu so Cara tries to explain it to him. Find out what the food items on the menu are and explain them in the same way as in the example.

Example:
Nick: Could you tell me what chicken tikka is, please?
Cara: It's an Indian dish. It's nice and spicy but not too hot.

Now you go on with:

1. Angus steak
2. Peas
3. Soft drinks
4. Boiled potatoes
5. Vegetable lasagne

MENU

Starter
- Tomato soup
- Prawn cocktail
- Country salad
- Fresh mussels

Main course
- Angus beef, chips and peas
- Chicken tikka with fried rice
- Fresh Scottish trout, boiled potatoes and salad
- Haggis and baked potatoes
- Vegetable lasagne

Dessert
- Warm apple pie and custard
- Fruit salad with cream
- Ice cream

Drinks
- Beer (lager or bitter)
- Wine (red, white or rosé)
- Spirits (especially all kinds of whisky)
- Mineral water
- Fruit juices
- Soft drinks (Irn-Bru, lemonade)

c) Now design the menu for German guests in German. ▶ SF 22 Mediation/translation

94 | Basic course | Advanced course | Cross-cultural business communication

Meeting people 12

‹R› **While listening**

A2.6 **d)** Listen to the dialogue and write down what Cara and Nick would like to have from the menu.

‹P› **After listening**

e) Place an order for Amy from the menu above.

f) Work in groups of three. Student A and Student B are guests in the restaurant. Student C is the waiter / waitress. Act out a dialogue using the menu on page 94.

5 Making conversation

Before reading

A2.7 **a)** Nick has made friends with Amy, the girl at the front desk. They arrange to meet in the local pub for a quiet drink. Amy said she'd be there at "half eight". Nick waits for an hour and then Amy arrives. Why do you think Nick has had to wait so long?

Nick:	It's nice here. Shall we sit over there?
Amy:	That's fine. Excuse me, are these seats taken?
Guest:	No, go ahead.
Nick:	Thanks. What are you having to drink, Amy?
Amy:	Oh, I think I'll have an orange juice. But I'm paying.
Nick:	No, no. I'll pay.

Nick waits, and Amy looks at him a little confused.

Amy:	Well, aren't you going to order?
Nick:	But the waiter hasn't come to our table yet?
Amy:	(laughing) No, Nick. In a pub you don't get served – you have to go to the bar and order the drinks there. And you have to pay for them at once.
Nick:	Oh, I didn't know that. Sorry.

Nick goes to the bar.

Barkeeper:	Next, please. Yes, sir?
Nick:	An orange juice and a large glass of beer, please.
Barkeeper:	You probably mean a pint of bitter, don't you?
Nick:	Yes, I think so.
Barkeeper:	There you go. That'll be 4.10, please.

‹R› **Understanding the text**

b) Explain how the English pub is different to a German pub.

c) Explain the following expressions:

1. Are these seats taken?
2. a pint
3. 4.10
4. Yes, sir?

After reading

d) Role play. Amy has invited Nick to a party where he meets other young foreign trainees from all over the world. Get into groups of five. Student A takes the role of Nick. You will find the other role cards on page 174. Circulate and start conversations. ▶ SF4 **Making conversation**

Facts

Here are some tips on how to make conversation:
- Never become too emotional or intense.
- Make sure you show interest and are polite.
- Avoid topics like politics, religion, personal problems or illnesses.

Role card: Nick

Name: Nick Müller
Home: Cologne, Germany
Placement : All Things Scottish, Perth
Journey to Scotland: direct flight to Glasgow
Marital status: single
Interests. Skiing and mountain-biking

Unit 13
Working in an office

1 In the office – answering telephone calls

Before reading

a) Nick spends the first week of his placement in the general office. Here he learns how the company works. What kind of activities do you think the people are doing in the photos?

b) What tasks do you think Nick has to do in the general office?

Understanding the text

A2.8 c) In his work in the office Nick has to answer the phone. Read the following dialogues and note the callers' requests.

Call 1
Nick: Hello, this is All Things Scottish. Nick Mueller speaking. Can I help?
Customer: Yes, this is John O'Shay from the tourist office in Motherwell. I'd like to order some more guide books.
Nick: Yes, fine. Which guide book was that exactly?

Call 2
Nick: Hello. This is All Things Scottish. You're speaking to Nick Mueller. How can I help you?
Customer: This is Mary Craddock. Can you put me through to the general manager, please?
Nick: One moment please. Just hold the line. I'll check if Mr McTell is free.

Facts

Spelling names
Example: Müller

M = capital m
ü = u – e
ll = double l

| 96 | Basic course | Advanced course | Cross-cultural business communication |

Working in an office 13

Call 3

Nick: All Things Scottish here. Nick Mueller speaking. Can I help you?
Customer: Greg Flannagan here. Can I speak to Mr Morgan, please?
Nick: Oh, I'm sorry, but Mr Morgan is in a meeting at the moment. Can I take a message?
Customer: Ay! Can you tell him to phone me back on 01356723987. The name is Flannagan. That's F – l – a double n – a – g – a – n.
Nick: I'll let him know, Mr Flannagan.

> **Facts**
> **Telephone numbers**
> Example: 023689921
>
> 0 = zero (US) or "Oh" (GB)
> 2368 = two – three – six – eight
> 99 = double nine

After reading

d) Practice the above telephone calls in pairs. Replace the names of the persons and other details.

2 Answering the telephone

While listening

A2.9 a) Listen to the phone call to find out who is talking.

b) Listen to the call again and fill in the memo sheet.

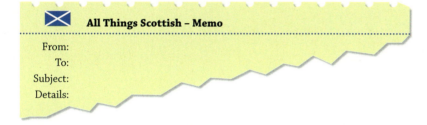

All Things Scottish – Memo
From:
To:
Subject:
Details:

After listening

c) Student A plays the role of the employee in the general office. Student B phones the company. Role card B is on page 175. Use the phrases in the dialogues above.

> **Role card: Student A**
> - 11067091 answers the phone correctly
> - asks what the caller wants
> - confirms that Mr McTell is in the office all day tomorrow
> - confirms that he/she will tell Mr McTell that the caller will phone again tomorrow

3 Making appointments

While listening

A2.10 a) Listen to another phone call and find out who is calling and why.

b) Copy Mr McTell's diary into your exercise book. Listen to the call again and fill in his appointments for next week.

c) Find out when the two businessmen can have their meeting.

d) Explain why they cannot meet earlier in the week.

Mr McTell's diary

	Monday	Tuesday	Wednesday	Thursday	Friday
9.00					

International business correspondence | Exam preparation | 97

13 Working in an office

4 Writing a business letter
▶ SF 23 Formal letters and e-mails

Understanding the text

a) Read the following business letter and find out what Mr McGregor is writing about.

All Things Scottish (ATS)
110 West Mill Street
Perth PH1 5PL
Scotland
5 UK
Tel +49(0)1738-450610-0   Fax +49(0)1738-450610-98
www.allthingsscottish.com

....

Your ref:
Our ref: M / Gd
10 13 March 20…

The Tourist Office
Attn Mr John O'Shay
69 High Street
Motherwell
15 ML1 2QN
Scotland

Dear Mr O'Shay

Your phone call of 3 March 20…

Thank you once again for your telephone call.
20 We are pleased to confirm that Mr McTell will be pleased to meet you on
Thursday, 17 March 20… at 11 o'clock in his office.

We look forward to seeing you at the arranged time.

Yours sincerely

Ian McGregor
25 All Things Scottish
Logistics Manager

---

98 | Basic course | Advanced course | Cross-cultural business communication

Working in an office **13**

b) After receiving a telephone call from Mr O'Shay from the Tourist Office in Motherwell, All Things Scottish wrote a letter of confirmation to him. Find the following in the letter on page 98.

1. salutation
2. letterhead
3. address
4. attention line
5. sender's job at the company
6. reason for writing
7. closing sentence
8. signature
9. complimentary close
10. references
11. subject line

After reading

c) The following letter is mixed up. Put the parts of the letter into the correct order.

1. Thank you for your letter of 19 November 20…
2. Yours sincerely
3. Purchasing Manager
4. We hereby confirm the date of the meeting – Monday 04 December
5. Your letter of 19 November 20…
6. Dear Ms Scott
7. We look forward to seeing you again in our company
8. 20 November 20…
9. Mr Grant
10. All Things Scottish
11. Our ref: GG / nm
12. Your ref: OS / lk
13. The Local Shop
14. Attn. Ms Scott
15. 14 Hibernian Way
16. Glasgow

d) Nick has to write a letter to a supplier in China. Mr Grant, the purchasing manager of All Things Scottish wants to visit them to discuss further purchases. Write a formal business letter to Mr Shusong of the Chinese Trading Company in Beijing. Their offices are at 123 Chang An Street in Beijing, China. The postal code is 017000.

In the letter you should

1. thank the Chinese company for their good cooperation in the past.
2. inform them that Mr Grant, ATS's purchasing manager, is visiting China and he will be in Beijing from 17 – 24 March.
3. ask them for an appointment to discuss further business.

Finish the letter politely.

International business correspondence | **Exam preparation** | **99**

Unit 14
Different countries, different cultures

1 Touring Scotland

Before reading

▶ SF 26 Describing illustrations and photographs

‹P› **a)** While Nick is in Scotland he goes on some tours around the country at the weekends. Look at some of the photos he has taken on his trips around Scotland and describe them.

b) Unfortunately, Nick is not quite sure which photo is which. Look at the entries in his blog and decide where the photos were taken. Two blog entries do not match.

Example: That looks like … because …

www.nickinscotland.com

- ▶ Sat 7th Ben Nevis / highest mountain in Scotland
- ▶ Sun 15th Oban / whisky distillery
- ▶ Sun 8th Loch Ness / didn't see the monster
- ▶ Sat 21st Aberdeen / North Sea oil
- ▶ Sat 14th Glasgow / largest city in Scotland
- ▶ Sat 28th Edinburgh / castle – capital of Scotland

c) Find the places which Nick visited on the map of Britain on the inside front cover.

100 | Basic course | Advanced course | Cross-cultural communication

Different countries, different cultures 14

2 Renting a car

While listening

a) Before Nick flies back to Germany, he wants to spend a weekend sightseeing in London. He is planning to drive down by car so he phones a car-hire firm to find out their prices. Listen to the phone call and write down how much it would cost to rent the following vehicles.

b) Listen again to the call and answer the questions.

1. Which seems to be the most suitable car for Nick? Why?
2. Where can he drop the car in London?
3. Why should he not drive into the centre of London?
4. How can he get into the centre according to John Samson?
5. When will Nick phone John Samson again?

After listening

c) John Samson has a busy day at the car-hire firm. The Linfords (2 adults and 2 children, aged 10 and 7) are going on holiday in Scotland and they would like to hire a car to travel around the country.

Work in pairs. Student A plays the role of Mr or Mrs Linford and phones John about renting a car for a week. Student B plays the role of John and gives Mr or Mrs Linford information about suitable cars and rates.

International business correspondence | Exam preparation | 101

14 Different countries, different cultures

3 An American in London

Before listening

a) While Nick is in London he is staying at a hotel. A lot of the guests come from overseas and this often causes communication problems. Think of situations where this might happen.

While listening

b) Listen to the conversation between an American guest and the receptionist at the hotel in London and describe the situation.

c) Listen to the conversation again and choose the right option. More than one option can be true.

1. The American has a room on the …
   a) ground floor   c) first floor
   b) second floor   d) third floor

2. The American has got a message on his …
   a) laptop   c) computer
   b) cell phone   d) television

3. He pays 220 pounds for his stay at the hotel …
   a) by credit card   c) in cash
   b) by check   d) in Euro bills

4. The following things are out of order at the hotel …
   a) the telephone in the guest's room
   b) the closet in the guest's room
   c) the computer at reception
   d) the elevator

5. The American guest wants to come back to Britain next year …
   a) on vacation   c) for a weekend trip
   b) on business   d) for his wedding anniversary

6. The American guest wants to know where he can find …
   a) a cinema   c) a bank
   b) a restroom   d) a gas station

After listening

d) The guest used the American English words on the right in the dialogue with the receptionist. Explain in British English what he meant.

- second floor • cell phone
- closet • bills • **elevator**
- restroom • vacation
- gas station • freeway
- French fries

Example: The American guest said that the elevator was out of order. In British English an 'elevator' is a 'lift'.

e) Decide in which English-speaking countries you could hear the following expressions.

1. Mountie
2. billboard
3. an Aussie
4. Gaelic football
5. a dingo
6. the All Blacks
7. a leprechaun
8. a kiwi

f) Use a dictionary or the Internet to find out what the expressions in exercise e) mean.

Different countries, different cultures 14

4 What you should know about Britain
Understanding the text

‹M› ▪ The teachers at Nick's college want Nick to design a handout for students doing placements in Britain in the future. Read Nick's tips and summarize them in German. ► **SF 22 Mediation/translation**

Ten useful tips for German students in Britain

1. Read as much as you can about Britain beforehand.
2. Only shake hands when you meet someone for the first time. After that the British don't like shaking hands.
3. Always try to be polite. Useful words like "please" and "thank you" help a lot! Remember: just answering a question with "yes" or "no" is seen as very impolite by the British. Try not to swear in English – people told me that it sounds unnatural coming from a foreigner!
4. In general, British people don't like close body contact with strangers. Keep a suitable distance.
5. British people often use first names. However, it depends on the rank and standing of the person you are talking to. I would never call the General Manager of the hotel by his first name. Always wait until the person you are talking to suggests using first names.
6. When you are out with British people in a pub, always be prepared to buy 'your round'. You go to the bar to order and you pay straight away.
7. Always remember to form a queue at the bus stop, at the baker's ... A true Brit forms a queue of one!
8. Dress code is important. In business a tie is a 'must' for men, and women should be careful not to wear 'showy' clothes. Jeans are a no-no.
9. Don't forget to drive on the left. And always look right before you cross the road. British pedestrians aren't so disciplined as we are in Germany: very often they don't wait for a 'green man' at the traffic lights, they just cross when nothing's coming.
10. Last but not least, smiling is always a good tactic. People seem to like you when you smile!

5 Test your English!

▪ This quiz is designed to find out if you know what to say in special situations. Choose the correct answer. More than one option can be correct.

QUIZ

1. What would you say if you met someone for the first time in a business situation?
   a) Good day.   c) Hello there.
   b) Pleased to meet you. d) Hallo.

2. How may a person in Britain answer an incoming telephone call? By saying …
   a) their name   c) where they are
   b) the phone number   d) Hi.

3. How would you ask to see the manager?
   a) Can I see the chief, please?
   b) Is it possible to see the boss, please?
   c) Where's the chef?
   d) Can I see the boss?

4. What would you say if you didn't understand something?
   a) Can you repeat that?
   b) Can you repeat that, please?
   c) Please?
   d) I didn't understand.

5. How would you ask somebody how you get to a city in Scotland?
   a) Which road do I take to get to Glasgow?
   b) How do I come to Dundee, please?
   c) Am I on the right street to Aberdeen?
   d) Could you tell me how I get to Edinburgh, please?

6. How do you finish a formal letter?
   a) Yours sincerely   c) Bye
   b) Best wishes   d) Yours

7. Nick wants to phone a hotel in London about accommodation. How would he start the phone call?
   a) Hello, this is Nick.
   b) Nick here.
   c) Hello, my name's Nick.
   d) Hello, this is Nick Müller speaking.

8. How should Nick ask for the price of a hotel room?
   a) How much do you demand?
   b) How much costs the room?
   c) How much does the room cost?
   d) How much is the room?

| International business correspondence | Exam preparation | 103

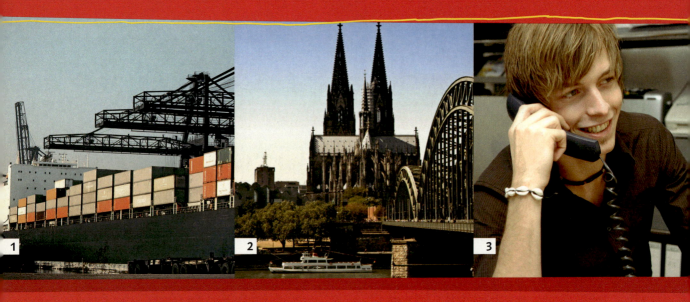

Unit 15
Enquiries

1 www.col-import.de

Before reading

a) Nick Müller is a trainee at a German company. Look at the photos above. What do the photos tell you about the work Nick does and the company for which Nick works?

‹R› Understanding the text

b) Read the home page of CNF and the e-mail on the right and answer the following questions.

1. What does CNF stand for?
2. Where is the company located?
3. What products does CNF deal with?
4. Where is the German company located?
5. What kind of business do they run?
6. What kind of customers do they supply?
7. How was the German company able to contact CNF?
8. What is the German company interested in?

c) Find words with a similar meaning in the texts on the right.

1. firm
2. goods
3. very good
4. relations
5. different
6. right now
7. get in touch with
8. understand
9. in the middle
10. latest
11. conditions
12. in the near future

104 | Basic course | Advanced course | Cross-cultural business communication

Enquiries **15**

CNF

http://www.cnf.com.cn/about

Home | About us | Worldwide

CNF is a leading Chinese export company. Our name stands for
Chinese Non-Food products. Our company is based in Hong
Kong and we offer a wide range of products for the American
and European market. As we have excellent connections to
producers in various branches of industry we can also offer you
products that are made to your specifications. At the moment
we can especially offer outdoor sports equipment at unbeatable
prices.

If you are interested, please contact:

CNF
Mr Ling Xiao
852 King's Road | Quarry Bay, Hong Kong
Telephone: + 852 1280 2477 | Telefax: + 852 1280 9865
E-mail: info@cnf.com.cn

Adresse: info@cnf.com.cn
Absender: r.springer@col-import.de
Betreff: Your web site

Dear Mr Ling

We learn from the CNF web site that you offer a wide range of non-food
products. We are a major German importer and wholesaler of such items
and supply discount outlets and supermarket chains in central Europe with
special offers and promotion material.

We would like to know more about your range of products. Could you
please let us have your current catalogue – if possible per download?

We are especially interested in your outdoor sports equipment. Please let
us know details and state your most favourable export prices together
with your terms of payment and delivery.

We usually place large orders so please quote possible quantity discounts.

We look forward to receiving your answer soon.

(Ms) Reinhild Springer
Purchasing manager
Col-Import AG

Facts

In East Asian names the family name comes first.

Example: Ling Xiao

Ling = family name
Xiao = first name

International business correspondence | Exam preparation | **105**

15 Enquiries

2 Useful phrases: Enquiry (Substitution table)

◻ **Opening**

We refer **to** We saw	your advertisement **for** (product) **in**			the (newspaper) **of** (date). the latest issue **of** (magazine).	
We understand We note We learn	**from** your	brochure sales literature web site	that you	produce export have a wide range **of**	(products).
Your company has been recommended **by** We have obtained your address **from**			a	business partner. customer.	

Your company / reasons for writing / request

We are	a	leading young rapidly-growing	German international	importer. wholesaler. manufacturer.	
We are	planning to	extend our range **of** introduce new		high-quality first-class reliable	(products).
	looking **for** a reliable		supplier **of** manufacturer **of**		
We	are especially interested **in** would like to know more **about**			your (product).	
Please	state quote let us know **about**		your most favourable prices and terms. your terms **of** payment and delivery. your earliest date **of** delivery. your delivery times. possible discounts.		
Could you please Would you please		send us let us have	your quotation **for** (products)? your latest catalogue? your current price list? a sample **of** (products)?		
We would	welcome appreciate		a quantity discount **of** … per cent. an introductory discount **of** … per cent. a demonstration **of** your (products). a visit **by** a representative.		

Closing

If your	prices terms	are competitive, meet our expectations, come **up to** our require- ments,	we will be	prepared able	to place to give	regular orders. substantial orders. a trial order.
			your products will sell well **in** this market.			
We	hope to hear **from** you				soon.	
	look forward **to** receiving your		answer reply		**in** the near future. shortly.	

106 | Basic course   Advanced course   Cross-cultural business communication

Enquiries 15

3 Practising words and phrases for enquiries

a) Complete the following word web with words from the substitution table on the left. Add other suitable words. ▶ SF 21 Word webs

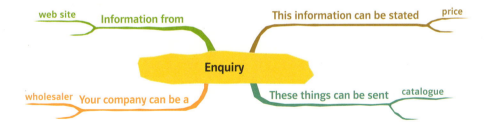

b) Rewrite the following letter. Replace the underlined words with similar words from the substitution table.

> Dear Ms Brown
>
> We [1] refer to your advertisement in the Globe Review. We [2] understand that you manufacture [3] high-quality shoes. We are a [4] leading German importer and we are planning to extend our range of these [5] goods. We [6] are especially interested in your range of trainers. Please [7] state your terms of payment. Could you please [8] send us your [9] current catalogue? If your prices [10] meet our expectations, we will be prepared to [11] give regular orders.
>
> We look forward to receiving your [12] answer [13] soon.
>
> Yours sincerely

c) Match the corresponding parts of an enquiry.

1.	If your prices are competitive,	a.	leading importer.
2	Could you please send us	b.	your latest catalogue?
3.	We are planning	c.	in the near future.
4.	We are especially interested	d.	your advertisement in …
5.	Please state your	e.	to introduce new products.
6.	We are a	f.	we will place regular orders.
7.	We refer to	g.	in your non-food products.
8.	We hope to hear from you	h.	terms of payment and delivery.

d) Put the sentences above in a suitable order and write the complete letter. Begin your letter with "Dear Sir or Madam" and finish it with "Yours faithfully".

International business correspondence | Exam preparation | 107

15 Enquiries

‹P› **4 Writing enquiries**
▶ **SF 23 Formal letters and e-mails**

a) Nick Müller has seen an interesting advertisement in the "Export-Expert-Worldwide" magazine. His boss Ms Springer leaves him a note in which she asks him to write an e-mail to the company.

Write the e-mail for Nick.

We at SEA-ECo

Our aim at SEA-ECo (South-East Asian Export Company) is to provide the best possible service at reasonable prices. Our motto is: *Value for money*.

We have contacts to manufacturers all over south-east Asia
5 and we can deliver non-food products for all purposes. We deliver immediately from stock by air or sea freight. We also offer low-cost production to your specifications at our partners' production plants in Vietnam, Malaysia and Indonesia.

10 At the moment our special offer covers a range of running shoes for men, women and children at unbeatable prices.

What can we do for you?
Don't delay – contact:

SEA-ECo
15 Attention Mr Adnan Nasution
P.O. Box 3215 ⋮ Jakarta 10032 ⋮ Indonesia
Tel: + 62 21 315 3476 ⋮ Fax: + 62 21 315 4267
E-mail: info@sea-eco.co.id

Col-Import AG
Von: R. Springer
An: N. Müller
Betreff: Anzeige im „Export-Expert-Worldwide" (liegt bei)

- Bitte E-Mail-Anfrage an SEA-ECo
- Katalog und Preisliste anfordern
- genauere Angaben zu den Sonderangeboten
- Lieferungsbedingungen und Lieferzeit bis Rotterdam
- mögliche Rabatte

b) Write the following letter of enquiry in English. Refer to the letter on page 98 for a suitable layout.

Situation:
You work for IABC (International Advanced Business Corporation) in 20095 Hamburg, Kleine Rosenstr. 6 – 10. Your company is a major trading company operating worldwide. Your boss, purchasing manager Ms Davenport, has received the leaflet of an Indian manufacturer of sari fabric from a business partner. As Ms Davenport is interested in the colours and patterns shown in the leaflet she asks you to write a letter of enquiry.

Your task:
Write the letter and use today's date. Include the following prompts:
- refer to the leaflet
- say how impressed you were by the colours and patterns
- present your company
- ask for further information (catalogue, price list)
- enquire about the terms of payment and delivery
- ask for samples
- say that you would like to find out about the quality of the fabric personally at their stand at the fashion fair in Istanbul
- ask if they are represented in Germany
- use a polite ending

Quality sari fabric!

Contact: Indian Fabrics, 273 / 1 Pandesara, Surat, Maharashtra, India 394221

108 | Basic course | Advanced course | Cross-cultural business communication

Enquiries 15

‹M› **c)** Write the following letter of enquiry in English using the German prompts below. Use today's date.

Situation:
Sie arbeiten im Einkauf der Firma *Domo-Import* in 32760 Detmold, Leonardo-da-Vinci-Weg 4.

Ihre Aufgabe:
Sie erkundigen sich nach Produkten der Firma *Scandinavian Exclusive Seating* (SES) in Norwegen (Adresse: Revierstredet 8, NO-0104 Oslo). Verwenden Sie dabei die folgenden Stichpunkte:
- Sie haben die Adresse und den Vorjahreskatalog des norwegischen Unternehmens von einem Kunden erhalten.
- Ihr Unternehmen ist Importeur und Großhändler von hochwertigen Möbeln.
- Sie interessieren sich insbesondere für exklusive Sitzmöbel (*seating furniture*) aus Leder.
- Sie machen dabei deutlich, dass eine umweltfreundliche Produktion für Ihre Kunden sehr wichtig ist.
- Sie bitten um die Zusendung des neuesten Katalogs und einer Preisliste.
- Für Sie ist eine kurze Lieferzeit wichtig, deshalb bitten Sie um entsprechende Angaben.
- Sie betonen, dass gute Verkaufsaussichten auf dem deutschen Markt bestehen, da der Markt für hochwertige Möbel wächst.
- Sie können umfangreiche Aufträge in Aussicht stellen und drücken die Hoffnung aus, dass das Angebot von SES wettbewerbsfähig ist.
- Sie schließen Ihren Brief höflich.

d) Do the following task in English. Use today's date.

Situation:
Als Mitarbeiter im Einkauf der *Dies & Das Handelsgesellschaft* in 18147 Rostock, Ost-West-Straße 34, sind Sie für das Aufspüren neuer Trends auf dem asiatischen Markt zuständig.

Ihre Aufgabe:
Eine Kollegin hat von einer Geschäftsreise eine Broschüre über Gartenspielgeräte mitgebracht. Sie schicken daraufhin eine Anfrage an das chinesische Unternehmen *Fujian Plastics Export Company*, 29 Qingtong Rd, 50–1101 Pudong New District, Shanghai, China 20120.
- Sie beziehen sich auf die Broschüre und bekunden Ihr Interesse an Gartenspielen.
- Sie stellen Ihr Unternehmen vor, das große Einzelhandelsketten und Discounter mit vielen Nonfood-Produkten aus aller Welt beliefert.
- Sie weisen darauf hin, dass Sie große Mengen benötigen und niedrige Preise sowie Mengenrabatte erwarten.
- Wichtig ist Ihnen dabei eine pünktliche und zuverlässige Lieferung, da Ihre Kunden Sonderverkäufe zu festen Terminen planen.
- Sie möchten die günstigsten Lieferungs- und Zahlungsbedingungen erfahren und bitten um die Zusendung von Mustern der angebotenen Kunststoff-Gartenspiele.
- Sie beenden Ihren Brief höflich.

| International business correspondence | Exam preparation | 109 |

15 Enquiries

5 An enquiry on the telephone

a) Listen to the telephone dialogue and find out the following:

1. the names of the persons
2. the countries where you think the persons are
3. the product they are talking about

b) Listen to the dialogue again and correct the following statements.

1. Peter Doblein is calling the *East Indian Trading Company*.
2. It is afternoon in Germany.
3. Mr Doblein has learned about the Indian company from a leaflet.
4. He is interested in garden tools.
5. The models mentioned are IC5 and IC6.
6. Mr Doblein would like to order 100 motors.
7. The goods and the information will arrive within two weeks.

6 Making telephone calls

▶ SF5 Making phone calls   ▶ SF7 Formal phone calls

a) Work in pairs. Prepare the following telephone call and present it to the class. Student A is Rajive Ranjan in Delhi – working for *ICT Industries* – and student B is Carl / Carla Holt from Berlin – working for *German Industries Import*. Carl / Carla is phoning ICT because he / she wants to enquire about their products.

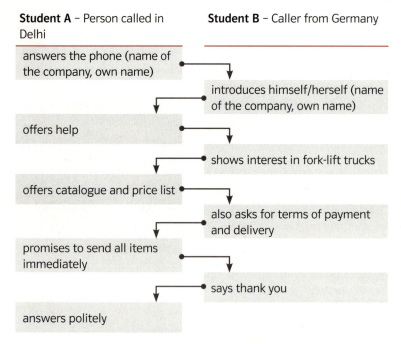

Student A – Person called in Delhi	Student B – Caller from Germany
answers the phone (name of the company, own name)	
	introduces himself/herself (name of the company, own name)
offers help	
	shows interest in fork-lift trucks
offers catalogue and price list	
	also asks for terms of payment and delivery
promises to send all items immediately	
	says thank you
answers politely	

Role card

Student A

- Sie interessieren sich für die neuen Regalsysteme (*shelving systems*).
- Sie haben die Produkte im Internet gesehen.
- Sie möchten gerne genauere Informationen.
- Sie wünschen sich einen aktuellen Katalog und eine Exportpreisliste.
- Sie bitten um ein Angebot mit Lieferungs- und Zahlungsbedingungen.
- Sie erkundigen sich nach Mengenrabatten.
- Sie freuen sich auf die Zusendung des Angebots.
- Sie verabschieden sich höflich.

b) Work in groups of three. Prepare and present the following telephone call. Student A (see role card on the right and role cards B and C on page 175) works for *Deutsche Büroausstattung GmbH* in Wolfsburg and calls a Swedish company under his / her own name. Student B is the receptionist, Ms Ella Lund, and student C the employee in the export department, Ms Klara Andersson. Both work for *SwedWoods* in Stockholm.

| 110 | Basic course | Advanced course | Cross-cultural business communication |

7 Useful phrases: Enquiry (German – English)

Enquiries 15

◾ Anfang	**Opening**
Wir beziehen uns auf	We refer to . . . .
Wir ersehen / entnehmen . . .	We understand / note / learn from . . .
Ihrer Anzeige in … vom … ,	your advertisement in … of …
Ihrem Prospekt / Informationsmaterial,	your brochure / sales literature
dass Sie … produzieren / exportieren.	that you produce / export . . . .
dass Sie ein großes Sortiment an … haben.	that you have a wide range of . . . .
Ihr Unternehmen wurde uns empfohlen von	Your company has been recommended to us by . . . .
Wir haben Ihre Adresse von … erhalten.	We have obtained your address from . . . .

Ihre Firma / Ihr Anliegen	**Your company / reasons for writing / request**
Wir sind Importeur / Großhändler / Hersteller von	We are a(n) importer / wholesaler / manufacturer of . . . .
Wir planen, . . .	We are planning to . . .
unser Sortiment an … auszuweiten.	extend our range of . . . .
neue Produkte einzuführen.	introduce new products.
Wir sind auf der Suche nach einem Lieferanten für	We are looking for a supplier of . . . .
Wir sind interessiert an	We are interested in . . . .
Wir würden gerne mehr erfahren über	We would like to know more about your . . . .
Bitte nennen Sie uns Ihre(n) . . .	Please state / quote / let us know about your . . .
günstigsten Preise und Bedingungen.	most favourable prices and terms.
Lieferungs- und Zahlungsbedingungen.	terms of payment and delivery.
frühesten Liefertermin.	earliest date of delivery.
Lieferzeiten.	delivery times.
möglichen Rabatte.	possible discounts.
Könnten / Würden Sie uns bitte . . . senden?	Could / Would you please send us / let us have . . . ?
Ihr Angebot für …	your quotation for …
Ihren neuesten Katalog	your latest catalogue.
Ihre aktuelle Preisliste	your current price list.
Wir würden uns freuen über . . .	We would welcome / appreciate . . .
einen Mengenrabatt von … Prozent.	a quantity discount of … per cent.
einen Einführungsrabatt von … Prozent.	an introductory discount of … per cent.
eine Vorführung Ihrer (Produkte).	a demonstration of your (products).
einen Besuch Ihres Außendienstmitarbeiters.	a visit by a representative.
ein Muster / Probeexemplar Ihres (Produkt).	a sample of your (product).

Ende	**Closing**
Wenn Ihre Preise / Bedingungen . . .	If your prices / terms . . .
wettbewerbsfähig sind, …	are competitive, …
unseren Erwartungen entsprechen, …	meet our expectations, …
unseren Anforderungen gerecht werden, …	come up to our requirements, …
werden wir in der Lage / bereit sein, . . .	we will be able / prepared to . . .
regelmäßige / umfangreiche Aufträge zu erteilen.	place regular / substantial orders.
einen Probeauftrag zu erteilen.	give a trial order.
Ihre Produkte werden sich hier gut verkaufen lassen.	Your products will sell well in this market.
Wir hoffen, bald von Ihnen zu hören.	We hope to hear from you soon.
Wir freuen uns darauf, von Ihnen zu hören / Ihre Antwort . . . zu erhalten.	We look forward to hearing from you / to receiving your answer / reply . . . .
bald / in Kürze / in naher Zukunft	soon / shortly / in the near future.

International business correspondence | Exam preparation | **111**

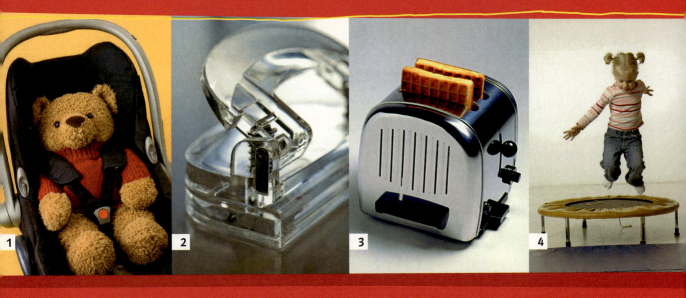

Unit 16
Offers

1 An offer from Hong Kong

Before reading

‹P› **a)** CNF is a leading Chinese export company. Describe the photos above and explain what range of products this company has on offer.

Understanding the text

‹R› **b)** Read CNF's offer on the right and check if your ideas were right.

c) Read the offer again and correct the following statements.

1. CNF is sending a catalogue and an import price list.
2. The company grants an introductory discount of 5% on all products.
3. The prices stated are ex works.
4. Delivery is made by sea immediately after receipt of order.
5. Payment must always be effected by letter of credit.
6. CNF produces its wide range of products itself.

d) Match the following expressions from the e-mail on the right.

1. special   a) equipment
2. introductory   b) credit
3. sports   c) offer
4. wide   d) questions
5. letter of   e) discount
6. branches of   f) range
7. further   g) industry

112 | Basic course | Advanced course | Cross-cultural business communication

Offers 16

> **From:** info@cnf.com.cn
> **To:** r.springer@col-import.de
> **Subject:** Offer
> **Attachments:** Catalogue and export price list
>
> Dear Ms Springer
>
> Thank you very much for your enquiry and for your interest in our products.
>
> We are pleased to make the following special offer. As an introductory discount we can grant you 5% on all of our outdoor sports equipment.
>
> The prices quoted are FOB Shanghai. Delivery is usually made by sea within four weeks after receipt of order. For first orders payment must be made by letter of credit. Regular customers are granted open account terms.
>
> As requested we are sending you our catalogue and export price list for further details. Please find them in the attachment. Apart from our selection of outdoor sports equipment we can also offer you a wide range of toys, household, office and outdoor products as we have excellent connections to producers in various branches of industry.
>
> If you have any further questions, please do not hesitate to contact us. We assure you that your order will be carried out promptly and carefully.
>
> We look forward to doing business with you.
>
> Yours sincerely
>
> Ling Xiao
> CNF sales manager

2 Terms of delivery (Incoterms® 2010) ▶ see the complete illustration on page 311

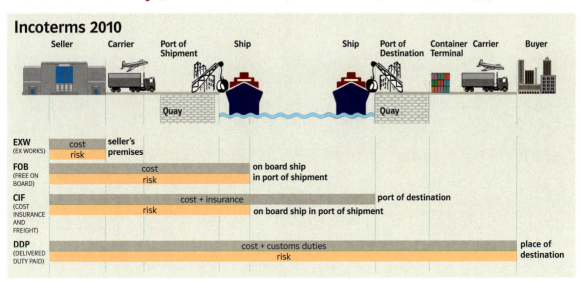

Study the diagram above and answer the following questions.

a) What do you think the abbreviation IN-CO-TERMS stands for?

b) Which of the terms is best for the seller? Give reasons.

c) Which one is the most favourable for the buyer? Explain your decision.

d) The seller is in Liverpool, the buyer is in Hamburg.
   1. Which is the correct Incoterm if the seller agrees to pay for all costs until the goods arrive at the port in Hamburg?
   2. Which is the correct term if the buyer agrees to pay for the transport by ship from Liverpool?

| International business correspondence | Exam preparation | 113 |

16 Offers

3 Useful phrases: Offer (Substitution table)

▫ Opening

Thank you **for** your Many thanks **for** your We refer **to** your	enquiry dated … . e-mail **of** … .		
We are pleased to	make submit	the following	quotation. offer.
We have pleasure **in** sending you			

Details

The prices	quoted stated	are	net. EXW. FOB (named port of shipment).	
We can We are willing to We are prepared to	offer you grant you give you	a … %	quantity introductory cash	discount.
Payment	should be must be has to be	made effected	**within** … days after delivery. **with** your order. **by** letter of credit (L/C).	
Delivery Shipment	can be will be	made arranged	**by**	air. rail. road. sea.
			within … days immediately.	**after** receipt **of** order.
This offer	is	valid firm	**until** … . **for** … weeks.	
As requested	we are sending you we will send you	our latest catalogue. our current price list.		

Closing

We hope We trust	that this offer	will come **up to** your expectations. will meet your requirements.	
If you have any further questions, Should you require any further information,		do not hesitate	to contact us. to get **in** touch **with** us.
We assure you You can be sure	that your order will be	executed dealt **with**	promptly. carefully.
We look forward **to**	doing business **with** you receiving your order welcoming you as our customer	soon.	

---

114 | Basic course   Advanced course   Cross-cultural business communication

Offers **16**

4 Practising words and phrases for offers

a) Match the expressions in the first box with expressions in the second
box that have a similar meaning.

1. quotation	a. give
2. willing	b. delivery
3. shipment	c. deal with
4. grant	d. prepared
5. quote	e. offer
6. come up to	f. get in touch with
7. contact	g. current
8. latest	h. firm
9. execute	i. state
10. valid	j. meet

b) The following phrases are written in the passive voice. Put them into
the active form.

Example: Our price list is attached. We attach our price list.

1. A 10 % discount can be granted. We can …
2. Payment should be made within four weeks. You …
3. Delivery can be arranged by sea.
4. Our catalogue will be sent tomorrow.
5. Shipment will be made by road.
6. Your order will be executed promptly.
7. Packing is not included in the price.
8. We can be contacted by e-mail.

c) Rewrite the following letter. Fill in the gaps with words from the
substitution table on page 114.

Dear Ms Collins

We [**1**] you for your enquiry dated March 10. We are pleased to [**2**] the following [**3**]. All our prices [**4**] in the price list are ex works. We can [**5**] you an [**6**] discount of 10 %. Payment must be [**7**] by letter of [**8**]. Delivery will be [**9**] by [**10**] within six weeks. Our offer is [**11**] until April 15. We hope that our offer will [**12**] up to your expectations. We [**13**] you that your order will be [**14**] promptly and carefully. We look forward to [**15**] you as our [**16**].

Yours [**17**]

d) Put the following parts of an offer in a suitable order. Then write the
complete letter in an appropriate form.

1. are net	2. with your order
3. this offer is valid	4. thank you for your enquiry
5. dear Mr Myers	6. and we assure you that your order
7. a 5 % quantity discount	8. delivery will be effected
9. we trust that this offer	10. the following quotation
11. dated August 12	12. for six weeks
13. payment must be made	14. we can offer you
15. you our latest catalogue	16. as requested we are sending
17. we have pleasure in sending you	18. will be executed promptly and carefully
19. we look forward to	20. on orders over 10,000 items
21. our prices	22. will meet your requirements
23. by rail	24. yours sincerely
25. receiving your order soon	

International business correspondence   Exam preparation   **115**

16 Offers

‹P› **5 Writing offers**
▶ SF 23 Formal letters and e-mails

a) Situation:
Mr Nasution, who works for the *South-East Asian Export Company*, has received an e-mail from Nick Müller in which Nick inquires about SEA-ECo's products.

Your task:
Write Mr Nasution's offer. Refer to Nick's wishes and the notes that Mr Nasution has already made.

From: n.mueller@col-import.de
To: info@sea-eco.co.id
Subject: Enquiry

Dear Mr Nasution

We refer to your advertisement in the "Export-Expert-Worldwide" of this month. We are especially interested in your special offer for running shoes for men, women and children. As our customers are planning various actions for the next season we require a substantial number of shoes on condition you offer standard quality at most favourable prices.

5 Please state your terms of payment and delivery CFR Rotterdam and your delivery times. Let us also know about possible quantity discounts that you could offer us. Moreover, we would appreciate it if you sent us some samples of your shoes.

As we require sports equipment in large quantities, we would be pleased to receive your catalogue and your export price list.

We look forward to receiving your quotation soon.

10 Yours sincerely

Nick Mueller
Purchasing assistant

Handwritten note:
US$ 8 men's and women's shoes · US$ 6 children's running shoes · CFR Rotterdam · delivery to Rotterdam within eight weeks · quantity discount: 5% on orders over 50,000 items · payment by letter of credit for first orders · catalogue and price list attached · free samples by air within two weeks

b) Situation:
Mr Rajesh Kumar from the *South Indian Trading Company* has just received the following telephone call.

Your task:
Write his offer to *Norddeutsche Handelsgesellschaft*. Make up any missing details.

RK: South Indian Trading Company. Rajesh Kumar speaking.
PD: This is Peter Doblein from Norddeutsche Handelsgesellschaft.
RK: Good afternoon, Mr Doblein. How can I help you?
PD: Good morning, Mr Kumar – I see – you are hours ahead of Central European time. Never mind. Well, I have seen your web site and I am interested in your new electric motors.
RK: Ah yes, we have had a lot of enquiries in the last few weeks. Which models are you especially interested in?
PD: Well, the ones that are particularly designed for outdoor use, for garden tools for example.
RK: Right, Mr Doblein. We've got the models EC5 und EC6 for that purpose. I can recommend them both.
PD: Would it be possible for you to send us some samples so that we can test the quality of the motors?
RK: Of course, Mr Doblein. We can send you a sample of each motor within a week. Would that be OK?
PD: That would be great. And could you please state your terms of payment and delivery and your delivery times?
RK: I'll be glad to arrange that for you. Would you please spell your name for me?
PD: It's P-E-T-E-R-D-O-B-L-E-I-N. The address is … Oh, I think I'll send you an e-mail.
RK: Thank you, Mr Doblein. You'll be receiving our samples and our sales literature within a week.
PD: Thank you for your help, Mr Kumar. Goodbye.
RK: You're welcome, Mr Doblein. Thanks for calling. Bye-bye.

116 | Basic course | Advanced course | Cross-cultural business communication

Offers 16

‹M› **c)** Write the following offer in English using the German prompts below. Use today's date.

Situation:
Sie arbeiten im Verkauf der Firma *Baufahrzeuge-Unger* in 48529 Nordhorn, Westfalenstraße 6, und Sie haben eine Anfrage des amerikanischen Unternehmens *Contractor's World*, Marbach Rd, San Antonio, Bexar County, Texas 78245, USA, erhalten (Ansprechpartnerin: Susan Fuller).

Ihre Aufgabe:
Beantworten Sie die Anfrage. Weisen Sie auf Ihr breites Angebot hin und bieten Sie insbesondere die neuen Schwerlastwagen *(heavy duty vehicles)* BU-2020 an, die sich für den Einsatz unter extremen Bedingungen – wie beispielsweise in Wüstenregionen *(deserts)* – eignen.
Da es sich um ein neues Modell handelt, könnten Sie einen Einführungsrabatt von 5% einräumen. Alle Preise in der beigefügten Preisliste verstehen sich FOB Hamburg. Die Lieferzeit beträgt in der Regel drei Monate. Wie gewünscht verschicken Sie Ihren aktuellen Katalog und Ihre Preisliste in der Anlage. Schließen Sie Ihren Brief höflich.

d) Write the following offer in English using the German prompts below. Use today's date.

Situation:
Sie arbeiten für das Maschinenbauunternehmen *Haller & Co KG* in 64293 Darmstadt, Robert-Bosch-Str. 15. Als Mitarbeiter im Verkauf betreuen Sie den asiatischen und australischen Markt.

Ihre Aufgabe:
Auf Grund einer Anfrage der Firma *Knox Productions*, 28 Falls Road, Marysville, Victoria, Australia 3779, schreiben Sie das folgende Angebot (Ansprechpartner: Rod Hogan).

- Beziehen Sie sich auf die Anfrage und danken Sie für das Interesse an Ihren Spezialmaschinen.
- Stellen Sie kurz Ihr Unternehmen vor, das eines der führenden Maschinenbauunternehmen *(mechanical engineering company)* in diesem Bereich in Deutschland ist.
- Erwähnen Sie, dass Ihr Unternehmen sehr zuverlässig ist und bereits Geschäftsbeziehungen zu verschiedenen Firmen in Australien unterhält.
- Verweisen Sie in Ihrem Angebot auf die beiligende Preisliste und Ihren Katalog, der separat verschickt wird *(under separate cover)*.
- Weisen Sie darauf hin, dass Sie auch Einzelanfertigungen vornehmen *(produce to specification)*.
- Die Lieferzeit für Ihre Produkte aus dem Katalog beträgt vier Monate.
- Die Lieferung erfolgt üblicherweise FOB Rotterdam.
- Bieten Sie an, dass Sie für weitere Fragen zur Verfügung stehen.
- Beenden Sie den Brief mit dem Hinweis auf prompte und sorgfältige Ausführung von Aufträgen und der Hoffnung auf baldige Geschäftsbeziehungen.

International business correspondence | **Exam preparation**

16 Offers

‹R› **6 An offer on the telephone**

A2.14 **a)** Listen to the telephone dialogue and find out the following:

1. the names of the persons
2. the countries where you think the persons are
3. the products they are talking about

b) Listen to the dialogue again and find out details about the following:

1. discount
2. terms of delivery
3. delivery time
4. terms of payment
5. fair

7 Making telephone calls
▶ SF 5 Making phone calls   ▶ SF 7 Formal phone calls

‹I› **a)** Work in pairs. Prepare the following telephone call and present it to the class. Student A is Dan / Dana Holding from Boston working for *Warehouse-Development-Now*. Student B is himself / herself working in the export department of *Regalsysteme Bremen*. Student B has received an e-mail from Boston in which Dan / Dana Brown enquired about the *Regalsysteme* products. Now he / she is making a call to the USA.

Student A – Person called in Boston	**Student B** – Caller from Germany
answers the phone (name of the company, own name)	
	introduces himself / herself (name of the company, own name); says why he / she is calling
thanks for the prompt call	
	offers special shelving systems for the American market
is very interested and wants further information	
	promises to send a catalogue and a price list
wants to know about the terms of payment and delivery	
	gives details about the terms and promises delivery within two months
thanks for the information	
	gives a polite answer and says goodbye
says goodbye	

Role card A

Student A (use your own name)

- Sie beziehen sich auf den Anruf von B und bedanken sich für das Interesse.
- Sie können ein großes Sortiment an österreichischen Spezialitäten anbieten *(specialities)*.
- Sie können frische Produkte per Luftfracht schnell versenden.
- Sie können andere Produkte per Bahn und Schiff liefern.
- Sie bieten einen aktuellen Katalog und eine Exportpreisliste an.
- Sie stellen Mengenrabatte in Aussicht.
- Sie nennen als Lieferbedingung „Lieferung ab Werk".
- Sie freuen sich auf eine mögliche Bestellung und verabschieden sich höflich.

‹M/I› **b)** Work in pairs (see role cards on the right and on page 175). Student A works for *AustriaCompact* in Salzburg and calls student B, Miranda / Michael Wonder, who works in the purchasing department of the supermarket chain *AmericanStore*. Student B tried to call student A an hour ago but he / she was not in. Now student A is calling back.

118 | Basic course | Advanced course | Cross-cultural business communication

Offers 16

8 Useful phrases: Offer (German – English)

◨ **Anfang** | **Opening**

Wir bedanken uns vielmals für Ihre Anfrage vom	**Many thanks for your enquiry dated . . . .**
Wir beziehen uns auf Ihre E-Mail vom	**We refer to your e-mail of . . . .**
Wir freuen uns, . . . unterbreiten zu können.	**We are pleased to submit . . .**
Wir freuen uns, Ihnen . . . zu senden.	**We have pleasure in sending you . . .**
das folgende Angebot	the following quotation.

Einzelheiten | **Details**

Die genannten Preise verstehen sich . . .	**The prices quoted are . . .**
ohne Abzug / ab Werk / FOB (frei an Bord).	net / EXW (ex works) / FOB (free on board).
Wir sind bereit, Ihnen . . .	**We are willing / prepared to . . .**
. . . anzubieten / zu gewähren.	offer / grant you . . .
einen Mengenrabatt	a quantity discount.
einen Einführungsrabatt	an introductory discount.
einen Barzahlungsrabatt	a cash discount.
Die Zahlung sollte . . . erfolgen.	**Payment should be made / effected . . .**
mit Ihrer Bestellung	with your order.
innerhalb von … Tagen nach Lieferung	within … days after delivery.
durch Akkreditiv	by letter of credit (L / C).
Die Lieferung . . .	**Delivery / shipment . . .**
kann erfolgen …	can be made / arranged …
auf dem Luftweg / per Bahn / LKW / Schiff.	by air / rail / road / sea.
Dieses Angebot ist gültig / verbindlich . . .	**This offer is valid / firm . . .**
bis … / … Wochen lang.	until … / for … weeks.
Wie gewünscht senden wir Ihnen . . .	**As requested we are sending you . . .**
unsere(n) aktuellsten Katalog / Preisliste.	our latest / current catalogue / price list.

Ende | **Closing**

Wir hoffen / glauben, dass dieses Angebot . . .	**We hope / trust that this offer . . .**
Ihre Erwartungen / Anforderungen erfüllen wird.	will meet your expectations / requirements.
Wenn Sie weitere Fragen haben, . . .	**If you have any further questions, . . .**
Sollten Sie weitere Informationen benötigen, . . .	**Should you require any further information, . . .**
zögern Sie nicht, …	do not hesitate …
sich mit uns in Verbindung zu setzen.	to contact us / to get in touch with us.
Wir versichern Ihnen . . . / Sie können sicher sein, . . .	**We assure you . . . / You can be sure . . .**
dass Ihr Auftrag … ausgeführt wird.	that your order will be executed / dealt with …
prompt / sorgfältig	promptly / carefully.
Wir freuen uns darauf, . . .	**We look forward to . . .**
mit Ihnen ins Geschäft zu kommen.	doing business with you.
Ihren Auftrag zu erhalten.	receiving your order.
Sie als unseren Kunden zu begrüßen.	welcoming you as our customer.

International business correspondence   Exam preparation   **119**

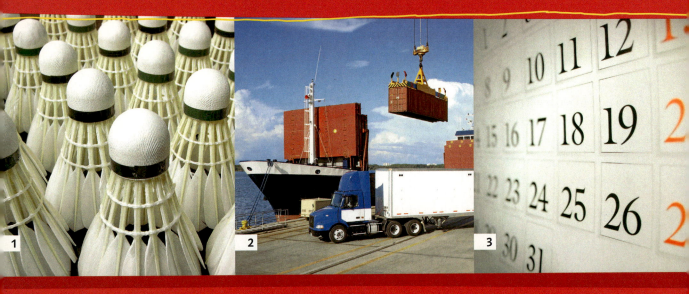

Unit 17
Orders

1 An order from *Col-Import*

Before reading

a) The photos above show some things that must be agreed on when placing orders. Match them with the expressions in the box below.

- time of delivery • terms of payment • price • terms of delivery
- goods ordered

‹R› Understanding the text

b) Make a list in your exercise book with the five items from the box above. Read *Col-Import's* order on the right and find the corresponding details in the letter.

Goods ordered	Price	Terms of ...		
20,000 badminton sets	@ US $ 2.50			

c) Read the order again and complete the following sentences.

1. This letter is *Col-Import's* first order with the Chinese company because …
2. *Col-Import* can only sell the products in Germany if …
3. If the importer and their customers are satisfied with the quality of the goods, …
4. *Col-Import* wants to be informed by the Chinese company if …

120 | Basic course | Advanced course | Cross-cultural business communication

Orders 17

From:	r.springer@col-import.de
To:	info@cnf.com.cn
Sent:	12/09/20…
Subject:	Order
Attachment:	Order No. 4564/AS/11

Attachment: Order No. 4564/AS/11.pdf

Col-Import AG
Industriestraße 27-39
50735 Köln / Cologne
Germany

Tel: 0049 (0)2236 3749582
Fax: 0049 (0)2236 3749584
E-Mail: info@col-import.de
Web: www.col-import.de

Mr Ling Xiao
CNF
852 King's Road
Quarry Bay
Hong Kong
P.R. China

Dear Mr Ling

Your ref.: LX
Our ref.: RS
Date: 12 September 20…

Order No. 4564 / AS / 11

Thank you very much for your offer of August 26, 20… and your catalogue and price list. We were very impressed by the wide range of products on offer and we are pleased to place the following order:

20,000 badminton sets "Easy play"	at US $ 2.50 each
5,000 trampolines "Hophop"	at US $19.50 each
10,000 garden croquet sets "July"	at US $ 6.90 each

As stated in your catalogue the products must meet EU safety standards.

Delivery must be executed by sea within 4 weeks FOB Shanghai. Payment will be effected by irrevocable, confirmed letter of credit. We also understand that you are willing to grant us an introductory discount of 5 per cent.

We trust that our order will be executed carefully. If the quality of your products meets our customers' requirements, we will be prepared to place further substantial orders with you.

Please acknowledge this order by return and inform us if there are any delays in delivery.

We look forward to doing business with you.

Yours sincerely

(Ms) Reinhild Springer
Purchasing manager

International business correspondence   Exam preparation   **121**

2 Useful phrases: Order (Substitution table)

Opening

Thank you **for** your Many thanks **for** your	offer quotation	**of** … .				
	catalogue. price list. samples.					
We are pleased to We would like to	place	the following the attached	order.			
Please	supply send us	the following	products goods	**on** the	terms conditions	stated below.

Details

Delivery Shipment	must be has to be	made executed	**within** … weeks. **by** (date) **at** the latest.
Payment will be	effected made arranged	**in** advance. **with** order. **on** delivery. **on** receipt **of** goods. **within** … days **after** receipt of goods. **by** transfer **of** the invoice amount. cash **against** documents. **by** irrevocable, confirmed letter **of** credit. according **to** your terms **of** payment.	

We note We understand	**from** your	offer quotation	that your prices include that you are willing to grant us	a discount **of** …%.
We expect				

Closing

Please confirm Please acknowledge	this order receipt **of** this order	**by** return. promptly.
Please	inform us let us know	when the goods have been shipped. if there are any delays **in** delivery.
We look forward **to**	doing business **with** you. receiving the goods **in / on** time.	

Orders **17**

3 Practising words and phrases for orders

a) Match the expressions in the first box with expressions in the second
box that have a similar meaning.

1. products	a. acknowledge
2. supply	b. shipment
3. note	c. send
4. confirm	d. quotation
5. make	e. promptly
6. delivery	f. goods
7. offer	g. conditions
8. has / have to be	h. understand
9. by return	i. effect
10. terms	j. must be

b) Fill in the correct prepositions.

Dear Ms Peters

Thank you [**1**] your offer [**2**] 15 September. Please send us the following goods [**3**] the terms stated below.

Delivery must be executed [**4**] the end of October [**5**] the latest. Payment will be effected [**6**] 30 days after receipt [**7**] goods. We note [**8**] your quotation that you are willing to grant us a quantity discount [**9**] 5 %.

Please confirm this order [**10**] return and inform us if there are any delays [**11**] delivery. We look forward [**12**] doing business [**13**] you.

Yours sincerely

c) The following order contains seven words which do not fit. Find them in
the letter and replace them by suitable words from the substitution table
on page 122.

Dear Mr Brown

Many thanks for your order of 20 January. We are pleased to execute the following order.

Delivery must be informed within four weeks. Discount will be effected by transfer of the invoice amount. We note that you are forward to grant us an introductory discount.

Please supply this order by return and inform us when the prices have been shipped.

Yours sincerely

d) Use the following prompts to make meaningful sentences in the passive
voice which can be used in an order. Use *will be*, *must be* or *should be*.

Example: supply the following goods on the terms stated below
The following goods <u>must be supplied</u> on the terms stated below.

1. make delivery within two weeks
2. effect payment with order
3. include a discount of five per cent
4. arrange shipment by air
5. confirm this order promptly
6. send the goods immediately

International business correspondence | Exam preparation | **123**

17 Orders

‹P› # 4 Writing orders

► **SF 23 Formal letters and e-mails**

a) Situation:
Nick Müller from *Col-Import* has received the following offer from
Mr Nasution, who works for the *South-East Asian Export Company*.

Your task:
Write Nick's order. Refer to the notes that his boss, Ms Springer, has
made in the margin.

From: nasution@sea-eco.co.id
To: n.mueller@col-import.de
Subject: Offer
Attachments: Catalogue and price list

Dank für das interessante Angebot, den Katalog und die Muster. Die Qualität der Schuhe entspricht unseren Erwartungen.

Dear Mr Mueller

We refer to your enquiry and are very glad about your interest in our special offer.
At the moment we can offer:

> men's running shoes "Fit" at US $8 per pair — *Bestellung: je 2.000 in US-Größe 9, 10, 11, 12*
> women's running shoes "Joy" at US $8 per pair — *Bestellung: je 1.500 in US-Größe 6, 7, 8*
> children's running shoes "Quick" at US $6 per pair

The shoes meet European standards and have already been sold in over 50 countries.

Delivery can be arranged CFR Rotterdam within eight weeks. Payment has to be made by irrevocable, confirmed letter of credit for first orders and by bank transfer on a regular basis. We can offer a quantity discount of 5% on orders over 50,000 items. *Lieferung muss innerhalb von 8 Wochen CFR Rotterdam erfolgen. Zahlung per Akkreditiv - wir erwarten Einführungsrabatt von 2%.*
Please find our catalogue and price list for our wide range of products in the attachment. The free samples of our running shoes that you required have already been dispatched.

We hope that this offer comes up to your expectations. If you have any further questions, do not hesitate to contact us.

We look forward to receiving your order soon.

Hoffnung auf sorgfältige und pünktliche Ausführung des Auftrags

Yours sincerely

Adnan Nasution
Export department

---

b) Situation: You work in the purchasing department of the British company
Technic-all in Birmingham.

Your task: Write an e-mail to Ms Alpana Ura, who works in the export
department of the *South Indian Trading Company*. Include the following
prompts.

- refer to her offer
- thank her for the two samples of electric motors
- their quality comes up to your expectations
- place an order for 1,000 motors (model EC5) and 500 motors (model EC6)
- delivery within two months
- terms of delivery FOB Goa
- payment by bank transfer when the goods have been shipped
- you want an acknowledgement of your order
- you expect to be informed if there is any delay in delivery

| Basic course | Advanced course | Cross-cultural business communication |

Orders 17

‹M› **c)** Write the following order in English using the German prompts below. Use today's date.

Situation:
Sie arbeiten im Einkauf der Firma *Domo-Import* in 32760 Detmold, Leonardo-da-Vinci-Weg 4, und Sie haben ein Angebot von Sven Olafsson von der Firma *Scandinavian Exclusive Seating* (SES) in Norwegen (Adresse: Revierstredet 8, NO-0104 Oslo) erhalten.

Ihre Aufgabe:
Schreiben Sie eine Bestellung an die norwegische Firma. Verwenden Sie dabei die folgenden Stichpunkte.
- Sie bedanken sich für die Zusendung von Katalog und Preisliste.
- Sie sind besonders von den Sitzmöbeln aus Leder beeindruckt.
- Umweltfreundliche Herstellung und Materialien können wichtige Argumente bei Ihren Kunden sein.
- Erste Bestellung von drei Polstergarnituren *(three-piece suites)* in Leder, Artikel-Nr. L342 „Purple" – damit sollen die Qualität und das Interesse der Kunden getestet werden.
- Lieferungsbedingungen: 6 Wochen ab Bestellung, FOB Oslo
- Zahlungsbedingungen: Überweisung bei Lieferung, 40 % Händlerrabatt *(trade discount)*
- Sie stellen weitere umfangreiche Aufträge in Aussicht.
- Sie bitten um eine Auftragsbestätigung und pünktliche Lieferung.
- Sie schließen mit einem freundlichen Schlusssatz.

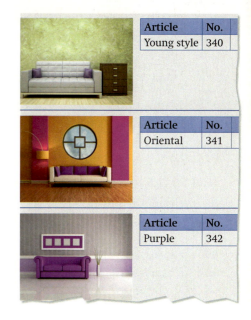

Article	No.
Young style	340

Article	No.
Oriental	341

Article	No.
Purple	342

d) Write the following order in English using the German prompts below. Use today's date.

Situation:
Als Mitarbeiter im Einkauf der *Dies & Das Handelsgesellschaft* in 18147 Rostock, Ost-West-Str. 34, sind Sie u.a. für das internationale Bestellwesen zuständig.

Ihre Aufgabe:
Auf Grund eines Angebots der *Fujian Export Company*, 29 Qintong Rd, 50-1101 Pudong New District, Shanghai, China 20120, schreiben Sie unter Ihrem Namen die folgende Bestellung an Frau Wang.
- Sie bedanken sich für das Angebot und die Muster, die Sie vor einigen Tagen erhalten haben.
- Sie entnehmen dem Informationsmaterial, dass die Produkte den europäischen Sicherheitsstandards entsprechen.
- Sie haben die Geräte in Ihrem Unternehmen getestet und möchten eine größere Probebestellung *(trial order)* aufgeben.
- Sie bestellen 2.000 Haartrockner *(hairdryer)* „Warm breeze" zum Stückpreis von 15,90 US-Dollar und 2.000 Toaster „Happy breakfast" zum Stückpreis von 27,10 US-Dollar.
- Die Produkte müssen der Qualität der Muster entsprechen.
- Die Lieferung soll bis zum Ende des nächsten Monats FOB Shanghai durchgeführt werden.
- Die Zahlung wird durch Akkreditiv erfolgen.
- Sie erwarten 5 % Mengenrabatt und stellen weitere große Aufträge in Aussicht.
- Sie bringen Ihre Hoffnung zum Ausdruck, dass sich erfolgreiche Geschäftsbeziehungen entwickeln werden.

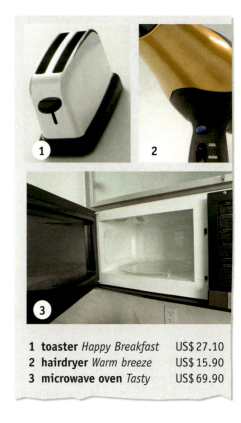

1 **toaster** *Happy Breakfast* US$ 27.10
2 **hairdryer** *Warm breeze* US$ 15.90
3 **microwave oven** *Tasty* US$ 69.90

| International business correspondence | Exam preparation | 125 |

17 Orders

‹R› 5 A trial order on the telephone

A2.15 a) Listen to the telephone dialogue and find out the following:

1. the names of the persons
2. the countries where the persons are
3. the product they are talking about
4. why this is a trial order

b) Listen to the dialogue again and find out details about the following:

1. the quantity of goods ordered
2. the prices
3. the quality of the product
4. the delivery time
5. the terms of payment
6. the discount

6 Making telephone calls

▶ SF 5 Making phone calls   ▶ SF 7 Formal phone calls

‹I› **a)** Work in pairs. Prepare the following telephone call and present it to the class. Student A is Amy / Alex Kowalski from Montreal working for *Inter-Top Canada*. Student B is himself / herself working in the purchasing department of a company in his or her home town. Student B has received an offer from *Inter-Top* and wants to order goods at his / her choice.

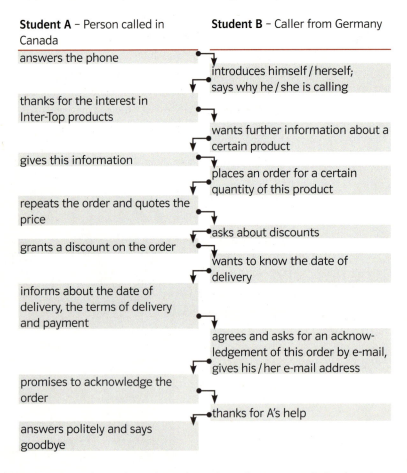

Student A – Person called in Canada
- answers the phone
- thanks for the interest in Inter-Top products
- gives this information
- repeats the order and quotes the price
- grants a discount on the order
- informs about the date of delivery, the terms of delivery and payment
- promises to acknowledge the order
- answers politely and says goodbye

Student B – Caller from Germany
- introduces himself / herself; says why he / she is calling
- wants further information about a certain product
- places an order for a certain quantity of this product
- asks about discounts
- wants to know the date of delivery
- agrees and asks for an acknowledgement of this order by e-mail, gives his / her e-mail address
- thanks for A's help

Role card A

Student A (use your own name)
- Sie beziehen sich auf das Angebot von GREEN LABEL.
- Sie sind interessiert an Gartenmöbeln aus Holz aus umweltfreundlicher Produktion.
- Sie wollen mehr über die Herkunft der Hölzer wissen.
- Sie erkundigen sich nach den Transportbedingungen und nach der Lieferzeit.
- Sie erkundigen sich nach dem Preis eines bestimmten Produktes und versuchen, einen Rabatt auszuhandeln.
- Sie stimmen den Zahlungsbedingungen zu.
- Sie bestellen eine bestimmte Anzahl des Produktes und betonen die Wichtigkeit einer pünktlichen Lieferung.
- Sie verabschieden sich höflich.

‹M/I› **b)** Work in pairs (see role cards on the right and on page 175). Student A works for the big chain of do-it-yourself stores (DIY) *BESSERKAUF* with its headquarters in Berlin and calls student B, Trisha / Tristan Cooling, who works in the export department of *GREEN LABEL*, a leading producer of garden furniture in Britain.

7 Useful phrases: Order (German – English)

◘ **Anfang**

Opening

Wir bedanken uns vielmals für Ihr Angebot vom	**Many thanks for your offer of . . . .**
Wir freuen uns, . . .	**We are pleased . . .**
den folgenden / anliegenden Auftrag zu erteilen.	to place the following / attached order.
Bitte liefern Sie uns die folgenden Artikel . . .	**Please supply / send us the following goods . . .**
zu den unten genannten Bedingungen.	on the terms / conditions stated below.

Einzelheiten

Details

Die Lieferung muss erfolgen . . .	**Delivery / Shipment must be made / executed . . .**
innerhalb von ... Wochen / Monaten.	within ... weeks / months.
bis spätestens zum	by ... at the latest.
Die Zahlung erfolgt . . .	**Payment will be effected / made / arranged . . .**
im Voraus.	in advance.
mit dem Auftrag / der Bestellung.	with order.
bei Lieferung.	on delivery.
bei Erhalt der Ware.	on receipt of goods.
innerhalb von ... Tagen nach Erhalt der Ware.	within ... days after receipt of goods.
durch Überweisung des Rechnungsbetrags.	by transfer of the invoice amount.
Kasse gegen Dokumente.	cash against documents.
durch unwiderrufliches, bestätigtes Akkreditiv.	by irrevocable, confirmed letter of credit.
entsprechend Ihren Zahlungsbedingungen.	according to your terms of payment.
Wir entnehmen Ihrem Angebot, . . .	**We note from your offer / quotation . . .**
dass Ihre Preise einen Rabatt von ...% beinhalten.	that your prices include a discount of ...%.
dass Sie bereit sind, uns einen Rabatt von ...% einzuräumen.	that you are willing to grant us a discount of ...%.
Wir erwarten einen Rabatt von . . . %.	**We expect a discount of . . . %.**

Ende

Closing

Bitte bestätigen Sie . . .	**Please confirm / acknowledge . . .**
diesen Auftrag umgehend.	this order by return.
den Erhalt dieses Auftrags prompt.	receipt of this order promptly.
Bitte informieren Sie uns, . . .	**Please inform us / let us know . . .**
sobald die Ware ausgeliefert wurde.	when the goods have been shipped.
wenn es Lieferungsverzögerungen geben sollte.	if there are any delays in delivery.
Wir freuen uns darauf, . . .	**We look forward to . . .**
mit Ihnen in Geschäftsbeziehungen zu treten.	doing business with you.
die Ware rechtzeitig / pünktlich zu erhalten.	receiving the goods in / on time.

International business correspondence | Exam preparation

Unit 18
Complaints

1 When things go wrong

‹P› **Before reading**

a) *Col-Import* has ordered some goods from CNF, a leading Chinese export company. Describe the photos above and explain what you think has gone wrong.

‹R› **Understanding the text**

b) Read *Col-Import's* complaints on the right and find out what really went wrong.

c) Read the complaints again and correct the following statements.

Order no. 2218:
1. *Col-Import* hasn't sent the goods on time.
2. The company delivered the wrong goods.
3. *Col-Import* is now happy with order no. 2218.
4. *Col-Import* needs the goods within a week.

Order no. 2249:
5. CNF sent order no. 2249 punctually to *Col-Import*.
6. *Col-Import* needs the goods for a trade fair exhibition.
7. *Col-Import* asks CNF to send another consignment.
8. *Col-Import* wants delivery within four weeks.

| Basic course | Advanced course | Cross-cultural business communication |

Complaints 18

From:	r.springer@col-import.de
To:	ling.xiao@cnf.com.cn
Date:	6 June, 20…
Subject:	Complaint
Attachments:	Order No. 2218

Dear Mr Ling

I'm writing with reference to our order no. 2218.

The goods arrived yesterday on schedule. However, they have given cause for complaint. When we unpacked the consignment we found out that the goods in carton nos. 7, 8 and 9 were damaged.

Could you send us replacements as soon as possible as we have planned a special promotion campaign for them next month?

Looking forward to hearing from you soon.

Yours sincerely

R. Springer
Purchasing manager
Col-Import AG

From:	r.springer@col-import.de
To:	ling.xiao@cnf.com.cn
Date:	11 August, 20…
Subject:	Complaint
Attachments:	Order No. 2249

Dear Mr Ling

I'm afraid I have to write to you again about our order no. 2249. We regret to inform you that the goods have not yet arrived. They should have been delivered by the end of last week.

This is a particular problem for us because we need the goods urgently for our special promotion campaign in various supermarkets in two weeks' time.

Please look into this problem for us immediately. We want to ask you to arrange for immediate dispatch of the consignment, otherwise we will hold you liable for any losses entailed.

We look forward to receiving the goods as soon as possible.

Yours sincerely

R. Springer
Purchasing manager
Col-Import AG

---

d) Find ten words in the two e-mails above with the help of the syllables in
the box.

> • ate • car • cere • com • con • di • dis • ence • er • im • lar • ly
> • me • ment • ment • par • patch • place • plaint • re • ref • sched
> • sign • sin • tic • ton • u • ule

International business correspondence   Exam preparation   **129**

18 Complaints

2 Useful phrases: Complaint (Substitution table)

◨ **Opening**

I am writing	**with** reference **to** our order	no. .... .
I am afraid I have to write **to** you	**about** our order	

We regret to inform you	that	the goods	have	given cause **for** complaint.
We are sorry to report		the consignment	has	not turned **out to** our satisfaction.
		the shipment		

Details

The goods	which	were ordered **on** …	have	not reached us yet.
The consignment		should have been delivered **by** …	has	not arrived yet.
			are	considerably overdue.
			is	

When we unpacked	the boxes	we found out that …	
When we opened	the crates	we discovered that …	
When we examined	the containers		
	the cartons		

… the goods	was	damaged.
… articles no. …	were	missing.
… the consignment	is	defective.
… the contents	are	not **up to** the standard we require.
… we had received the wrong goods.		

Please	look into this	matter	immediately.
We ask you to		problem	as soon as possible.
Could you			
	send us replacements		
	ship the consignment		

We are willing to	keep	the goods	**at** a reduced price **of** …. .
We are prepared to		the consignment	if you grant us a reduction **of** …. .

Unless the consignment arrives **by** …,	we must	cancel our order.
Should you not be able to deliver **by** …,	we will have to	look **for** another supplier.
We want to ask you **for** immediate dispatch, otherwise		hold you liable **for** the loss entailed.

Closing

We hope	that you will settle the matter as soon as possible.
We trust	that you will understand our position.
We are sure	

We look forward	**to** receiving the goods	immediately.
Looking forward	**to** hearing **from** you	soon.

130 | Basic course | Advanced course | Cross-cultural business communication

Complaints 18

3 Practising words and phrases for complaints

a) Match the expressions in the first box with suitable expressions in the second box in order to make meaningful sentences.

1.	The consignment was	a.	are damaged.
2.	The amount of delivered goods	b.	not arrived yet.
3.	Some items	c.	unpacked immediately.
4.	We need the goods	d.	is incorrect.
5.	Please send us	e.	urgently.
6.	The goods have	f.	replacements.
7.	The consignment has given	g.	keep the goods.
8.	Please look into	h.	to hearing from you soon.
9.	We are willing to	i.	cause for complaint.
10.	We look forward	j.	this matter immediately.

b) Create a word web with words from the substitution table on page 130. Add other words that you already know. ▶ SF 21 Word webs

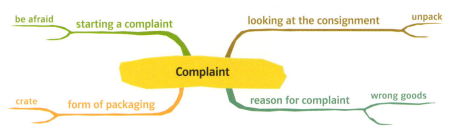

c) Rewrite the following letter. Fill in the gaps with words from the substitution table.

> Dear Mr Williams
>
> We are [1] with reference to our order no. 67D. We [2] to inform you that when we [3] the crates we discovered that we had received the [4] goods. In another crate a number of the items are not up [5] the standard that we require.
>
> Could you [6] into this problem immediately? We would ask you to send us [7] as soon as possible. If you are not able to guarantee delivery of the goods by next week, we will have to [8] our order.
>
> Yours sincerely
>
> Paul Morrison

d) Put the following parts of a complaint in a suitable order. Then write the complete letter in an appropriate form.

1.	the articles in crates 3 and 4	2.	could you look into the problem immediately
3.	this is very inconvenient for us because	4.	dear Mr Scholes
5.	we found that	6.	we want to ask you to arrange for
7.	we need the goods urgently	8.	looking forward to receiving your reply
9.	yours sincerely	10.	I'm writing with reference to our order no. 654
11.	when we opened the crates	12.	we regret to inform you that the consignment you sent us is not in order
13.	were damaged	14.	immediate dispatch of the replacements

International business correspondence | Exam preparation | 131

18 Complaints

‹P› 4 Writing complaints
▶ SF 23 Formal letters and e-mails

a) Situation:
Nick Müller, who works for *Col-Import*, has had a very busy week. And sometimes in business things don't always go as well as expected.

Your task:
Write his letters / e-mails of complaint (n.mueller@col-import.de) to the following suppliers:

1. *Col-Import* received 3,000 pairs of trainers from the firm *Train IT* in Vietnam yesterday (e-mail address: info@train-it.vn). The problem is that the trainers are the wrong colours. *Col-Import* would keep them but they wish a reduction in price.

2. *Col-Import* placed an order for 2,000 pairs of jeans from a Tunisian firm called *The Jeans Company* two months ago. Their e-mail address is expo@TJC.tn. When the goods arrived *Col-Import* discovered that in crates no. 17 and no. 18 the jeans were damaged and cannot be sold in this condition. You need replacements immediately.

3. *Col-Import* ordered 7,000 electronic toys from the South Korean firm *Park Ltd* five weeks ago. Their e-mail address is export@park-ltd.kr. Unfortunately the toys haven't arrived yet. *Col-Import* needs the articles urgently because of the coming Christmas season.

Complaints 18

‹M› **b)** Write the following complaint in English using the German prompts below. Use today's date.

Situation:
Sie arbeiten im Einkauf der Firma *Col-Import*. Vor kurzem haben Sie bei der amerikanischen Firma *PRINT-IT* eine Lieferung von 1000 T-Shirts bestellt (E-Mail-Adresse: smalling@print-it.us). Die Auftragsnummer war D-7818 und Ihre Kontaktperson war Mr Wesley Smalling. Als die Lieferung gestern bei der Warenannahme geprüft wurde, musste man dort feststellen, dass nur 500 T-Shirts geliefert wurden. Die bestellten T-Shirts mit dem Aufdruck von kalifornischen Universitäten fehlten.

Ihre Aufgabe:
Schreiben Sie an Herrn Smalling eine E-Mail:
- Beziehen Sie sich auf Ihre Bestellung von vor sechs Wochen.
- Beschreiben Sie die Mängel in der Lieferung.
- Bitten Sie Herrn Smalling, die restlichen T-Shirts sofort zu schicken.
- Machen Sie einen Vorschlag für eine finanzielle Regelung, die die möglichen Nachteile für Ihre Firma ausgleicht.
- Schließen Sie Ihren Brief höflich.

c) Write the following complaint in English using the German prompts below. Use today's date.

Situation:
Sie arbeiten für das Sportartikelunternehmen *Sports & Co KG* in Offenbach. Als Mitarbeiter im Einkauf betreuen Sie den lateinamerikanischen und den mexikanischen Markt. Letzte Woche lieferte Ihnen die Firma *Mextiles* aus Mexiko 5000 Baseballkappen. Als die Verpackung geöffnet wurde, entdeckten Mitarbeiter Ihres Unternehmens leider, dass 500 der Baseballkappen fehlerhaft waren. Teilweise waren die Kappen ausgeblichen (*faded*). Einige Kappen waren verschmutzt. Ihr Ansprechpartner, den Sie gut kennen, ist Herr Luis Hernandez.

Ihre Aufgabe:
Schreiben Sie eine E-Mail an Luis Hernandez (E-Mail-Adresse: l.hernandez@mextiles.mx):
- Beginnen Sie Ihre Mängelrüge freundlich.
- Schildern Sie die vorhandenen Mängel.
- Bitten Sie um umgehende Stellungnahme zu diesem Vorfall.
- Weisen Sie auf Ihre langjährigen Geschäftsbeziehungen hin.
- Bitten Sie um eine schnelle Regelung des Problems.

| International business correspondence | Exam preparation | 133 |

18 Complaints

5 A complaint on the telephone

A2.16 a) Listen to the telephone dialogue and find out the following:

1. the names of the persons
2. the countries where you think the persons are
3. the problem they are talking about

b) Listen to the dialogue again and find out details about the following:

1. what articles and how many articles were ordered
2. when they were ordered
3. what the problem seems to be
4. what the seller promises
5. why delivery is so urgent

6 Making telephone calls
▶ SF 5 Making phone calls   ▶ SF 7 Formal phone calls

a) 1. Work in pairs. Prepare the following telephone call and present it to the class. Student A is Don/Donna Busby from Chicago working for *Electronics R Life*. Student B is himself/herself working in the export department of *Kameras & Co* in Magdeburg. Student B has received an e-mail from Chicago in which Don/Donna Busby made a complaint about the consignment of 300 hi-tech cameras made in Germany. Now he/she is making a call to the USA.

Student A – Person called in Chicago	**Student B** – Caller from Germany
answers the phone	
	introduces himself/herself; says why he/she is calling and apologizes for the complaint
asks about reasons	
	explains what has gone wrong – problems in production – many members of staff off sick flu
wants to know when he/she can expect the goods	
	promises delivery within the next month
shows understanding, but wants a reduction on the agreed price	
	agrees to a 5% reduction
wants an e-mail from the German caller to confirm the details	
	promises to confirm delivery and reduction immediately
says thank you and goodbye	
	apologizes once more and then says goodbye

Role card A

Student A (use your own name)

- Sie beziehen sich auf den Auftrag Nr. 7779 von vor 3 Monaten.
- Sie beschweren sich darüber, dass zehn Panels defekt waren, als Sie die Lieferung öffneten.
- Sie bitten um sofortigen Ersatz für die defekten Panels.
- Sie wünschen einen Rabatt wegen der Mängel.
- Sie freuen sich über die baldige Ersatzlieferung.
- Sie verabschieden sich höflich.

2. Now write the e-mail for *Kameras & Co* in which you confirm the details of your telephone call with the American company.

b) Work in pairs (see role cards on the right and on page 175). Student A works for *Grünbau GmbH* in Mainz and calls student B, Layla/Larry Schneyder, who works in the sales department of *Solar Panels Inc.* in Los Angeles.

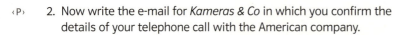

134 | Basic course | Advanced course | Cross-cultural business communication

Complaints 18

7 Useful phrases: Complaint (German – English)

◼ **Anfang**	**Opening**
Ich schreibe Ihnen in Bezug auf unseren Auftrag	**I am writing with reference to our order . . . .**
Wir bedauern, Sie informieren zu müssen, dass . . .	**We regret to inform you that . . .**
Es tut uns leid, Ihnen mitteilen zu müssen, dass . . .	**We are sorry to report that . . .**
die Lieferung Anlass zu einer Beschwerde gibt.	the consignment has given cause for complaint.
die Lieferung nicht zu unserer Zufriedenheit ausgefallen ist.	the shipment has not turned out to our satisfaction.
Einzelheiten	**Details**
Die Waren, die wir am . . . bestellt haben, . . .	**The goods which we ordered on . . .**
Die Lieferung, die bis zum . . . hätte erfolgen müssen, . . .	**The consignment which should have been delivered by . . .**
haben / hat uns noch nicht erreicht.	have / has not yet reached us.
sind / ist noch nicht eingetroffen.	have / has not arrived yet.
sind / ist lange überfällig.	are / is considerably overdue.
Als wir die Kisten auspackten . . .	**When we unpacked the crates . . .**
Als wir die Kartons untersuchten, . . .	**When we examined the cartons . . .**
fanden wir heraus / entdeckten wir, dass . . .	we found out / discovered that . . .
der Inhalt fehlte.	the content was missing.
die Waren defekt waren.	the articles were defective.
die Lieferung nicht dem Standard entspricht, den wir erwarten.	the consignment was not up to the standard we require.
wir die falschen Waren erhalten haben.	we had received the wrong goods.
Bitte prüfen Sie die Angelegenheit / das Problem . . .	**Please look into this matter / problem . . .**
Bitte senden Sie uns Ersatz . . .	**Please send us replacements . . .**
Bitte liefern Sie . . .	**Please ship the consignment . . .**
sofort / so bald wie möglich.	immediately / as soon as possible.
Wir sind bereit, . . .	**We are willing / prepared to . . .**
die Ware zu einem reduzierten Preis von . . . zu behalten.	keep the goods at a reduced price of . . . .
die Lieferung zu behalten, wenn Sie uns einen Nachlass von . . . % gewähren.	keep the consignment if you grant us a reduction of . . . %.
Wenn die Lieferung nicht bis zum . . . eintrifft, . . .	**Unless the consignment arrives by . . . , . . .**
Sollten Sie nicht in der Lage sein, bis zum . . . zu liefern, . . .	**Should you not be able to deliver by . . . , . . .**
Wir möchte Sie um die sofortige Auslieferung bitten, ansonsten . . .	**We want to ask you for immediate dispatch, otherwise . . .**
müssen wir unsere Bestellung stornieren.	we must cancel our order.
werden wir uns nach einem anderen Lieferanten umsehen.	we will have to look for another supplier.
müssen wir Sie für den damit verbundenen Schaden haftbar machen.	we must hold you liable for the loss entailed.
Ende	**Closing**
Wir hoffen / vertrauen darauf / sind sicher, dass . . .	**We hope / trust / are sure that . . .**
Sie die Angelegenheit so bald wie möglich erledigen.	you will settle the matter as soon as possible.
Sie unsere Position verstehen.	you will understand our position.
Wir freuen uns, . . .	**Looking forward to . . . / We look forward to . . .**
die Ware sobald wie möglich zu erhalten.	receiving the goods as soon as possible.

International business correspondence | Exam preparation | 135

1 2 3

Unit 19
Reminders

1 A reminder

Before reading

a) Look at the photos above and say what you think has happened.

Understanding the text

b) Read the reminder on the right and check if your ideas were right.

c) Read the reminder again and correct the following statements.

1. *Col-Import* has received payment for the invoice no. C1793.
2. The company sent the goods in November.
3. Mr Freund has attached a copy of the offer.
4. He has asked *gardentools.co.uk* to send the goods back.
5. If the British company has already paid, Mr Cleverly should phone Mr Freund.
6. *Col-Import* won't answer any more questions about the order.
7. *Col-Import* wants payment within six weeks.
8. Mr Freund works in the marketing department.

After reading

d) Imagine you were Mr Cleverly. What would you do in this situation?

| 136 | Basic course | Advanced course | Cross-cultural business communication |

Reminders 19

From: d.freund@col-import.de
To: c.cleverly@gardentools.co.uk
Sent: 20/11/20…
Subject: Reminder
Attachment: Reminder of 20 November 20…
Invoice No. C1793

▶

Garden Tools
Alington Avenue
Dorchester
Dorset DTI 12 AB
Great Britain

Col-Import AG
Industriestraße 27–39
50735 Köln / Cologne
Germany
Tel: 0049 (0)2236 3749582
Fax: 0049 (0)2236 3749584
E-Mail: d.freund@col-import.de
Web: www.col-import.de

Your ref.: CL
Our ref.: DF
Date: 20 November 20…

Dear Mr Cleverly

Invoice No. C1793

Our records show that we have not received payment yet for our invoice no. C1793, dated 13 October 20… .

Your order was dispatched from our warehouse on 14 October 20… . According to our agreed terms, payment should have been made by 13 November 20… .

This is probably a simple oversight on your part, but please give this matter your prompt attention.
Please find attached a copy of the invoice for your reference.

If you have already settled the invoice in the meantime, please disregard this e-mail. Moreover, should you have any questions regarding payment, please do not hesitate to contact us.

We look forward to receiving your payment soon.

Yours sincerely

Dietmar Freund
Sales Department
Col-Import AG

19 Reminders

2 Useful phrases: Reminder (Substitution table)

◘ **Opening**

I am writing to inform you that Our records show that May I draw your attention **to** the fact that Please accept this as a friendly reminder that	we have not received payment **for** our invoice no. … yet.	
	our invoice no. …	is now overdue. was due **on** … (date).
Your order was executed The goods were dispatched The items left our warehouse	**on** … (date).	

Details

According **to** our	agreed terms	payment should have been made **by** … (date).
	terms **of** payment	
I am enclosing Please find attached	a copy **of** our invoice (**for** your reference).	
We are sure that you have mistakenly overlooked this This is probably a simple oversight **on** your part This may simply be a problem **with** your bank	but please	settle your account immediately. give it your prompt attention. make your payment **within** … days.
If you fail to meet our deadline, If we do not receive payment by …,	we will have to	change our terms of payment. stop future deliveries. take legal steps.

Closing

If payment has already been effected, If you have settled the invoice **in** the meantime, If we should have overlooked your payment,	please	let us know **at** once. disregard this letter. accept our apologies.
If you have any further questions regarding payment, Should you require any further information,	do not hesitate	to contact us. to get **in** touch **with** us.
We look forward **to**	an early settlement **of** your account. receiving your payment soon. doing business **with** you **in** the future.	

3 Practising words and phrases for reminders

a) Rewrite the following letter. Fill in the gaps with words from the substitution table above.

Dear Ms Neville

Our records [**1**] that we have not yet received [**2**] for our [**3**] no. 218. The goods were [**4**] from our [**5**] on 23 January 20… . According to the agreed [**6**] payment should have been [**7**] by 22 February 20… .

I am sure that you have mistakenly [**8**] this, but we would be grateful if you could give this matter your prompt [**9**] and [**10**] your account within the next few days. If you have paid the bill in the [**11**], please [**12**] this letter. If you have any further [**13**] regarding payment, please do not [**14**] to get in [**15**] with us.

We look forward to [**16**] payment from you soon.

Yours sincerely

138 | Basic course | Advanced course | Cross-cultural business communication

Reminders 19

b) Match the verbs in the first box with suitable expressions in the second box. Refer to the substitution table on the left.

1. receive	a. your account
2. be	b. your prompt attention
3. contact	c. our apologies
4. enclose	d. payment
5. give	e. due
6. settle	f. this letter
7. disregard	g. a copy of the invoice
8. accept	h. us

c) The following phrases are written in the active voice. Put them into the passive form.

Example: We attach our invoice. Our invoice is attached.
1. We have not received payment yet.
2. You agreed to these terms.
3. We dispatched the goods from our warehouse last month.
4. You should have made payment by 10 December.
5. You should settle your account within the next few days.
6. We enclose a copy of your order.
7. You have always paid your bills promptly in the past.
8. If you have settled the invoice in the meantime, please disregard this letter.

d) Put the following parts of a reminder in a suitable order. Then write the complete letter in an appropriate form.

1. according to our agreed terms	2. with reference to our invoice no. 665
3. but please give it your prompt attention	4. yours sincerely
5. the goods were dispatched	6. I am enclosing
7. dear Mr Martin	8. if you have any questions concerning payment,
9. from our warehouse last month	10. I am sure
11. please disregard this reminder	12. a copy of the invoice
13. I am writing to inform you	14. that payment is now overdue
15. you have mistakenly	16. for your reference
17. if you have already settled the invoice,	18. please do not hesitate to contact me
19. payment should have been made by 30 May	20. overlooked this
21. that our records show	

International business correspondence   Exam preparation   139

19 Reminders

‹P› 4 Writing reminders
▶ SF 23 Formal letters and e-mails

a) Situation:
You work for *Keramikwerke Hannover AG*, Lindenstr. 112, 30559 Hannover (e-mail address: ms@keramik-hannover.de) and have dealt with the British firm *Cups, mugs and more* in Bath for a long time now. Two months ago you sent them a consignment of 200 German beer mugs. Unfortunately you still haven't received payment from the British firm, which is extremely unusual as they usually pay on time. Their address is 24 High Street, Bath, BA1 5 AW, England (e-mail address: e_fisher@cupsandmugs.co.uk).

Your task:
Write a polite reminder as an attachment to an e-mail to Eric Fisher from *Cups, mugs and more*:
- Be very tactful, as they are very good customers of your firm and normally very reliable with regard to payment.
- Enquire if they have received your delivery.
- Ask them what has gone wrong.
- Suppose that there has been an oversight or a problem with the bank.
- Tell them to disregard your reminder if payment has been effected in the meantime.
- Apologize for any inconvenience that you may have caused.
- Express your wish to do further business with the other company.

b) Situation:
You work for *IMPOTEX Germany* in Bremen. Your e-mail address is g.braun@impotex-germany.de. An Irish company, *Multistore*, based in Cork, Ireland ordered 1,000 calculators from you two months ago. You dispatched the goods promptly. Payment should have been effected by the end of last month but you haven't heard anything from them since you delivered the goods. Their e-mail address is st-willis@multistore.ie.

Your task:
Write a reminder to Steven Willis at *Multistore*:
- Inform him that you have not received payment yet.
- Let him know that you require payment for the goods.
- Let him also know that you expect his company to settle the invoice within a week.
- Be polite.

Reminders 19

‹M› **c)** Write the following offer in English using the German prompts below. Use today's date.

Situation:
Sie arbeiten im Verkauf der Firma *Frank Elektro GmbH* und haben am 8. Mai an die britische Firma *Cool Kitchens Ltd* in Newcastle-upon-Tyne 500 Design-Toaster per LKW geliefert. Ihre Rechnung ging am 9. Mai heraus. Die Firm *Cool Kitchens* ist bereits ein guter Kunde Ihres Unternehmens und hat immer rechtzeitig ihre Rechnungen bezahlt. Darüber hinaus ist anzunehmen, dass das Unternehmen der *Frank Elektro GmbH* weitere Aufträge erteilen wird. Die Zahlung sollte bei Erhalt der Ware erfolgen. Leider ist die Zahlung noch nicht eingegangen, obwohl die Lieferung vor etwa drei Wochen eingetroffen sein müsste. Ihre Kontaktperson bei *Cool Kitchens* ist Ms McFadden. Ihre E-Mail-Adresse lautet mcfadden@cool-kitchens.co.uk.

Ihre Aufgabe:
Schreiben Sie eine Erinnerung an die britische Firma:
- Formulieren Sie Ihr Schreiben äußerst höflich und zurückhaltend.
- Beziehen Sie sich auf Ihre Lieferung und Ihre Rechnung.
- Weisen Sie darauf hin, dass weder eine Zahlung noch irgendeine Nachricht von *Cool Kitchens* vorliegt.
- Äußern Sie Ihr Bedauern.
- Drücken Sie die Vermutung aus, dass es sich um ein Versehen handelt.
- Bitten Sie den Kunden, den Erhalt der Ware zu bestätigen und die Zahlung innerhalb von einer Woche vorzunehmen.
- Weisen Sie darauf hin, dass Ihre E-Mail gegenstandslos ist, wenn die britische Firma bereits gezahlt haben sollte.
- Schließen Sie die E-Mail höflich mit der Hoffnung auf weitere gute Geschäftsbeziehungen.

Frank Elektro GmbH

E-mail: expo@frank-elektro.de

Date: 09 May 20...

Invoice No. FE 104579A

Delivery:
500 design toasters "silver star"   9.800

Terms of payment:
Payment on receipt of goods

d) Write the following offer in English using the German prompts below. Use today's date.

Situation:
Sie arbeiten für das Unternehmen *Bornkessel & Schultheis GmbH* in Berlin (E-Mail-Adresse: amex@bornschult.de). Als Mitarbeiter/in im Verkauf betreuen Sie den nordamerikanischen Markt. Vor drei Monaten hatten Sie der Firma *Up and away* in Toronto, Kanada, 250 Kiteboards geliefert. Trotz zweier Mahnschreiben an die kanadische Firma haben Sie bis zum heutigen Datum nichts von dem Unternehmen gehört. Ihr Ansprechpartner dort ist Mr Craig Duvall. Seine E-Mail-Adresse ist c.duvall@upaway.ca.

Ihre Aufgabe:
Auf Grund dieses Zahlungsverzugs schreiben Sie die dritte Mahnung:
- Verweisen Sie auf die bereits erfolgten Mahnungen.
- Drängen Sie auf sofortige Zahlung.
- Weisen Sie das kanadische Unternehmen auf mögliche Konsequenzen hin, wenn keine Reaktion erfolgt.

International business correspondence   Exam preparation   141

19 Reminders

‹R› 5 A reminder on the telephone

A2.17 a) Listen to the telephone dialogue and find out:

1. the names of the persons
2. the countries where you think the persons are
3. the problem they are talking about

b) Listen to the dialogue again and find out details about the following:

1. the delivery date
2. the payment agreement
3. the original invoice number
4. the mistake that happened

6 Making telephone calls

▶ SF 5 Making phone calls   ▶ SF 7 Formal phone calls

‹I› **a)** Work in pairs. Prepare the following telephone call and present it to the class. Student A is Linford / Lynn Walker and works in *The Mountain Shop* in Aviemore, Scotland. Student A receives a call from Germany. Student B is himself / herself working in the sales department of *Weyrauch und Fischer GmbH* in Munich. *Weyrauch und Fischer GmbH* haven't received payment for their invoice no. AS34, dated six weeks ago.

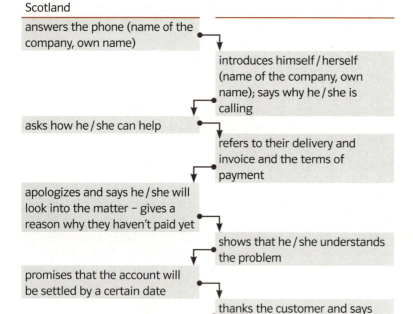

Student A – Person called in Scotland

- answers the phone (name of the company, own name)
- asks how he / she can help
- apologizes and says he / she will look into the matter – gives a reason why they haven't paid yet
- promises that the account will be settled by a certain date
- apologizes again and says goodbye

Student B – Caller from Germany

- introduces himself / herself (name of the company, own name); says why he / she is calling
- refers to their delivery and invoice and the terms of payment
- shows that he / she understands the problem
- thanks the customer and says goodbye

Role card A

Student A (use your own name)

- Sie melden sich mit Ihrem Namen.
- Sie beziehen sich auf Ihre Lieferung Nr. 221 und die Rechnung Nr. 545.
- Sie erinnern Ihren Gesprächspartner, dass die Zahlung noch nicht bei Ihrer Bank eingegangen ist, obwohl die Zahlungsfrist drei Wochen überschritten ist.
- Sie zeigen Verständnis für den Irrtum.
- Sie erläutern die Konsequenzen, wenn die Zahlung nicht erfolgt: Rückgabe der Ware auf eigene Kosten.
- Sie freuen sich auf die baldige Zahlung.
- Sie verabschieden sich freundlich.

‹M/I› **b)** Work in pairs (see role cards on the right and on page 175). Student A works for *SwissWorks AG* in Zurich, Switzerland name and calls student B, Barry / Brenda Bailley, who works in the purchasing department of *Jenkinson and Bro Ltd* in Swansea, Wales.

| Basic course | Advanced course | Cross-cultural business communication |

7 Useful phrases: Reminder (German – English)

◾ **Anfang**

Deutsch	**Opening**
Unseren Unterlagen entnehmen wir, dass …	**Our records show that …**
Ich möchte Sie informieren, dass …	**I am writing to inform you that …**
Darf ich Ihre Aufmerksamkeit darauf richten, dass …	**May I draw your attention to the fact that …**
Bitte betrachten Sie dieses Schreiben als freundliche Erinnerung, dass …	**Please accept this as a friendly reminder that …**
wir bisher noch keine Zahlung für unsere Rechnung erhalten haben.	we have not received payment for our invoice yet.
unsere Rechnung Nr. … nun überfällig ist.	our invoice no. … is now past due.
unsere Rechnung Nr. … am … fällig war.	our invoice no. … was due on … .
Ihr Auftrag wurde am … ausgeführt.	**Your order was executed on … .**
Die Ware wurde am … ausgeliefert.	**The goods were despatched on … .**
Die Ware verließ unser Lager am … .	**The items left our warehouse on … .**

Einzelheiten	**Details**
Entsprechend den vereinbarten Zahlungsbedingungen …	**According to our agreed terms of payment …**
sollte die Zahlung bis zum … erfolgt sein.	payment should have been made by … .
In der Anlage finden Sie …	**I am enclosing … / Please find attached …**
eine Kopie unserer Rechnung.	a copy of our invoice (for your reference).
Wir sind sicher, dass Sie dies übersehen haben …	**We are sure that you have overlooked this …**
Dies ist wahrscheinlich ein reines Versehen Ihrerseits …	**This is probably a simple oversight on your part …**
Das Problem könnte bei Ihrer Bank liegen, …	**This may simply be a problem with your bank …**
aber bitte …	but please …
begleichen Sie die Rechnung unverzüglich.	settle your account immediately.
schenken Sie ihm Ihre unverzügliche Aufmerksamkeit.	give it your prompt attention.
zahlen Sie innerhalb von … Tagen.	make your payment within … days.
Wenn Sie diesen Termin nicht einhalten, …	**If you fail to meet our deadline, …**
Wenn wir Ihre Zahlung nicht bis zum … erhalten, …	**If we do not receive payment by …, …**
werden wir … müssen.	we will have to …
unsere Zahlungsbedingungen ändern	change our terms of payment.
zukünftige Lieferungen einstellen	stop future deliveries.
rechtliche Schritte einleiten	take legal steps.

Ende	**Closing**
Wenn Sie in der Zwischenzeit gezahlt haben, …	**If payment has been effected in the meantime, …**
Wenn Sie bereits die Rechnung beglichen haben, …	**If you have already settled the invoice …**
Falls wir Ihre Zahlung übersehen haben, …	**If we should have overlooked your payment, …**
lassen Sie es uns sofort wissen.	let us know at once.
betrachten Sie diesen Brief als gegenstandslos.	disregard this letter.
möchten wir uns bei Ihnen entschuldigen.	accept our apologies.
Wenn Sie weitere Fragen in Bezug auf die Zahlung haben, …	**If you have any further questions regarding payment, …**
Sollten Sie weitere Informationen benötigen, …	**Should you require any further information, …**
zögern Sie nicht, sich mit uns in Verbindung zu setzen.	do not hesitate to contact us / get in touch with us.
Wir freuen uns auf …	**We look forward to …**
einen schnellen Ausgleich Ihres Kontos.	an early settlement of your account.
Ihre baldige Zahlung.	receiving your payment soon.
weitere Geschäftsbeziehungen mit Ihnen.	doing business with you in the future.

Unit 20
Youth unemployment

🔊 A2.18

Lost in nowhere land

According to the latest figures the number of school-leavers in Britain who are not in education, employment or training (the so-called Neets) has increased to nearly 1 million.
5 What are the reasons for this development?

Many young people are really worried about the future. They have worked hard to pass their exams. They have written lots of applications and CVs. They have applied to a large number of firms but
10 they have only received rejections. The consequences for young people can be serious. Some experts even speak of the "lost generation" when they talk about the young unemployed. If they do not find an apprenticeship or another way
15 of getting into employment over a longer period, the young people won't get used to working or gain work experience. This may result in a lifetime of unemployment and poverty. Experts also say that this first failure can put people on the road to
20 crime or homelessness.

There seem to be quite a lot of educational, economic and social factors which stop young people finding employment – unhelpful careers advice, poor training and job opportunities in
25 many professions, and a lack of support from families and schools over a long period are just a few examples.

When Terence Packer, 17, from Exeter left school with one GCSE, he completed a BTec in
30 sport. He then thought that he was qualified enough to find a job leading sporting activities for young people but he soon found out that employers wanted job experience, which he did not have. Terence had done some coaching in his
35 holidays, however, that did not seem sufficient.

Of course, it is hard for Terence who feels qualified and is eagerly looking for a job but cannot find one. "You see, I'm still living with my mum and she helps me in many ways but I feel I should earn my own money and pay her instead of 40 her paying for me."

When Aruna Nun, who is now eighteen, was twelve her mother fell ill and she had to care for her little brothers and sisters. She did not have enough time for school so things went downhill 45 very quickly. She did poorly in her GCSEs and only found a placement for a few months. "My brothers and sisters are a little older now so that I could start a proper job and help at home in the evening. I would like to be a teaching assistant or work in 50 childcare, but of course, there is no chance for me on the job market. That's why I'm thinking about doing a childcare course at college this autumn."

The government is trying to reduce youth unemployment and is aiming to create new jobs by 55 giving employers thousands of pounds for each job which is given to a young person. The government is also appealing to companies to support young people and give them a job, training opportunities or at least a job placement so that they can get work 60 experience. In this way the government hopes to get young people into careers.

Critics say that the government is not doing enough to solve the problem of youth unemployment. They say that there are still too 65 many young people hanging around at home or on the streets instead of doing a proper job. In the long run it is not only these young people who will suffer.

(568 words)

144 | Basic course | Advanced course | Cross-cultural business communication

Exam preparation | Youth unemployment **20**

‹R› **1 Reading comprehension**

a) Decide which of the following statements are true. More than one option may be correct.

1. Many young people are worried about the future because …
   a) most of their job applications have not been successful.
   b) it is so difficult to get work experience.
   c) a lack of work experience can lead to lifelong unemployment.
   d) they have not managed to pass their exams.

2. Quite a few young people have difficulties finding jobs …
   a) because they do not get enough help from their families.
   b) because there are not enough training facilities in a lot of jobs.
   c) because they do not get careers advice.
   d) for a number of different reasons.

3. Terence Parker and Aruna Nun …
   a) did not finish school.
   b) both have little job experience.
   c) do not know what jobs they would like to have.
   d) live at home.

4. The government …
   a) is paying money to companies that employ young people.
   b) is supporting young people by giving them jobs.
   c) wants young people to have the chance to get job experience.
   d) wants to give a job placement to every young person.

5. The author is convinced that …
   a) all young people are not qualified enough to find a job.
   b) the government will solve the problem of youth unemployment in the near future.
   c) there are many different reasons why young people have difficulties finding jobs.
   d) the situation of many young people is not easy and can have negative effects in the future.

b) Do the following tasks in complete sentences. Use your own words.

1. Describe the experiences of young school-leavers on the job market.
2. Give reasons for the problems young people have during their job search.
3. Describe Terence's situation.
4. Based on the text, explain how young people can improve their chances of finding a good job.
5. Explain the measures that are taken by the government to change the job situation of young people.

2 Comment

‹P› ▪ Choose either composition 1 or composition 2.
   ► **SF16 Writing a composition/comment**

1. "Young people today are either too lazy or not qualified enough to get a good job." Discuss.
2. "Life today is a lot more difficult for young people than it used to be." Discuss.

International business correspondence | Exam preparation | 145

3 Composition – Cartoon

‹P› ■ Describe and analyze the cartoon.   ► SF 27 Describing cartoons

4 Mediation

‹M› ■ Da Ihre Tante in Exeter in Großbritannien wohnt, interessieren Sie sich für eine Ausbildung dort. Um Ihren Eltern weitere Informationen über Ausbildungsmöglichkeiten zu geben, übertragen Sie den folgenden Auszug aus einer Broschüre des Exeter College ins Deutsche.
► SF 22 Mediation/translation

Do an apprenticeship – start your career!

You are
¬ motivated
¬ willing to learn at college and at your workplace
¬ sure which area of work you would like to work in
¬ able to find a company that will give you a job?*

At the start of the programme you
¬ must be at least 16 years old
¬ have completed year 11 at school
¬ are not on a full-time course
¬ have lived in the EU for at least three years

*If you are not able to find an employer, you can also do a full-time apprenticeship at our college.

Debbie Cooper

"I'm glad that I had the chance of starting an apprenticeship last year. I'm in my second year now and I'm enjoying it. My employer has really helped me to improve my skills. Moreover I go to college once a week. When I've finished my apprenticeship successfully I'm sure I'll find a suitable job.

‹M/P› **5 Composition – Letter of application**
▶ SF 23 Formal letters and e-mails

**Looking for an apprenticeship
at a successful company?**

Why not come to SunLife Supermarkets?

You like
» working in a team?
» helping customers?
» doing your work efficiently?

Then we look forward to getting your application!

At SunLife Supermarkets you will get the perfect training.
And there are lots of careers opportunities after you have
finished your apprenticeship successfully.

Essential requirements:
» You need to be friendly and polite.
» You must be able to work in a team.
» You must be prepared to work at weekends.

If you are interested, please send your letter of application to:

Sunlife Supermarkets
Stowford Rise
Exeter
Ex10 9GA, UK

■ Ihre Tante hat Ihnen die obige Stellenanzeige der Supermarktkette
SunLife zugeschickt. Schreiben Sie einen Bewerbungsbrief an SunLife
unter Verwendung der folgenden Informationen:

1. Ihr Name, Geburtstag, Geburtsort
2. Schulbildung:
   Städtische Gesamtschule in … von … bis …
   Berufskolleg in … von … bis …
3. Ausbildungswunsch: Verkäufer – Kontakt mit Kunden, gute Aufstiegsmöglichkeiten, sichere Zukunft
4. Abschlussnoten: Englisch 2, Deutsch 3, Mathematik 2, Wirtschaft 2, Datenverarbeitung/Computer 1
5. Arbeitserfahrung: 3mal in der Woche abends an der Kasse im Supermarkt von Januar 20… bis
   Dezember 20…
6. Ihre Hobbies und Interessen
7. Berufswunsch: leitende/r Angestellte/r im kaufmännischen Bereich

Unit 21
New jobs

A2.19

Can a new superstore help a rundown area?

When a new superstore opened in a Manchester suburb about a year ago local people hoped that the sun would shine again on their district. The store is one of the so-called 'regeneration partnership stores' which are meant to develop deprived areas, attract further investment and find at least 20% of its staff among local, long-term unemployed or disabled people.

Before the opening of the new store, 80 local people were given an extra training course for eight weeks, which was financed by the local council. About £1,000 of public money was spent on each applicant. "The money is well spent," says one official, "it helps to get long-term unemployed people back to work and it saves the community a lot of money in benefits."

The regeneration partnership model came to Britain from the US where community activists managed to persuade a big American bank to open a branch in Harlem, one of the poorest parts of New York. "It may not always be the answer to an area's problems but the idea is that this kind of new project can be the start of a wider development, attracting further businesses and in this way creating new jobs," the official adds.

"Of course, not all shop owners are happy about the arrival of a big competitor. But I believe we can transform the area and existing businesses can survive if they manage to offer additional services instead of competing in the same fields. We have established a business forum in which businesses and the town council work together. When the long-term unemployed find work, their spending power will increase. The business climate here will also improve, which in turn will attract other shop owners, bars and restaurants."

One year on, not all the wishes have come true. Some retailers are doing quite well while others have been hit hard. The local convenience store has lost a third of its business and has had to dismiss two of its assistants. Local retailers have realized that many shoppers just drive to the big supermarket and then drive home again.

Studies have not clearly shown whether large retail chains really create new jobs or make people lose them. Some groups fear that independent small shops could have disappeared from Britain by 2020. They claim that small businesses create more jobs than the big superstores which only employ one person per £95,000 of turnover – compared to small shops where it is £42,000.

(419 words)

| 148 | Basic course | Advanced course | Cross-cultural business communication |

1 Reading comprehension

‹R› **a)** Fill in the following grid with information from the text. Only note down key words.

1.	something special about the new store	
2.	the employees	
3.	the origin of the idea	
4.	arguments for the new store	
5.	negative effects	
6.	worries about the future	

b) Use your key words to write a summary of the text.

c) Do the following tasks in complete sentences. Use your own words.

1. Describe the origin of 'regeneration partnership'.
2. Explain the basic idea behind the project.
3. Give reasons for the council's interest in the new superstore.
4. Describe the benefits of the project for the long-term unemployed.
5. Give reasons for the other shop owners' fear.

2 Composition – Cartoon

‹P› ▪ Describe and analyze the cartoon.   ▶ SF 27 Describing cartoons

'Errrm...I think I'll phone a friend !'

21 New jobs | Exam preparation

3 Composition – Diagram

‹P› ▪ Describe and analyze the statistics. ►SF 28 Describing diagrams

Unemployment in per cent						
Country	2000	2002	2004	2006	2008	2010
Germany	7.5	8.4	9.8	9.8	7.3	7.5
Spain	11.1	11.1	10.6	8.5	11.3	19.0
Great Britain	5.4	5.1	4.7	5.4	5.6	7.7
EU (27)	8.7	8.9	9.0	8.2	7.0	9.6
Norway	3.4	3.9	4.5	3.4	2.6	3.3
USA	4.0	5.8	5.5	4.6	5.8	9.7

Source: EU Commission, EUROSTAT, OECD, February 2010.

4 Mediation

‹M› You are chatting with an English-speaking friend about your future jobs.
You have just read the following leaflet. Summarize the main aspects
for your friend in English. ►SF 22 Mediation / translation

Ein Beruf mit Zukunft für Dich!

Wenn Du Dich heute für einen Beruf entscheidest,
musst Du darauf achten, dass Du mit deiner
Ausbildung gute Chancen auf dem Arbeitsmarkt
hast. Diese Anforderung sollte Dein Wunschberuf
5 auf jeden Fall erfüllen.

Es ist natürlich gar nicht so leicht vorauszusagen,
welche Berufe eine Zukunft haben und welche
nicht, denn die Arbeitswelt verändert sich ständig.
Diese Veränderung kann man am besten am zu-
10 nehmenden Einsatz von Computer und Internet
erkennen. So sind in den letzten Jahren die Berufe
der Informationstechnik sehr wichtig geworden.
Heute werden viel mehr Computerspezialisten
gebraucht als früher. Zurzeit werden deshalb viel
15 mehr Menschen als früher für diese Berufe aus-
gebildet. In ein paar Jahren kann sich die Situation
aber schon wieder ändern, mit Sicherheit werden
wieder neue Berufsfelder hinzukommen.

Berufe mit Zukunft
20 Nach Vorhersagen von Fachleuten gibt es einige
Berufsbereiche, die als besonders zukunftssicher
eingeschätzt werden. In diesen Bereichen erwarten
die Experten, dass auch zukünftig Fachkräfte benötigt werden.

1. Berufe im IT-Bereich 25
2. Klassische Produktions- und Dienstleistungsberufe
3. Soziale, pflegende, beratende und unterrichtende
   Berufe
4. Berufe im Bereich des Umweltschutzes

Neben den existierenden Berufen werden jedes 30
Jahr Berufe neu entwickelt oder neu geregelt. Sie
entstehen, weil Unternehmen für neue Aufgaben
und Tätigkeiten speziell ausgebildete Fachleute
brauchen. Bei solchen Berufen kannst Du also davon ausgehen, dass Du in Zukunft gute Chancen 35
auf dem Arbeitsmarkt hast. Hier ist die Konkurrenz
in den ersten Jahren gering, sodass die Chancen auf
einen Arbeitsplatz recht gut sind. Eine Garantie
kann Dir natürlich niemand geben.

Manchmal ist es natürlich nicht leicht, einen Be- 40
trieb in der Nähe zu finden, der genau diese neue
Berufsausbildung schon anbietet. Hier heißt es
dann, flexibel zu sein. Das kann auch bedeuten,
dass Du schon in jungen Jahren eine weite Anfahrt
zu Deinem Ausbildungsplatz hast oder sogar um- 45
ziehen musst. Aber denke daran: Eine gute, zu-
kunftssichere Ausbildung ist die beste Garantie
für ein erfolgreiches Berufsleben! (309 Wörter)

150 | Basic course | Advanced course | Cross-cultural business communication

5 Composition – Advertisement
▶ SF 26 Describing illustrations and photographs

a) Describe the advertisement for Newcastle.

b) Analyze the advertisement and its possible effects.

6 Commercial correspondence – Enquiry
▶ SF 23 Formal letters and e-mails

Situation:
Sie arbeiten bei der deutschen IT-Firma **Meyer und Mehr** (Elbbrückenstr. 122 in 01097 Dresden). Letzte Woche war Ihre Chefin, Frau Silvia Meyer, auf einer Messe in Leipzig. Dort hat sie unter anderem den Verkaufsstand einer britischen Firma besucht, die IT-Ausrüstungen (*equipment*) vertreibt. Frau Meyer war sehr interessiert und der britische Verkaufsleiter hat ihr seine Visitenkarte gegeben. Allerdings hat Ihre Chefin leider die anderen Informationsblätter verlegt.

Ihre Aufgabe:
Ihre Chefin möchte, dass Sie an den britischen Verkaufsleiter schreiben und nähere Informationen über das angebotene Sortiment einholen. Sie sollen die aktuelle Preisliste und weitere Informationen über Lieferungs- und Zahlungsbedingungen anfordern. Ihre Firma möchte eventuell von der britischen Firma in großer Stückzahl einkaufen. Schreiben Sie die Anfrage.

Mr Wayne Thomas
Sales Manager

161 – 163 Penarth Road, Cardiff
CF14 3AG, Wales
Tel: 0044 29 2076 6547
E-mail: w.thomas@bootit.co.uk

Unit 22
Modern technology

Just google it!

It sounds like an American fairy tale. What began in a friend's garage in the middle of the 1990s has since become a billion dollar business and the most powerful media brand in the world.

Google's success story started in 1996 when Larry Page and Sergey Brin were both students at Stanford University in California. They began developing a new kind of search engine that would produce better results than any of the existing ones. At the beginning their search engine was part of the university website but in 1997 the domain name, google.com, was registered.

The word 'Google' seems to be a misspelling of the word 'googol', which represents a number with one hundred zeros. 'Google' has since entered dictionaries and 'to google' now means 'to use the Google search engine to obtain information on the Internet'.

At the beginning Brin and Page were against having advertising in their search engine, but they soon changed their minds. They allowed text ads, but not pop-up advertising. The ads were – and still are – text-based, and users like the clear and simple page design which keeps loading times short. Since 2000 Google has been selling advertisements which are related to the key words that a user enters. In this way advertising is targeted only at users who are interested in a topic. Advertisers pay per click on their links and this ingenious idea has made the company highly profitable. Today, 99 % of Google's earnings come from advertising while the big advantage for its users is that all of the services are free.

Google's most popular service is its web search engine, which has a market share of about 60 %. Other products include, for example, Google Earth and Google Maps, and the company has also

entered the mobile phone market. In recent years Google's street view service has taken pictures of millions of public and private buildings, which has led to a lot of criticism with regard to people's privacy. The images of city streets are often so detailed that you can see cars or pedestrians clearly. Politicians have even raised doubts about national security because satellite pictures may show targets that are at risk.

The search engine itself is often referred to as 'Big Brother' because it records and stores its users' personal searches. Google also scans the e-mails of people who use the company's e-mail-service. This all helps Google to target advertising as exactly as possible. Theoretically, Google would be able to start a file for every user, listing their interests, their appointments, their photos – and even their love affairs.

That is the price users have to pay although experts say that the company cannot afford to assign its data to individuals and sell this to interested third parties. The long-term economic damage to the company would be much greater than any short-term profits.

(476 words)

Exam preparation | Modern technology 22

1 Reading comprehension

a) Decide which of the following statements are true. More than one option may be correct.

1. At the beginning the Google search engine …
   a) did not have its own website.
   b) allowed text advertisements.
   c) was developed by a very small team.
   d) did not even have a name.

2. Companies like to advertise on Google's website because …
   a) of the pop-up advertisements.
   b) of the short loading times.
   c) of the connection between the advertisements and the search terms that users enter.
   d) they only have to pay when a Google user visits their website.

3. According to the text Google has …
   a) doubts about national security.
   b) a lot of information about its users.
   c) different services on offer.
   d) taken photos of its users.

4. Many experts believe that …
   a) Google will make a lot of money by selling their users' data to interested companies.
   b) Google could have higher profits in the long run by selling their users' data.
   c) companies are interested in the users' data.
   d) Google is not able to collect users' data and connect the information with individuals.

5. The author points out that …
   a) using Google has its advantages and dangers.
   b) Google is one of the leading media companies in the world.
   c) Google's is a typical American success story.
   d) Google's services have a market share of about 60 %.

b) Do the following tasks in complete sentences. Use your own words.

1. Describe the development of Google in its first years.
2. Outline Google's changing attitude to advertising.
3. Explain the success of the Google search engine according to the text.
4. Give reasons why Google's activities may not always work to the advantage a) of society and b) of its users.

International business correspondence | Exam preparation | 153

2 Comment

‹P› ■ Choose either composition 1 or composition 2.
▶ SF 16 Writing a composition / comment

1. "Many young people are very careless with their personal data on the Internet and especially in social networks." Discuss.
2. "The Internet will bring together people of different races and religion, and make the world a more peaceful place." Discuss.

3 Composition – Cartoon

‹P› ■ Describe and analyze the following cartoons.
▶ SF 27 Describing cartoons

4 Composition – Advertisement

‹P› ▶ SF 26 Describing illustrations and photographs

a) Describe the advertisement.
b) Analyze the advertisement and its possible effects.

5 Mediation

‹M› ■ Für den bilingualen Wirtschaftslehreunterricht bereiten Sie ein Referat über den Einsatz von Robotern in der Produktion vor. Zu Ihrer Vorbereitung haben Sie das folgende Informationsblatt erhalten. Fassen Sie die wesentlichen Gesichtspunkte auf Englisch zusammen.
► SF 22 Mediation / translation

Warum Sie in Roboter investieren sollten

Der Einsatz von Robotern bietet viele Vorteile – in einem breiten Spektrum von Anwendungsmöglichkeiten. Dabei ist vor allem darauf hinzuweisen, dass die Integration von Robotertechnik in die Produktion zu einer Steigerung sowohl der Produktivität als auch der Effektivität führt.

Die „International Federation of Robotics" hat eine Studie veröffentlicht, die die wichtigsten Gründe aufzählt, die für eine derartige Investition sprechen.

Die Kosten: Der Einsatz von Robotern senkt die Arbeitskosten. Es entfallen beispielsweise die Kosten für die Mitarbeiterentlohnung, für Gesundheitsvorsorge und Sicherheit.

Die Produktionsleistung: Anders als menschliche Arbeitskräfte können Roboter problemlos in langen Schichten, über Nacht und am Wochenende eingesetzt werden. Roboter arbeiten schneller als menschliche Arbeitskräfte und fallen selten aus. Sie können offline programmiert werden, sodass die laufende Produktion nicht angehalten werden muss.

Die Qualität: Roboter sorgen für eine gleich bleibend hohe Produktqualität, Nachteile durch menschliche Einflüsse wie z. B. Müdigkeit oder Krankheit sind ausgeschlossen.

Die Arbeitsbedingungen: Roboter verrichten extrem harte und gefährliche Arbeiten und verbessern damit die Arbeitsbedingungen der Mitarbeiter. Die Qualifikation und Motivation der Mitarbeiter können durch die Schulung an Robotern gesteigert werden.

(177 Wörter)

‹M/P› ## 6 Commercial correspondence – Offer
► SF 23 Formal letters and e-mails

Situation:
Sie arbeiten bei **Santech**, Langenstr. 94 – 96, 28195 Bremen. Ihre Firma stellt Nanoroboter *(nanorobots)* für medizinische Zwecke her. Letzte Woche erhielten Sie eine Anfrage von der Stadt Birmingham, England. Sie möchten Nanoroboter in einigen ihrer Krankenhäuser einsetzen. Ihr Ansprechpartner bei der Stadt Birmingham ist Mr Robert Flynn.

Ihre Aufgabe:
Schreiben Sie ein Angebot an Mr R. Flynn, Birmingham City Council, Health Department, Mainstream Industrial Park, Birmingham, B7 4SN, England. Ihr Angebot lautet wie folgt: Alle Preise sind FOB Bremen und Ihre Firma bietet einen Mengenrabatt von 10 % auf Bestellungen über 50.000 Euro an. Normalerweise verlangt Ihre Firma 20 % Anzahlung. Die Lieferung erfolgt innerhalb von 60 Tagen nach Auftragseingang. Das Angebot ist drei Monate gültig. Sie legen den neuesten Prospekt sowie eine aktuelle Preisliste bei. Beenden Sie Ihren Brief höflich.

Unit 23
Plastic money for young people

A2.21

Cash isn't cool anymore

**Your children have got pre-paid mobiles. How boring!
The new must-have is the pre-paid credit card.**

A massive campaign for pre-paid cards is targeting teenagers and children as young as eleven. The cards are expected to replace traditional pocket money in the future. The average age at which children receive their first mobile phone is now just eight and about 20% already use their parents' credit cards to buy goods on the Internet. So it seems to be a logical step forward to give teenagers their own credit cards.

The concept of pre-paid credit cards is similar to that of the cards used in mobile phones – you load money onto a pre-paid card and you can spend it in your favourite stores or shop online. You can also withdraw money from cash machines, pay bills or use the card on journeys abroad. When the card is empty you just top it up again by loading more money onto it. As with any other card you have to sign the back when you receive it and use a PIN (personal identification number) when you want to make transactions.

The big advantage for parents is that the pre-paid card is not a real credit card and children can only spend the money their parents have put onto the card. Therefore, it is impossible to get into debt. This kind of card is considered to be a good way of teaching children how to manage money. It is also safer for children as they do not need to carry cash anymore. The card is protected by a PIN and can be cancelled if it is stolen.

So what are the disadvantages of the card? Well, for credit card companies it is good business. Not only do they reach a lot of new, young customers, they also earn a lot of money. For example, there is an 'issuing fee' of about £10 when you get the card. There may also be an additional monthly fee, a 'reload fee' when you top up your card and a fee of £1 every time you use it.

The difficulty for card companies and internet shops comes when they must check the ages of teenage customers. Cards have already been sent out to 11-year-olds without their parents' knowledge, and one father discovered that his 15-year-old son had bought cigarettes and alcohol on the Internet. His son only had to click the button "I'm over 18" and he could use his pre-paid card to order what he wanted.

Some credit card companies are working on solutions: When they send pre-paid cards directly to children, they have agreed to send notification letters to their parents, too. Moreover, companies are working on the development of a database which can help to check the identity and the age of young customers.

Experts believe that if children are educated, pre-paid cards can be a sensible and safe alternative to cash, and can teach them to handle their money – even in the virtual world of the Internet.

(507 words)

Exam preparation | Plastic money for young people 23

‹R› **1 Reading comprehension**

a) Fill in the following grid with information from the text. Only note down key words.

1. the campaign for credit cards	
2. the concept	
3. advantages	
4. possible disadvantages	
5. problems of the companies	
6. the experts' view	

b) Use your key words to write a summary of the text.

c) Do the following tasks in complete sentences. Use your own words.

1. Describe the way in which a pre-paid credit card works.
2. Explain the advantages of a pre-paid credit card for young people.
3. Give reasons why parents may be worried about this development.
4. Explain how credit card companies and other firms can profit from the introduction of the pre-paid credit card.

2 Composition – Diagram

‹P› ◘ Describe and analyze the diagram. ► SF 28 Describing diagrams

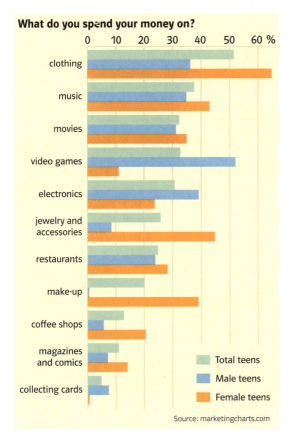

157 | International business correspondence | Exam preparation

3 Plastic money for young people

3 Composition – Cartoon

‹P› ■ Describe and analyze the following cartoons. ▶ SF 27 Describing cartoons

"Emily, have you been shopping online during class?"

"If everyone does their shopping online, the malls will close and we won't have anywhere to hang out."

4 Mediation

‹M› ■ Ein E-Mail-Freund aus Neuseeland möchte Sie besuchen kommen. Sie haben gerade die folgende Seite im Internet gefunden und möchten Ihren Freund über die Möglichkeit einer Kreditkarte für Jugendliche informieren. Fassen Sie dafür die wesentlichen Informationen aus dem folgenden Text auf Englisch zusammen. ▶ SF 22 Mediation / translation

http://www.thisisme.uk

Kreditkarten jetzt auch für unter 18jährige!

Kreditkarten für Jugendliche – das sind so genannte „vorbezahlte" Karten, die im Grunde die gleichen Funktionen haben wie herkömmliche Karten. Der Karteninhaber kann damit bei Millionen von Geschäften einkaufen. Praktisch ist es insbesondere, dass mit einer
5 solchen Karte auch im Internet oder bei telefonischen Bestellungen bezahlt werden kann. Die Voraussetzung ist allerdings, dass sich ein entsprechendes Guthaben auf der Karte befindet, denn der Kaufbetrag wird sofort beim Kauf von der Karte abgebucht.

Diese Kreditkarten eignen sich insbesondere für Schülerinnen und
10 Schüler, die im Ausland, z. B. in den USA oder in Australien, für ein Jahr die Schule besuchen wollen. Ebenso sind sie sicherlich geeignet für Studentinnen und Studenten, die im Ausland – insbesondere in Übersee – studieren, oder für junge Leute, die im Ausland als Au-pair arbeiten wollen. In vielen Ländern wie beispielsweise in Großbritannien, den USA oder Kanada sind Kreditkarten viel weiter verbreitet als in Deutschland. Dort sind sie oft außer Bargeld die einzige Möglichkeit zu bezahlen.
15 Da normale Kreditkarten in der Regel aber erst an Kunden abgegeben werden, die älter als 18 Jahre sind, stehen junge Leute im Ausland schnell ohne Geld da.

Die Lösung für diese Fälle: die guthabenbasierte Kreditkarte.

(201 Wörter)

‹M/P› **5 Commercial correspondence – Order**
▶ SF 23 Formal letters and e-mails

Situation:
Sie arbeiten in Ihrer Stadt im Einkauf einer Warenhauskette. Ihr Chef, Jochen Beyer, möchte Waren bei einer irischen Firma einkaufen, da Ihre Warenhäuser eine „Irische Woche" durchführen wollen.
Sie haben ein Angebot von der Firma **All Things Irish** (E-Mail-Adresse: mark-owen@all-things-irish.com) bekommen: Alle Preise gelten ab Werk, die Zahlung soll bei Auftragserteilung erfolgen, der Versand erfolgt innerhalb einer Woche nach Auftragseingang. Das Angebot ist 6 Monate gültig.

Ihre Aufgabe:
Ihr Chef hat die zu bestellenden Produkte bereits in der Preisliste markiert. Schreiben Sie anhand der angegebenen Mengen Ihre Bestellung. Wiederholen Sie die angegebenen Bedingungen und weisen Sie darauf hin, dass Sie damit einverstanden sind und dass Transport und Versicherung durch Ihr Unternehmen arrangiert werden. Sie beenden Ihre E-Mail höflich mit dem Wunsch nach guten zukünftigen Geschäftsbeziehungen.

Drinks
- X Barry's Tea Picnic Hamper — 80 Euros — *1000 Stück*
-    Guinness Beer (4 pack) — 8 Euros
- X Butler's Hot Chocolate — 3 Euros — *5000 Stück*

Specialities
- X Waterford Crystal wine glasses (2) — 30 Euros — *1000 Stück*
-    Irish dance shoes — 40 Euros
- X Irish Fruit Soda Bread — 2 Euros — *10.000 Stück*

Books
- X Irish recipes — 10 Euros — *500 Stück*
- X Ireland by bike — 6 Euros — *500 Stück*
-    *Dubliners* by James Joyce — 5 Euros

Unit 24
Business, transport and ecology

A2.22

Meals on wheels

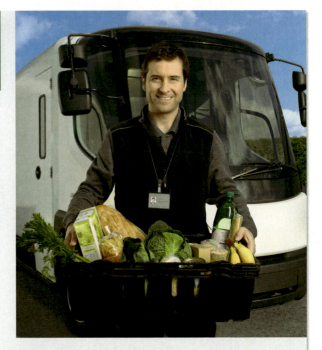

The food delivery company, Food4U, has revolutionized the way we shop and will continue to do so in the future, as Oliver Smalling, one of the founder members of the company, reveals in this interview.

"We decided about 5 years ago that the massive developments in computer technology would create a generation of people who wouldn't always want to go to a traditional supermarket to do their weekly shopping. So, we built up a company with no shops but with a high level of service: our customers could buy their groceries online and we would deliver them to their house.

At that time we had no idea about groceries. We just knew that everybody has to eat and so we looked for a way of getting this food into their kitchens without them having to go to the supermarket. To get more information about our potential customers we had looked at the evolution of grocery retailing over the last 50 years. There has been a drastic change in consumer behaviour over this time. For example, the first self-service supermarket was opened in 1950. Shoppers were horrified that they had to walk around and select the groceries that they wanted to buy themselves. But as a result of the lower prices customers got used to this system of shopping very quickly. The next development was in the 1980s, when the first out-of-town hypermarkets emerged. Shoppers soon got used to driving their cars to these stores where they could park and load their cars full with the week's groceries. So our idea is a logical part of this chain in consumer behaviour. We make it even more comfortable for our customers – they just order their groceries from home via the Internet and we deliver the goods.

We focus very strongly on the environmental aspects of our business. We maintain that we are "greener" than the traditional supermarkets because we don't have the vast number of energy consuming stores. Moreover, by delivering the goods with one of our ecologically friendly vans we can serve up to 40 families who would all have to use a lot of fuel to get their groceries. We also promote locally grown food which helps to keep the carbon footprint of the goods we sell as low as possible.

We have built up a company which is different and more efficient and ecologically friendly than our competitors. Our annual sales for last year were higher than we expected. And we are still expanding – we intend to look for markets in other European countries, too.

Nearly all countries in the western world today have large supermarket chains but they also have young populations who have grown up on Facebook and PlayStations. This generation will shop online and we want to be there to serve."

(469 words)

1 Reading comprehension

‹R› **a)** Decide which of the following statements are true. More than one option may be correct.

► **SF12 Multiple choice exercises**

1. The company decided to start up
   a) a new type of retailing service.
   b) a new chain of supermarkets.
   c) an Internet grocery business.
   d) an out-of-town outlet.

2. The company observed how grocery retailing has developed through
   a) looking at the price of the goods.
   b) studying surveys on retailers.
   c) analyzing the ways people buy things.
   d) counting the new supermarkets in the UK.

3. The company is environmentally friendly because it
   a) works together with traditional supermarket chains.
   b) uses transport in an ecologically sensible way.
   c) sells goods from producers in the neighbourhood.
   d) does not own a lot of stores to heat.

4. The company plans in the future to
   a) get bigger.
   b) expand its services to all other countries
   c) increase its sales in Europe.
   d) concentrate its business in the UK.

5. The impression we get of the company is that it is
   a) efficient.
   b) successful.
   c) progressive.
   d) environmentally friendly.

b) Do the following tasks on the text.

1. Describe what kind of company "FOOD4U" is.
2. Outline the reasons why Oliver and his colleagues decided to found the company.
3. Sum up the development of grocery retailing in the UK.
4. Explain how the company can be described as environmentally friendly.
5. Describe how they see the future.

2 Comment

‹R› ■ Choose either composition 1 or composition 2.

► **SF16 Writing a composition/comment**

1. "In the future we won't be able to find so many shops in our town centres." Discuss.
2. „Ecologically speaking, online shopping makes more sense than having a lot of shops and outlets." Discuss.

Composition – Advertisement

- Describe the advertisement and analyze its message.
  ► SF 26 Describing illustrations and photographs

4 Composition – Cartoon

- Describe the cartoons and analyze their message. ► SF 27 Describing cartoons

5 Mediation – Planung einer Geschäftsreise
▶ SF 22 Mediation/translation

- Ein Geschäftsmann plant eine zweitägige Geschäftsreise nach Manchester, zu der er seine Frau mitnehmen möchte. Seine Assistentin hat ihnen die folgenden Informationen herausgesucht. Entscheiden Sie sich für ein Hotel, ein Restaurant sowie je eine Freizeitaktivität für den Geschäftsmann und seine Frau und begründen Sie Ihre Auswahl.

http://www.traveltips.com

HOTELS
Radisson Edwardian, Peter Street, Manchester, conveniently located in the centre of town, 263 luxurious rooms and suites, prices from 105 pounds per person

RoomZZ, Princess Street, Manchester, 5 minutes' walk from Deansgate (town centre), each apartment has air conditioning and really comfortable beds, small kitchen available, prices from 79 pounds per unit

RESTAURANTS
The New Emperor, Chinatown, George Street, a modern Cantonese restaurant popular with the local Chinese community, won recommendations, very authentic and of high standard

Akbar's, Princess Street, reputation as one of the best Indian restaurants, in the North of England, menu includes classic, refined and creative Indian dishes

Mr Thomas's Chop House, Cross Street (city centre), one of the oldest bars in Manchester, unique Victorian atmosphere, friendly staff, fine wine and beer, food of high quality

THINGS TO DO AT THE WEEKEND
Shopping
- Triangle Centre (town centre)
- Trafford Centre (20 min tram ride from town)
- Local markets

Sport
Premier League football at Old Trafford (home to Manchester United)

Local attractions
The Quays: waterfront location, (15 min tram ride from town) Entertainment, leisure facilities, cultural facilities including the famous Lowry (art and entertainment)

6 Business letter – complaint

- Writing a complaint ▶ SF 23 Formal letters and e-mails

Situation: Sie buchten bezüglich einer Geschäftsreise Ihrer Chefin, Frau Dr. Sanders, einen Aufenthalt in dem Hotel „Grand View" in Dublin. (13.09. bis 17.09.201… Nr. 68119K). Sie haben Anlass zur Beschwerde:

a. Das Hotel, das Frau Dr. Sanders gebucht hatte, hatte laut Homepage des Hotels 4 Sterne. In Wirklichkeit hatte es aber nur 2 Sterne.
b. Das Zimmer auf der 2. Etage war zur Hauptstraße ausgerichtet und entsprechend laut.
c. Frau Dr. Sanders war weder mit dem Essen (teilweise nicht warm), noch mit dem Personal (unfreundlich, mangelhafte Englischkenntnisse) zufrieden.

Ihre Aufgabe: Schreiben Sie einen Beschwerdebrief an das Grand View Hotel, 56–58 Trinity Street, Dublin, Ireland oder eine E-Mail an das Hotel, grandviewhotel@freenet.com.ie, in dem Sie die Gründe für Ihre Beschwerde ausführen. Bitten Sie das Hotelmanagement Stellung zu nehmen und einen Vorschlag zu machen, wie die Unannehmlichkeiten für Frau Dr. Sanders ausgeglichen werden könnten.

Unit 25
Globalisation and fair trade

Fair trade or not?
by Penny Skinner

The ethics were simple in the early days of Fairtrade. It was a rebel brand. Fairtrade helped people in poor countries and was against the capitalists in the rich countries. But, in the late 90s the green and blue hippy label started appearing on the shelves of some leading supermarkets. This is when ethics and big business started to mix. Since then the Fairtrade movement has experienced a big boost. Overall, the value of Fairtrade goods has gone up from about 30 million pounds to over 800 million pounds in the last ten years. These statistics – and the behaviour of the retailers – suggest that Fairtrade is becoming "mainstreamed". But do ethics still play a role in this world of big business? The Fairtrade Foundation maintains that they do, and that over 7 million farmers and their communities in the developing world have been given a better life as a result of customers buying Fairtrade products.

Nevertheless, it is still important to urge companies and retailers to remember the human rights of the workers throughout the whole supply chain. And sometimes these words seem to fall on open ears. For example, Tesco, Marks and Spencer and Next, who are all major retailers in the UK, have recently taken clothes made in Uzbekistan off their shelves after they found out that child labour was being used there to produce them.

Moreover, Dan Rees from the Ethical Trading Initiative (ETI), which works with several major companies to improve the lives of workers in the global supply chain, says,

"Retailers and brands have a huge influence in the world. Nearly 20 million people in Bangladesh, for example, depend on the clothes industry for their livelihood. If retailers in western countries use their power to improve the working conditions of many of these workers, then they will have shown that they really intend to act in an ethically acceptable way, too." Dan Rees goes on to say, "And if consumers continually asked the retailers what they were doing about the workers in such countries, then things would really start to change."

So, at the end of the day, we, the consumers, have the power. But very often it is extremely difficult to look behind the hype which many of the big companies use. "Greenwashing" is the term used to describe the PR scam in which big companies boast about small changes. One typical example can be found in the coffee business. A few years ago four of the biggest coffee companies "greenwashed" themselves by changing a part of their products to Fairtrade products. In fact, the change amounted to only 1% of their total coffee bean purchases. What about the other 99% of their products?

Even Britain's International Development Minister has called on the industry to come clean. He has also reminded Fairtrade to give customers more information about where the products really come from. The Fairtrade Foundation appears to be reacting to this criticism. Fairtrade 2.0 is on its way, and not before time.

(510 words)

Exam preparation | Globalisation and fair trade 25

1 Reading comprehension

‹R› **a)** Copy the grid below and make notes in it about the article.

1. Development of Fairtrade	
2. Ethical Trading Inititiative	
3. Consumer power	
4. Greenwashing	
5. Changes in policy	

b) Use the information you have found out in exercise a) to write a summary of the text.

c) Do the following tasks on the text in complete sentences. Use your own words.

1. Describe how Fairtrade has developed over the last ten years.
2. Explain the aims of Fairtrade.
3. Outline what some clothes retailers have recently done.
4. Sum up what Dan Rees from ETI maintains.
5. Explain the term "greenwashing".
6. Describe some possible future developments.

2 Comment

‹P› ■ Choose either composition 1 or composition 2.
▶ **SF16** Writing a composition/comment
1. "Consumers have to use their moral right to choose the products they buy." Discuss.
2. "Globalisation is causing one of the biggest changes in our society today." Discuss.

3 Composition – Cartoon

‹P› ■ Describe and analyze the cartoon. ▶ **SF27** Describing cartoons

International business correspondence | Exam preparation | 165

25 Globalisation and fair trade

‹P› **4 Composition – Advertisement**
▶ SF 26 Describing illustrations and photographs

a) Describe what you can see in the advertisement.

b) By using the AIDA formula (see page 31) analyze the advertisement and its effects.

‹P› **5 Composition – Diagram**
▶ SF 28 Describing diagrams

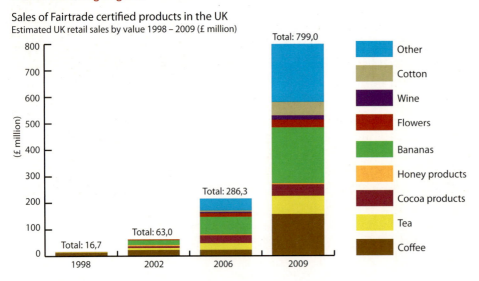

■ Describe and analyze the statistics to show how Fairtrade has developed over the last ten years.

166 | Basic course | Advanced course | Cross-cultural business communication

‹M› 6 Mediation
▶ SF 22 Mediation/translation

- You have found this extra information on the Internet and want to inform an English-speaking friend about it. Write a summary of the contents in English for him. Do not translate word for word.

> **Probleme beim Fairtrade-Kakao noch ungelöst!**
> von Adelheid Kornfeld
>
> Im weltweiten Kakaogeschäft wird viel Geld verdient, allerdings nicht mit dem Rohstoff, sondern mit der Schokolade. Vom Preis einer handelsüblichen Tafel bekommen die Bauern nur einen Bruchteil (rund 3 Cent). Der Anteil von Fairtrade am Weltmarkt
> 5 liegt bei gerade einmal 0,1 %. Die meisten Produzenten für Fairtrade-Kakao sind dabei gezwungen, ihren Kakao ohne das Fairtrade-Siegel zu normalen Weltmarktkonditionen zu verkaufen, da bislang nicht ausreichend Abnehmer vorhanden sind. Die größten Lieferländer sind zurzeit die Dominikanische Republik mit
> 10 einem Anteil von 48,6 % am Fairtrade-Markt und Ghana mit einem Anteil von 45,5 %.
>
> (88 Wörter)

‹M/P› 7 Commercial correspondence – Reminder
▶ SF 23 Formal letters and e-mails

Situation:
Sie arbeiten bei der Firma **Cool It**, einem Logistikunternehmen, das sich auf den Transport von tiefgekühlten Lebensmitteln in ganz Europa spezialisiert hat. Ihre Firma hat ihren Hauptsitz in der Wartburgstraße 100–103, 44579 Castrop-Rauxel, Deutschland (E-Mail: your *first name.name*@cool-it.de). Vor zwei Monaten lieferten Sie 500 Speiseeispackungen von der Firma **Ice and Simple** in Bristol, UK, an eine Supermarktkette mit Firmensitz in Hamburg. Die Zahlungsbedingungen waren: Zahlung innerhalb 30 Tage nach Ausführung der Lieferung. Die Rechnungsnummer war L7129-GB. Sie haben leider bisher keine Zahlung von der englischen Firma erhalten.

Ihre Aufgabe:
Schreiben Sie unter dem heutigen Datum eine Mahnung an die englische Firma, **Ice and Simple**, 135 Perry Road, Bristol BS41, England. Ihre Kontaktperson in der Firma ist Mr Bryan Robson (b.robson@ice_simple.co.uk). Beschreiben Sie die Situation. Die Rechnung muss innerhalb von 10 Tagen beglichen werden. Fehlende Angaben sind sinnvoll zu ergänzen.

Video lounge

1 Applying for a job placement ▶ Unit 2 D4   Jobs in Action

Before watching

a) Describe the photo.

b) What kind of situation do you think this is?

While watching

c) Watch the film and find out the following:

1. the names of the two people;
2. the type and name of the company.

d) Watch the film again and answer the following questions.

1. Why does the applicant want to work there?
2. What skills must a good employee have?
3. How does the applicant see her future?
4. Which areas will she work in as part of the placement?

After watching

e) Do you think the applicant will get the job placement? Why / why not?

2 Manufacturing ▶ Unit 5 D2   BBC Motion Gallery

Before watching

a) Describe the photo and guess what they produce at Vestas Technology.

b) What do you think the man's job is?

While watching

c) Watch the first two minutes of the film and find out if your ideas were right.

d) Watch the complete film and do the multiple choice exercise. Find the most suitable options according to the film. More than one answer may be true.

1. The island …
   a) is normally known for tourism.
   b) has changed in the last 20 years.
   c) is home to a number of industries.
   d) has a strong economy.

2. The business park shown in the film is …
   a) in Newport.
   b) in Portsmouth.
   c) near the Isle of Wight.
   d) on the Isle of Wight.

168

3. Vestas…
   a) is a Swedish firm.
   b) employs 1,600 people.
   c) sells wind turbines all over the world.
   d) exports turbines by sea.

4. The company has …
   a) performed nearly as well as expected.
   b) has profited from government money.
   c) has been growing quickly.
   d) has been very successful locally.

5. According to Graham Biss …
   a) productivity has been rising.
   b) productivity has been falling.
   c) the idea of partnership has attracted new companies.
   d) the business park is full up with businesses.

6. Graham Biss adds that they …
   a) are only 30 minutes away from a big airport.
   b) have no traffic problems on the island.
   c) are two hours away from London.
   d) are ten minutes from the beach.

After watching

d) Use the answers to the exercises above to give a summary of the film.

3 Ecology and/or economy? Unit 7 A — BBC Motion Gallery

Before watching

a) Which part of North America is shown in the map?

b) What kind of conflict would you expect in this area?

While watching

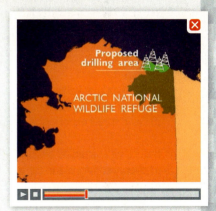

c) Watch the first 30 seconds of the film and find out if your answers to a) and b) were right.

d) Watch the complete film. Find out if the following statements are true or false according to the film.

1. Alaska is relatively well developed.
2. The wildlife there is protected by a national refuge.
3. The Arctic National Wildlife Refuge (ANWR) is a haven for wild animals.
4. The people living in the first village shown in the film can make a lot of money from the caribou.
5. Native people think there is no danger to wildlife in that area.
6. There are rich oil fields inside the ANWR.
7. Oil drilling would take place in the caribou area.
8. Oil drilling is already affecting caribou life.
9. Oil is slowly running out on the west coast.
10. All native people of that area are against drilling for oil there.
11. Many things were paid for in the second village by oil companies' taxes.
12. More drilling would bring more money to the area.

After watching

e) "There should be no drilling for oil in national parks." Refer to the film to find arguments for and against this statement. Think of more arguments for and against, and state your personal point of view.

Video lounge

4 Travel and tourism ▶ Unit 8 A   BBC Motion Gallery

Before watching

a) Describe the photo and guess what the video is about.

While watching

b) Watch the beginning of the film and find out if your guess was correct.

c) Watch the complete film and find the most suitable options according to the film. More than one answer may be true.

1. Nick …
   a) first studied accountancy.
   b) turned to studying tourism.
   c) applied to computer companies.
   d) started work as a tour leader in the United States.

2. As a tour leader you work …
   a) in a mild climate.
   b) in a foreign country.
   c) with different people.
   d) with different cultures.

3. Derek Moore is looking for persons who …
   a) want to travel.
   b) like working with animals.
   c) speak at least five languages.
   d) have travel experience.

4. Before he started as a tour leader Nick …
   a) prepared for his job for three months.
   b) went to libraries to inform himself.
   c) watched films about the history of the country.
   d) informed himself about geography, culture, food of the country.

5. A tour leader must always remember that …
   a) he is part of the service industry.
   b) he must be self-centred.
   c) his interests come second.
   d) the guests are important.

After watching

d) Prepare a short report about the advantages and disadvantages of the work as a tour leader.

e) Are you interested in such a job and are you suitable for it? Say why/why not.

Video lounge

5 American immigration ▶ Unit 10 C   BBC Motion Gallery

Before watching

a) Describe the photo.

b) What kind of scene do you think this is?

While watching

c) Watch the film and find out:

1. where the action takes place;
2. what different groups of people are involved;
3. why they do what they do.

d) Watch the film again and answer the following questions.

1. What special kind of "travel industry" is shown in the film?
2. What are the people called who want to cross the border?
3. Why do they take water with them?
4. How many of these people try to cross the border each week?
5. How many get caught trying to cross?
6. What town do they want to reach?
7. How many volunteers work on the border?
8. What percentage of workers in the service industry are migrants?

After watching

e) Explain the following parts of the film commentary.

1. "Meet the people who travel between worlds – the Third and the First."
2. "America can't live without them – but can it live with them?"

6 A job placement at reception ▶ Unit 11 2   Jobs in Action

Before watching

a) Describe the photo.

b) What kind of scene do you think this is?

While watching

c) Watch the film and find out about the problems the new trainee has.

d) Watch the film again and find out the following information:

1. the departments which the new trainee will get to know;
2. the caller's family name;
3. the date of his arrival;
4. the number of nights he wants to stay at the hotel;
5. the type of room he wants to book;
6. the name of his credit card.

After watching

e) Describe the difficulties that you had when you started a job placement.

Role cards

Unit 1
C Why we are here

d) **Role card B**

Young European

Think up the following information:
- a name
- a country of origin
- reasons for coming to Britain
- a workplace
- free time activities
- plans for the future

Unit 2
B3 A job for you?

a) **Role card B**

Linda Smith

1. Exeter/1990
   Example: I was born in Exeter in 1990.
2. 1990 – 2006
3. since 2006
4. 2006 – 2008
5. customer service at R.S. Reynolds
6. since 2010
7. babysitting
8. five years ago
9. always
10. last month

Unit 2
D4 Role play: Having an interview

a) **Role card B**

Employer

Prepare questions about:
- education
- work experience
- skills and qualifications
- personality and character
- interests and hobbies

Be prepared to say something about:
- the work placement
- your company

Unit 3
C2 A sales talk

b) **Role card B**

Customer

You are a well-informed customer who asks critical questions. You can only speak English.

Think about:
- the disadvantages of the product
- better prices and offers
- the quality of the product, etc.

Unit 3
D4 Should advertising be banned?

a) **Role card B**

Company representative

You sell products to children and teenagers.

Possible arguments:
- information about new products
- children want to have a choice
- new jobs are created

Role card C

Parent

You are against this type of advertising in magazines and on TV.

Possible arguments:
- manipulation
- waste of money
- dangers (ads for alcohol, cigarettes, etc.)

Unit 4
D3 Big brother at school?

Role card B

Head teacher

You are in favour of CCTV cameras at college because you expect students to behave better then.

On the other hand, you can understand the students' arguments.

Role card C

Teacher

You are not sure if it is a good idea having CCTV cameras in classrooms.

The cameras could help to make life at college easier and safer for everybody but on the other hand you would feel observed every minute of the day.

Role card D

Police spokesperson

You are very much in favour of CCTV cameras.

You give examples of schools where the introduction of cameras has helped to reduce the crime rate.

Unit 6
B5 "Water, water, everywhere . . ."

a) ### Role card B

Talk about the following things:
- dangers of overfishing
- no need for exotic seafood
- economic help for poor fishermen

Role card C

Talk about the following things:
- polluted rivers
- environmental problems caused by industry
- governments must act

Role card D

Talk about the following things:
- clean up your own environment
- local action
- join environmental organizations

Unit 8
D4 Developing an economy

Role card B

Mining company

- Write down arguments in favour of your project on one card.
  Think about:
  - ways of using the area that are economically and ecologically correct,
  - the advantages for the people and the local government
- Write down arguments against the other two projects on another card. Think about the negative things that could happen if the local government decided in favour of one of the other two groups.

Role card C

Manufacturing company

- Write down arguments in favour of your project on one card.
  Think about:
  - what you want to produce
  - ways of using the area that are economically and ecologically correct
  - the advantages for the people and the local government
- On another card write down arguments against the other two projects. Think about the negative things that could happen if the local government decided in favour of one of the other two groups.

Role card D

Travel organization

- Write down arguments in favour of your project on one card.
  Think about:
  - ways of using the area that are economically and ecologically correct,
  - the advantages for the people and the local government
- On another card write down arguments against the other two projects. Think about the negative things that could happen if the local government decided in favour of one of the other two groups.

Unit 11

2 Finding accommodation – Making phone calls

c) Role card B

Receptionist at the Scotsman's Hotel

Name:	Donna McAllister
Hotel number:	Glencoe 62275
Room availability:	10 rooms free for all of next month
Rates:	Full board £60; half board £40
Long stay offer:	15% reduction
Distance to All Things Scottish:	a ten-minute walk
Booking:	e-mail or online booking form No deposit required

Unit 12

5 Making conversation

d) Role card B

Student B

Name:	Frank Flottmann
Home:	Boston, USA
Placement:	Green Hotel, Dundee
Journey to Scotland:	flight to Heathrow – great; train trip to Scotland – terrible
Marital status:	single
Interests:	American football

Role card C

Student C

Name:	Svetlana Bazkova
Home:	St Petersburg, Russia
Placement:	ComputerRUS, Aberdeen
Journey to Scotland:	direct flight to Glasgow
Marital status:	single
Interests:	computer games

Role card D

Student D

Name:	Min Leh
Home:	Beijing, China
Placement:	Social Services Department, Edinburgh
Journey to Scotland:	on business in London and drove up
Marital status:	married, 1 child
Interests:	cooking

Role card E

Student E

Name:	Katie O'Neill
Home:	Dublin, Ireland
Placement:	McFarry's Logistics, Glasgow
Journey to Scotland:	ferry, rough crossing
Marital status:	single
Interests:	ballroom dancing

Role cards

Unit 13
2 Answering the telephone

c) Role card B

Name:	Kieron Burns
Company:	The Scottish Shop in Dundee
Reason for call:	Wants to talk to Mr McTell about a new order of books
	Tells the receptionist that he will phone back at 2 o'clock tomorrow

Unit 15
6 Making telephone calls

b) Role card B

- Sie melden sich mit Firmennamen und eigenem Namen.
- Sie fragen, wie Sie helfen können.
- Sie verbinden den/die Anrufer(in) mit der Exportabteilung.

Role card C

- Sie melden sich mit Ihrem Namen.
- Sie freuen sich über das Interesse des Anrufers / der Anruferin.
- Sie sichern die Zusendung der gewünschten Materialien zu.
- Sie versprechen ein Angebot für Ihr Regalsystem „Flex 3000".
- Sie werden auch die verschiedenen Mengenrabatte auflisten.
- Sie bedanken sich noch einmal für das Interesse.
- Sie verabschieden sich freundlich.

Unit 16
7 Making telephone calls

b) Role card B

- Sie melden sich mit Ihrem Namen.
- Sie freuen sich über den schnellen Rückruf des Anrufers/der Anruferin.
- Sie interessieren sich für typisch österreichische Produkte, insbesondere Nahrungsmittel.
- Sie fragen nach dem Versand von frischen Produkten.
- Sie erkundigen sich nach Katalog und Preisliste.
- Sie fragen nach Lieferbedingungen und Rabatten.
- Sie stellen einen Probeauftrag in Aussicht, wenn die Waren im Katalog Ihren Erwartungen entsprechen.
- Sie bedanken sich noch einmal für den Anruf.
- Sie verabschieden sich freundlich.

Unit 17
6 Making telephone calls

b) Role card B

- Sie melden sich mit Ihrem Namen und dem Namen Ihrer Firma.
- Sie freuen sich über das Interesse des Anrufers/der Anruferin.
- Sie sind bereit, dem Anrufer folgende Punkte zu erläutern:
  - Herkunft des Holzes
  - Transport der Ware
  - Lieferzeit
  - Preis
  - Zahlungsbedingungen
- Sie erklären sich bereit, dem Kunden einen kleinen Rabatt auf den Katalogpreis einzuräumen.
- Sie versprechen pünktliche Lieferung.
- Sie bedanken sich für das Vertrauen des Kunden und verabschieden sich freundlich.

Unit 18
6 Making telephone calls

b) Role card B

- Sie melden sich mit Ihrem Namen und Ihrer Firma.
- Sie entschuldigen sich für die Mängel.
- Sie geben einen möglichen Grund an – schlechte Verpackung bei der Speditionsfirma.
- Sie stimmen einer Ersatzlieferung zu.
- Sie erwähnen, dass der Kunde die defekten Teile auf Ihre Kosten zurückschicken sollte.
- Sie stimmen einem zehnprozentigen Rabatt auf die neu gelieferten Teile zu.
- Sie versprechen baldige Lieferung.
- Sie verabschieden sich höflich.

Unit 19
6 Making telephone calls

b) Role card B

- Sie melden sich mit dem Namen Barry/Brenda Bailley.
- Sie fragen, was Sie für den Anrufer/die Anruferin tun können.
- Sie bestätigen den Erhalt der Ware und der Rechnung.
- Sie entschuldigen sich für die versäumte Zahlung.
- Sie geben Gründe dafür an: Urlaubszeit / einige Mitarbeiter krank.
- Sie akzeptieren die eventuellen Konsequenzen.
- Sie versichern, dass die Zahlung unverzüglich erfolgen wird.
- Sie entschuldigen sich nochmals und verabschieden sich höflich.

175

Skills files

Language study skills

1 Learning habits

Cultural awareness

2 Cross-cultural communication

Speaking and listening

3 Having a discussion
4 Making conversation
5 Making phone calls
6 Social calls
7 Formal phone calls

Reading

8 Reading comprehension
9 Anticipating, skimming, scanning
10 Surviving without a dictionary
11 Using a dictionary
12 Multiple choice exercises
13 Multiple matching exercises
14 Short answer questions
15 Gapped summary

Writing

16 Writing a composition/comment
17 Writing a summary
18 Writing the minutes
19 Connectives
20 Collecting words
21 Word webs
22 Mediation/translation
23 Formal letters and e-mails
24 Letter to the editor
25 Personal letters and e-mails

Describing and analyzing

26 Describing illustrations and photographs
27 Describing cartoons
28 Describing diagrams
29 Analyzing films

Presentations and projects

30 Group work and projects
31 Internet research
32 Giving a talk or presentation
33 Taking notes
34 Creating a poster

Language study skills | **Skills files**

1 Learning habits
Lerngewohnheiten

Welcher Lerntyp bin ich?

1. Ich bin ein eher visueller Lerntyp, d.h. ich lerne am besten, indem ich Lerninhalte über das Auge aufnehme, z.B. Bilder anschaue, Texte lese.
   D.h. besorgen Sie sich privat häufig englischsprachige Texte, z.B. Comics, Internet, etc. Lesen Sie möglichst viel.

2. Ich bin ein eher auditiver Lerntyp, d.h. ich lerne am besten, indem ich Lerninhalte über das Ohr aufnehme, z.B. Musik höre, Gespräche führe, jemandem zuhöre.
   D.h. versuchen Sie die Liedtexte, die Sie hören, zu verstehen und übersetzen Sie diese ins Deutsche. Schauen Sie Nachrichten im Fernsehen auf Englisch an.
   Es könnte für Sie beispielsweise hilfreich sein, wenn Sie die Lesetexte in diesem Buch anhand der CD im Workbook anhören, um sich neue Vokabeln besser einprägen zu können.

3. Ich bin ein eher kinästhetischer Lerntyp, d.h. ich lerne am besten, indem ich Lerninhalte über meinen Tastsinn aufnehme, z.B. wenn ich mich bewege, experimentiere, Erfahrungen mache, aktiv werden kann.
   D.h. benutzen Sie Selbstlernprogramme (E-Learning) oder versuchen Sie mit englisch- oder amerikanischsprechenden Leuten ins Gespräch zu kommen, z.B. im Irish Pub, in Sportclubs, etc.

Diese drei Lerntypen sind nur die grundlegenden Lerntypen. Studien belegen, dass Menschen besonders schnell und gut lernen, wenn möglichst viele Lernkanäle angesprochen werden, d.h. dass Lernen mit allen Sinnen am effektivsten ist. Nach Möglichkeit sollten neue Lerninhalte demnach durch Lesen, Ansehen, Aktivwerden, Anhören und Sprechen aufgenommen werden. Es könnte für Sie beispielsweise hilfreich sein, wenn Sie die Lesetexte in diesem Buch anhand der CD im Workbook anhören, um sich neue Vokabeln besser einprägen zu können.

Weitere Informationen zu Lerntypen und Online Tests finden Sie im Internet (siehe Stichworte).

Key Words
- Lerntypentest
- Lerntypenbestimmung
- Lerntypentheorien

Skills files | Cultural awareness

Tipps für alle Lerntypen, um optimal Sprache zu lernen

Lernen Sie regelmäßig!
Lernen Sie regelmäßig Vokabeln und Grammatik, nicht erst kurz vor Ihrer Klausur. Wenn Sie jeden Tag fünf Vokabeln lernen und diese am Wochenende wiederholen, haben Sie schon 25 neue Vokabeln oder englische Redewendungen in einer Woche gelernt.

Nutzen Sie Songtexte, DVDs, Zeitschriften, Internet!
Die englische Sprache begegnet Ihnen mittlerweile überall: in der Werbung, im Fernsehen, im Radio, in Zeitschriften etc. Also halten Sie Ihre Augen und Ohren offen. Sehen sie sich Ihren Lieblingsfilm auf DVD doch einmal in der englischen Sprache an.

Analysieren Sie Ihre Fehler!
Machen Sie in jeder Klausur immer wieder dieselben Fehler? Versuchen Sie konkret an Ihren Fehlern zu arbeiten. Nehmen Sie sich die zwei Fehler, die Sie in der letzten Klausur am häufigsten gemacht haben, vor und gehen Sie die Erläuterungen in Ihrer Grammatik noch einmal genau durch. Vielleicht können Sie auch noch ein paar Übungen im *Workbook* dazu machen.

Vermeiden Sie lange und komplizierte Sätze!
Gewöhnen Sie sich schnell an, im Unterricht in der englischen Sprache zu kommunizieren. Wenn Sie Ihre Sätze einfach halten, machen Sie auch nicht so viele Fehler und fühlen sich sicherer.

2 Cross-cultural communication
Interkulturelle Kommunikation

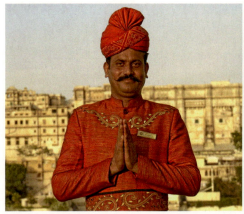 

Wenn Sie ins Ausland reisen oder in Ihrem Heimatland auf Menschen aus anderen Ländern treffen, sollten Sie sich eventuell auftretender kultureller Unterschiede bewusst sein. Diese Unterschiede können sich auf unterschiedliche Glaubensvorstellungen, Meinungen, Werte und Normen beziehen.

Deshalb sollten Sie folgende Regeln beachten:
- Respektieren Sie alle Menschen.
- Seien Sie gegenüber dem „Anderssein" aufgeschlossen.
- Interpretieren Sie Verhaltensweisen, die Sie nicht verstehen, nicht als unnormal oder falsch.
- Gehen Sie nicht davon aus, dass es nur einen richtigen Weg gibt zu kommunizieren (Ihren!).
- Informieren Sie sich, wenn möglich, vorher über die kulturellen Hintergründe der anderen Person/des anderen Landes.

Informationen zu kulturellen Hintergründen finden Sie im Internet (siehe Stichworte).

Key Words
- kulturelle Unterschiede
- Kulturunterschiede
- Tabus und Regeln
 + (Name des Landes)

Tipps: Kulturelle Unterschiede

Bekleidung: Wenn Sie ins Ausland reisen, sollten Sie auf Ihre Kleidung achten und sie möglichst den örtlichen Traditionen anpassen. In manchen Ländern gelten kurze Hosen, Miniröcke oder ausgeschnittene Tops als unangemessene Bekleidung in der Öffentlichkeit.

Gestik: Vermeiden Sie ausladende Gestik mit den Händen und Armen. Einige in westlichen Ländern übliche Gesten haben in anderen Ländern keinerlei Bedeutung (z. B. mit den Schultern zucken) oder aber eine gegensätzliche Bedeutung (z. B. bedeutet das Kopfschütteln in Indien „Ja").

Begrüßung: Es gibt verschiedene Begrüßungsarten auf der ganzen Welt (z. B. ist eine Verbeugung die traditionelle Begrüßung in Japan). Um sicher zu gehen, ist es manchmal angebracht, darauf zu warten, wie Ihr Gegenüber die Begrüßung einleitet.

Gesprächsthemen: Seien Sie vorsichtig bei der Wahl der Gesprächsthemen. In den meisten Ländern, so auch in westlichen Industriestaaten, gelten Sexualität, Religion, Politik, Krankheit und Tod als Tabuthemen. Themen, mit denen Sie in den meisten Ländern nicht falsch liegen, sind beispielsweise das Wetter, Sport und Reisen.

Humor: Seien Sie vorsichtig mit Sarkasmus und Humor, da es kulturell bedingt ein unterschiedliches Empfinden darüber gibt, was lustig ist.

Alkohol: In einigen Ländern gilt ein generelles Alkoholverbot und in vielen Ländern ist es verboten, Alkohol in der Öffentlichkeit zu trinken.

Kommunikationsregeln für den Aufenthalt in Amerika

Begrüßung: In der Regel begrüßen Sie sich in den USA, wie in Deutschland, mit einem kurzen Händeschütteln.

Anrede: In der Regel spricht man sich in den USA mit dem Vornamen an. Häufig lassen sich auch Kollegen und Vorgesetzte mit dem Vornamen anreden. Dies ist jedoch kein Zeichen von Freundschaft, Sie sollten trotzdem weiterhin Respekt zeigen.

Höflichkeit: In den USA ist Höflichkeit besonders wichtig und wird sehr ernst genommen. Nach der Begrüßung wird in der Regel gefragt *„How are you?"* In einem Gespräch sollten Sie auch die Worte *will*, *must* oder *want* vermeiden. Gerne gehört sind dagegen *please*, *might* und *would like to*.

Einladungen: Wenn Sie in den USA eingeladen werden, sollten Sie ein kleines Geschenk mitbringen.

Restaurantbesuch: Im Restaurant warten Sie, bis man Ihnen einen Platz zuweist. Setzten Sie sich nicht einfach an einen freien Tisch.

Warteschlangen: Ob Sie auf den Bus warten, eine öffentliche Toilette aufsuchen möchten, auf dem Postamt sind oder im Supermarkt, es ist immer wichtig, dass Sie sich an das Ende der Reihe stellen und geduldig warten.

Polizeikontrolle: Wenn Sie in den USA von der Polizei angehalten werden sollten, dann legen Sie die Hände auf das Lenkrad und machen so lange nichts, bis Sie zu etwas aufgefordert werden.

Bevor Sie im Ausland arbeiten, sollten Sie sich bei Freunden/Bekannten/Verwandten/Lehrern erkundigen, die bereits in dem Land waren!

3 Having a discussion
An einer Diskussion teilnehmen

Diskussionen dienen dem Austausch von Meinungen und Ideen zu einem bestimmten Thema. Sie können uns auch neue Aspekte liefern, wenn wir uns mit unbekannten Themen beschäftigen.
Ob Sie die Diskussion leiten oder an der Diskussion teilnehmen, Sie sollten sich immer gut vorbereiten und sich an die folgenden Regeln halten.

Regeln und Redemittel für die Diskussionsleitung

- Sorgen Sie für einen geordneten Diskussionsablauf und guten Diskussionsstil, d.h. achten Sie besonders auf die Höflichkeit der Diskussionsteilnehmer.

- Halten Sie Ihre eigene Meinung zurück und bleiben Sie immer neutral.

- Geben Sie eine Einführung in das Diskussionsthema und stellen Sie die Diskussionsteilnehmer vor.

  (As you know,) our discussion today is about …
  On my right/left I have … (name of person or group), who is/are in favour of … / against …

- Bestimmen Sie die Reihenfolge der Wortmeldungen.

  Who would like to open the discussion?
  …, would you like to open the discussion?
  The next person to speak is …, followed by … and then …

- Sorgen Sie dafür, dass alle Teilnehmer die gleichen Chancen haben, zu Wort zu kommen.

  Is there anything you would like to say, …?

- Bringen Sie Vielredner dazu, sich kurz zu fassen.

  I'm sorry to interrupt you, but I'm afraid I have to stop you there.
  Sorry, but I must give the others a chance to put forward their arguments now.

- Sorgen Sie dafür, dass immer nur ein Teilnehmer spricht.

  Please wait your turn. You'll have a chance to speak in a minute!
  If you'd just let … finish, please.

- Notieren Sie sich die wichtigsten Ideen/Argumente und fassen Sie die Diskussion am Ende zusammen.

  Time is running out, so I'd like to sum up what we've been discussing.
  We heard from … that …

- Bedanken Sie sich am Ende der Diskussion bei den Teilnehmern für die Teilnahme an der Diskussion.

  Thank you for taking part in the discussion!

Regeln und Redemittel für Diskussionsteilnehmer

- Stellen Sie zunächst sicher, dass Sie das Diskussionsthema richtig verstanden haben.

- Entscheiden Sie, welche Meinung Sie vertreten.

- Wenn Sie ausreichend Zeit haben, kann es sinnvoll sein, sich mit den Gegenargumenten auseinanderzusetzen. Überlegen Sie sich schon vorher, was Sie den Argumenten der anderen Diskussionsteilnehmer entgegensetzen können.

- Sprechen Sie kurz und bleiben Sie beim Thema.

- Bereiten Sie sich gut auf die Diskussion vor, indem Sie sich vor Beginn der Diskussion Argumente zurechtlegen und diese stichpunktartig aufschreiben. Sie sollten Ihre Argumente immer erläutern und begründen können. Es ist auch hilfreich, wenn Sie sich Beispiele überlegen.

> Firstly … secondly … finally …
> First I would like to point out …
> In addition / Moreover / Besides / Furthermore …
> Another significant advantage is …
> On the one hand … on the other hand …
> Consequently / That is why / Therefore …
> However / In contrast to / Nevertheless …
> I think / feel / believe / am of the opinion that …
> To my mind …
> In my opinion …

- Bleiben Sie immer höflich und denken Sie daran, dass es um das Thema geht und nicht um die Personen. Also attackieren Sie nur die Argumente.

> I'm sorry, but I (completely) disagree.
> That's an interesting point, but …
> You've missed the point (entirely).

- Falls Sie etwas nicht richtig verstanden haben und einen Diskussionsteilnehmer unterbrechen möchten, seien Sie höflich.

> Sorry to interrupt, but could you please explain/ repeat the point you just made?

- Gehen Sie auf die Meinungen der anderen Diskussionsteilnehmer ein.

> You are (quite/absolutely) right.
> That's a very good point!
> Absolutely!/Exactly!
> I agree (with you/Laura).
> Andrea made a very valid point when she said that …
> I partly agree with Sven. What he didn't mention was …

Weitere Redemittel für Diskussionsteilnehmer

- Vorschläge machen:

> I suggest that we …
> We would propose that you …
> What do you think about …?
> If I were you, I would …
> Why don't we …

- Auf Vorschläge reagieren:

> That's a good idea! / Fine!
> OK. / Yes, why not?
> OK, if you want, I don't really mind.
> I'm not sure that will work.
> I think it would be a better idea to talk about …
> What about …?

- Nach einer Meinung fragen:

> What do you think about …?
> How do you feel about …?
> What is your view on/about …?
> In your opinion what is the best solution?
> What would you say?

- Mit Zwischenreden umgehen:

> Can I just finish what I was saying, please?
> Just a second, I haven't quite finished.
> Would you let me / allow me to make my point, please.
> I'll just finish what I wanted to say if you don't mind.
> You could at least let me finish my sentence!

- Das Thema wechseln:

  > There is something else I'd like to say …
  > Have you ever thought of …?
  > On the other hand …
  > I'd like to bring up another point.

- Zum eigentlichen Thema zurückkehren:

  > Let's get back to what we were saying/discussing.
  > Let's get back to the point.
  > As I was saying before, …
  > This discussion is getting away from the original topic.
  > What we should really be talking about is …

- Nachfragen bei Verständnisschwierigkeiten:

  > Did I get that right?
  > Do you really mean that …?
  > Could you explain what you just said / the point you just made again, please?
  > Could you give me/us an example, please?

- Missverständnisse aufklären:

  > I'm sorry, but …
  > … that's not what I meant to say (at all)!
  > … you've got me (completely) wrong.
  > … you've (completely) misunderstood me.
  > Sorry, I didn't make myself clear. I'll try and explain again.

4 Making conversation
Smalltalk

Als Smalltalk bezeichnet man eine leichte Unterhaltung ohne Tiefgang. Dabei bietet sich eine gute Möglichkeit, Interesse zu zeigen, freundlich zu kommunizieren und Konflikte zu vermeiden. Bei vielen gesellschaftlichen Ereignissen, z. B. Partys, verbringt man die ganze Zeit mit Smalltalk.

Der Smalltalk hat als gesellschaftlicher Brauch eine hohe Bedeutung, indem er besonders dem unverbindlichen Kennenlernen oder der Auflockerung der Atmosphäre dient. Ein geschäftliches Treffen, ein Telefonat, ein Bewerbungsgespräch etc. können Sie immer mit ein paar Minuten Smalltalk einleiten (und beenden).

Bedenken Sie: „How are you?" ist keine Frage, auf die Sie mit Ihrem persönlichen Befinden antworten sollten. So ist die Frage nicht gemeint, sondern sie stellt in der Regel nur die Einleitung für den Smalltalk dar.

Beliebte Themen für Smalltalk

- das Wetter (besonders in Großbritannien)
- Anfahrt zu dem Ort des Gesprächs
- der eigene Wohnort / Wohnort des Gesprächspartners.
- die eigene Familie / die Familie des Gesprächspartners (wenn man die Familie kennt!)
- ein aktueller Film oder eine bekannte Fernsehserie
- Auswahl an Sehenswürdigkeiten, Einkaufsmöglichkeiten, Restaurants etc., die eine bestimmte Stadt bietet
- Sport (z. B. aktuelle internationale Sportveranstaltungen)
- Urlaub
- Schule/Universität/Beruf
- Hobbys und Interessen
- ein Thema aus den aktuellen Nachrichten, das nicht kontrovers ist

Ungeeignete Themen für Smalltalk

- Religiöse Themen
- Politische Themen
- Probleme am Arbeitsplatz
- Beziehungs- oder Familienprobleme

Redemittel

- Ein Gespräch beginnen:

> Hi!
> Hello!
> Do you mind if I join you?
> Nice to see you (again)!
> How are you?
> How are you doing? (informal)
> How are things? (informal)

- Ein Thema finden:

> Did you see … on TV last night / at the weekend?
> Have you seen the new [James Bond] film yet?
> Did you read about [that terrible train crash] in the newspaper this morning?
> Terrible/Beautiful weather, isn't it?
> How was your journey?
> Have you ever been here before?
> Who do you think is going to win [the football match] this evening?

- Auf den Gesprächspartner eingehen:

> Really?
> I don't believe it!
> Well, I've never heard of anything like that before!
> That's the funniest / most interesting / strangest thing I've heard in ages!
> I couldn't agree more!

- Füllwörter:

> Well, …
> Actually, …
> Let's see, …
> Let me think, …

- Frageanhängsel:

> You know …, don't you?
> He's …, isn't he?
> It hasn't …, has it?

- Das Gespräch beenden:

> It was nice talking to you!
> Excuse me, I've got to go now.
> Hope to see you again soon.
> Hope you get home safely.
> Give my regards to …
> Don't forget to say hello to … for me!
> Have you got my mobile number / my e-mail address so that we can stay in contact?

5 Making phone calls
Telefongespräche führen

Im modernen Berufsleben gehören Telefonate in englischer Sprache zum Alltag. Mit etwas Vorbereitung können Ihnen solche Gespräche erheblich leichter fallen.

Vorbereitung auf das Telefongespräch

- Machen Sie sich Stichpunkte in der englischen Sprache oder machen Sie sich eine grobe Skizze über die Punkte, die Sie ansprechen möchten. Das ist besonders wichtig, wenn Sie Geschäftsanrufe tätigen.
- Wenn möglich, finden Sie den Namen und die Durchwahl der Kontaktperson bereits vor dem Telefonat heraus.
- Denken Sie darüber nach, was die Kontaktperson möglicherweise sagen oder fragen wird, und bereiten Sie entsprechende Antworten darauf vor.
- Seien Sie darauf vorbereitet, Wörter zu buchstabieren, insbesondere Namen und Adressen.
- Haben Sie keine Angst, Fehler zu machen.

Während des Telefongesprächs

- Sprechen Sie langsam und deutlich. Stellen Sie Ihre Anfragen eindeutig und sachlich.
- Wenn Sie ein geschäftliches Telefongespräch führen, nennen Sie immer Ihren Vornamen und Ihren Familiennamen und reden Sie die Kontaktperson mit *Mr*, *Mrs* oder *Ms* und ihrem Familiennamen an.
- Wenn Sie ein privates Telefongespräch führen, reicht es, sich mit Ihrem Vornamen zu melden.
- Erwarten Sie nicht, jedes einzelne Wort zu verstehen. Wenn Sie aber meinen, etwas Wichtiges nicht verstanden zu haben, dann fragen Sie nach.

→ **Regeln und Redemittel finden Sie auf der folgenden Seite.**

Regeln und Redemittel

- Wenn die Person wiederholen soll, was sie gesagt hat:

  I'm sorry I didn't quite catch what you said.
  Could you repeat that, please?

- Wenn die Person etwas noch einmal erklären soll:

  I'm sorry, I'm afraid I don't understand what you
  mean. Could you explain that again, please?
  I'm afraid I couldn't quite follow you. Did you
  mean …?

- Wenn die Person langsamer sprechen soll:

  Could you speak a little more slowly, please?

- Seien Sie höflich! Denken Sie daran, „bitte" zu sagen, wenn Sie nach Informationen fragen, und „danke", wenn Ihnen geholfen wurde.

  please = bitte
  you're welcome / not at all = bitte schön; gern
  geschehen

- Nennen Sie Telefonnummern immer als einzelne Zahlen. Wenn die gleiche Zahl zweimal hintereinander vorkommt, können Sie *double* sagen (z. B. *44 = double 4*). Für die Ziffer *0* sagt man sowohl im Britischen als auch im Amerikanischen *Oh*. Im Amerikanischen können Sie außerdem auch *zero* sagen.

  07145 12206 = Oh (zero) – seven – one – four –
  five – one – double two – oh (zero) – six

- Wenn Sie Namen nennen, ist es oftmals hilfreich, wenn Sie diese buchstabieren.

  Would you like me to spell …?
  Would you like me to spell that for you?
  It's spelt …
  I'll just spell that for you. It's …

- Fordern Sie die Kontaktperson höflich dazu auf, Namen etc. zu buchstabieren, um Verwirrung zu vermeiden.

  Could you spell …, please?
  Could you spell that for me, please?
  Would you mind spelling …?
  Would you mind spelling that for me, please?

- Wiederholen Sie die Informationen (Zeiten, Namen, Adressen, Preise etc.), um sicher zu gehen, dass Sie alles richtig verstanden haben.

  Let me just check that I've understood all the
  information you've given me. …
  Let me just check that I've understood all the
  information you're asked for correctly. …
  I'll just repeat that back to you to make sure I've
  got everything down correctly. …
  Let me just check that I've spelt your name
  correctly. …

- Wenn Sie die Kontaktperson nicht richtig hören können, bitten Sie sie, lauter zu sprechen.

  I'm sorry, (it's a very bad line,) I didn't quite catch
  that! Could you speak up a bit, please?
  Sorry, it's very loud at my end. Would you mind
  speaking up a bit?

- Wenn Sie denken, dass Sie sich verwählt haben, fragen Sie nach und entschuldigen Sie sich. Legen Sie nicht einfach auf.

  Is that (+ number you want)?
  I'm sorry, I think I've dialled the wrong number.

- Wenn Sie vermuten, dass sich ein Anrufer verwählt hat, erklären Sie ihm dies höflich. Legen Sie nicht einfach auf.

  I'm sorry, but I think you've got the wrong number.
  This is (+ number / name / company name).
  I'm sorry, there's no one here with that name. This
  is (+ your number / name / company name).

Skills files | Speaking and listening

6 Social calls
Private Telefongespräche

Wenn Sie ein privates Telefongespräch in englischer Sprache führen möchten, können Sie im Wesentlichen den Vorgaben in **Skills File 5** (Telefongespräche führen) folgen. Auch die Formulierungen in **Skills File 4** (Smalltalk) können hilfreich sein.

Redemittel

- Begrüßung:

  Hello!
  Hello, this is …[1]
  Hello …[2]! It's me …[1]

- Ein Gespräch beginnen:

  How are you?
  How are you doing?
  It's great to hear from you!
  I just thought I'd call and find out how you are.
  I just wanted to ring and let you know that …

- Jemand anderen sprechen wollen:

  Could I speak to …[3], please?
  Is …[3] in, please?
  Do you know when …[3] will be back, please?

- Einen Gesprächspartner weiterreichen:

  Just a second, I'll go and find him/her.
  Hold on a minute, I'll see if he/she is in.

- Eine Nachricht weitergeben:

  Could you give …[3] a message, please?

- Eine Nachricht entgegennehmen:

  I'm afraid he/she can't come to the phone right now. Can I take a message?
  I'm sorry, but he/she isn't in at the moment. Would you like me to take a message?

- Zurückrufen:

  Would it be OK to ring back later?
  What time can I ring back?
  I'll ring back in about half an hour, if that's OK.
  Could you give …[3] my number, please, and ask him/her to ring me back?
  You can try ringing again in about [15 minutes] if you want to.
  He/She should be back at about [11 pm].
  Shall I ask him/her to call you back?

- Sich verabschieden:

  Thanks for ringing!
  It was great to hear from you!
  Speak to you again soon, I hope!
  Bye!
  Take care.
  All the best.

[1] Ihr Name [2] Name der Person, die am anderen Ende der Leitung ist [3] Name der Person, die Sie sprechen möchten

Speaking and listening | Skills files

7 Formal phone calls
Förmliche Telefongespräche

Wenn Sie ein Telefongespräch mit einem Geschäftspartner führen möchten, können Sie im Wesentlichen den Vorgaben in **Skills File 5** (Telefongespräche führen) folgen. Die Grundlage für ein erfolgreiches Geschäftstelefonat wird in den ersten Minuten gelegt. Sorgen Sie deshalb dafür, dass Sie von Beginn an freundlich sind und deutlich sprechen.

Redemittel

- Begrüßung:

> Good morning / Good afternoon …[1]!
> (This is) …[2] speaking.
> Can I help you?
> What can I do for you?

- Jemand anderen sprechen wollen:

> Could I speak to …[3], please?
> Can you put me through to …[3], please?
> I'd like to speak to someone in your [sales] department.

- Einen Gesprächspartner weiterverbinden:

> Please hold (the line).
> One moment please.
> I'll connect you with …[3]
> I'll connect you with the [sales] department.
> I'll put you through to …[3]

- Wenn jemand nicht zu sprechen ist:

> I'm sorry, …[3] isn't here.
> I'm sorry, …[3] isn't available at the moment / today.

- Nach der richtigen Durchwahl usw. fragen:

> Can you give me …[3]'s extension number, please?
> I can give you his/her extension number [voice mail number, fax number, e-mail address]. It's …

- Den Grund für den Anruf nennen:

> I'd like to receive more information about …
> I'm calling about …

- Eine Nachricht weitergeben:

> Could you pass on a message, please?

- Eine Nachricht entgegennehmen:

> Would you like to leave a message?
> Can I take a message?
> Would you like me to pass on a message?

- Eine Nachricht auf einem Anrufbeantworter oder einer Mailbox hinterlassen:

> Hello, this is …[2] at …[1]. I'm sorry to have missed you.
> I'd be grateful if you could ring me back this morning/afternoon.
> You can get me on my mobile. The number is …
> I'll be in the office all afternoon so you can reach me there.

- Einen Rückruf vereinbaren:

> Shall I ask him/her to call you back?
> Could you call back later, please?
> Could you ask him/her to call me back, please? My number is …[4]
> Can I call back later?
> I'll call back later if that's OK.
> When would be the best time to call back?

- Sich verabschieden:

> Thanks for your call!
> Thanks for calling!
> Thank you very much for your help!
> Sorry I couldn't be of more help.
> Have a nice day!
> Goodbye!

1 Name Ihrer Firma **2** Ihr Name **3** Name der Person, mit der Sie sprechen wollen **4** Ihre Telefonnummer

8 Reading comprehension
Leseverstehen

Die Units in diesem Buch enthalten fiktionale und nicht-fiktionale Texte, die Sie im Unterricht lesen werden. Um über diese Texte sprechen zu können, sollten Sie lernen, möglichst schnell zu lesen. Das Gelesene gleichzeitig auch gut zu verstehen, mag Ihnen schwierig vorkommen, z. B. durch unbekanntes Vokabular oder komplizierte Textstrukturen. Deshalb ist es wichtig, systematisch zu lesen, um die Textinhalte zu erfassen.

Tipps: Schwierige Texte leichter verstehen

Überblick gewinnen
Sie überfliegen den gesamten Text recht zügig und ermitteln, was der Inhalt ist. Es ist manchmal hilfreich, die Gesamtaussage des Textes in einem Satz aufzuschreiben, um sich diese besser einprägen zu können.
Beispiel: *The text is about …*

Textaufgaben lesen
Lesen Sie die Fragen, die an den Text gestellt werden. Falls es keine Aufgaben gibt, stellen Sie selber Fragen an den Text!
Beispiel: *Who?, What?, When?, Where?, Why?, How?*

Detailliertes Lesen
Beim zweiten Lesedurchgang lesen Sie den Text Abschnitt für Abschnitt und markieren die wichtigsten Textaussagen oder Schlüsselbegriffe bzw. notieren sich diese auf einem Blatt.

Tipp: Nutzen Sie die Abschnitte als Lesehilfe, d. h. in der Regel wird in jedem neuen Abschnitt ein neuer, weiterführender Aspekt des Themas genannt.
Beispiel: Fragen Sie nach jedem Abschnitt: „Welche Funktion hat dieser Abschnitt?" oder „Welche neuen Aspekte hat dieser Abschnitt aufgeworfen?"

Nachschlagen
Je nach Schwierigkeitsgrad des Textes wird es einzelne Begriffe oder gar ganze Sätze geben, die unverständlich geblieben sind. Klären Sie Unbekanntes mit einem Wörterbuch.
Wenn Sie ganze Sätze nicht verstehen, bitten Sie zunächst einen Mitschüler um Hilfe.
▶ **SF 10 Surviving without a dictionary**
▶ **SF 11 Using a dictionary**

Zusammenfassung mit eigenen Worten
Fassen Sie die wichtigsten Aspekte des Textes mit eigenen Worten zusammen. Lösen Sie sich vom Text und finden Sie Ihre eigenen Worte.

Reading | Skills files

9 Anticipating, skimming, scanning
Antizipieren, Skimming, Scanning

Um die Fragen zu einem Text richtig beantworten zu können, benötigen Sie eine Kombination verschiedener Lesestrategien. Die bekanntesten Lesestrategien sind das Antizipieren, das Skimming und das Scanning.

Antizipieren ist die Leseerwartung, die an einen Text gestellt wird. Es bedeutet, dass Sie vorhersagen, worum es in dem Text gehen könnte, ohne den Text gelesen zu haben. Wenn Sie sich bereits vor dem ersten Lesen Gedanken über den Inhalt des Textes gemacht haben und evtl. sogar Ihr Vorwissen zu dem Thema aktiviert haben, wird es Ihnen leichter fallen, auch schwierige Texte zu verstehen.

Skimming bedeutet, einen Text zu überfliegen, um möglichst schnell einen Gesamteindruck vom Inhalt zu erhalten. Danach sollte es Ihnen möglich sein, in einem Satz den Inhalt wiederzugeben.

Scanning bedeutet, einen Text gezielt auf bestimmte Informationen hin zu filtern.

Antizipieren

Bevor Sie den Text lesen, haben Sie bestimmte Erwartungen, die sich beim späteren Lesen bestätigen lassen oder die Sie verwerfen müssen. Versuchen Sie vorherzusagen, worum es in dem Text gehen könnte.

Beim Antizipieren ist es hilfreich folgende Punkte zu beachten:
* Textsorte (Handelt es sich um einen fiktionalen Text, z.B. Romanauszug, Kurzgeschichte, oder handelt es sich um einen nicht-fiktionalen Text, z.B. Zeitungsartikel, Internetseite, Sachtext, Reisebericht?)
* Erscheinungsdatum und Erscheinungsort des Textes (Geben Erscheinungsdatum und -ort einen Hinweis auf das mögliche Thema des Textes, besonders bei Zeitungsartikeln?)
* Layout und Illustrationen (Bilder, Graphiken)

Skimming

Nach dem Antizipieren überfliegen Sie den Text, um sich einen Gesamtüberblick zu verschaffen. Diese Technik kann beispielsweise besonders hilfreich sein, wenn Sie sich in Ihrer Abschlussprüfung zwischen zwei Texten entscheiden können. Skimming heißt auch, dass Sie ungefähr drei- bis viermal schneller lesen als gewöhnlich.

Beim Skimming ist es hilfreich folgende Punkte zu beachten:
* Lesen Sie die Überschrift und die Untertitel, um herauszufinden, worum es in dem Text geht.
* Versuchen Sie, sich ganze Abschnitte anzusehen und nicht Wort für Wort zu lesen.
* Lesen Sie nur den ersten und den letzten Satz jedes Abschnittes.

Scanning

Diese Technik des selektiven Lesens kann besonders hilfreich sein, wenn Sie Fragen zum Text beantworten sollen und nur nach relevanten Informationen suchen.

Beim Scanning ist es hilfreich folgende Punkte zu beachten:
* Lesen Sie die Fragen/Aufgaben zum Text sorgfältig durch.
* Lassen Sie Ihre Augen über den Text fliegen und fokussieren Sie dabei Schlüsselbegriffe. Lesen Sie den Text nicht Wort für Wort.
* Markieren Sie Schlüsselbegriffe oder wichtige Details im Text oder notieren Sie diese.
* Versuchen Sie, anhand Ihrer Notizen die Fragen mit Ihren eigenen Worten zu beantworten.

Skills files | Reading

10 Surviving without a dictionary
Umgang mit Texten ohne Wörterbuch

Auch wenn Ihnen ein Wörterbuch zur Verfügung steht, lesen Sie den Text mindestens einmal vollständig durch, ohne die unbekannten Wörter nachzuschlagen. Versuchen Sie, die Hauptaussage des Textes zu verstehen.

Texterschließung ohne Wörterbuch

- Überlegen Sie, ob der Kontext, in dem das unbekannte Wort auftaucht, Ihnen hilft, das Wort zu verstehen. So können z. B. angrenzende Worte oder Sätze dabei helfen.
- Manche englische Wörter werden gleichermaßen in der deutschen Sprache verwendet.
  Beispiele: *computer, crash, deadline, international, laptop, loyal, tourist* …
- Manche englische Wörter sind der deutschen Bezeichnung sehr ähnlich.
  Beispiele: *cloning, economy, electricity, globalisation, industry, politics, president, technology* …
  Aber achten Sie hier besonders auf „falsche Freunde"!
  Beispiele: *brave* = mutig; *sea* = Meer; *sensible* = vernünftig; *to spend money* = Geld ausgeben
- Manche englische Wörter ähneln Wörtern, die Sie aus anderen Fremdsprachen kennen.
  Beispiele: *announce* (French: annoncer), *organic* (Latin: organicus), *solar* (Latin: solaris)
- Bei zusammengesetzten Wörtern kennen Sie vielleicht zumindest einen der beiden Wortteile.
  Beispiele: *high-class, lifestyle, part-time, salesperson, subculture, work experience*
- Bei manchen Wörtern hilft es, sie laut auszusprechen, weil der Klang des Wortes hilft, die Bedeutung zu finden.
  Beispiele: *bang, clap, crisps, hiss, moo, ouch, ping, whisper*
- Versuchen Sie, die Wortfamilie zu ermitteln (siehe unitbegleitendes Vokabular im SB auf den Seiten 248 bis 291). Ein Teil des Wortes könnte mit einem Ihnen bereits bekannten englischen Wort zusammenhängen. Achten Sie auch auf Vorsilben und Nachsilben.

Vorsilben

- Folgende Vorsilben geben Worten eine negative oder gegensätzliche (≠) Bedeutung:

in-	active ≠ inactive
im-	possible ≠ impossible
il-	literate ≠ illiterate
ir-	relevant ≠ irrelevant
anti-	anti-smoking
counter-	counterrevolution
mis-	to misunderstand
un-	happy ≠ unhappy
de-	to stabilise ≠ to destabilise
dis-	to like ≠ to dislike

- Folgende Vorsilben zeigen einen Anstieg (+) oder eine Abnahme (−) an:

out- (+)	to grow – to outgrow
over- (+)	to heat – to overheat
sub- (−)	standard – substandard
super- (++)	natural – supernatural
under- (−)	to pay – to underpay

- Weitere Vorsilben:

inter-	international	pro-	pro-abortion
post-	post-war	re-	reread
pre-	pre-school	trans-	transatlantic

Nachsilben

- Nachsilben bestimmen den Wortstamm und bilden oft aus Verben und Adjektiven Nomen.

-ation	to nationalize – nationalization	-ing	to begin – beginning	-ness	happy – happiness
-ence	to differ – difference	-y	difficult – difficulty	-or	to act – actor
-er	to teach – teacher	-ment	to improve – improvement		

11 Using a dictionary
Richtiger Umgang mit dem Wörterbuch

Einsprachige Wörterbücher

Das einsprachige Wörterbuch soll bei der Beseitigung von Verständnisproblemen helfen, z. B. wenn Sie einen Text lesen oder einen Text produzieren möchten. Das einsprachige Wörterbuch hilft Ihnen, Wortbedeutungen aus dem Kontext zu entnehmen.

Das Wörterbuch kennenlernen

- Bevor Sie zum ersten Mal mit Ihrem einsprachigen Wörterbuch arbeiten, sollten Sie sich einen Überblick verschaffen, d. h. Sie blättern durch das Wörterbuch und lernen die wichtigsten Hilfen kennen. Nur wenn Sie wissen welche Informationen das Wörterbuch bietet und wo diese stehen, können Sie das Wörterbuch optimal nutzen.
- Achten Sie beispielsweise auf:
  - den Aufbau des Wörterbuchs (Vorspann, Wörterverzeichnis, Nachspann)
  - die Anleitung zur Benutzung
  - das Verzeichnis der Abkürzungen und Symbole
  - verschiedene Listen, z. B. unregelmäßige Verben, Namenslisten
  - Illustrationen und Schaubilder
  - Überblick über die grundlegende Grammatik.
- Nachdem Sie sich einen groben Überblick verschafft haben, schauen Sie sich den Aufbau eines Eintrags genauer an, z. B. das Wort *success*. In einem guten einsprachigen Wörterbuch werden Sie zu dem Eintrag folgende Informationen finden:
  - Schreibung und Worttrennung
  - die verschiedenen Wortarten (Nomen, Verb, Adjektiv, Adverb)
  - Aussprache (anhand von Lautschrift)
  - unregelmäßige Formen
  - die verschiedenen Bedeutungen des Wortes, auch innerhalb einer Wortart
  - Synonyme und Definitionen
  - Beispielsätze zum typischen Gebrauch des Wortes
  - Redewendungen, in denen das Wort verwendet wird.

Skills files | **Reading**

Mit dem einsprachigen Wörterbuch arbeiten

- Bevor Sie ein Wort nachschlagen, ermitteln Sie die Wortart im Satzzusammenhang, z. B. Nomen, Adjektiv, Verb etc.
- Wenn Sie den Eintrag für das gesuchte Wort gefunden haben, lesen Sie nicht den gesamten Eintrag, sondern beschränken Sie sich auf die Verwendung Ihres Wortes in der gesuchten Wortart.
- Lesen Sie dann alle weiteren Informationen, die Ihnen das Wörterbuch zu dem entsprechenden Stichwort in der gesuchten Wortart gibt, z. B. Beispielsätze oder grammatische Informationen.
- Nehmen Sie sich Zeit zum Lesen des Eintrags und versichern Sie sich, dass Sie die richtige Bedeutung des Wortes gefunden haben. Achten Sie dabei insbesondere auf den Textzusammenhang.

Zweisprachige Wörterbücher

Das zweisprachige Wörterbuch (Englisch-Deutsch, Deutsch-Englisch) soll insbesondere bei der Übertragung von Texten in die andere Sprache helfen, z. B. wenn Sie einen Text übersetzen möchten. Es kann aber auch verwendet werden, um unbekannte Wörter in einem fremdsprachigen Text schnell zu verstehen.

Das Wörterbuch kennenlernen

Bevor Sie zum ersten Mal mit dem Ihrem zweisprachigen Wörterbuch arbeiten, sollten Sie sich mit dem Wörterbuch vertraut machen. (Siehe Das Wörterbuch kennenlernen auf Seite 191, den ersten Punkt)

- Nachdem Sie sich einen groben Überblick verschafft haben, schauen Sie sich den Aufbau eines Eintrags genauer an, z. B. das Wort *success*. In einem guten zweisprachigen Wörterbuch werden Sie zu dem Eintrag folgende Informationen finden:
  - Schreibung und Worttrennung
  - die verschiedenen Wortarten (Nomen, Verb, Adjektiv, Adverb)
  - Aussprache (anhand von Lautschrift)
  - unregelmäßige Formen
  - die verschiedenen Übersetzungen des Wortes, auch innerhalb einer Wortart
  - Beispielsätze zum typischen Gebrauch des Wortes
  - Redewendungen, in denen das Wort verwendet wird.

Mit dem zweisprachigen Wörterbuch arbeiten

- Bevor Sie ein Wort nachschlagen, ermitteln Sie die Wortart im Satzzusammenhang, z. B. Nomen, Adjektiv, Verb etc.
- Wenn Sie den entsprechenden Eintrag für das Wort gefunden haben, lesen Sie aber nicht den gesamten Eintrag, sondern beschränken Sie sich auf die Verwendung Ihres Wortes in der gesuchten Wortart.
- Lesen Sie zudem alle weiteren Informationen, die Ihnen das Wörterbuch zu dem entsprechenden Stichwort in der gesuchten Wortart gibt, z. B. Beispielsätze.
- Nehmen Sie sich Zeit zum Lesen des Eintrags und versichern Sie sich, dass Sie die richtige Bedeutung des Wortes gefunden haben, ob also die Übersetzung im Textzusammenhang passt.

12 Multiple choice exercises
Multiple Choice Übungen

Multiple Choice Aufgaben unterscheiden sich grundlegend von den Ihnen wahrscheinlich geläufigeren Aufgabentypen, z. B. Fragen zum Text oder dem Schreiben eines Essays.

Bei Multiple Choice Aufgaben wird von Ihnen verlangt, die richtige(n) Antwort(en) aus verschiedenen Antwortmöglichkeiten zu erkennen und nicht eine eigenständige Antwort zu produzieren.

Die meisten von Ihnen werden Multiple Choice Aufgaben als einfacheren Aufgabentyp bezeichnen, weil die richtige Antwort auf jeden Fall dabei ist und Sie zur Not raten können.

Allerdings verlangen Multiple Choice Aufgaben ein detailliertes Textverständnis, z. B. im Hinblick auf die Bedeutung einzelner Wörter oder die Verwendung des richtigen Tempus.

Multiple Choice Aufgaben lösen

- Lesen Sie den Text, um sich einen allgemeinen Überblick zu verschaffen.
- Lesen Sie die Aufgabe gründlich und stellen Sie sicher, dass Sie diese richtig verstanden haben. Es gibt unterschiedliche Aufgabentypen zum Multiple Choice.
  Beispiel 1: *Find the most suitable option according to the text. Only one option is true.* (Es darf nur eine richtige Möglichkeit angekreuzt werden.)
  Beispiel 2: *Write down the correct answers: T (true) or F (false). Only answer if you are sure. Wrong answers will result in a loss of credits.* (Es können mehrere Antworten richtig sein, die Sie ankreuzen müssen. Es kann aber auch sein, dass nur eine Antwortmöglichkeit richtig ist. Es gibt Punktabzüge für falsch gegebene Antworten.)
- Lesen Sie den Text ein zweites Mal und markieren Sie die entsprechenden Abschnitte zu den Aufgaben im Text oder notieren Sie sich diese stichpunktartig auf einem gesonderten Blatt.
- Beantworten Sie die Aufgaben in der angegebenen Reihenfolge. In der Regel beziehen sich die Aufgaben in chronologischer Reihenfolge auf den Text.
- Unterstreichen Sie wichtige Schlüsselbegriffe in der jeweiligen Aufgabe. Das wird Ihnen helfen, sich auf die Informationen zu konzentrieren, die benötigt werden, um die richtige(n) Antwort(en) auszuwählen.
- Lesen Sie alle Antwortmöglichkeiten, bevor Sie eine Antwort auswählen.
- Streichen Sie Antwortmöglichkeiten durch, bei denen Sie sich sicher sind, dass sie falsch sind. Das wird Ihnen helfen, die richtigen Antwortmöglichkeiten einzugrenzen.
- Wenn Sie sich nicht sicher sind, dann versuchen Sie nicht, die richtige Antwort zu erraten. In den Prüfungen bekommen Sie in der Regel Punktabzüge für falsche Antworten.

Skills files | Reading

13 Multiple matching exercises
Zuordnungsaufgaben

Bei der Bearbeitung von Zuordnungsaufgaben wird von Ihnen verlangt, einem Text oder einem Foto etwas zuzuordnen. Die bekannteste Art der Zuordnungsaufgaben ist es, Textabschnitten Überschriften zuzuordnen. Bei dieser Aufgabenart geht es in der Regel darum zu überprüfen, ob Sie die Bedeutung eines Abschnitts verstanden haben.

Zuordnungsaufgaben lösen

- Lesen Sie den Text bzw. sehen Sie sich die Fotos/Schaubilder an, um sich einen allgemeinen Überblick zu verschaffen.
- Lesen Sie die Aufgabe und die Antwortmöglichkeiten und stellen Sie sicher, dass Sie diese richtig verstanden haben. Es gibt unterschiedliche Aufgabentypen zum *multiple matching*.
  Beispiel 1: *Look at the photos. Match them with the words in the box. Two words do not match.* (visuelle Vorlage)
  Beispiel 2: *Listen to the texts and match them with the photos/headings.* (Hörverstehen)
  Beispiel 3: *Match the following headings with the suitable paragraphs in the text. Two of the headings do not fit.* (Leseverstehen)
  Beispiel 4: *Read the text in detail and match the key points with the headings in the text.* (Leseverstehen)
- Lesen Sie den Text ein zweites Mal und markieren Sie die entsprechenden Hinweise zu den Antwortmöglichkeiten im Text oder notieren Sie sich diese stichpunktartig.
- Wenn Sie die Antwortmöglichkeiten zugeordnet haben, dann überprüfen Sie Ihre Wahl, indem Sie den Text noch einmal lesen.
- Es gibt häufig mehr Auswahlmöglichkeiten als für die Aufgabe notwendig. Streichen Sie dann zuerst die Antwortmöglichkeiten, die offensichtlich nicht passen bzw. nicht zugeordnet werden können. Das wird Ihnen helfen, die richtigen Antwortmöglichkeiten einzugrenzen.

14 Short answer questions
Kurzantworten geben

Bei dieser Aufgabe handelt es sich ausdrücklich um eine Textverstehensaufgabe und nicht um Textproduktion. Deshalb sollen Sie hier nicht in eigenen Worten antworten, sondern nur zeigen, dass Sie den richtigen Abschnitt im Text gefunden haben und die entsprechenden Wörter oder Ausdrücke übernehmen können.

Bei dieser Aufgabenart kann es sich handeln um:
- Fragen, die Sie mit Hilfe von Wörtern oder Phrasen aus dem vorliegenden Text beantworten sollen. Sie müssen nur diese Kurzantwort geben und keine eigenen Formulierungen benutzen.
  Beispielfrage: *When did he leave the restaurant?* – **Beispiellösung:** at noon
- unvollständige Sätze, die Sie anhand von Wörtern oder Formulierungen aus dem Text vervollständigen sollen.
  Beispielaufgabe: *Listen to the CD again and complete the following sentences.*
  Sarah works on Fridays, Saturdays and ... – **Beispiellösung:** Tuesdays
- unbekannte Wörter, die aus dem Kontext erschlossen werden sollen.
  Beispielaufgabe: *Find a word in the text that has the same meaning as ...*
- Pronomina, die einem Substantiv zugeordnet werden sollen.
  Beispielaufgabe: *What does the word 'it' (line 21) refer to?*

15 Gapped summary
Zusammenfassung anhand eines Lückentexts

Gapped summary ist eine Aufgabe zur Überprüfung des Textverständnisses. Dabei verlangt die Aufgabenstellung das Vergleichen eines (längeren) Textes mit einem zweiten kürzeren Text, in dem die wichtigsten Textinformationen des ersten Textes zusammengefasst sind, bei dem jedoch die Schlüsselwörter entfernt worden sind. Sie sind nun aufgefordert, diese Schlüsselwörter im ersten Text zu finden und in die Lücken im zweiten Text einzusetzen. Dabei sollen Sie sich keine eigenen Wörter ausdenken, sondern nur Wörter aus dem ersten Text übernehmen.

Beispiel für einen Lesetext:

> Yamasaki, who died in 1986, would have been horrified by the deconstruction of the World Trade Center on September 11, 2001, when two planes flown by terrorists crashed into the twin towers of
> 5 the WTC.

Beispiel eines gapped summary:
The author points out how [1. …] the architect would have been if he had lived to experience the catastrophe caused by terrorists.

Lösung: 1. `horrified`

16 Writing a composition/comment
Eine Stellungnahme schreiben

Eine Stellungnahme dient der argumentativen Auseinandersetzung mit einem bestimmten Thema. Es handelt sich hierbei um einen klar strukturierten Aufsatz, in dem verschiedene Aspekte zu einem Thema näher beleuchtet werden. Am Ende steht immer Ihre persönliche Meinung, die Sie anhand von Argumenten begründen müssen. Ein argumentativer Aufsatz wird im Präsens (Gegenwart) geschrieben.

Skills files | Writing

Formulierung der Aufgabenstellung

- Erläutern Sie einen vorgegebenen Sachverhalt und beurteilen Sie diesen kritisch, indem Sie zuerst verschiedene Aspekte anführen und anschließend Begründungen/Beispiele einbringen, die Ihre Sichtweise unterstützen.
  Beispiele: *Comment on this statement: "Teenagers should not have their own computers because it is too dangerous."*
  There is a lot of discussion in the media about genetic engineering. What do you think? Write a composition in about 150 words.
- Befassen Sie sich argumentativ mit dem vorgegebenen Thema/Problem, beleuchten Sie alle Seiten des Themas/Problems und fassen Sie die wichtigsten Aspekte zusammen. Gewichten Sie die Argumente, bevor Sie eine eigene begründete Meinung abgeben.
  Beispiel: *Discuss the sentence, "The world is getting smaller." Use information from the texts and your own ideas to write a comment in about 250 words."*

Vorbereitung der Stellungnahme

- Definieren Sie das Thema eindeutig unter Berücksichtigung der Aufgabenstellung.
- Schreiben Sie stichpunktartig alle Ideen auf, die Sie zu dem Thema haben.
- Sortieren Sie Ihre Ideen in einer Tabelle, einem Diagramm oder einem Word web.
  ► SF 21 Word webs
- Falls notwendig und möglich, sammeln Sie weitere Fakten, Argumente, Statistiken zu dem Thema, z. B. im Internet oder in der Bücherei.
- Formulieren Sie Ihre eigene Meinung zu dem Thema.

Verfassen der Einleitung

- Ihre Einleitung soll das Thema/Problem darstellen und das Interesse des Lesers wecken. Sie können z. B.
  - ein bedeutsames Zitat anführen,
  - eine provokative Aussage machen,
  - eine persönliche Erfahrung schildern,
  - die aktuelle öffentliche Meinung darstellen,
  - aktuelle Statistiken benennen.

- Zudem sollen Sie in Ihrer Einleitung:
  - den Inhalt Ihres Kommentars kurz vorstellen.
  - einen kurzen Überblick über das Thema/Problem zum gegenwärtigen Zeitpunkt und in der Vergangenheit geben.

Redewendungen

- Einleitungssätze:

> According to the latest statistics …
> It is a well-known fact that …
> Today there is a lot of discussion about …
> Today many people are worried about …

Writing | Skills files

Verfassen des Hauptteils

- Ordnen Sie zunächst Ihre gesammelten Argumente. Eine Möglichkeit ist es, die Argumente vom schwächsten Argument zum stärksten Argument anzuordnen.
- Der Hauptteil muss übersichtlich gegliedert sein. Deshalb sollten Sie für jedes neue Argument mit einem neuen Absatz beginnen. Innerhalb eines Absatzes nennen Sie Ihr Argument und in den weiteren Sätzen erläutern Sie dieses anhand von Beispielen, Statistiken und/oder gesammelten Fakten.
- Setzen Sie Ihre Sätze in Bezug zueinander, indem Sie passende Bindewörter verwenden. ▶ **SF 19 Connectives**
- Verwenden Sie geeignete Adverbien, um Argumente hervorzuheben oder abzuschwächen.

Redewendungen

- Argumente strukturieren:

  > Firstly …, secondly …, finally …
  > Moreover …
  >
  > In addition …
  > Next …
  > Then …

- Gegensätze ausdrücken:

  > On the one hand … on the other hand …
  > However …
  > In contrast …

- Begründungen angeben:

  > That's why …
  > It follows that …
  > Because (of)…
  > So …
  > Therefore …

- Adverbien:

  > absolutely – after all – almost – at least – completely – extremely – fortunately – hardly – in fact – mainly – of course – particularly – perhaps – really – sadly – very

Verfassen des Schlussteils

- Im letzten Teil Ihrer Stellungnahme, ziehen Sie Schlussfolgerungen aus den im Hauptteil aufgeführten Argumenten. Die Schlussfolgerungen sollen das Gesagte kurz zusammenfassen.
- Im Anschluss daran geben Sie Ihre eigene Meinung zu dem Thema. Nennen Sie keine neuen Argumente im Schlussteil.

Redewendungen

- Schlussfolgerungen:

  > In conclusion …
  > As a result …
  > All in all …
  > In short …
  > On the whole …
  > In my opinion …
  > In my view …
  > To my mind …

Skills files | Writing

17 Writing a summary
Eine Inhaltsangabe schreiben

Eine Inhaltsangabe ist ein kurzer Text, in dem Sie die wichtigsten Aspekte eines vorliegenden Textes mit eigenen Worten wiedergeben. Wenn Sie die Inhaltsangabe zu einem Text schreiben, zeigen Sie, dass Sie das Wesentliche des Textes verstanden haben. Eine Inhaltsangabe ist immer eine objektive Darstellung/Version des Originaltextes.

Regeln zum Schreiben einer Inhaltsangabe

- Interpretieren oder kommentieren Sie den Text nicht, sondern schreiben Sie objektiv, worum es in dem Text geht.
- Berücksichtigen Sie wichtige Fakten, Aspekte, Ereignisse.
- Klammern Sie alle unwichtigen Details des Textes aus. Verwenden Sie keine Statistiken, Zahlen oder Zitate.
- Kürzen Sie lange Sätze und vereinfachen Sie den Wortschatz des Textes.
- Schreiben Sie Ihre Inhaltsangabe im Präsens (Gegenwart).
- Fassen Sie sich kurz! Ihre Inhaltsangabe sollte maximal ein Fünftel bis ein Drittel der Länge des Originaltextes haben.

Inhaltsangaben von nicht-fiktionalen Texten

Wenn Sie eine Inhaltsangabe von einem nicht-fiktionalen Text, z. B. Zeitungsartikel, Bericht, Sachtext usw. schreiben sollen, dann folgen Sie den folgenden Schritten:

- Lesen Sie den Originaltext sorgfältig, um das Hauptthema herauszufinden.
- Unterstreichen Sie den Satz, in dem das Hauptthema/die Hauptthese genannt wird.
- Formulieren Sie einen Einleitungssatz für Ihre Inhaltsangabe, der, wenn möglich, Textsorte, Titel des Textes, Autor, Erscheinungsort, Erscheinungsdatum und Hauptthema beinhalten sollte.
  Beispiel: *The newspaper article* "The answer is blowing in the wind" *written by Rick Martin and published in* The Daily USA *on November 12, 2010 is about the first big wind farm project in Nebraska.*
- Lesen Sie nun den Text ein zweites Mal und unterstreichen Sie alle wichtigen Fakten, Ideen, Argumente im Text, die das Hauptthema hervorheben. Hinweis: Keine vollständigen Sätze, sondern nur Stichpunkte.
- Fassen Sie nun die Hauptideen des Textes mit eigenen Worten zusammen. Sie können entweder eine Liste mit Stichpunkten erstellen oder einen Satz zu jedem Abschnitt des Originaltextes schreiben.
- Schreiben Sie einige oder alle Ihrer Sätze um, indem Sie die Intention des Autors hinzufügen. (Siehe Formulierungen zur Autorenintention.)
- Setzen Sie Ihre Sätze in Bezug zueinander, indem Sie passende Bindewörter verwenden.
  ▶ SF 19 Connectives

Redewendungen

- Formulierungen zur Autorenintention:

The author/writer opens with …
He/she points out that …
He/she suggests that …

He/she shows that …
He/she emphasizes …
He/she explains …
He/she concludes with …
He/she finishes with …

Inhaltsangaben von fiktionalen Texten

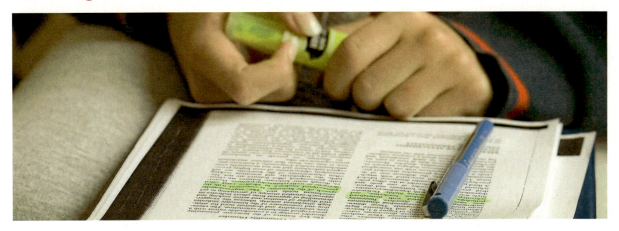

Wenn Sie eine Inhaltsangabe von einem fiktionalen Text, z. B. Kurzgeschichte, Romanauszug, Gedicht usw. schreiben sollen, dann folgen Sie den nachstehenden Schritten:

- Lesen Sie den Originaltext einmal sorgfältig, um herauszufinden, wer der Hauptcharakter ist und in welcher Situation sich dieser gerade befindet.
- Unterstreichen Sie den/die Hauptcharakter(e) und den Satz, der die Situation am besten beschreibt, in der der Hauptcharakter sich gerade befindet.
- Formulieren Sie einen Einleitungssatz für Ihre Inhaltsangabe, der folgende Punkte beinhalten sollte: Textsorte, Titel des Textes, Autor, Erscheinungsort, Erscheinungsdatum und Hauptcharakter/Situation.
  Beispiel: *The extract from the novel "Cloning Miranda" written by Carol Matas deals with Miranda, a teenage girl, who finds that she has a sister who has been cloned only to save Miranda's life.*
- Lesen Sie nun den Text ein zweites Mal und unterteilen Sie den Text – wenn möglich – in zwei Teile. Der zweite Teil beginnt, wenn sich in der Handlung/Situation etwas ändert oder ein neuer Aspekt hinzukommt. Unterstreichen Sie den Wendepunkt im Text.
- Fassen Sie nun die Handlung des Textes mit eigenen Worten zusammen. Beschreiben Sie hierzu, was passiert und wie die Ereignisse miteinander verbunden sind. Die untenstehenden Redewendungen können dabei hilfreich sein.
- Setzen Sie Ihre Sätze in Bezug zueinander, indem Sie passende Bindewörter verwenden.
  ▶ SF 19 Connectives

Redewendungen

> The scene/story/extract/action takes place in …
> It is set in …
> It takes place in the present/past/future.
>
> The main character is …
> There are two/three/etc. main characters.
> We get to know … by …
> He/She is confronted with …
>
> There is a conflict between …
> The turning point …
> At the beginning … / at the end …

Skills files | Writing

18 Writing the minutes
Ein Protokoll schreiben

Ein Protokoll hält die Inhalte einer Konferenz, Besprechung, Diskussion, eines Referats oder einer Unterrichtsstunde fest. Dadurch ist es den Teilnehmern zu einem späteren Zeitpunkt möglich, die besprochenen Punkte nachzuvollziehen.

Formen des Protokolls

Es gibt verschiedene Formen des Protokollierens, die sich für verschiedene Anlässe eignen. Die beiden geläufigsten Formen – das Verlaufsprotokoll und das Ergebnisprotokoll – finden Sie im Folgenden erklärt:

	Verlaufsprotokoll	Ergebnisprotokoll
Kopfteil	Der Kopfteil sollte möglichst folgende Basisinformationen enthalten: Datum • Uhrzeit (Beginn und Ende) • Ort • Anwesende/Teilnehmer bzw. auch Abwesenheit eingeladener Personen • Leiter der Veranstaltung • Anlass/Thema der Veranstaltung • Tagesordnung	
Hauptteil	• Das Verlaufsprotokoll ist die ausführlichere Form des Protokolls. Es wird Wert gelegt auf den Prozess der Ergebnisfindung. • Geben Sie das Gehörte in zeitlicher Reihenfolge wieder. Dazu gehört auch der Inhalt von Vorschlägen, Diskussionen, Beschlüssen und Abstimmungsergebnissen.	• Das Ergebnisprotokoll ist die Kurzform des Protokolls. Es wird Wert gelegt auf das Festhalten der Ergebnisse der Veranstaltung. • Geben Sie nur die Ergebnisse des Gehörten wieder. Sie müssen deutlich formuliert sein und in der Reihenfolge der Tagesordnungspunkte dokumentiert werden.
Schlussteil	Der Schlussteil Ihres Protokolls sollte Ihre elektronische Signatur oder Kürzel sowie das Datum der Veranstaltung enthalten. Am Ende Ihres Protokolls weisen Sie auf mögliche Anlagen hin, z. B. Arbeitsblätter, die dem Protokoll angehängt werden.	

Protokolle schreiben

- Hören Sie erst genau zu, bevor Sie anfangen zu schreiben. Schreiben Sie erst dann, wenn ein Teilabschnitt beendet ist.
- Reduzieren Sie das Gehörte auf die Hauptaspekte und schreiben Sie diese stichpunktartig auf.
- Verwenden Sie Abkürzungen, die für Sie zu einem späteren Zeitpunkt aber auch noch verständlich sind. Schreiben Sie Namen und wichtige Begriffe möglichst vollständig auf.
- Schreiben Sie knapp und sachlich. Die eigene Meinung oder Wertungen gehören nicht in ein Protokoll.
- Verfassen Sie das Protokoll im Präsens (Gegenwart) in ganzen Sätzen.
- Gliedern Sie das Protokoll durch sinnvolle Absätze.

Writing | Skills files

19 Connectives
Bindewörter (Konjunktionen)

Bindewörter sind Wörter oder Formulierungen, die Satzglieder, Sätze oder Textabschnitte miteinander verbinden. Diese Bindewörter geben Ihrem Text eine klare Struktur und sie erleichtern es dem Leser, Ihren Ausführungen zu folgen.

Die folgenden Bindewörter sind nur eine kleine Auswahl. Sie sollten eine persönliche Liste mit Bindewörtern führen, die Sie immer wieder erweitern können.

- Eine Reihenfolge anzeigen / Gliederung:

firstly …, secondly …, finally … first of all next then later ultimately	**Beispiel:** Next the author describes the activities of the different organizations which help in Zimbabwe.

- Gedanken/Argumente hinzufügen:

another also as well in addition / additionally too moreover furthermore last but not least	**Beispiel:** Another significant advantage of solar energy is that it doesn't pollute our air.

- Beispiele geben:

for example for instance	**Beispiel:** The government of the USA is a good example of a presidential federal government.

- Die eigene Einstellung verdeutlichen:

obviously undoubtedly/ doubtlessly clearly generally luckily fortunately unfortunately happily/sadly for …	**Beispiel:** Obviously it is wrong to say that tourism always damages our environment.

- Eine eigene Meinung abgeben:

in my opinion in my view to my mind Without a doubt	**Beispiel:** To my mind this is not the solution to the economic problems of the people living in this area.

- Begründungen angeben:

consequently therefore as a result this is why because of so	**Beispiel:** This is why more than thirty food companies in Britain have signed a promise to reduce their food transport miles.

- Vergleiche anstellen:

compared with on the one hand … on the other hand … in the same way similarly	**Beispiel:** Compared with the situation five years ago children watch TV for longer periods of time.

- Gegensätze ausdrücken:

in contrast to however despite / in spite of	**Beispiel:** Despite all of the arguments mentioned in the text I do not agree with the author's position.

- Schluss:

in conclusion as a result all in all in short on the whole finally to sum up	**Beispiel:** To sum up, I am absolutely against the author's demand that pupils in German schools wear uniforms.

201

20 Collecting words
Vokabeln systematisch lernen

Wenn Sie eine Sprache lernen, ist es unerlässlich, dass Sie Vokabeln lernen. Je mehr Vokabeln Sie kennen, desto leichter wird es Ihnen fallen, Texte zu verfassen.

Tipps: Neue Vokabeln systematisch sammeln

Alphabetisch (A–Z): Diese Methode ist geeignet, wenn Sie Vokabeln schnell nachschlagen möchten. Allerdings müssen Sie das englische Wort bereits kennen. Wenn Sie einen Text verfassen möchten, ist dies meist nicht der Fall. Deshalb sollten Sie diese Methode mit einer der folgenden kombinieren.

Synonyme oder Antonyme: Sammeln Sie alle Synonyme, d. h. bedeutungsgleichen Wörter, und schreiben Sie diese zusammen auf.
Beispiel: *small, little, tiny*
Oder Sie schreiben Antonyme, d. h. Gegensätze, zusammen auf.
Beispiel: *small ≠ big.*

Wortfamilien: Wenn Sie sich ein Wort notieren, können Sie die anderen Formen (Wortarten) dieses Wortes hinzufügen, d. h. Nomen, Verb, Adjektiv, Adverb. Dadurch erweitern Sie Ihren Wortschatz besonders schnell.
Beispiel: *economy, to economize, economical, economically, economic.*

Wortfelder: Sammeln Sie Vokabeln anhand von thematischen Zusammenhängen.
Beispiel: das Wortfeld *globalisation: industry, travelling, culture, communication, brands, poverty, culture, technology, environment, multiculturalism* usw.

Word webs: Beginnen Sie mit dem Wortfeld, zu dem Sie Vokabeln sammeln möchten, z. B. *globalisation*, und schreiben Sie alles auf, was Ihnen zu diesem Wortfeld einfällt. Strukturieren Sie Ihre Einfälle in einem Word web. ▶ **SF 21 Word webs**

Kollokationen: Machen Sie sich eine Liste von Wörtern, die oft im Zusammenhang miteinander verwendet werden.
Beispiele: *to draw a conclusion, to make a promise* (Verb + Nomen), *extremely beautiful* (Adverb + Adjektiv), *a handsome man, a tall woman, a powerful computer* (Adjektiv + Nomen) usw.

21 Word webs
Wortnetze

Ein Wortnetz eignet sich überall dort, wo Gedanken zu einem bestimmten Thema gesammelt und dargestellt werden sollen, um sich das Thema sinnvoll zu erschließen oder um einen Überblick zu erhalten. Die Grundstruktur eines Wortnetzes ist immer gleich.

Wozu nutzt man Wortnetze?

Brainstorming: Um Ideen zu einem Thema zu sammeln und zusammenzutragen.
Erörterung von Themen: Um Argumente zu strukturieren. Beginnen Sie mit dem Thema der Diskussion und fügen Sie *arguments for* (Thesen) und *arguments against* (Antithesen) hinzu.
Vokabellernen: Um sich neue Wortfelder zu erschließen. Beginnen Sie mit einem Oberthema und fügen Sie alle Wörter hinzu, die sich auf diesen Begriff beziehen.

Erstellen eines Wortnetzes

Sie benötigen ausreichend Platz zum Erstellen des Wortnetzes, z. B. ein ausreichend großes Blatt Papier, Plakat, Tapete, Flipchart. Außerdem brauchen Sie Stifte in verschiedenen Farben.

1. Im Mittelpunkt steht das Hauptthema, zu dem Ideen gesammelt werden sollen, in einem aufgemalten Kreis. Das Thema kann als Stichpunkt formuliert werden, aber auch als Fragestellung.

2. Sammeln Sie nun Ideen und fügen Sie diese in aufgemalten Kreisen mit einer Linie an das Hauptthema an. Wichtig ist, dass die Ideen bzw. Hauptpunkte noch relativ allgemein gehalten sind.

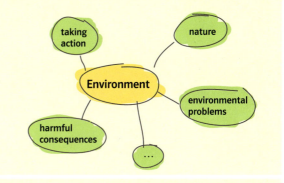

3. Wenn Sie genügend Hauptpunkte gefunden haben, dann hängen Sie daran Unterpunkte in aufgemalten Kreisen an, die sich thematisch auf die Hauptpunkte beziehen.

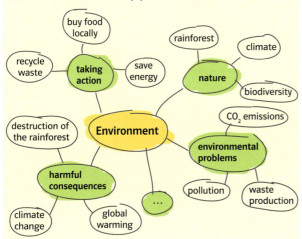

4. Anstelle von Kreisen können Sie auch Linien für die Haupt- und Unterpunkte verwenden.

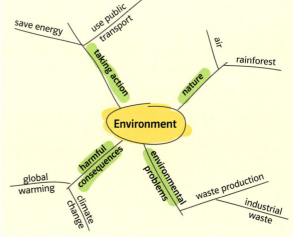

Skills files | Writing

22 Mediation/translation
Mediation/Übersetzung

Mediation ist die sinngemäße Übertragung der wichtigsten Inhaltspunkte eines Textes in eine andere Sprache. Der Sinn einer Mediation besteht nicht darin, den Text wortwörtlich zu übersetzen (vgl. Übersetzung), sondern bei einer Mediation geht es darum, die wesentliche Botschaft eines Textes oder einer Äußerung in eine andere Sprache zu übertragen.

Bearbeitung einer Mediationsaufgabe

- Überfliegen Sie den Text, um sich einen allgemeinen Überblick über den Text zu verschaffen *(Skimming)*. ►SF 9 **Anticipating, skimming, scanning**
  Um welche Textsorte handelt es sich? Worum geht es in dem Text? (Hauptthema)
- Lesen Sie die Aufgabenstellung sorgfältig durch. Finden Sie heraus, welche Art von Text Sie verfassen und welches Sprachniveau Sie verwenden sollen.
  Beispiele für Textsorten sind informativer Text, Gedicht, Geschäftsbrief, Handzettel, Werbeanzeige, Schaubild usw. Wer ist der Adressat Ihrer Mediation? Z. B. Geschäftspartner, Freund, Chef usw.
- Lesen Sie nun den Text ein zweites Mal. Während Sie lesen, sollten Sie die wichtigsten Begriffe notieren, um die Aufgabe zu bearbeiten *(Scanning)*.
  ►SF 9 **Anticipating, skimming, scanning**
  Schreiben Sie sich nur Schlüsselbegriffe auf, keine ganzen Sätze. Achten Sie auf Bindewörter wie *but*/aber; *however*/jedoch; *in contrast* / im Gegensatz usw. Diese Bindewörter leiten oft neue Gesichtspunkte ein.
- Wählen Sie nur die für die Aufgabenstellung relevanten Punkte aus und fassen Sie diese mit Ihren eigenen Worten zusammen.
  Die Gliederung Ihres Textes muss nicht übereinstimmen mit der Gliederung des Originaltexts. Achten Sie darauf, dass Sie den Text nicht einfach übersetzen.
- Lesen Sie sich nun Ihren Text noch einmal durch und überprüfen Sie, ob Sie alle relevanten Punkte des Originaltexts in eigenen Worten verständlich wiedergegeben haben.
  Überprüfen Sie, ob Sie:
  - alle wichtigen Aspekte des Originaltexts genannt haben,
  - keine Beispiele, die im Originaltext genannt werden, einbezogen haben,
  - den Text adressatengerecht verfasst haben,
  - die Textsorte berücksichtigt haben,
  - den Text in der Zielsprache verständlich verfasst haben. (vgl. auch „Falsche Freunde" auf Seite 205),
  - den Text übersichtlich gestaltet haben.

Bearbeitung einer Übersetzungsaufgabe

Die **Übersetzung** eines Textes von einer Sprache in eine andere Sprache unterscheidet sich grundlegend von der Mediation. Wenn Sie einen Text übersetzen, dann müssen Sie diesen Wort für Wort in die andere Sprache übertragen. Der Sinn einer Übersetzung besteht darin, den Text so genau wie möglich in der Zielsprache wiederzugeben. Manchmal müssen Sie dazu die Satzstellung ändern oder idiomatische Ausdrücke sinnvoll anpassen.

- Überfliegen Sie den Text, um sich einen allgemeinen Überblick über den Text zu verschaffen *(Skimming)*.
- Schreiben Sie sich stichpunktartig auf, worum es in dem Text geht, bevor Sie mit der detaillierten Übersetzung beginnen. Verwenden Sie hierzu bereits die Zielsprache des zu verfassenden Textes.

Rohfassung

- In der Rohfassung Ihrer Übersetzung sollten Sie nicht wortwörtlich übersetzen. Versuchen Sie aber, sich so nah wie möglich an die Wortwahl des Originaltextes zu halten. Lassen Sie keine Lücken in Ihrer Übersetzung. Wenn Sie die genaue Übersetzung nicht kennen, dann schreiben Sie zunächst das Wort in der Sprache des Originaltexts auf.
- Für eine Übersetzungsaufgabe erhalten Sie in der Regel eine längere Bearbeitungszeit. Schreiben Sie deshalb Ihre erste Fassung mit einem Bleistift oder am PC, so dass Sie Wörter ändern und verbessern können.

Zweite Fassung

- Lesen Sie die erste Fassung sorgfältig durch und versuchen Sie die noch fehlenden Wörter oder Satzteile zu übersetzen.
- Versuchen Sie zunächst die Bedeutung der noch fehlenden Wörter aus dem Kontext zu erschließen. ▶ **SF 10 Surviving without a dictionary**
  Wenn es Ihnen nicht gelingt, die Wörter aus dem Kontext zu erschließen, dann schlagen Sie diese in einem Wörterbuch nach. ▶ **SF 11 Using a dictionary**
- Dann vergleichen Sie Ihre zweite Fassung Wort für Wort mit dem Originaltext. Stellen Sie sicher, dass Sie keine Satzteile ausgelassen haben.

Endfassung

- Lesen Sie Ihre Übersetzung noch einmal sorgfältig und überprüfen Sie, ob sie einwandfrei deutsch bzw. englisch klingt. Falls nicht, überarbeiten Sie diese Passagen noch einmal. Überlegen Sie hier genau, was Sie sagen möchten und wie Sie dies auf Deutsch bzw. Englisch normalerweise ausdrücken würden.
- Lesen Sie sich nun Ihren Text noch einmal durch und überprüfen Sie, ob Ihr Text dem Originaltext entspricht. Überprüfen Sie, ob Sie:
  - sinngemäß alles übersetzt haben. Nur wenn Sie ein Wort nicht übersetzen können und dieses nicht im Wörterbuch finden, dann paraphrasieren Sie, d.h. umschreiben Sie das Wort.
  - den Schreibstil des Originaltexts übernommen haben.
  - keine falschen Freunde in Ihren Zieltext eingebaut haben (vgl. auch „Falsche Freunde" unten).
  - Redewendungen richtig übersetzt haben.

Falsche Freunde

Falsche Freunde *(false friends)* sind Wörter, die in zwei verschiedenen Sprachen zwar ähnlich aussehen oder ähnlich klingen, aber dennoch unterschiedliche Bedeutungen haben.

Beispiele:

actual ≠ aktuell; = tatsächlich
become ≠ bekommen; = werden
brave ≠ brav; = mutig
gift ≠ Gift; = Geschenk

handy ≠ Handy; = geschickt, handlich
rent ≠ Rente; = Miete
sensible ≠ sensibel; = vernünftig
still ≠ still; = immer noch

Skills files | Writing

23 Formal letters and e-mails
Formelle Briefe und E-Mails

Formelle Briefe

Wenn Sie einen Brief an einen Geschäftspartner verfassen möchten, müssen Sie sich an bestimmte formale Vorgaben halten. Diese Vorgaben sind nicht einheitlich geregelt, sondern unterscheiden sich in den verschiedenen Kulturkreisen – auch innerhalb des englischsprachigen Raums. Bei englischsprachigen Geschäftsbriefen sollten Sie sich an den britischen Vorgaben orientieren, es sei denn, Sie schreiben an ein Unternehmen in den USA.

Es gibt verschiedene Anlässe für formelle Briefe: Anfragen, Angebote, Beschwerden, Bestellungen, Bewerbungsschreiben, Mahnungen, Mitteilungen, Rechnungen und Reservierungen.

Your Books

342 Beaconsfield Road
Liverpool L256EE
England
Tel +44(0)151-1092687
Fax +44(0)151-1092688
www.yourbooks.co.uk
info@yourbooks.com

1 Your ref:
2 Our ref: Ab/Bc

3 15 March 20_

4 Confetti & Co
80 Tottenham Court Road
London WI6 8HR
England

5 Dear Sir or Madam

6 Your advertisement for balloons on the Internet

We refer to your advertisement for your balloons, which we found on the Internet last week.

We are a well established publishing company with subsidiaries all over the world. Our company is planning an introductory day for our new trainees. Therefore we would like to order your balloons for decoration.

Furthermore we saw your special March offer on the Internet and would be pleased if you could send us a confirmation of the validity of your stated prices. Moreover we would be grateful for information about terms of delivery and payment.

We look forward to receiving your answer soon.

7 Yours faithfully

8 *Matt Smith*

9 Matthew Smith
10 Training Manager

---

1 Im Amerikanischen stehen die Bezugszeichen ganz am Ende des Briefs unter den Anlagen.

2 Bezugszeichen des Absenders

3 Das Datum steht normalerweise unterhalb der Bezugszeichen. Es kann aber auch in der ersten Zeile oberhalb der Adressen oder in der ersten Zeile unterhalb der Adressen stehen.
Schreibweisen im Britischen Englisch: Tag, Monat, Jahr; im Amerikanischen Englisch: Monat, Tag, Jahr

4 Die Empfängeradresse steht unter dem Datum.

5 Anrede

6 Betreffzeile

7 Grußformel am Ende des Briefes

8 Unterschrift

9 Vollständiger Name

10 Position

Der folgende Beispielbrief zeigt Ihnen, wie ein Bewerbungsschreiben in Großbritannien in der Regel aufgebaut ist.

1 Lessingstr. 84
44147 Dortmund
Germany

Ms Angela Kelly
Maytree Nursery School
14 Moss Way
Leeds
LS2 9NQ
England

15 February 20_

Dear Ms Kelly

2 **Your advertisement in the Leeds Times of 6 February**

3 With reference to your advertisement in the Leeds Times of 6 February, I would like to apply for the position of a nursery school teacher.

4 After completing my education at Cologne College for Social Care I have been working with *Kindertagesstätte Regenbogenland* in Dortmund since August 20_. I now have great experience in developing the nursery learning environment and developing lesson plans. I feel well qualified for the position advertised.

5 I am particularly interested in this job as I would very much like to gain work experience abroad. As well as speaking fluent English and Spanish, I have working knowledge of French. My mother tongue is of course German.

I can supply references from former employers if you wish.

6 I enclose my curriculum vitae and certified translations of my certificates. Please do not hesitate to contact me if you should require further information.

7 I look forward to hearing from you.

Yours sincerely

Jasmin Kramer
Jasmin Kramer

8 Encs.

---

1 Ihre Adresse ohne Angabe des Namens gehört in die Ecke oben links.

2 Betreffzeile

3 Sagen Sie, worauf Sie sich beziehen (z. B. Anzeige, Telefonat), und nennen Sie den Anlass für den Brief.

4 Stellen Sie sich vor, indem Sie die wichtigsten Qualifikationen und Erfahrungen benennen.

5 Nennen Sie weitere Qualifikationen.

6 Erwähnen Sie die Anlagen Ihres Briefes und weisen Sie darauf hin, dass Sie weitere Zeugnisse usw. senden können.

7 Abschlussworte

8 Encs. = Enclosures (Anlagen)

Formelle E-Mails

Mittlerweile werden verstärkt keine formellen Briefe mehr geschrieben, sondern formelle E-Mails. Sie nehmen zum einen weniger Zeit in Anspruch und sie sind zum anderen schneller beim Empfänger.

Wenn Sie eine formelle E-Mail schreiben, dann müssen Sie den gleichen Kommunikationsregeln folgen wie beim formellen Brief.

Beim Aufbau Ihrer formellen E-Mail gibt es jedoch Unterschiede zum formellen Brief. Das Beispiel zeigt Ihnen, wie eine formelle E-Mail in Großbritannien in der Regel aufgebaut ist:

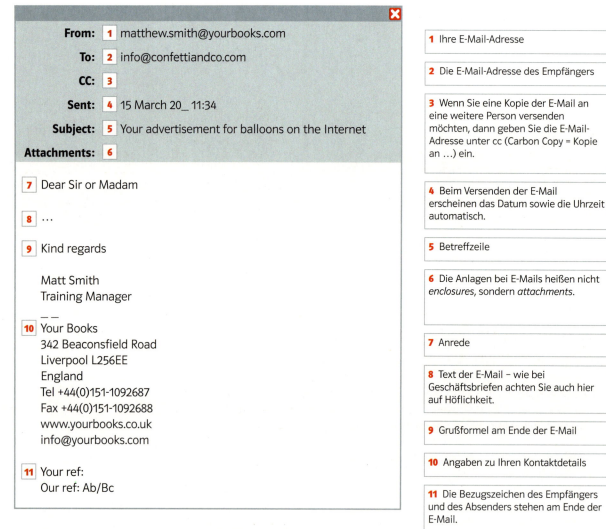

→ Redewendungen finden Sie auf der folgenden Seite.

Writing | Skills files

Redewendungen

• Anreden:

> Dear Sir or Madam   Dear Mr Albee
> Dear Sir   Dear Ms Howard
> Dear Madam

• Schlussformeln:

> Yours faithfully (Britisch)
> Yours sincerely (Britisch; wenn Sie die Person
>   namentlich kennen)
> Best wishes / Best regards / Kind regards (Britisch
>   und Amerikanisch)
> Sincerely (Amerikanisch)

• Bezugnahme:

> We refer to your advertisement …
> Referring to your advertisement …
> We refer to your offer of August 26, 2010.
> Your firm has been recommended to us by …

• Briefanlass und Geschäftsvorstellung:

> We wish to point out that …
> We should appreciate it if you would …
> We are a medium-sized company importing a wide
>   range of …

• Informationen/Services erbitten:

> Would you please send us …?
> We would be grateful for details of …
> We would like to ask for/to …
> A visit by your representative would be
>   appreciated.

• Nachrichten übermitteln:

> We are pleased to inform you that …
> You will be pleased to hear that …
> We are really sorry to inform you that …

• Abschlussworte:

> We hope to hear from you soon.
> We look forward to hearing from you soon.
> We look forward to an early reply.
> We hope this information will help you.

• Struktur:

> therefore / for this   so far / up to now
>   reason   still
> if / provided that   as
> however/but   so that
> besides / in addition

24 Letter to the editor
Der Leserbrief

Der Leserbrief gehört zu den formellen Briefen. In der Regel schreibt man einen Leserbrief an eine Zeitung oder Zeitschrift, wenn man einen Artikel über ein umstrittenes Thema gelesen hat und seine Sichtweise zu diesem Thema äußern möchte. ► SF 23 Formal letters

Tipps: Verfassen eines Leserbriefs

Lesen Sie den Zeitungsartikel sorgfältig durch und machen Sie sich Notizen zu Aspekten, auf die Sie in Ihrem Leserbrief eingehen möchten.

Sammeln Sie Ideen für Ihre Argumente und strukturieren Sie diese.

Fassen Sie sich kurz. Der Stil eines Leserbriefs ist knapp und klar. Wichtig ist, dass Sie sachlich bleiben.

Schreiben Sie den Leserbrief auf dem Computer und senden Sie ihn per E-Mail.

Bevor Sie Ihren Leserbrief absenden, lesen Sie ihn nochmals sorgfältig durch und korrigieren Sie alle gefundenen Fehler.

Skills files | Writing

Aufbau des Leserbriefs und Redewendungen

- Anrede:

> To the editor
> Editor:
> Dear editor
> Dear Sir / Dear Madam / Dear Sir or Madam

- In der Einleitung sollten Sie zunächst den Bezug zu dem Zeitungsartikel herstellen. Nennen Sie neben dem Thema auch die Quelle des Artikels, auf den Sie sich beziehen.

> I refer to your report/article on energy consumption in today's / last week's edition of *USA Worldwide*.
> With reference to the article on energy consumption (*USA Worldwide*, 12 June 2010) I would like to point out that …
> I am writing with reference to the article on energy consumption you published in yesterday's issue of *USA Worldwide*.

- Machen Sie Ihre eigene Position zu dem Thema deutlich.

> I completely agree with your statements on …
> I entirely disagree with …
> I am completely opposed to …

- Im Hauptteil begründen Sie Ihre Position sachlich und zeigen Hintergrundwissen.

- Der Hauptteil besteht aus klar voneinander abgrenzbaren Argumenten, die Sie bestenfalls mit Beispielen veranschaulichen.

> One should not forget that …
> My first/second/final argument …
> Another aspect is that …
> To my mind …

- Im Schlussteil bekräftigen Sie noch einmal Ihre Position zu dem Thema, indem Sie Schlussfolgerungen ziehen und Forderungen aufstellen bzw. Lösungsvorschläge machen.

> I am sure many readers will agree with me when I claim that …
> In conclusion, I would say that …
> All in all, …
> Together, we can …

- Achtung: Wiederholen Sie Ihre Argumente nicht!

- Der Leserbrief endet ohne Grußformel nur mit Vornamen und Familiennamen.

  ► **SF 16 Composition** ► **SF 19 Connectives**

Beispiel:

From: michael.martin@webs.com
To: james.sullivan@press.com
Subject: Letter to the editor: "Food pantries falling short"

To the editor

I am writing about the article "Food pantries falling short" in the Aug. 10 *Press*. The Stanton family represents one in 10 of Michigan households that suffer from hunger. These households are a fraction of the 38 million who go hungry every day in the United States.

These are not statistics; they are humans in the image of God going hungry. The U.S. Conference of Mayors reported that requests for food assistance increased by an average of 12 percent in 24 cities surveyed. More than half of those in need had children, and while many were employed they were unable to put food on their table.

So what can we do? We cannot continue to read articles like this and remain idle. How we treat the hungry in our midst speaks volumes about our hearts, our character and our priorities. This is indeed a moral issue, an issue of justice and one that demands our immediate action.

In addition to donating food to local pantries, we can also call on our legislators to make a difference. A new piece of legislation called the Hunger-Free Communities Act would commit the federal government to cutting hunger in the U.S. in half by 2015, and eliminate it by 2020. This bill needs to be passed as soon as possible.

Together, we can end hunger. The question is only when we will choose to solve this problem.

Michael Martin

25 Personal letters and e-mails
Persönliche Briefe und E-Mails

Persönliche E-Mails

In den meisten Fällen werden keine persönlichen Briefe mehr geschrieben und mit der Post verschickt, sondern E-Mails. Sie können Ihre E-Mail zwanglos formulieren, so als würden Sie ein Gespräch mit der Person führen. Im Allgemeinen sollten Sie aber denselben Regeln folgen, die für das Schreiben eines Briefes gelten. Bedenken Sie, dass der ausländische Freund einen bestimmten Kommunikationsstil von Ihnen erwarten könnte.

Beispiel:

From: nicole.volk@webs.de
To: sandra_brown@fast.ca
Subject: Hey there! :-)

1 Hi Susan

2 Just a few lines to let you know I'm still alive!

3 How are things in Canada? You're on your snowboard every day, aren't you?
4 I really must say, I envy you having so much snow!!! We don't, so I haven't gone snowboarding this winter yet.

Suppose I won't go snowboarding this winter anyway, cause now I'm busy at college with exams. I've been working really hard at school. Hopefully I'll remember everything!

Last weekend I stayed at Sandra's place. :-) Do you remember that girl from volleyball classes? We studied together and went to a party that really rocked. I met this guy … :D We'll see how things work out …

Please drop me a line when you have a minute ASAP. We must keep in touch.

5 Love

Nicole

6 Königstr. 34
70173 Stuttgart
Germany

1 Beginnen Sie Ihre E-Mail mit einer Anrede: *Dear + name* (formell) *Hi + name* (informell).

2 Das erste Wort nach der Anrede wird immer groß geschrieben.

3 Gruppieren Sie Ihre Informationen in Sinnabschnitten.

4 Sie können Frageanhängsel verwenden, z. B. *aren't you?, don't you?*

5 Beenden Sie Ihre E-Mail mit einer entsprechenden Schlussfloskel, z. B. *All the best / Best wishes / Bye for now / Love / Lots of love and kisses …*

6 Sie schreiben Ihre Adresse nicht zu Beginn der E-Mail, sondern erst am Ende unterhalb Ihres Namens. Es ist auch üblich die Adresse wegzulassen.

Persönliche E-Mails verfassen

- Wenn Sie eine persönliche E-Mail schreiben, müssen Sie nicht in vollständigen Sätzen schreiben.
  Beispiel: Suppose I won't go snowboarding this winter anyway, cause I'm busy at college with exams.

Redemittel

- Freundliche Formulierungen:

Well, …	go back to a topic
Anyway …	summarize the topic
By the way …	change the topic
Of course …	say something is obvious
(Un)luckily …	show good or bad fortune
To be honest …	say what you really mean

- Abkürzungen und Emoticons:

Beispiele für Abkürzungen:		Beispiele für Emoticons/ Smileys:	
LOL	laughing out loud		
2BCTND	to be continued	:-)	smiling, happy
AKA	also known as	:D	large grin
ASAP	as soon as possible	:o	shocked, surprised
CM	call me	:O	shouting
F2F	face to face		

Persönliche Briefe

Einen persönlichen Brief schreiben Sie an jemanden, den Sie gut kennen, z. B. an einen Freund oder einen Verwandten. Es gibt ebenfalls keine festen Regeln.

Es gibt verschiedene Kommunikationsanlässe: Freundschaftlicher Brief, Liebesbrief, Einladung, Entschuldigung, Glückwunsch/Kondolenz und Danksagung.

26 Describing illustrations and photographs
Bilder und Fotos beschreiben

Wenn Sie ein Bild analysieren möchten, dann beschreiben Sie das Bild sowohl optisch, d. h. das Aussehen des Bildes, als auch inhaltlich, d. h. den Informationsgehalt. Die Bildanalyse soll so genau sein, dass sich ein blinder Mensch theoretisch das Bild genau vorstellen kann.

Erster Eindruck

- Beschreiben Sie zunächst die Bildart, die Sie sehen, und welche Situation das Bild zeigt.
- Wenn angegeben, nennen Sie die Quellenangabe des Bildes, z. B.: Von wem stammt das Bild? Wer hat es erstellt? Wann ist das Bild entstanden? Welchen Titel trägt das Bild? Wo wurde es veröffentlicht?

Beschreibung des Bildes / des Fotos

- Beschreiben Sie nun detailliert, was Sie auf dem Bild sehen können. Gehen Sie hierbei so vor, dass Sie mit dem wichtigsten Aspekt des Bildes beginnen (im Vordergrund, im Fokus), und nennen Sie erst dann die Details, die im Hintergrund zu sehen sind.
- Achten Sie darauf, dass Sie nur beschreiben und noch nicht interpretieren!
- Was genau zeigt das Bild? Beantworten Sie möglichst die w-Fragen „wer?", „wo?", „was?".
- Beschreiben Sie zudem, wenn möglich, die Körpersprache der Menschen, d. h. Gestik und Mimik, die Beziehung der Menschen zueinander, die Verwendung von Farben, Licht und Symbolen.

Interpretation und Intention

- Versuchen Sie nun, das Bild zu interpretieren, d.h. ziehen Sie Schlussfolgerungen aus dem Beschriebenen hinsichtlich der Intention (Absicht) des Malers/Fotografen.
  - Welche Atmosphäre vermittelt das Bild? Warum wird diese Atmosphäre vermittelt?
  - Welche Botschaft möchte der Maler/Fotograf weitergeben? Und was möchte er/sie damit bewirken?
  - Welche Zielgruppe wird angesprochen?

Wirkung / persönliche Meinung

- Im letzten Teil Ihrer Bildanalyse formulieren Sie Ihren persönlichen Eindruck, den das Bild bei Ihnen hinterlassen hat. Versuchen Sie hierzu immer Beispiele dafür zu geben, welche Elemente des Bildes genau zu Ihrer persönlichen Meinung über das Bild geführt haben.
  - Wie wirkt das Bild auf Sie? Ablehnend oder anziehend?
  - Welche Gefühle weckt das Bild in Ihnen?
  - Bestätigt das Bild die Wirklichkeit oder zeigt es Widersprüche?

Tempus

- Wenn Sie beschreiben, welchen Gegenstand / welche Person Sie in einem Bild sehen, dann verwenden Sie die einfache Form des Präsens. ►GF16 **Present simple**
  Beispiele:
  There is a young person in the foreground.
  The photo shows …
- Wenn Sie jedoch beschreiben, was die Person in dem Bild gerade tut, dann müssen Sie die Verlaufsform des Präsens verwenden. ►GF17 **Present continuous**
  Beispiel: *The young person is holding a sign with one hand.*

Redemittel: Bilder und Fotos beschreiben

- Beschreibung der Bildart und der gezeigten Situation:

  The picture is a/an illustration/painting/collage/still (from a film) / electronic image …
  The (colour/black-and-white) photograph shows …
  This is a (painting) showing a typical … scene/ situation …
  This (collage) illustrates …
  In this (still) you can see (that) …

- Beschreibung von Farben und Licht:

  The colours are bright/dark.
  The photograph is clear / in focus / blurred / not in focus / well-lit.
  The day the photograph was taken on was sunny/ cloudy.

- Beschreiben, wo sich etwas im Bild befindet:

  on the right-hand/left-hand side of the illustration
  At the top/bottom of the photo you can find …
  in the upper right-hand corner
  in the lower left-hand corner
  In the centre of the picture there is …
  In the foreground/background you can see …

- Interpretation und Intention:

  The person in the picture looks … (+ adjective)
  The painting gives you the impression that …
  The artist wants to express that …
  Perhaps his/her intention is to show that …
  The illustration is aimed at children …
  Considering the … in the photo you could draw the conclusion that …

Skills files | Describing and analyzing

- Beschreibung der Atmosphäre:

This creates a/an … atmosphere.
The main factors that contribute to this
    atmosphere are …
The atmosphere is cosy, friendly, funny, happy,
    lively, peaceful, warm …
It is chilly, dark, depressing, desperate, sad, scary,
    serious, terrifying …
The atmosphere is boring, exotic, hectic,
    mysterious …
The … in the photo conveys an atmosphere of
    great sadness/happiness.

- Persönliche Meinung:

The impression I get from this illustration is that …
The illustration makes me feel …
The colours/light the artist has chosen make/makes
    me feel … (+ adjective)
In my opinion the painting is supposed to …
To my mind the photograph would be better if …
    (+ past simple)
My first thought when I saw the (photograph)
    was …
The (collage) is shocking/brilliant/breathtaking/
    terrifying/impressive/realistic …
The (painting) reminds me of …

27 Describing cartoons
Karikaturen beschreiben

Eine Karikatur ist eine satirische (spöttische) Darstellung von Menschen oder
gesellschaftlichen Situationen. Charakteristisch für Karikaturen ist, dass sie die Realität
übertrieben und verformt darstellen mit dem Ziel, einen gesellschaftlichen Zustand, eine
Person oder eine Institution zu kritisieren. Meistens besteht eine Karikatur aus einem Bild und
einem kurzen Text innerhalb des Bildes, z. B. als Sprechblase, oder unterhalb des Bildes als
Bildunterschrift.

Eine Karikatur bedient sich in der Regel zahlreicher Stilmittel, um die Komik einer Situation
oder die Eigenheiten einer Person überspitzt darzustellen.

Beispiele:

exaggeration	Übertreibung	Eigenschaften werden überdimensioniert und überzogen dargestellt.
irony	Ironie	Das Gegenteil des Gesagten ist gemeint.
pun	Wortspiel	Beruht auf der Mehrdeutigkeit und Verdrehung von Wörtern
simile	Vergleich	Veranschaulichung einer Aussage, indem sie durch *like* oder *as* mit einem anderen Bereich in Beziehung gesetzt wird
symbol	Symbol	Etwas Konkretes verweist auf etwas Abstraktes.

Wenn Sie eine Karikatur beschreiben und analysieren möchten, beachten Sie „Redemittel:
Bilder und Fotos beschreiben" auf Seite 213.
▶ SF 26 Describing illustrations and photographs

→ Redemittel finden Sie auf der folgenden Seite.

Redemittel: Karikaturen beschreiben

- Die Karikatur beschreiben:

  The cartoon consists of an illustration of …
  The illustration shows …
  There is a caption below the cartoon, which says "…".
  In the (first) speech bubble it says "…"
  The text in the speech bubble is spoken by …

- Die Botschaft der Karikatur:

  The cartoonist's message might be that …
  His point seems to be that …
  Probably his intention is to show that …
  The cartoonist is criticizing the behaviour of …
  He is making fun of …
  He is making a sarcastic comment on …

- Interpretation der Karikatur:

  The figure is a caricature of …
  The cartoonist exaggerates character traits.
  The person's body language shows that …
  From his/her facial expression you can conclude that …
  … symbolizes / stands for / is a symbol of …

- Persönliche Meinung:

  I think / I don't think the cartoon is (very) funny because …
  I think / I don't think the cartoon is easy to understand because …
  I agree / I don't agree with the point the cartoonist is making because …

28 Describing diagrams
Diagramme beschreiben

Diagramme sind graphische Darstellungen von numerischen Daten oder Informationen. Sie veranschaulichen Informationen und erleichtern es dem Leser, komplizierte Sachverhalte aufzunehmen.

Je nachdem, was ein Diagramm verdeutlichen soll, werden unterschiedliche Arten von Diagrammen eingesetzt. Im Folgenden finden Sie eine Auswahl der am häufigsten verwendeten Arten von Diagrammen.

Pie chart: Ein Tortendiagramm ist in mehrere Kreissektoren unterteilt, die Teile des Ganzen anzeigen. Es eignet sich besonders, um Anteile darzustellen.	**Bar chart:** Ein Säulendiagramm oder Balkendiagramm ist ein Diagramm, das die Häufigkeitsverteilung verschiedener Sektoren veranschaulicht. Es eignet sich besonders, um einige wenige Daten miteinander zu vergleichen.	**Line graph:** Ein Liniendiagramm stellt den funktionellen Zusammenhang von zwei Merkmalen graphisch dar. Es eignet sich besonders gut, um die Entwicklung von Werten graphisch darzustellen.

Skills files | **Describing and analyzing**

Diagramme beschreiben

- Nennen Sie zunächst die Art des Diagramms, den Titel, die Quelle, Erscheinungsort und -jahr sowie die Maßeinheiten und Parameter.
- Beschreiben Sie das Diagramm nun detailliert. Machen Sie sich zunächst Notizen. Je nach Art des Diagramms können Sie:
  - den Verlauf der Entwicklung differenziert beschreiben,
  - Einzelwerte vergleichen,
  - Gemeinsamkeiten und Unterschiede benennen,
  - den Kurvenverlauf, die Säulenverteilung, die Sektorverteilung beschreiben,
  - Maximal- und Minimalwerte angeben.
- Achten Sie darauf, dass Ihre Beschreibung nicht zu detailliert ausfällt. Konzentrieren Sie sich nur auf auffällige Entwicklungen oder Zahlen.
- Mit Hilfe Ihrer Notizen formulieren Sie vollständige Sätze, um das Diagramm zu beschreiben.
- Versuchen Sie nun, das Diagramm zu interpretieren, d.h. ziehen Sie Schlussfolgerungen aus dem Beschriebenen und überprüfen Sie gegebenenfalls die Zuverlässigkeit der Quelle.
- Fassen Sie die wichtigsten Ergebnisse des Diagramms in ein bis zwei Sätzen zusammen.

Redemittel: Diagramme beschreiben

- Bestandsaufnahme der Informationen:

> The pie chart "US Exports" published in *The Daily USA* in New York in 20… shows in percentage terms what the USA exported in the year 20…

- Beschreibung:

> The chart/graph/diagram shows …
> It shows the development from … to …
> The table shows the change of … from … to …
> The chart gives an overview of …
> The time scale runs vertically.
> The weight scale runs horizontally.
> On the y-axis/x-axis you can see …

- Einen Anstieg beschreiben:

> There is a noticeable upward trend between … and …
> By 2009 figures reached their highest level.
> The number grew/increased.
> The number of … rose slightly/sharply/slowly.

- Eine Abnahme beschreiben:

> We notice a downward trend between … and …
> By 20 … figures reached their lowest level.
> The number declined/decreased.
> The number fell slightly / slowly / sank sharply.
> The number of … remained unchanged/steady.

- Unveränderte Werte:

> Figures remained steady / Figures did not change.

- Zahlen und Daten:

> the figures for the last year / the last month, etc.
> the latest figures
> the total number of …
> a significant / an insignificant number of …
> a high percentage of …
> a majority/minority of …
> percentage/amount

- Mengenbezeichnungen:

> a total of
> over/under
> nearly/almost/ approximately
> exactly
> more/less than
> the same number as
> the same amount of
>
> from over/under
> one in five
> half / a third / a quarter / two thirds
> 100 per cent
> twice/three times as many
> on average

- Interpretation:

> The biggest change can be seen in …
> This leads to the assumption that …
> This suggests a relation between … and …

- Schlussfolgerung:

> The drastic change may be due to …
> All in all you can say that …
> To sum up … we can say that …

29 Analyzing films
Filmanalyse

Die Filmanalyse unterscheidet sich nicht wesentlich von der Analyse von geschriebenen Texten und auch Bildern. Bei der Textanalyse untersuchen Sie z. B. die Charaktere, den Handlungsverlauf und den Handlungsort; bei der Bildanalyse beschreiben und interpretieren Sie z. B. die Körpersprache von Menschen, die Verwendung von Farben und Licht und die Atmosphäre. ▶ **SF 26 Describing illustrations and photographs**

Diese Aspekte werden Sie auch bei der Filmanalyse näher betrachten.
In der Regel untersuchen Sie in der Schule keine ganzen Filme, sondern nur kurze Filmausschnitte, sogenannte Filmsequenzen.

Filmarten

Spielfilm *(feature film)* Ein Spielfilm ist ein Film mit einer fiktionalen Handlung, die manchmal auch der Wirklichkeit (z. B. realen Personen oder Ereignissen) nachempfunden sein kann.

Dokumentarfilm *(documentary)* Ein Dokumentarfilm befasst sich mit tatsächlichen Gegebenheiten und Ereignissen. Deshalb können Sie den Dokumentarfilm nicht genauso analysieren wie den Spielfilm: Es gibt in der Regel keinen Handlungsverlauf, weil keine Geschichte erzählt wird, sondern der Schwerpunkt liegt auf der Sachlichkeit des Films. Ein Dokumentarfilm soll Informationen zu einem bestimmten Thema bereitstellen.
Deshalb analysieren Sie bei einem Dokumentarfilm zunächst vor allem die Darstellung des Themas, die Vorgehensweise und Intention des Regisseurs und die Wirkung des Filmes auf den Zuschauer.
Zusätzlich müssen Sie die Gestaltungselemente des Dokumentarfilms analysieren, die denen des Spielfilms gleichen.

Werbefilm *(commercial)* Ein Werbefilm ist ein kurzer Film, in dem für ein Produkt oder eine Dienstleistung geworben wird. Charakteristisch für den Werbefilm ist, dass er Menschen beeinflussen soll, ein bestimmtes Produkt zu kaufen. (Siehe AIDA-Formel zur Analyse von Werbefilmen.) ▶ **Unit 3, Seite 31**

Quellenangabe

- Schreiben Sie eine Quellenangabe.
  Beispiel: The feature film "Twilight", directed by Catherine Hardwicke and produced in the USA in 2008, is about a teenage girl who falls in love with a vampire.

Skills files | Describing and analyzing

Gesamteindruck und Empfindungen

- Welchen Gesamteindruck haben Sie von der Filmsequenz? Welche Empfindungen ruft sie in Ihnen hervor?

> My first thought when I saw the film sequence was …
> The film sequence is shocking/brilliant/ breathtaking/terrifying/impressive/realistic …

- Worum geht es in der Sequenz grob? Achten Sie auf Handlungsverlauf (plot); Einsatz eines Erzählers (narrator); Handlungsort und -zeit (setting); Spannungsaufbau (suspense); Atmosphäre (atmosphere).

> This sequence is about …
> This sequence presents the different aspects of …

> This sequence discusses the problem of … / the theme of …
> The film makes use of a narrator.
> The narrator wants to inform/influence/ manipulate/convince the viewer.
> The director makes use of voiceover with the aim of …
> The story/extract is set in …
> The scene/action takes place in the present/past/ future …
> Suspense is created by / arises from …
> The main cause of suspense is …
> The conflict between … and … creates suspense.
> The atmosphere in this sequence is …
> ► **SF 26 Describing illustrations and photographs**

Die Charaktere bzw. Darsteller

- Beschreiben Sie die Charaktere (Spielfilm) bzw. die Darsteller (Dokumentarfilm) der Filmsequenz.

> The main character is …
> There are two/three/etc. main characters.
> We get to know … by …
> He/She is confronted with …

- Achten Sie auf das Aussehen (appearance).

> general: pretty, handsome, beautiful, ugly
> body: fat, obese, slim, thin, tall, small
> face: round/square/wrinkled face; pale/tanned skin; bright/dull eyes; long/pointed/flat nose; curly/ straight/short/long hair
> clothes: jacket, trousers, shirt, skirt, dress; fashionable, clean, dirty, tidy, neat, worn-out

- Achten Sie auf das Verhalten und die Beziehungen der Charaktere zueinander (behaviour and relationships).

> negative character traits: aggressive, anxious, bad- tempered, dishonest, narrow-minded, pessimistic, rude, shy, unfair

> positive character traits: brave, friendly, honest, open-minded, optimistic, polite, reasonable, self-confident
> This character represents …
> The character is in a conflict (with) …
> The character finds himself/herself in an inner conflict …
> There is a relationship between … and …

- Achten Sie auf die Sprache (language and how the characters communicate with one another).

> The character has got a soft/loud/pleasant/coarse/ funny voice.
> The character speaks quietly/loudly.
> There is little dialogue in this sequence.
> There is a long dialogue between … and … in this sequence.
> They are shouting at each other.
> The character's monologue is focusing (mainly) on …
> The scene begins/ends with a monologue.
> This scene presents an important dialogue between … and …

Describing and analyzing | Skills files

Die Szene im Kontext des Films

- Setzen Sie die Filmszene in den Kontext des Gesamtfilms.

- Führt die Szene dazu, dass die Handlung voranschreitet? / …, dass Spannung aufgebaut wird? / … , dass neue Charaktere eingeführt werden? / … , dass ein Konflikt aufkommt? / …, dass ein Wendepunkt eingeleitet wird?

> The course of the action is …
> There is a conflict between …
> The turning-point …
> At the beginning … / at the end …
> The film sequence introduces new characters.

Gestaltungselemente

- Wie wird die Filmszene gefilmt? Achten Sie auf:
  - Kameraabstände *(distance between the camera and the object)*
  - die Kameraperspektive *(camera position)*
  - Kamerabewegung *(camera movement)*

> The director uses a long shot / static shot / over-the-shoulder shot in order to show …
> The scene is shot from … point of view / high-angle / eye-level.
> The medium shot / close-up / tracking shot is used to create a/an … effect.
> The viewer sees this scene in a … shot.

- Wie wird das gefilmte Material am Ende nachbearbeitet?
  - Montage-Technik: Schnitt-Technik *(cut)*; Übergänge *(fade, wipe etc.)*
  - Special effects, z.B. Farben *(black-and-white, coloured)*; Zeitraffer, Zeitlupe *(fast motion, slow motion)*; Standbild *(freeze frame)*; Bildteilung *(split screen)*; Texteinblendungen *(text inserts)*

> The intensity of the colour green/red/blue in this scene puts emphasis on …
> The director's use of black-and-white stresses …
> The use of slow motion emphasizes the moment / the character's situation.
> The use of fast motion highlights the speed of the scene.
> The text inserts add authenticity to the documentary.

- Wie werden die gefilmten Szenen vertont? Achten Sie auf:
  - Dialoge, Monologe, Erzählerkommentar
  - den Einsatz von Filmmusik
  - sonstige Geräusche, z.B. Straßenlärm, Anrufbeantworter
  - Lautstärken

> The film music/sound builds suspense …
> The film music/sound provides a shift from one scene to another.
> There is light piano music in the background.
> The music/sound makes the scene more cheerful/ sad/melancholic/aggressive/romantic/ authentic/dramatic, etc.
> The background noises give the scene more authenticity.
> The background noises / the sound effects stress the atmosphere.

- Wie werden Beleuchtungseffekte eingesetzt?

- Gibt es wiederkehrende Objekte als Symbole?

> There is hardly any light in the scene.
> The director makes use of back light / semi-darkness / darkness / artificial illumination …
> The director makes use of symbols.
> The … symbolizes / stands for / is a symbol of …

219

30 Group work and projects
Gruppenarbeit und Projekte

Gruppenarbeit

Die Arbeit in Gruppen bietet die Chance, sich mit einem Unterrichtsinhalt im Team auseinanderzusetzen. Viele Aufgaben lassen sich besser und schneller in einer Gruppe lösen. Gruppenarbeit dient dem Zweck, gemeinsam zu einer Lösung zu kommen, indem Sie miteinander kommunizieren und Ideen austauschen.

Gruppenzusammensetzung
- Die optimale Gruppengröße beträgt in der Regel 3 – 5 Personen.
- Gruppen können nach verschiedenen Prinzipien gebildet werden: nach Interesse, nach Sympathie, nach Zufall, nach Stärken und Schwächen. Dabei sollte darauf geachtet werden, dass die Gruppen ungefähr gleich stark gebildet werden und dass sie sich gegenseitig unterstützen.

Vorbereitung der Gruppenarbeit
- Richten Sie sich Ihren Arbeitsplatz so ein, dass Sie gut arbeiten, aber auch gut miteinander kommunizieren können.
- Erstellen Sie sich einen Arbeitsplan. Berücksichtigen Sie hierbei die Zeit, die Ihnen zur Bearbeitung der Aufgabe zur Verfügung steht.
- Verteilen Sie Aufgaben an die einzelnen Gruppenmitglieder. Beachten Sie, dass jeder ungefähr dieselbe Menge an Arbeit hat. Manchmal ist es sinnvoll, schriftlich festzuhalten, wer welche Aufgabe übernimmt.
- Für den Interaktionsprozess in der Gruppe kann es hilfreich sein, dass Sie den einzelnen Gruppenmitgliedern Funktionen zuordnen, z. B. Gruppenleiter, Zeitwächter, Schriftführer, Streitschlichter usw.
- Stellen Sie fest, welche Materialien Sie benötigen, und legen Sie fest, wer welche Materialien besorgt.
Wenn die Gruppenarbeit über eine Unterrichtseinheit hinausgeht, sollten Sie sich überlegen, ob es eine Möglichkeit gibt, die Materialien aufzubewahren, so dass Sie immer Zugang dazu haben.
- Einigen Sie sich auf eine geeignete Form, um die Ergebnisse zu präsentieren, wenn sie nicht bereits vorgegeben wurde.

Durchführung der Gruppenarbeit

- Gehen Sie immer höflich und respektvoll miteinander um. Lassen Sie alle ausreden und fallen Sie niemandem ins Wort.
- Sie tragen alle die Verantwortung für die Qualität Ihrer Arbeitsergebnisse. Deshalb unterstützen Sie sich gegenseitig und helfen Sie einander bei Problemen.
- Wichtige Arbeitsergebnisse sollten von jedem Gruppenmitglied schriftlich festgehalten werden und nicht nur von einem Schriftführer. So kann es Ihnen nicht passieren, dass Ihnen bei der Präsentation der Arbeitsergebnisse Informationen fehlen.
- Bemühen Sie sich als Arbeitssprache Englisch einzusetzen.

Redemittel

- Die eigene Meinung ausdrücken:

In my opinion/view …   We should …
I think (that) …   It would be a good idea
I would like to …   to …

- Jemanden unterbrechen:

Sorry, may I interrupt you for a second?
Wait a minute …
I'm sorry to interrupt but …

- Das Thema wechseln:

Before I forget …
There is something else I wanted to say …
By the way …

- Zum eigentlichen Thema zurückkehren:

Let's get back to …
To get back to what we were talking about …
As I was saying …

- Überraschung ausdrücken:

Really?   I don't believe it!
Are you serious?

- Zugeständnisse machen:

I (partly) agree with   Yes, that's true, but …
   you, but …

- Interesse zeigen:

Tell me about your idea.   I'd love to …
Absolutely …

- Rückmeldung geben:

That's very kind of you.   I see.
Are you sure?   I like your idea.

- Jemanden auffordern, etwas zu tun:

Could you possibly …?
Could I ask you to …?
Do you think you could … please?

- Vorschläge machen:

If I were you I would …
You could try …
How about …?

- Füllwörter:

Well, …   I mean …
Anyway …   In fact …
Actually …

- Höflichkeitsfloskeln:

Please.   No worries.
You're welcome.   Don't worry.
Thank you.

Projekte

Projekte zeichnen sich dadurch aus, dass Sie mit dem Lehrer gemeinsam ein Thema und die Arbeitsziele festlegen. Bei der Lösung der Aufgabe, der Beschaffung der Materialien/ Informationen und der Erstellung eines Produktes arbeiten Sie jedoch selbstständig in Gruppen.

Skills files | Presentations and projects

Erfolgreiche Durchführung eines Projektes

- Lesen Sie die Aufgabenstellung sorgfältig und stellen Sie sicher, dass alle Gruppenmitglieder die Aufgabe verstanden haben. Oft ist es bei Projekten der Fall, dass zu Beginn nur das allgemeine Ziel bekannt ist und sich die detaillierten Ziele erst in der Gruppe ergeben, z. B. durch spezifische Betrachtungsweisen des Themas.
  Folgende Fragestellungen zum Verstehen des Arbeitsauftrags können hilfreich sein:
  – Was sollen Sie genau tun und mit welchem Ziel?
  – Gibt es eine zeitliche Begrenzung?
  – Welche Entscheidungen können Sie frei treffen?
  – Sind noch Fragen offen?
- Führen Sie in der Gruppe ein Brainstorming durch:
  – Was wissen Sie bereits über das Thema? Erstellen Sie ein Word web. ▶ SF 21 Word webs
  – Welche Aspekte des Themas möchten Sie bearbeiten?
  – Wo finden Sie die Informationen zu dem Thema?
- Planen Sie die Arbeit in Gruppen:
  – Erstellen Sie einen Plan, auf dem festgehalten wird, wer welche Aufgabe übernimmt.
  – Erstellen Sie einen Terminplan, auf dem Sie festhalten, wann bestimmte Aufgaben erledigt sein müssen.
  – Legen Sie fest, wie Sie Ihre Arbeit koordinieren. Wann treffen Sie sich, evtl. auch außerhalb des Unterrichts? Wie tauschen Sie Informationen aus?
- Entscheiden Sie gemeinsam in der Gruppe, wie Sie Ihre Arbeitsergebnisse präsentieren möchten, falls dies nicht in der Aufgabenstellung festgelegt ist.
  Ideen für Präsentationen: Handzettel, Broschüre, Poster, Plakat, Wandzeitung, Video, Hörspiel, Kurzvortrag, PowerPoint-Präsentation …
- Vergessen Sie nicht, alle Quellen zu notieren, die Sie verwendet haben. Sie müssen immer angeben können, wo Sie Informationen, Bilder usw. gefunden haben.

31 Internet research
Suche im Internet

Es gibt mittlerweile Millionen von Webseiten im Internet. Das Problem ist jedoch, unter der Vielzahl die gewünschten Informationen zu finden. Sie werden nur sofort fündig, wenn Sie die einschlägige Internet-Adresse bereits kennen oder Sie durch einen Link direkt weitergeleitet werden. Falls beides nicht der Fall ist, müssen Sie auf Suchmaschinen zurückgreifen. Suchmaschinen sind Spezialprogramme, mit deren Hilfe Sie sich Ihrem Ziel durch die Eingabe entsprechender Stichwörter nähern können.

Presentations and projects | Skills files

Thema formulieren und eingrenzen

- Bevor Sie sich an den PC setzen, um im Internet nach Informationen zu suchen, sollten Sie sich genau überlegen, welche Informationen Sie benötigen, damit Sie nicht die Orientierung verlieren. Denn das Hauptproblem bei der Recherche im Internet liegt darin, dass man viel Zeit damit verbringt, eine Fülle an unwichtigen und überflüssigen Informationen zu sichten. Um dies zu vermeiden, können Sie z. B. …
  - das Thema präzisieren und evtl. eingrenzen,
  - sinnvolle Stichwörter zum Thema sammeln,
  - themenbezogene Wortfelder erstellen.

Suchanfragen richtig stellen

- Wenn Ihre Suchanfrage zu ungenau ist, werden Sie eine Vielzahl von Informationen erhalten, die zu allgemein sind. Wenn Sie z. B. Informationen zum Thema *TV viewing habits of children* suchen, reicht es nicht aus, das Stichwort *Media* einzugeben. Suchmaschinen bedienen sich teilweise leider unterschiedlicher Suchbegriffe.
  Folgende Eingabearten sind bei den meisten Suchmaschinen möglich:
  - Mehrere Wörter ohne Anführungszeichen
    Beispiel: *TV viewing habits*
    Ergebnis: Alle Texte, in denen entweder *TV* oder *viewing* oder *habits* vorkommen, werden angezeigt.
  - Mehrere Wörter mit Anführungszeichen
    Beispiel: „*TV viewing habits*"
    Ergebnis: Es werden nur Texte angezeigt, in denen die exakte Wortfolge vorkommt.
- Wenn Sie zu wenige Treffer erlangen, überprüfen Sie die Schreibweise, verwenden Sie weniger Begriffe oder versuchen Sie es mit einem anderen Stichwort.
- Wenn Sie zu viele Treffer erlangen, verwenden Sie spezifischere Begriffe oder fügen Sie Stichwörter hinzu.
- Spezielle Begriffe, die aber nicht zu ausgefallen sind, bringen meist gute und eingegrenzte Ergebnisse.

Informationen finden

- Um möglichst schnell und gezielt Informationen zu finden, können Sie Techniken wie Skimming und Scanning verwenden.
  ► **SF9 Anticipating, skimming, scanning**
- Wenn Sie nach einzelnen Wörtern auf einer Seite suchen möchten, können Sie auch Strg+F drücken. Es erscheint dann ein Suchfeld, in das Sie das betreffende Wort eingeben können.

Informationen verarbeiten

- Denken Sie daran, dass jeder User beliebige Informationen im Internet veröffentlichen kann. Die von Ihnen gefundenen Informationen müssen also nicht immer korrekt sein. Um wertloses Material von wertvollem Material zu unterscheiden, können folgende Fragen hilfreich sein:
  - Wer hat die Webseite veröffentlicht? (z. B. kommerziell vs. nicht kommerziell, Privatperson vs. öffentliche Institution, usw.)
  - Verfolgen die Autoren ein bestimmtes Interesse? (Soll z. B. etwas verkauft werden?)
  - Werden Fakten dargelegt oder Meinungen?
  - Sind die Informationen aktuell? (Wann z. B. wurde die Webseite zum letzten Mal aktualisiert? Von wann sind die Jahreszahlen/Statistiken?)

Skills files | Presentations and projects

Favoriten

- Wenn Sie die gesuchten Informationen gefunden haben und später noch einmal auf die Seite zurückgreifen möchten, können Sie die Seite in die Liste der Favoriten aufnehmen. Ihr Browser speichert diese Liste, so dass Sie die Seite jederzeit anzeigen können, ohne erneut suchen zu müssen. Je nach Browser kann diese Liste auch Lesezeichen oder Bookmark heißen. Sie finden die Favoriten in der Menüleiste. Dort klicken Sie auf „Lesezeichen hinzufügen", während Sie die Seite, die Sie speichern möchten, geöffnet haben. Sie können die Seite auch direkt auf dem Desktop speichern, sodass Sie schnell auf diese Seite zugreifen können.

32 Giving a talk or presentation
Ein Referat halten, Arbeitsergebnisse präsentieren

Eine Präsentation oder ein Referat ist eine vorbereitete Vorstellung von Inhalten oder Ergebnissen zu einem bestimmten Thema. Ziel einer Präsentation ist es, die Zuhörer zu informieren.

In der Schule finden häufig Gruppenpräsentationen statt, so dass Sie sich untereinander absprechen sollten, wer welchen Teil übernimmt. ▶ SF 30 Projects and group work

Brainstorming

- Verschaffen Sie sich zunächst einen Überblick über das Thema, indem Sie ein Wortnetz zu dem Themenbereich erstellen. ▶ SF 21 Word webs
- Sie sollten sich auch Folgendes genau überlegen:
  - Welches Ziel verfolge ich mit der Präsentation?
  - An wen ist die Präsentation adressiert?
  - Welche Hilfsmittel und Medien kann ich verwenden, um erfolgreich zu präsentieren?

Materialsuche

- Sammeln Sie Informationen zu dem Thema. Sie können z. B. in Bibliotheken, Zeitungen, Schulbüchern, Lexika oder dem Internet recherchieren. Oder Sie befragen einen Experten zu dem Thema. ▶ SF 31 Internet research

Konzipierung und Aufbau der Präsentation

- Da Sie möglichst frei sprechen sollten und dies in der Fremdsprache noch etwas schwerer fällt, ist es sinnvoll, wenn Sie sich einen Ablaufplan Ihrer Präsentation erstellen. Sie können z. B. eine Tabelle erstellen, in der die Gliederung, der zeitliche Ablauf und der Einsatz von Medien ersichtlich werden. Den Ablaufplan können Sie sich auf Ihren Rednertisch legen, um während der Präsentation bei Bedarf einen Blick darauf werfen zu können.
- In der Regel können Sie Ihre Präsentation anhand der klassischen Dreiteilung aufbauen: Einstieg – Hauptteil – Schlussteil, wobei Sie den Einstieg und den Schlussteil kurz halten sollten, der Hauptteil kann ausführlicher sein.
- Einstieg: Anrede der Zuhörer und sich vorstellen – Thema vorstellen – Gliederung vorstellen. Dabei ist es sinnvoll, das Interesse der Zuhörer zu wecken. Beginnen Sie z. B. mit einem Zitat, einer Karikatur oder einer provokanten Frage, um die volle Aufmerksamkeit zu erhalten.
- Hauptteil: Gut strukturierte Ausführungen (z. B. chronologische Anordnung der Hauptaspekte) – Beispiele geben – visuelle Hilfsmittel hinzuziehen
- Schlussteil: Zusammenfassung der Hauptaspekte – Dank an die Zuhörer.

Stichwortkarten

- Reduzieren Sie Ihren Vortrag auf die wichtigsten Stichpunkte und schreiben Sie diese auf Karteikarten. Die Stichwortkarten sollten keinesfalls den ganzen Text Ihres Vortrags enthalten. Sie sollten es auch vermeiden, vollständige Sätze aufzuschreiben. Sie können sich auch Stichworte zu Beispielen oder Vokabeln auf den Stichwortkarten notieren.
- Sie sollten die Stichwortkarten so aufteilen, dass Sie während des Vortrags nicht durcheinander geraten. Es ist sinnvoll, für den Einstieg und den Schlussteil jeweils eine Stichwortkarte vorzubereiten. Für den Hauptteil sollten Sie je nach Länge Ihres Vortrags mehrere Karten vorbereiten, z. B. je Hauptaspekt eine Karte.

Visuelle Hilfsmittel

- Die meisten Menschen nehmen nur 30 % über das Ohr auf, aber ca. 70 % über das Auge. Überlegen Sie sich deshalb, welche visuellen Hilfsmittel Ihre Präsentation angemessen unterstützen können.
- Weniger ist mehr! Überfrachten Sie Tafelanschrieb, Plakate, Folien, Handzettel usw. möglichst nicht. Strukturieren Sie diese übersichtlich.   ▶ SF 34 **Creating a poster**

Vortragsweise

- Wenn Sie nur ablesen, werden sich Ihre Zuhörer schnell langweilen. Sie sollten daher möglichst frei sprechen und nur hin und wieder auf Ihre Stichwortkarten zurückgreifen.
- Sprechen Sie nicht so, wie Sie schreiben, sondern versuchen Sie, natürlich zu sprechen, so dass Ihre Zuhörer Ihnen folgen können. Formulieren Sie möglichst kurze und unkomplizierte Sätze. Verzichten Sie, wenn möglich, auf Fachbegriffe, die Ihren Zuhörern unbekannt sind. Falls Sie doch auf Fachbegriffe zurückgreifen müssen, schreiben Sie diese an die Tafel.
- Nutzen Sie Wiederholungen, um Wichtiges zu betonen.

Stimme und Körpersprache

- Sprechen Sie langsam: So haben Sie länger Zeit, um Ihre Sätze im Englischen zu formulieren.
- Machen Sie Pausen: Die Zuhörer hören das Gesagte vielleicht zum ersten Mal.
- Halten Sie Blickkontakt mit den Zuhörern. Achten Sie auch auf die Reaktionen der Zuhörer.
- Versuchen Sie, Ihre Aussagen durch Gestik und Mimik zu unterstreichen.

Redemittel für die Präsentation

- Einstieg:

  Good morning, my name is …
  Good morning, let me introduce our group. …
  Can everybody hear me alright?
  Can everybody see the board/poster/screen?
  Let me start by saying a few words about …
  The topic of my presentation today is …

- Hauptteil:

  Let me give you an example.
  If you look at the screen, you'll see that …
  As you can see on the board/poster/screen …
  That proves my point.
  I'd like to move on to …
  Before we go any further, let's look at …

- Struktur und Zeitangaben:

  My presentation will last fifteen minutes.
  I will talk for fifteen minutes.
  My presentation is split into four key areas.
      Firstly, … Secondly, … Thirdly, … Finally, …
  There will be time for questions at the end.
  If you have any questions, feel free to interrupt me.

- Schlussteil:

  Finally …
  I'd like to finish/conclude by saying that …
  To summarize … / To conclude …
  Thank you very much for your attention.
  Thank you very much for listening.
  If you have any questions, please feel free to ask.

33 Taking notes
Die Mitschrift im Unterricht

Informationen, die im Unterricht mündlich präsentiert werden, sind in der Regel die zentralen Lerngegenstände und beinhalten einen großen Teil des prüfungsrelevanten Materials. Mitschriften entstehen im Unterricht durch das Aufschreiben der relevanten Informationen von verschiedenen Quellen, z. B. Unterrichtsgesprächen, Referaten, Hörverständnistexten, Interviews, Filmanalysen usw.

Unabhängig von der Quelle ist bei der Mitschrift besonders wichtig, dass Sie lernen, richtig zuzuhören. In der Regel kann der Mensch nämlich lediglich 30 % des Gehörten behalten. Da die englische Sprache nicht Ihre Muttersprache ist, wird es Ihnen noch schwerer fallen, das gesprochene Englisch zu verstehen und Informationen aufzunehmen. Die folgenden Tipps helfen Ihnen, Ihr Zuhörerverhalten zu verbessern.

Tipps zum richtigen Zuhören

Wenn Sie nichts oder nur schlecht hören können, verändern Sie Ihre Position. Setzen Sie sich dorthin, wo Sie den Sprecher sehen können und wo Sie nicht von Ablenkungen gestört werden.

Akzeptieren Sie die Tatsache, dass Sie nicht alles verstehen werden.

Achten Sie auf die Hauptaussagen des Gesprochenen. Versuchen Sie, Wichtiges von Unwichtigem zu unterscheiden. Konzentrieren Sie sich erst auf Details, wenn Sie die Hauptaussagen verstanden haben.

Auch wenn Sie für eine Zeit lang dem Gesprochenen nicht folgen können, lassen Sie sich nicht ablenken. Bleiben Sie konzentriert bei der Sache. Oft werden die wichtigen Informationen vom Sprecher im weiteren Verlauf wiederholt.

Machen Sie sich Notizen, während Sie zuhören. Scheuen Sie sich nicht nachzufragen, wenn Sie etwas nicht verstanden haben.

Übersetzen Sie das Gehörte nicht in Ihre Muttersprache.

Vorbereitung

- Vor Unterrichtsbeginn sollten Sie kurz Ihre Notizen zur vorangegangen Unterrichtsstunde lesen. Dadurch werden Sie sich an den bereits besprochenen Lernstoff erinnern und es wird Ihnen helfen, dem neuen Lernstoff zu folgen.
- Sie sollten immer die Materialien für die Unterrichtsstunde vollständig mitbringen, d.h. Bücher, Hefte, verschiedenfarbige Stifte, Papier, usw.

Notizen erstellen

- Hören Sie erst genau zu, bevor Sie anfangen zu schreiben. Wenn Sie sofort drauflos schreiben, kann es passieren, dass Sie die wichtigste Information verpassen, weil Sie sich gerade auf die Mitschrift konzentrieren.
- Hören Sie auf „Signalsätze", die anzeigen, dass das Folgende besonders wichtig ist, z.B. *Remember that …, The most important point …, In conclusion …*
- Schreiben Sie so schnell und effizient wie möglich, indem Sie nur das Wesentliche schreiben und Kurzsätze bzw. Stichworte aufschreiben. Verwenden Sie Abkürzungen, Symbole und Wortverkürzungen (siehe Tabelle).

Symbole		Abkürzungen		Wortverkürzungen	
&, +	and	p., l.	page, line	med	medicine
=	the same as	i.e.	that is	govt	government
≠	not the same as	e.g.	for example	impt	important
♀	female	cf	compare	yth	youth
♂	male	w/	with	tgt	target
%	percent	w/o	without	cert	certificate

- Informationen, die Sie beim Zuhören nicht verstanden haben, markieren Sie mit einem Fragezeichen (?), so dass Sie später nachfragen oder nachschlagen können.

Skills files | Presentations and projects

Überarbeiten der Notizen

- Formulieren Sie Kurzsätze und Stichworte in längere Sätze um.
- Abkürzungen, Symbole und Wortverkürzungen sollten ausgeschrieben werden.
- Beantworten Sie Fragen zu Wörtern oder Informationen, die Sie nicht verstanden haben. Schlagen Sie nach oder fragen Sie Ihre Mitschüler oder Ihren Lehrer.
- Vergleichen Sie Ihre Mitschrift mit der Mitschrift Ihrer Mitschüler. So können Sie Ihre Mitschriften gegenseitig ergänzen.

34 Creating a poster
Ein Plakat erstellen

Ein Plakat ist eine informative, großformatige und übersichtlich gestaltete Form, Arbeitsergebnisse zu präsentieren. In der Regel stehen Plakate nicht für sich alleine, sondern sind als visuelle Unterstützung von Präsentationen gedacht.

Informationen beschaffen und verarbeiten

Bevor Sie mit der Gestaltung des Plakats beginnen, müssen Sie sich mit dem Inhalt beschäftigen. Sammeln Sie Informationen zu Ihrer Aufgabe, lesen Sie Texte, trennen Sie wichtige Informationen von Unwichtigem und fassen Sie schließlich die Inhalte zusammen.

Gliederung der Inhalte

- Auf einem Plakat sollten nie vollständige Sätze stehen, sondern Stichpunkte oder Halbsätze. Deshalb überarbeiten Sie Ihre Zusammenfassungen nun noch einmal, indem Sie Sätze umformulieren und kürzen oder durch Bilder und Symbole ersetzen. Fragen Sie sich an dieser Stelle immer: Welche Botschaft soll das Plakat vermitteln?
- Finden Sie eine passende Überschrift für das Plakat. Die Überschrift sollte nicht zu lang sein, aber für den Leser verständlich. Verwenden Sie also nur Abkürzungen in Überschriften, die allgemein bekannt sind.

Aufbau und Anordnung planen

- Überlegen Sie, ob die Inhalte Ihres Plakats besser im Hochformat oder im Querformat zur Geltung kommen und wie Sie die Überschriften, Textelemente und Bilder anordnen.
- Wenn Sie sich für eine klassische Anordnung der Inhalte entscheiden, dann halten Sie sich an den Aufbau, so wie er im nebenstehenden Schaubild dargestellt ist.
  - Überschrift: über den gesamten Kopf des Plakats,
  - Einleitung: oben links,
  - Schlussfolgerungen: unten links,
  - Sachinformationen und Ergebnisse: füllen den restlichen Platz.

Überschrift

Einleitung

Sachinformationen und Ergebnisse

Schlussfolgerungen

Schrift und Farben

- Ihre Schrift sollte so groß sein, dass sie von allen Positionen des Raumes lesbar ist. Versuchen Sie, gerade zu schreiben. Verwenden Sie möglichst Druckbuchstaben und dicke Stifte.
- Heben Sie Wichtiges durch Farben, Unterstreichungen, Umrahmungen oder Schraffierungen hervor. Verwenden Sie jedoch maximal 3 Farben pro Plakat.

Grammar files

1 **Indefinite article**
Unbestimmter Artikel

2 **Definite article**
Bestimmter Artikel

3 **Plural**
Mehrzahl

4 **Some important prepositions**
Zeitliche und Räumliche Präpositionen,
Präpositionen der Art und Weise

5 **Possessive case**
Genitiv

6 **Comparison of adjectives**
Steigerung der Adjektiven

7 **Adjective and adverb**
Adjektiv und Adverb

8 **Word order with adverbs and adverbials**
Wortstellung bei Adverbien und adverbialen
Bestimmungen (a. B.)

9 **Some or any?**

10 **Some/any + -one/-body/-thing/-where**

11 **Much – many – a lot of**

12 **Little / a little – few / a few**

13 **Modal auxiliaries**
Modale Hilfsverben

14 **Defining relative clauses**
Notwendige Relativsätze

15 **Non-defining relative clauses**
Nicht notwendige Relativsätze

The tenses Die Zeiten

16 **Present simple**

17 **Present continuous**

18 **Past simple**

19 **Past continuous**

20 **Present perfect simple**

21 **Present perfect continuous**

22 **Past perfect simple**

23 **Future with 'going to'**

24 **Will-future**

25 **Question tags**
Frageanhängsel

26 **Reported speech**
Indirekte Rede

27 **Conditionals**
Bedingungssätze

28 **Passive voice**
Passiv

29 **Infinitive**
Infinitiv

30 **Gerund**
Gerundium

31 **Participle**
Partizip

1 Indefinite article
Unbestimmter Artikel

Form

a	college	vor **gesprochenen** Konsonanten
	student	
	university	
an	interview	vor **gesprochenen** Vokalen
	address	
	hour	

Verwendung

| I have bought **a** book for you. | für zählbare Begriffe in der Einzahl |
| He is **a** teacher. | vor Berufsbezeichnungen |

2 Definite article
Bestimmter Artikel

Form

the	course	vor **gesprochenen** Konsonanten
	language	Aussprache [ðə]
	European	
the	engineer	vor **gesprochenen** Vokalen
	office	Aussprache [ði:]
	hour	

Verwendung

the people of London	bei Substantiven (Personen, Dingen,
the life of Lucy Jordan	Abstrakta), wenn sie näher bestimmt sind
the University of Manchester	oder werden
the United States	für Ländernamen im Plural
the Thames, **the** North Sea	für Flüsse und Meere
the Browns	für Eigennamen im Plural
On their tour they visited **the** church.	für die konkrete Bedeutung als Gebäude

Verwendung von Substantiven ohne Artikel

Der Artikel wird abweichend vom Deutschen **nicht** verwendet:

nature, life, time, people	für abstrakte Begriffe und Sammel-bezeichnungen, wenn sie nicht näher bestimmt sind oder werden
Trafalgar Square, Buckingham Palace	für Ortsbezeichnungen
Switzerland, Normandy, Lake Windermere	für Länder, Berge und Seen im Singular
church, school, college When does church begin?	für Gebäudebezeichnungen, wenn die normale Nutzung gemeint ist

3 Plural
Mehrzahl

Form

student college	student**s** college**s**	Die meisten Nomen bilden den Plural durch Anhängen von -s.
universit**y** cit**y**	universit**ies** cit**ies**	Konsonant + y wird zu -ies.
addre**ss** mat**ch**	address**es** match**es**	Nach Zischlauten (z. B. s, ss, ch, sh) wird -es angehängt.
man woman child life	**men** **women** **children** **lives**	Einige Nomen haben unregelmäßige Pluralformen.

Verwendung

information, weather, nature, knowledge, work, furniture	Einige Nomen treten nur im Singular auf.
trousers, jeans, glasses, clothes, thanks, customs, savings	Einige Nomen treten nur im Plural auf.
news, the United States, the United Nations, economics, mathematics, electronics **Example:** No news **is** good news.	Einige Nomen treten nur in der Pluralform auf, das Verb steht jedoch im Singular.
family, government, staff, team, band	Sammelnamen – Plural, wenn eher auf die einzelnen Mitglieder hingewiesen wird – Singular, wenn die Gruppe eher in ihrer Gesamtheit gemeint ist

4 Some important prepositions
Zeitliche und Räumliche Präpositionen, Präpositionen der Art und Weise

Zeitliche Präpositionen

on 20th September **on** Saturday **on** weekdays	**at** six o'clock **at** the age of 16 **at** night	**by** day, **by** Wednesday
	at noon **at** midnight	twelve minutes **to** five
in 1992 **in** the morning **in** the evening	**at** the weekend	(a) quarter **past** six, half **past** nine

Räumliche Präpositionen

go **to** the cinema go **to** college I've been **to** Scotland
at home **at** school **at** the supermarket

Präpositionen der Art und Weise

go **by** bus, car, bike
go **on** foot

5 Possessive case
Genitiv

's-Genitiv

Verwendung bei Personen, Tieren, Zeiten, Personenkollektiven

Henry**'s** exam the baker**'s** (shop)	Nomen im Singular + **'s**
his parents' computer shop the Greens' house	Nomen im Plural + **'**
people**'s** faces children**'s** books	bei Nomen im Plural **ohne** s Anhängung von **'s**
today**'s** newspaper two weeks' pay	Bei Zeiten gelten die gleichen Regeln.
Britain's social problems the party's policy	häufig auch bei Staaten, Städten und Institutionen

of-Genitiv

Verwendung bei Sachen

the title **of** the book the price **of** the computers	Der *of*-Genitiv wird im Singular und im Plural verwendet.

6 Comparison of adjectives
Steigerung von Adjektiven

Form

cheap small	cheap**er** small**er**	cheap**est** small**est**	Steigerung der kurzen Adjektive mit -er und -est
nice	nic**er**	nic**est**	stummes -e entfällt
heavy	heav**ier**	heav**iest**	-y wird zu -ier und -iest
big	bi**gg**er	bi**gg**est	Nach kurzen Vokalen wird der Endkonsonant ver- doppelt.
good bad little	**better** **worse** **less**	**best** **worst** **least**	Einige Adjektive haben unregelmäßige Steigerungsformen.
careful difficult	**more** careful **more** difficult	**most** careful **most** difficult	Alle dreisilbigen und mehrsilbigen Adjektive und alle zweisilbigen Adjektive, die nicht auf -er, -le, -y, -ow enden, werden mit *more* und *most* gesteigert.
careful difficult	**less** careful **less** difficult	**least** careful **least** difficult	Eine Verminderung der Adjektive ist mit *less* und *least* möglich.

Verwendung

In town centres walking is often **as fast as** going by car.	Gleichheit wird mit *as … as* ausgedrückt.
Travelling by plane is **faster than** travelling by train. Travelling by car is **more expensive than** walking.	Ungleichheit kann mit Hilfe des Komparativs und *than* ausgedrückt werden.
A bicycle is **not so expensive as** (isn't **as expensive as**) a car. A bicycle is **less expensive than** a car.	Eine andere Form Ungleichheit auszudrücken, ist *not so … as* oder umgangssprachlich *not as … as*. Wie im Deutschen kann man auch „weniger als" verwenden.
The Concorde was **the fastest** airliner from Paris to New York.	Der Superlativ wird nur benutzt, wenn mehr als zwei Dinge miteinander verglichen werden.

7 Adjective and adverb
Adjektiv und Adverb

Form

Adjective	Adverb	
cheap	cheap**ly**	Das Adverb wird gebildet aus Adjektiv + -ly.
lazy	laz**ily**	-y wird zu -ily
horrible	horrib**ly**	-le wird zu -ly
economic	econom**ically**	-ic wird zu -ically
fast good	**fast** **well**	Einige Adverbien bilden unregelmäßige Formen.

Adjective	Adverb	Adverb	
late	**late** (spät)	**lately** (in letzter Zeit)	Einige Adverbien bilden mehrere Formen.
hard	**hard** (hart)	**hardly** (kaum)	
near	**near** (nah)	**nearly** (beinahe)	

Steigerung von Adverbien

quickly carefully	more quickly more carefully	most quickly most carefully	Alle abgeleiteten Adverbien auf -ly werden mit *more* und *most* gesteigert.
well badly fast	better worse faster	best worst fastest	Unregelmäßige Adverbien haben eigene Steigerungsformen.

Verwendung

There are many **new computers** on the market. **They** are still **expensive**.	Adjektive beziehen sich auf Nomen oder Pronomen.
We can't **control** the technology **exactly**. Comics are **really popular** with children. Modern computers work **extremely quickly**. **Fortunately, she** e-mailed the information to me in time.	Adverbien beziehen sich auf Verben, … Adjektive, … Adverbien, … und ganze Sätze.
He **felt nervous** about his new job.	Nach Verben, die einen Zustand beschreiben (z. B. *feel*, *look* (= aussehen), *smell, taste, sound, be, become, get, seem, appear, keep*) folgt ein Adjektiv.

Grammar files

8 Word order with adverbs and adverbials
Wortstellung bei Adverbien und adverbialen Bestimmungen (a. B.)

Die folgenden Satzstellungen sind üblich.

At nine o'clock he caught the bus **to work**.	Adverbien / a. B. der Zeit stehen am Anfang oder Ende des Satzes. Adverbien / a. B. des Ortes stehen in der Regel am Ende des Satzes.
Mr Woods **always** travels to work by train. He has never missed a train in his life. The train arrives **punctually**.	Adverbien / a. B. der Häufigkeit (z. B. *never, sometimes, often, usually, always*) stehen vor dem Vollverb. Adverbien / a. B. der Art und Weise stehen in der Regel nach dem Verb (den Verben).
The bus drove **slowly** through **London during the rush hour**.	Treten mehrere Adverbien / a. B. zur gleichen Zeit auf, gilt die Regel: Art und Weise vor Ort und Zeit.

9 Some or any?

Verwendung

I need **some** help with this program. **Some** newspapers in Britain only appear on Sundays.	in Aussagesätzen vor unbestimmten Mengen (etwas) oder Anzahlen (einige)
They didn't make **any** money with the new campaign. Some TV stations do not show **any** adverts.	in verneinten Sätzen vor unbestimmten Mengen oder Anzahlen (kein oder keine)
Have they done **any** research on the new product? Have you got **any** ideas for a new logo?	in Fragesätzen vor unbestimmten Mengen (etwas) oder Anzahlen (welche?)
Would you like me to show you **some** examples?	in Fragesätzen, wenn sie eine Aufforderung, Bitte oder ein Angebot enthalten und wenn die Antwort „ja" erwartet wird.
We never needed **any** electronic devices in the past.	nach Wörtern mit negativer Bedeutung

10 Some/any + -one/-body/-thing/-where

Somebody wants to see you. We haven't been **anywhere** this weekend. Have you got **anything** to say?	Die Regeln zum Gebrauch von *some* und *any* gelten auch für diese Formen.

235

Grammar files

11 Much – many – a lot of

Form

much **a lot of**	viel	nicht zählbar
many **a lot of**	viele	zählbar

Verwendung

He spends **a lot of** time practising his communication skills. **A lot of** (many) people have computers in their homes.	In Aussagesätzen wird in der Regel *a lot of* bevorzugt.
I don't have **a lot of/much** money to spend on computers. There aren't **a lot of/many** experts on the staff.	In verneinten Sätzen kann man beide Formen gebrauchen.
How **much** money do you earn? How **many** adverts did they show? They spend too **much** time in front of the screen.	Nach *how* und *too* muss *much* oder *many* stehen.

12 Little/a little – few/a few

Form

We had **little** help during our training. John had only **a little** time to explain. Last week I spent **less** money than the week before. His latest film made the **least** money.	wenig ein bisschen weniger am wenigsten	unzählbar
Few computers never break down. There are **a few** good adverts on TV. There are **fewer** cars on the roads on Sundays. **The fewest** immigrants are from Norway.	wenige ein paar weniger die wenigsten	zählbar

13 Modal auxiliaries
Modale Hilfsverben

Form

Modale Form	Ersatzform	Bedeutung
must	**have to**	müssen
can	**be able to**	können
can	**be allowed to**	dürfen
mustn't **can't**	**not be allowed to**	nicht dürfen
can't	**not be able to**	nicht können
needn't	**not have to**	nicht brauchen/nicht müssen

Verwendung

Cars **must/have to** stop when the lights are red. You **needn't/don't have to** pay in that car park. John **can't/isn't able to** find a parking space.	In der Gegenwart kann entweder die modale Form oder die Ersatzform benutzt werden.
We **had to** turn right at the traffic lights. He **didn't have to** wait as the lights were green. Jane **couldn't/wasn't allowed to** leave her car outside the house, as there was a "No Parking" sign.	Mit Ausnahme von *could* oder *couldn't* können die modalen Hilfsverben keine anderen Zeiten bilden. Für die anderen Zeiten werden die Ersatzformen verwendet.
You **should** go home now. There **may** be some rain today. You **might** even lose your job.	Für einige modale Hilfsverben gibt es keine genau passenden Ersatzformen.

14 Defining relative clauses
Notwendige Relativsätze

Verwendung

Ein Relativsatz ist notwendig, wenn die darin enthaltene Information nötig ist, um zu erkennen, welche Person oder Sache gemeint ist.

The man **who/that** is getting on the bus is on his way to the office. The boy **who/that** was on the platform was waiting for a friend.	Bei Personen werden die Relativpronomen *who* oder *that* verwendet.
The bus **which/that** is at the lights is going to London. The train **which/that** is leaving right now is heading for Bristol.	Bei Sachen wird *which* oder *that* verwendet.
He greeted the man **(who)** he saw on the platform. He read the paper **(which)** he had bought that morning.	Wenn das Relativpronomen Objekt des Relativsatzes ist, kann es weggelassen werden.
The woman **whose** name I always forget is coming to see us.	*Whose* (dessen/deren) wird als possessives Relativpronomen gebraucht.

15 Non-defining relative clauses
Nicht notwendige Relativsätze

Verwendung

Ein Relativsatz ist nicht notwendig, wenn die darin enthaltene Information nicht nötig ist, um zu erkennen, welche Person oder Sache gemeint ist.

Henry's wife, **who is 58**, was waiting for him at the station.	Ein Relativsatz wird durch Kommas vom Hauptsatz getrennt.
The train, **which was an Intercity**, left punctually.	*that* darf hier nicht verwendet werden.
Henry, **who I met at the station**, is retiring next week.	In nicht-notwendigen Relativsätzen darf das Relativpronomen nicht entfallen.

The Tenses
Die Zeiten

16 Present simple

Form

I/you/we/they he/she/it	**live** **lives**	in Leeds.	Aussage
I/you/we/they he/she/it	**do not (don't) live** **does not (doesn't) live**	in Birmingham.	Verneinung

Do **Does**	I/you/we/they he/she/it	**(not)**	**live**	in Liverpool?	(verneinte) Frage
Why Why	**do** you **does** she	**(not)** **(not)**	**work** **like**	on Saturdays? baseball?	

Besonderheiten

Who **How many students**	**likes** **live**	basketball? at home?	Ist das Fragewort Subjekt oder Teil des Subjekts, wird *do/does* nicht verwendet.

Besonderheiten bei der Schreibung der s-Endung

watch, kiss	watch**es**, kiss**es**	*-es* nach Zischlauten
carry, try	carr**ies**, tr**ies**	*-ies*, wenn die Endung *-y* in der Grundform hinter einem Konsonanten steht
go, do	go**es**, do**es**	Ausnahmen beachten!

Verwendung

She **has** a brother.	bei einem Dauerzustand
She **(usually) goes** to college by bus. He **(often) helps** at home.	bei regelmäßigen oder wiederholten Handlungen (oft mit Häufigkeitsadverbien wie *usually, normally, often, sometimes, never, always* – sogenannte *tense markers*)
She **doesn't smoke**.	bei Gewohnheiten
He **has** a flat in Mayfield. I **think** that this **is** a good idea.	bei bestimmten Verben, wenn sie einen Zustand beschreiben, z. B. *be, have, look, think, see, know, like, want*
The train **arrives** at 8 o'clock tomorrow morning.	bei Fahrplänen und Veranstaltungsprogrammen (mit Zukunftsbezug)

17 Present continuous

Form

I you/we/they he/she/it	**am** **are** **is**	**(not)**	**reading** a book.	Aussage und Verneinung
Am **Are** **Is**	I you/we/they he/she/it	**(not)**	**reading** a magazine?	Frage und verneinte Frage Die Kurzform der Verneinung wird mit *aren't* und *isn't* gebildet.

Besonderheiten bei der Schreibung

come, take	co**ming**, ta**king**	*-e* entfällt
sit, run	si**tt**ing, ru**nn**ing	Verdoppelung der Konsonanten am Wortende nach kurzen Vokalen

Verwendung

They **are talking** about their courses.	bei Handlungen, die im Moment des Sprechens stattfinden
She **is studying** for her exam this year. She **is working** at home today.	bei Handlungen, die vorübergehend stattfinden, nicht aber unbedingt im Augenblick
She **is having** a good time. A lot of people **are thinking** about their future.	bei bestimmten Verben (siehe *present simple*), wenn sie eine vorübergehende Handlung und keinen Zustand beschreiben
I **am meeting** him tomorrow.	bei zukünftigen Handlungen (mit Zeitbestimmung)
Some students **are always complaining**.	zur gefühlsbetonten Darstellung von Handlungen in Verbindung mit *always*

Grammar files

18 Past simple

Form

She You	work**ed** need**ed**	in Glasgow a new car.	last year.	Aussagen Grundform + -ed (Infinitiv)

Besonderheiten

mov**e**	mov**ed**	stummes -e entfällt
tr**y**	tr**ied**	Konsonant + y wird zu ie
sto**p**	sto**pped**	Lautverdopplung
go meet	**went** **met**	unregelmäßige Verben haben besondere Formen für das *simple past* dabei wird die 2. Form verwendet

He We	**did not** **(didn't)**	**need** **lose**	special software. the money.	Verneinung

Did	you they it	**(not)**	**move** **live** **take**	to Glasgow? in Birmingham? more than six months?	(verneinte) Frage
Why did	he	**(not)**	**stop**	in Liverpool?	

Verwendung

Jane **moved** to Glasgow seven years ago. First she **worked** for a computer company.	bei Handlungen zu einem bestimmten Zeit- punkt oder in einem abgeschlossenen Zeit- raum in der Vergangenheit (oft mit einer Zeitbestimmung wie z. B. *yesterday, last year, in 1988, … ago, from … until – tense markers*)

19 Past continuous

Form

I/He/She/It	**was**	**(not)** **(wasn't)**	**standing**	on the platform.	(verneinte) Aussage
We/You/They	**were**	**(not)** **(weren't)**			

Verwendung

As/while he **was driving** to the airport, it started to rain. A lot of passengers **were waiting** at the counter when Jason went into the bank.	Für eine Handlung, die schon im Gange war, als eine neue Handlung eintrat, wird die Verlaufsform verwendet.
While **I was reading** a book, my friend **was writing** a letter.	Bei gleichzeitigem Verlauf zweier Handlungen steht die Verlaufsform in beiden Fällen.
What **did** you **do** when Susan **came** in? When she **came** in **I put down** my newspaper and talked to her.	Für Handlungen, die nacheinander statt-fanden, wird in beiden Fällen *past simple* benutzt.

20 Present perfect simple

Form

I/You/We/They	have	(not) (haven't)	**had** a car for three years.	(verneinte) Aussage *have/has* + 3. Form
He/She/It	has	(not) (hasn't)	**sold** 20 million CDs. **been** to Scotland.	

Have	I/you/we/they	(not)	**made** a loss?	(verneinte) Frage
Has	he/she/it		**taken** a photo? **been** here?	

Verwendung

I **have repaired** the car.	bei Handlungen in der Vergangenheit ohne Zeitangabe – das Ergebnis ist oft wichtiger als die Zeitangabe
They **have sold** 50,000 cars **up till now**.	mit Zeitbestimmungen, die einen Zeitraum beschreiben, der noch andauert, z.B. *today, this week, so far, in the last ten years* – *tense markers*
He has **already paid** the bill.	mit bestimmten Adverbien wie z.B. *ever, never, always, yet, just, already* – *tense markers*
How long have you **known** about this particular book? The Browns **have lived** there **for** over three years. We **have lived** here **since** 2006.	bei nicht abgeschlossenen Zuständen mit *how long, since* und *for* – *since* bezieht sich dabei auf einen Zeitpunkt, *for* auf einen Zeitraum Im Deutschen wird hier das Präsens verwen-det, z.B. *Wir leben hier seit 2006.*

Grammar files

21 Present perfect continuous

Form

I/you/we/they	**have**	**been standing.**	*Present simple* von *have* + *been* + *-ing*-Form

Verwendung

How long have you been waiting? I've been waiting … – for half an hour. – since ten o'clock.	bei Handlungen, die in der Vergangenheit begonnen haben und noch andauern – meist in Verbindung mit *how long, since, for* Im Deutschen wird hier das Präsens verwendet – z. B. Ich warte schon seit 10 Uhr.

22 Past perfect simple

Form

I/You/He/She/ It/We/They	**had**	**(not)** **(-n't)**	**travelled** to Paris.	(verneinte) Aussage

Verwendung

After he **had arrived** at the hotel, he went to his room. When **I** arrived at the station, the ticket office **had** already **closed**.	für Handlungen oder Zustände, die vor einem Zeitpunkt in der Vergangenheit abgeschlossen waren

23 Future with 'going to'

Form

I He/She/It We/You/They	**am ('m)** **is ('s)** **are ('re)**	**(not)**	**going to** watch TV.	(verneinte) Aussage
Am **Is** **Are**	I he/she/it we/you/they	**going to have**	a cup of coffee?	Frage

Verwendung

She **is going to answer** the phone.	bei Absichten und Vorhaben
That fax machine **is going to break** down.	bei Vorhersagen, die aufgrund bereits bekannter Fakten oder bisheriger Erfahrungen sicher oder logischerweise in Erfüllung gehen müssen

24 Will-future

Form

I/You/He/She/It We/They	**will** **will not (won't)**	**use** alternative energy. **waste** water.	Aussage Verneinung
Will	I/you/he/she/it we/they	**use** talking computers?	Frage

Verwendung

Computers **will probably do** most of the work.	bei Vorhersagen mit *hope/suppose/expect* und *probably*
Just a minute, **I'll help** you with your shopping.	bei Entscheidungen, die im Moment des Sprechens getroffen werden
I'll phone you tomorrow, I promise.	bei Versprechen
Will you **make** some coffee, please?	um eine Bitte auszudrücken

25 Question tags
Frageanhängsel

Form

Aussagesatz	Frageanhängsel	
You can drive, Pollution is increasing, Trams will improve our public transport service,	**can't you?** **isn't it?** **won't they?**	Das Hilfsverb wird in dem Frageanhängsel wiederholt. Ist der Aussagesatz positiv, so wird das Frageanhängsel verneint.
Statistics aren't always correct,	**are they?**	Ist der Aussagesatz verneint, so wird das Frageanhängsel bejaht.
We enjoyed the journey, She usually goes to Britain,	**didn't we?** **doesn't she?**	Wenn der Aussagesatz kein Hilfsverb enthält, wird das Frageanhängsel mit *to do* in der Zeit des Aussagesatzes gebildet.

Verwendung

Frageanhängsel werden verwendet:

Air travel is really comfortable, **isn't it?**	beim Wunsch nach Bestätigung
You didn't walk here, **did you?**	bei Überraschung
Oh, it's not another traffic jam, **is it?**	bei Verärgerung
Well, that's a really new idea, **isn't it?**	bei ironischen Aussagen

26 Reported speech
Indirekte Rede

Form

Bei Aussagen ändern sich die Zeitformen, wenn das einleitende Verb in der Vergangenheit steht.

"We are protesting about pollution." → Harry said they **were protesting** about pollution. "He doesn't buy cans." → June told me he **didn't buy** cans.	*Present tenses* werden zu *past tenses*.
"Watson's opened four supermarkets in 2008." → Fred pointed out that Watson's **had opened** four supermarkets in 2008. "They have started a bus service." → He added that they **had started** a bus service.	*Simple past* und *present perfect* werden zu *past perfect*.
"There will be more 'green' products." → Sue went on to say that there **would be** more 'green' products.	*will* wird zu *would*.

Weitere Änderungen bei Aussagen

"I can save more energy." → Harry told me that **he** could save more energy.	Die Pronomen werden angepasst.
"We are meeting the town planner tomorrow." → Sue added that they were meeting the town planner **the next day**. "I bought the car three days ago." → He said that he had bought the car **three days before**.	Orts- (z. B. *here* wird zu *there*) und Zeitbestimmungen werden angepasst.

Fragen

"What are you doing about waste?" → **They asked what we were doing** about waste. "When did you introduce bicycle routes?" → **We wanted to know when they had introduced** bicycle routes.	Bei Fragen wird die Wortstellung geändert.

Verwendung

Indirekte Rede wird benutzt, wenn berichtet werden soll, was jemand gesagt oder gefragt hat.

27 Conditionals
Bedingungssätze

Form

Typ 1

If-Satz	Hauptsatz	
If **we fit** a shower, If **you go** to Paris,	**we will** save water. **you can** see the Eiffel Tower.	*Present simple* wird für das Verb im If-Satz, Futur mit *will* für das Verb im Hauptsatz verwendet.
If **you want** to stay alive,	don't drink and drive!	Im Hauptsatz kann in manchen Fällen ein modales Hilfsverb mit Verb oder ein Imperativ stehen.

Typ 2

If-Satz	Hauptsatz	
If the government **developed** solar energy,	there **would be** less pollution.	*Past simple* wird für das Verb im If-Satz, *Conditional I (would)* für das Verb im Hauptsatz verwendet.
If I **were** Environment Minister,	I **could** put my ideas about energy into practice.	*could* oder *might* sind Alternativen zu *would* im Hauptsatz.

Typ 3

If-Satz	Hauptsatz	
If Tom and Kate **had insulated** their roof years ago,	they **would have saved** a lot of money.	*Past perfect* wird für das Verb im If-Satz, *Conditional II (would have)* für das Verb im Hauptsatz verwendet.

Verwendung

Typ 1 wird verwendet, wenn es sich um eine erfüllbare Bedingung in der Gegenwart oder Zukunft handelt: "Was passiert / wird passieren, wenn …?"

Typ 2 wird verwendet, wenn es sich um eine unerfüllbare Bedingung in der Gegenwart handelt: "Was würde passieren, wenn …?"

Typ 3 wird verwendet, wenn über eine nicht mehr erfüllbare Bedingung in der Vergangenheit gesprochen wird: "Was wäre passiert, wenn …?"

Grammar files

28 Passive voice
Passiv

Form

The robots **are equipped** with sensors. This motor **was not made** in Great Britain. **Will** the new car **be sold** in Japan?	Form von *be* in der jeweiligen Zeit + Partizip Perfekt (3. Form) des Verbs
Now the wheels **can be fitted**. The car **must be tested** first.	Bei der Benutzung von Hilfsverben wird das Hilfsverb + *be* + Partizip Perfekt (3. Form) des Verbs verwendet.

Verwendung

These cars **were made** in Germany. The handbook **is written** in English.		hauptsächlich in der Schriftsprache, wenn der Ausführende unbekannt, unwichtig oder selbstverständlich ist
This information **is checked by** the central computer.		Wenn der Ausführende allerdings genannt werden soll, dann benutzt man die Präposition *by (by-agent)*.
It is said **It is reported** **It is believed** **It is supposed**	that computers will become even more important in the future.	bei Verben des Meinens und Berichtens
He is said to be rich.		
English **is spoken** here. = Man spricht Englisch. We **will be told** the result later. = Man wird uns später das Ergebnis sagen.		Im Deutschen wird ein Aktivsatz mit ‚man' bevorzugt.

29 Infinitive
Infinitiv

Verwendung

ohne *to*

We **must write** a report about our trip to England.	nach den meisten Hilfsverben
Our new teachers **make us work** very hard, but on Friday they **let us go** home early.	nach *make* und *let* + direktem Objekt

mit *to*

The teacher **asked me to show** my photos of Newcastle. She **told them to wait** outside for a moment.	nach bestimmten Verben (*ask/tell/advise/expect* etc.)
This is not **easy to understand**. I am **surprised to hear** that.	nach Adjektiven
I do not know **what to do**.	nach Fragewörtern

Grammar files

30 Gerund
Gerundium

Verwendung

Drinking and **driving** is dangerous.	als Subjekt
I **enjoy swimming.**	als Objekt nach Verben ohne Präpositionen, wenn eine allgemeingültige Situation beschrieben wird: z.B. *enjoy/like/dislike/hate/stop/start/avoid/suggest/mind/love/recommend/prefer*
I **look forward to seeing** you again. He is **tired of waiting** here. They saw the **danger of destroying** the environment.	nach Verben/Adjektiven/Substantiven mit Präpositionen
He has helped me a lot **by giving** me that map of Newcastle. The child crossed the road **without looking**.	nach Präpositionen mit adverbialer Bedeutung, z.B. *by/without/instead of*
Normally I enjoy swimming but today I **would prefer to play** tennis. I **remember learning** those rules. = *Ich erinnere mich daran, dass ich die Regeln gelernt habe.* I **must remember to learn** these rules. = *Ich muss daran denken, diese Regeln zu lernen.*	Statt des Gerundiums wird der Infinitiv verwendet, wenn es sich um eine Ausnahmesituation handelt (oft mit *would*) oder wenn die Bedeutung des Satzes die Verwendung des Gerundiums nicht zulässt, z.B. bei *stop/start/remember*.

31 Participle
Partizip

Form

Es gibt zwei Formen des Partizips.

waiting/going/watching	Partizip Präsens
waited/gone/watched	Partizip Perfekt

Verwendung

The weather forecast for the **coming** week … The weather in New York last week was rather **mixed**.	als Adjektiv
You can find several families **living** in one flat. There are a lot of restaurants there especially **built** for the tourists.	anstelle von Relativsätzen
After talking to the press they started their demonstration. **Having discussed** the problem with the President personally, they flew home to California.	als Verkürzung von Adverbialsätzen (*after/before/because/while* etc.)

247

Unit vocabulary

Videotraining: Englische Aussprache

Perfekte englische Aussprache leicht gemacht: Mit dem Lernprogramm zur englischen Lautschrift können Sie alle Laute einüben. Wählen Sie einfach in der Navigation rechts den entsprechenden Reiter (*Vowels* oder *Consonants*) aus und dann klicken Sie auf das gewünschte phonetische Symbol. Sprechen Sie die Worte laut nach.
Unter www.klett.de geben Sie einfach den Online-Link 808201-1000 ein. Von dort aus können Sie die Webanwendung online starten.

Abkürzungen und Zeichen

etw.	= etwas	=	entspricht	Vor den Vokabeln
pl.	= Plural	↔	ist das Gegenteil von	finden Sie immer
sing.	= Singular	→	verwandt mit	die jeweiligen
so./sb.	= someone/somebody	CD	Vokabel aus Hörtext	Übungsnummern
sth.	= something			
BE	= britisches Englisch			
AE	= amerikanisches Englisch			

1 Preparing for the world of work

A

above [əˈbʌv]	oben	above = over; There's a nice picture above the table in Becky's room.
impression [ɪmˈpreʃn]	Eindruck	She has made a good impression.
blog [blɒg]	Internet-Tagebuch	a diary on the Internet
below [bɪˈləʊ]	unten	below = under; The TV magazine is on the shelf below the TV. Look, down there!
business studies [ˈbɪznɪsˌstʌdɪz]	Betriebswirtschaftslehre	subject at college in which you learn about the production and the buying and selling of goods and services
ICT [ˌaɪsiːˈtiː]	Informations- und Kommunikationstechnologie (Kurzform)	information and communication technology
Geneva [dʒəˈniːvə]	Genf	big city in Switzerland
Switzerland [ˈswɪtsələnd]	Schweiz	country south of Germany
full-time (F/T) [ˌfʊlˈtaɪm]	Vollzeit-, ganztags	full-time ↔ part-time
marketing [ˈmɑːkɪtɪŋ]	Marketing	Using advertisements etc. to try to sell products.
placement [ˈpleɪsmənt]	Praktikum	A position you have for a short time with a company in order to learn about the work there.
advertising agency [ˈædvətaɪzɪŋ ˌeɪdʒənsi]	Werbeagentur	company that plans advertisements for other companies
market research department [ˌmɑːkɪt ˈriːsɜːtʃ dɪˌpɑːtmənt]	Marktforschungsabteilung	part of a company that tries to find out about customers' wishes
concerning [kənˈsɜːnɪŋ]	betreffend, bezüglich	regarding

Unit vocabulary

	dislike ['dɪslaɪk]	Abneigung	What are your likes and dislikes? = What do you like and what don't you like?
	personality [ˌpɜːsn'æləti]	Persönlichkeit	personality → person
B 1	**leaver** ['liːvə]	Schulabgänger(in)	The student left school. He is a school leaver.
	adult ['ædʌlt]	Erwachsene(r)	Tickets cost $3 for children (under 18) and $5 for adults.
	Geography [dʒɪ'ɒgrəfi]	Geographie	In Geography lessons we learn about different countries.
	Science [saɪəns]	Wissenschaft	Achtung Aussprache: Das erste 'c' wird nicht gesprochen.
	Biology [baɪ'ɒlədʒi]	Biologie	You learn about animals and trees in Biology lessons.
	Physics ['fɪzɪks]	Physik	Science = Biology, Chemistry, Physics
	project ['prɒdʒekt]	Projekt	I'm busy with the school project.
	presentation [ˌprezn'teɪʃn]	Präsentation	We've got lots of information for our presentation to the class.
	essay ['eseɪ]	Aufsatz	In school I had to write an essay about why children are not allowed to smoke.
	term [tɜːm]	Trimester, Begriff	In Britain, one of the three periods of time between the school holidays: the autumn term, the spring term and the summer term.
	placement ['pleɪsmənt]	Praktikum, Platzierung	During a work placement you can see if you like the job.
	prompt [prɒmpt]	Stichwort	keyword
	website ['websaɪt]	Website, Internetseite	You can find lots of information about London on the website.
B 3	**lunchtime** ['lʌntʃtaɪm]	Mittagszeit	lunchtime → lunch
	library ['laɪbrərɪ]	Bibliothek	There are many interesting books in our library.
	project ['prɒdʒekt]	Projekt, Vorhaben	This week we are doing a German project.
	normally ['nɔːməlɪ]	normalerweise	usually, regularly
C	**nationality** [ˌnæʃn'æləti]	Nationalität	nationality → national
	cosmopolitan atmosphere [kɒsməˌpɒlɪtn 'ætməsfɪə]	weltoffene Atmosphäre	New York City has a cosmopolitan atmosphere because of the different cultures living there.
	multicultural [ˌmʌltɪ'kʌltʃərəl]	multikulturell	London and New York are multicultural cities.
	stay [steɪ]	Aufenthalt	stay → to stay
	paperboy ['peɪpəbɔɪ]	Zeitungsausträger	
	chef [ʃef]	Koch, Köchin	A false friend: der Chef = the boss; der Koch = the chef
	to socialize ['səʊʃəlaɪz]	ausgehen	When you socialize, you go out with or meet your friends.
	to settle ['setl]	einleben	I have just moved here. I still have not settled in.
	suitable ['suːtəbl]	geeignet	Warm jackets and thick shoes are suitable for cold weather.
	European [jʊərə'piːən]	europäisch	Germany and England are European countries.
	salesperson ['seɪlzˌpɜːsn]	Verkäufer(in)	person who sells goods
	practice ['præktɪs]	Praxis, Übung	rooms where a dentist treats his patients
	bank employee ['bæŋk ɪmˌplɔɪiː]	Bankkaufmann, Bankkauffrau	person who works at a bank
	doctor's assistant ['dɒktəz əˌsɪstənt]	medizinische(r) Fachangestellte(r)	person who helps at the doctor's
	to assist [ə'sɪst]	assistieren, helfen	to help
	to advise (sb. to do sth.) [əd'vaɪz]	(jmdm.) raten (etwas zu tun)	If you advise sb. to do sth., you tell them it would be a good idea.
	industrial [ɪn'dʌstrɪəl]	Industrie-	industrial → industry
	merchant ['mɜːtʃənt]	Kaufmann, Kauffrau	person who buys and sells
	assistant tax consultant [əˌsɪstənt ˌtæks kən'sʌltənt]	Steuerfachangestellte(r)	person who helps other people to save money
	dental assistant [ˌdentl ə'sɪstənt]	zahnmedizinische(r) Fachangestellte(r)	person who helps at the dentist's
	to save [seɪv]	sparen, retten	I am saving my money to buy a new bike.
	European [jʊərə'piːən]	Europäer(in)	Europe → European
	journalist ['dʒɜːnəlɪst]	Journalist(in)	A journalist writes for a newspaper.
	to interview ['ɪntəvjuː]	befragen	The journalist interviewed Brad Pitt about his latest movie.

Unit vocabulary

	to act out [ækt 'aʊt]	ausführen, durchspielen	to act → action
	role [rəʊl]	Rolle	Brad Pitt plays a role in the new film.
	country of origin [ˌkʌntrɪ əv 'ɒrɪdʒɪn]	Herkunftsland	Your country of origin is the country you were born in.
	workplace ['wɜːkpleɪs]	Arbeitsplatz	workplace → work → worker → to work
D 1	situation [ˌsɪtjʊ'eɪʃn]	Situation	what is happening at the moment
	sales talk ['seɪlz ˌtɔːk]	Verkaufsgespräch	The salesman is very good at sales talk: he sells a lot of products.
	location [ləʊ'keɪʃn]	Einrichtung, Standort, Lage	The hotel was in a good location.
	top [tɒp]	Top, Oberteil	Hannah wore her new top last night.
	salad ['sæləd]	Salat	Would you like vegetables or a green salad?
	right-hand ['raɪthænd]	rechtsseitig, rechts stehend	In Germany the cars drive on the right-hand side of the road.
	the background [ðə 'bækgraʊnd]	der Hintergrund	You can see mountains in the background of the picture.
	left-hand ['lefthænd]	linksseitig, links stehend	In England the cars drive on the left-hand side of the road.
	the foreground [ðə 'fɔːgraʊnd]	der Vordergrund	foreground ↔ background
	to scream [skriːm]	schreien	Don't scream at me!
	to consist of [kən'sɪst ɒv]	bestehen aus	to be made up of
CD	to get changed [get 'tʃeɪndʒd]	sich umziehen	It is getting warmer. I think I will get changed and put a T-shirt on.
	to take orders [teɪk 'ɔːdəz]	Bestellungen entgegennehmen	The waiter took our orders. We wanted some cake and tea.
	tip [tɪp]	Trinkgeld	Before you leave a café or restaurant, you normally leave a tip.
D 2	to scan [skæn]	scannen, durchsuchen	To look at sth. (a text etc.) very carefully because you are looking for special details.
	cash desk ['kæʃ ˌdesk]	Kasse	the place in a shop where you pay
	storage room ['stɔːrɪdʒ ˌruːm]	Lagerraum	room where you keep things
	incoming goods department [ˌɪnkʌmɪŋ'gʊdz dɪˌpɑːtmənt]	Wareneingang	place at a company where the goods arrive
	stocks [stɒks]	Vorrat	goods that are kept in a shop for sale

2 Getting a job

A 1	personnel [ˌpɜːsən'el]	Personal	The personnel manager looks for the right person for the right job.
	manufacturing [ˌmænjə'fæktʃərɪŋ]	Herstellung	manufacturing → to manufacture
	research [rɪ'sɜːtʃ]	Forschung	research → to research
	to operate ['ɒpəreɪt]	bedienen	If you operate a machine, you make it do its work.
	raw material [ˌrɔː mə'tɪərɪəl]	Rohstoff	Germany must import a lot of its raw materials.
	recipe ['resɪpɪ]	Rezept	I have a good recipe for chocolate cookies.
	sweet [swiːt]	Süßigkeit	The children eat too many sweets.
	phrase [freɪz]	Ausdruck	'Good' is a word, 'be good at' is a phrase.
	brand [brænd]	Marke	The Levis brand is known all over the world.
	headquarters [ˌhed'kwɔːtəz]	Zentrale, Stammsitz	Many international companies have their headquarters in the USA.
	home-made [ˌhəʊm'meɪd]	hausgemacht	Did you buy that cake? – No, it's home-made.
	huge [hjuːdʒ]	riesig	very big
	confectionery [kən'fekʃənrɪ]	Süßwaren	sweets and chocolates
	ever since [ˌevə 'sɪns]	seitdem	I've been a fan of Tokio Hotel ever since I heard their first song.
	frozen ['frəʊzn]	gefroren	The lake was frozen in the cold weather.
	business field ['bɪznɪs ˌfiːld]	Geschäftsbereich	Big companies often operate in different business fields (production, banking, insurance).
	convenience food [kən'viːnɪəns ˌfuːd]	Fertiggericht	food which is frozen or dried so that it can be cooked easily

250

Unit vocabulary

A 2	**sharp** [ʃɑːp]	steil, stark, scharf	sharp → sharply
	steady ['stedɪ]	stetig	steady → steadily
B 1	**to expand** [ɪk'spænd]	(sich) ausdehnen, expandieren	to expand → expansion
	superstore ['suːpəstɔː]	großer Supermarkt	In a superstore you can buy nearly everything.
	independent [ˌɪndɪ'pendənt]	unabhängig	independent → to depend → independence
	dealer ['diːlə]	Händler(in)	A dealer buys and sells things.
	retailer ['riːteɪlə]	Einzelhändler(in)	A retailer is a person who sells goods to consumers.
	letter ['letə]	Buchstabe	There are four letters in the word 'joke'.
B 3	**yourself** [jɔː'self]	selbst	You shouldn't talk about yourself all the time.
	fluency ['fluːənsɪ]	Sprachbeherrschung, Sprachgewandtheit	fluency → fluent
B 4	**bracket** ['brækɪt]	Klammer	These are brackets: ( ).
	chain [tʃeɪn]	Kette	A supermarket chain is a large number of shops that belong to the same person.
	to type [taɪp]	tippen	It's easier to read a text that has been typed than one that has been written by hand.
	loaf of bread [ˌləʊf_əv 'bred]	Brotlaib	I went to the bakery and bought a loaf of bread.
C	**application** [ˌæplɪ'keɪʃn]	Bewerbung	application → to apply → applicant
	curriculum vitae [kəˌrɪkjələm 'viːtaɪ]	Lebenslauf	curriculum vitae (CV) = résumé
	permanent ['pɜːmənənt]	dauerhaft	for a longer time
	fluent [fluːənt]	flüssig	If you are fluent in English, you can speak it easily and well.
	ignorant ['ɪgnərənt]	ignorant	ignorance → to ignore → ignorant
	qualification [ˌkwɒlɪfɪ'keɪʃn]	Qualifikation	If you have a driving licence, you have the qualification to be a driver.
	accountancy [ə'kaʊntənsɪ]	Rechnungswesen, Buchführung	keeping the books in a company
	essential [ɪ'sentʃl]	wichtig	very important
	requirement [rɪ'kwaɪəmənt]	Anforderung	requirement → to require
	with reference to [wɪð 'refrəns tuː]	betreffend, bezüglich	
	advert ['ædvɜːt, əd'vɜːtɪsmənt]	Anzeige	advert = advertisement
	open-minded [ˌəʊpn'maɪndɪd]	aufgeschlossen, unvoreingenommen	
	to gather ['gæðə]	(sich) sammeln	collect
	retail trade ['riːteɪl ˌtreɪd]	Einzelhandel	companies that sell goods to consumers
	shelf, pl. **shelves** [ʃelf, ʃelvz]	Regal	You keep books on a shelf.
	control [kən'trəʊl]	Kontrolle	Are there any problems? – No, everything is under control.
	checkout ['tʃekaʊt]	Kasse, Abschlusskontrolle, Auschecken	That supermarket has ten checkouts.
	reputation [ˌrepjə'teɪʃn]	Ansehen, Ruf	The firm has a reputation for quality products.
	rewarding [rɪ'wɔːdɪŋ]	lohnend	rewarding → reward
	to enclose [ɪn'kləʊz]	beifügen	If you enclose sth., you put it in with the letter you want to send.
	challenge ['tʃælɪndʒ]	Herausforderung	His new job was a real challenge.
	further education [ˌfɜːðər edjʊ'keɪʃn]	höhere Schulbildung, Aus- und Weiterbildung	you can get further education at a college
	intermediate [ˌɪntə'miːdɪət]	Zwischen-, dazwischen liegend	being between two levels
	secondary school ['sekəndrɪ ˌskuːl]	weiterführende Schule	a kind of high school between primary school and college or university
	active ['æktɪv]	aktiv	action → to act out → active
	driving licence ['draɪvɪŋ ˌlaɪsəns]	Führerschein	

251

Unit vocabulary

D 1	candidate ['kændɪdət]	Bewerber(in)	someone who is trying to get a job
	motor mechanic ['məʊtə mɪˌkænɪk]	Kfz-Mechaniker(in)	someone who repairs cars
	nursery school ['nɜːsərɪ ˌskuːl]	Vorschule	a school for young children between three and five years of age
	bank clerk ['bæŋkˌklɑːk]	Bankkaufmann/-frau	person who works in a bank
	electrician [ˌelɪk'trɪʃn]	Elektriker(in)	someone who repairs electric equipment
CD	convinced [kən'vɪnst]	überzeugt	
	to support [sə'pɔːt]	unterstützen	If you support people, you agree with them and help them.
	to intend [ɪn'tend]	beabsichtigen	intention → to intend
	to get an insight [ˌget ən 'ɪnsaɪt]	einen Einblick bekommen	
	on offer [ɒn 'ɒfə]	im Angebot	There is 50 % off the shoes. They are on offer.
	applicant ['æplɪkənt]	Bewerber(in)	applicant → to apply → application
D 2	word web ['wɜːd ˌweb]	Wortnetz	a diagram you can make to collect ideas about a topic
	social ['səʊʃl]	sozial, gesellschaftlich	Rich people and poor people often come from different social backgrounds.
	reliable [rɪ'laɪəbl]	zuverlässig	someone you can depend on is reliable
	character ['kærɪktə]	Charakter, (Roman-)Figur	the kind of person you are
D 3	plant [plɑːnt]	Fabrikanlage	factory
	purchasing ['pɜːtʃəsɪŋ]	Einkauf	buying goods
	administration [ədˌmɪnɪ'streɪʃn]	Verwaltung, Regierung, Behörde	the management of an office

3 Marketing and advertising

A 1	target ['tɑːgɪt]	Ziel	aim, goal
A 2	heading ['hedɪŋ]	Überschrift	Each part of the article has got a different heading.
	ending ['endɪŋ]	Ende	ending → to end
	lonely ['ləʊnlɪ]	einsam	I'm often alone, but I don't feel lonely.
	cafeteria [ˌkæfə'tɪərɪə]	Kantine, Cafeteria	cafeteria → café
	truthful ['truːθfəl]	ehrlich	honest
	trainer ['treɪnə]	Turnschuh	running shoe
	similar ['sɪmɪlə]	ähnlich	similar ↔ different; similar → similarly
	logo ['ləʊgəʊ]	Firmenemblem	a design or symbol that a company uses to advertise its products
	tick [tɪk]	Häkchen	Put a tick next to the correct answer.
	stripe [straɪp]	Streifen	The US flag is called the 'stars and stripes'.
	silver ['sɪlvə]	Silber	Rings are made of gold or silver.
	confused [kən'fjuːzd]	verwirrt	If you are confused, you do not understand what is happening.
A 3	no-name product [ˌnəʊneɪm 'prɒdʌkt]	Billigprodukt, ohne Markenname	no-name product ↔ branded product
	packaging ['pækɪdʒɪŋ]	Verpackungsmaterial	packaging → to pack
A 4	consumer [kən'sjuːmə]	Konsument(in), Verbraucher(in)	someone who buys or uses goods or services
	item ['aɪtəm]	Punkt, Gegenstand	thing
	mobile phone [ˌməʊbaɪl 'fəʊn]	Mobiltelefon, Handy	mobile phone (BE) = mobile, cellphone (AE); false friend: handy (English) = praktisch (German)
	cosmetics [kɒz'metɪks]	Kosmetik	make-up
	common ['kɒmən]	gemeinsam, gebräuchlich	What do these boys have in common? – They both play football; common → commonly
B 1	portrait ['pɔːtrət]	Portrait, Konterfei	painting or photograph of a person
	art [ɑːt]	Kunst	Becky likes art at school because she's good at drawing.
	unlimited [ʌn'lɪmɪtɪd]	grenzenlos, unbegrenzt	His knowledge seemed unlimited.
	to try on [traɪ 'ɒn]	anprobieren	That's a nice T-shirt, Lisa. Why don't you try it on?
	to exchange [ɪks'tʃeɪndʒ]	umtauschen, austauschen	This CD doesn't work. I would like to exchange it.

Unit vocabulary

B 2	**dialogue** ['daɪəlɒg]	Dialog, Gespräch	dialogue *(BE)* = dialog *(AE)*
	underlined [ˌʌndə'laɪnd]	unterstrichen	underlined → to underline
	to act out [ækt 'aʊt]	aufführen	The actor acted out his role perfectly.
B 3	**to get dressed** [get ˌ'drest]	sich anziehen	to put clothes on
	to drop [drɒp]	(herunter)fallen, fallen lassen	to drop → drop (of water)
B 4	**to unpack** [ʌn'pæk]	auspacken	unpack ↔ pack
	commercial [kə'mɜːʃl]	Werbespot	During TV shows there are commercials for cars, coffee, mobiles …
C 1	**advertiser** ['ædvətaɪzə]	Inserent(in), Werbefachmann/-frau	advertiser → to advertise → advertisement
	to behave [bɪ'heɪv]	sich benehmen	You're silly! You behave like a little child.
	in particular [ɪn pə'tɪkjʊlə]	im Besonderen	in particular = especially
	at risk [ət 'rɪsk]	gefährdet	at risk → to risk → risk (of death)
	County Council [ˌkaʊntɪ 'kaʊnsəl]	etwa: Kreisverwaltung	local government of a county in Britain
	tip [tɪp]	Tipp, Hinweis	I can give you tips for your trip to England.
	extract ['ekstrækt]	Auszug	An extract from a book is just a small part of the story.
	right [raɪt]	Recht	Children don't have the right to drive cars. It's illegal.
	trader ['treɪdə]	Händler(in)	trader → to trade → trade
	additional [ə'dɪʃnl]	zusätzlich	additional → to add → additionally
	confirmation [ˌkɒnfə'meɪʃn]	Bestätigung	The confirmation comes as an e-mail.
	to cancel ['kænsəl]	absagen	One of the singers was ill, so the concert was cancelled.
	regulation [ˌregjʊ'leɪʃn]	Regelung, Vorschrift	Don't risk accidents, watch the traffic regulations!
	cooling-off period [ˌkuːlɪŋˌɒf ˌpɪərɪəd]	Widerspruchsfrist	Within the cooling-off period the buyer can get his money back.
	auction ['ɔːkʃn]	Versteigerung	You can buy things cheaply in an auction.
	platform ['plætfɔːm]	Plattform	The train leaves from platform 3.
	to trust [trʌst]	vertrauen	to trust someone = to believe that someone is honest
	feedback ['fiːdbæk]	Rückmeldung, Feedback	You get feedback when the other person says something about what you said or did.
	to be based [bɪ 'beɪst]	Geschäftssitz haben	Your company is based in London.
	bid [bɪd]	Gebot	an offer to pay a particular sum of money in an auction; bid → to bid
	postage ['pəʊstɪdʒ]	Porto, Postgebühr	If you don't want your letter to come back, put enough postage on it.
	payment ['peɪmənt]	Bezahlung	payment → to pay
	scam [skæm]	Betrug	a banking scam
	text message ['tekst ˌmesɪdʒ]	Textmitteilung, SMS	SMS = short message service
	premium rate number [ˌpriːmɪəmˌreɪt 'nʌmbə]	Sonderrufnummer	At a premium rate of £2.50 you can buy a game for your mobile phone.
	to delete [dɪ'liːt]	löschen	When you type a wrong letter on your PC, you can delete it again.
	ringtone ['rɪŋtəʊn]	Klingelton	My best friend has his favourite song as a ringtone on his mobile phone.
	wallpaper ['wɔːlˌpeɪpə]	Hintergrundbild, Tapete	My boyfriend has my picture as a wallpaper on his computer screen.
	alert [ə'lɜːt]	Alarm	a signal that warns of a danger
	short code ['ʃɔːt ˌkəʊd]	Kurzwahlnummer	To get the latest football news send an SMS with 'football' to the short code 72404.
	to change one's mind [ˌtʃeɪndʒ wʌnzˌ'maɪnd]	seine Meinung ändern	I've changed my mind. I don't want to go out with you anymore.
	summary ['sʌmərɪ]	Zusammenfassung	a very short version of a text which gives only the most important points
	certain ['sɜːtn]	bestimmt, gewiss	If you say you have certain things to do, you mean definite things, but you don't say what they are.
	detailed ['diːteɪld]	detailliert	detailed → detail
	relevant ['reləvənt]	relevant, bedeutend	relevant ↔ irrelevant
	to purchase ['pɜːtʃəs]	kaufen	to purchase → a purchase

Unit vocabulary

	local council [ˌləʊkl ˈkaʊnsəl]	etwa: Gemeinderat	government of a town in Britain
	task [tɑːsk]	Aufgabe	a piece of work, especially sth. that is difficult or that you don't enjoy doing
C 2	contract [ˈkɒntrækt]	Vertrag	to agree in a contract (= einen Vertrag abschließen)
	to persuade [pəˈsweɪd]	überreden	If you want to persuade someone to do something, it's important to find good arguments.
D 1 CD	expert [ˈekspɜːt]	Experte/Expertin	a person who knows a lot about a subject
	quiet [kwaɪət]	Ruhe	quiet ↔ noise
	cooking [ˈkʊkɪŋ]	Kochen	cooking → to cook → the cook
	missing [ˈmɪsɪŋ]	fehlend, vermisst	Not all the letters have arrived. Two are missing.
	crime [kraɪm]	Verbrechen, Kriminalität	Stealing money is a crime.
	to be on [bɪ ˈɒn]	zu sehen sein (Sendung)	to be shown
	fascinated [ˈfæsɪneɪtɪd]	fasziniert	fascinated → fascinating → fascination
	climate [ˈklaɪmət]	Klima	The kind of weather that is typical of a country or an area.
	extreme [ɪkˈstriːm]	extrem	Extreme weather means that it is very cold, very hot and/or very windy in an area.
	catastrophic [ˌkætəˈstrɒfɪk]	katastrophal	catastrophic → catastrophe
	hurricane [ˈhʌrɪkən]	Wirbelsturm, Hurrikan	Tornados and hurricanes are very bad storms.
	level [ˈlevl]	Niveau, Pegelstand	He plays football at a very high level.
	lifetime [ˈlaɪftaɪm]	Lebensdauer, Lebenszeit, Lebzeiten	as long as a person lives
	planet [ˈplænɪt]	Planet	The Earth is a planet.
	slogan [ˈsləʊgən]	Slogan, Werbespruch	a short phrase that a company uses to advertise its products
	gender [ˈdʒendə]	Geschlecht	The gender of a girl is female.
	to create [krɪˈeɪt]	schaffen	to create → creative → creativity
	flyer [ˈflaɪə]	Flugblatt	flyer → to fly
D 2	agency [ˈeɪdʒənsɪ]	Agentur	NASA is the US space agency.
	jingle [ˈdʒɪŋgl]	Jingle, kurze Tonfolge in der Werbung	a short melody which is easy to remember
	storyline [ˈstɔːrɪlaɪn]	Handlung	The movie has a boring storyline.
	script [skrɪpt]	Drehbuch	The actor didn't want to act in the film because he didn't like the script.
	to market [ˈmɑːkɪt]	vermarkten, verkaufen	to sell
	promotion [prəˈməʊʃn]	Werbung, Promotion	promotion → to promote
	uniqueness [jʊˈniːknəs]	Einzigartigkeit	uniqueness → unique
	discount [ˈdɪskaʊnt]	Rabatt, Nachlass	Let's buy this MP3 player, it's really cheap. There's a 50% discount on it!
	billboard [ˈbɪlbɔːd]	Plakatwand, Werbetafel	board on which posters and adverts are displayed outdoors
	merchandising [ˈmɜːtʃəndaɪzɪŋ]	Verkaufsförderung, Merchandising, Vermarktung	In a merchandising campaign a football club sells products with the club's logo.
	sponsoring [ˈspɒnsərɪŋ]	Sponsoring, Förderung, finanzielle Unterstützung	A famous beer brand is the sponsor of the tennis championship.
	distribution [ˌdɪstrɪˈbjuːʃn]	Vertrieb, Verteilung	distribution → to distribute
	retailing [ˈriːteɪlɪŋ]	Einzelhandel	retailing → to retail → retailer
D 3	formula [ˈfɔːmjələ]	Formel	You need formulas in mathematics.
	theory [ˈθɪərɪ]	Theorie	theory ↔ practice
	marketing [ˈmɑːkɪtɪŋ]	Marketing	using advertisements etc. in order to sell products
	to attract [əˈtrækt]	anziehen	to attract → attraction → attractive
	to analyze [ˈænəlaɪz]	analysieren	to examine the details of something carefully in order to understand or explain it
D 4	to ban [bæn]	verbieten	In Germany they have banned smoking in schools.
	representative [ˌreprɪˈzentətɪv]	Vertreter(in)	representative → to represent
	ban [bæn]	Verbot	a ban → to ban

Unit vocabulary

4 Media in our lives

A 1	**bar chart** [ˈbɑː ˌtʃɑːt]	Säulendiagramm, Balkendiagramm	bar graph
A 2	**to tend (to)** [tend]	zu etwas neigen	to tend → tendency
	screen [skriːn]	Bildschirm	TVs and computers have screens.
	monitor [ˈmɒnɪtə]	Monitor, Bildschirm	You can see pictures or texts on the monitor of a PC.
	electronic [ˌelekˈtrɒnɪk]	elektronisch	Electronic equipment includes things like televisions, computers etc.
	surprising [səˈpraɪzɪŋ]	überraschend	surprising → surprise → to surprise
	educational [ˌedʒʊˈkeɪʃnl]	lehrreich, bildend	There's a lot of rubbish on TV, but there are also some educational programmes.
	constant [ˈkɒnstənt]	beständig, andauernd, konstant	constant → constantly
	average [ˈævərɪdʒ]	Durchschnitt	a typical amount
	scientist [ˈsaɪəntɪst]	Wissenschaftler(in)	scientist → science → scientific
	brain [breɪn]	Gehirn	Your brain controls your feelings, and how you think and move.
	to confuse [kənˈfjuːz]	verwirren	to confuse → confused
	aged [eɪdʒd]	im Alter von	aged → age
	overweight [ˌəʊvəˈweɪt]	übergewichtig	overweight → weight → to weigh
	dramatic [drəˈmætɪk]	dramatisch	dramatic → drama
	conclusion [kənˈkluːʒn]	Schlussfolgerung	conclusion → to conclude
	to summarize [ˈsʌməraɪz]	zusammenfassen	to summarize → summary
	consequence [ˈkɒnsɪkwəns]	Konsequenz, Folge	the result of something
	to affect [əˈfekt]	auswirken, beeinflussen	to influence
B 1	**to influence** [ˈɪnflʊəns]	beeinflussen	to influence → the influence
B 2	**messaging service** [ˈmesɪdʒɪŋ ˌsɜːvɪs]	Dienst zur Versendung von (Sofort-)Nachrichten	ICQ and Skype are instant messaging services.
	browser [ˈbraʊzə]	Browser	a computer program that helps to find and read documents on the Internet
	icon [ˈaɪkɒn]	Icon, Symbol, Bildschirmsymbol	You find icons for the computer programs on the desktop.
	to click [klɪk]	klicken	to press for a short time
	desktop [ˈdesktɒp]	Desktop, Benutzeroberfläche	the background image on your computer screen
B 3	**managing director** [ˌmænɪdʒɪŋ dɪˈrektə]	Geschäftsführer(in), Mitglied der Geschäftsführung	managing director → to manage → management
	telecommunications [ˌtelɪkəˌmjuːnɪˈkeɪʃnz]	Telekommunikation	communications → to communicate
	to go ahead [ˌgəʊ əˈhed]	fortfahren	to continue
	to secure [sɪˈkjʊə, sɪˈkjɔː]	absichern, bewirken, schützen	to secure → security
	mobile [ˈməʊbaɪl]	mobil, beweglich	mobile → mobile phone
	web [web]	Netz	(short form of) World Wide Web
	server [ˈsɜːvə]	Server, zentrale Einheit im Netzwerk	server → to serve → service
	to update [ʌpˈdeɪt]	aktualisieren	The server needed to have the latest software so I updated it.
	innovation [ˌɪnəʊˈveɪʃn]	Neuerung	innovation → to innovate
B 4	**adjective** [ˈædʒɪktɪv]	Adjektiv	'good, polite, old, new' are adjectives
	button [ˈbʌtn]	Knopf, Taste	It's easy to take a picture – just press the button.
	to download [ˈdaʊnləʊd]	herunterladen	You can download interesting information from the Internet.
	file [faɪl]	Datei	Don't forget to save the file!
	electricity [ɪˌlekˈtrɪsəti]	Elektrizität	You need electricity for a microwave, a hairdryer, a refrigerator, …
	wireless [ˈwaɪələs]	drahtlos	WLAN = wireless local area network
	to steal [stiːl]	stehlen	Robin Hood stole money from rich people and gave it to poor families.

255

Unit vocabulary

environment [ɪnˈvaɪərənmənt]	Umwelt, Umgebung, Umfeld	the world (or area) we live in
recyclable [ˌriːˈsaɪkləbl]	wiederverwertbar, wiederverwendbar	recyclable → to recycle → recycling
harmful [ˈhɑːmfəl]	schädlich, nachteilig	damaging, bad
toxic [ˈtɒksɪk]	giftig	poisonous
material [məˈtɪərɪəl]	Material	things that help you to make or write sth.
in addition [ɪn əˈdɪʃn]	zusätzlich, außerdem	When Sarah fell, she broke her arm and, in addition, she broke her glasses.
to print [prɪnt]	drucken	to print → printer
complicated [ˈkɒmplɪkeɪtɪd]	kompliziert	not easy, difficult
whereas [weəˈræz]	während	People can think for themselves, whereas a computer cannot.
publishing date [ˈpʌblɪʃɪŋ ˌdeɪt]	Veröffentlichungsdatum	publishing date → to publish → publication
according to [əˈkɔːdɪŋ tə]	laut, entsprechend	According to the weather forecast, it will be warm and sunny tomorrow.
comment [ˈkɒment]	Kommentar, Stellungnahme	a statement of your opinion
to comment [ˈkɒment]	kommentieren, Stellung nehmen	to give one's opinion on something
World Wide Web [ˌwɜːld waɪd ˈweb]	weltweites Netz innerhalb des Internets	WWW
network [ˈnetwɜːk]	Netz, Netzwerk	Which network does your mobile phone use?
programming language [ˈprəʊɡræmɪŋ ˌlæŋɡwɪdʒ]	Programmiersprache	programming language → program → programmer
HTML [ˌeɪtʃtiːemˈel]	eine Programmiersprache für das World Wide Web	Hypertext Markup Language
software [ˈsɒftweə]	Software (Computerprogramme)	software ↔ hardware
worldwide [ˌwɜːldˈwaɪd]	weltweit	worldwide → world
crime [kraɪm]	Verbrechen	Stealing money is a crime.
criminal [ˈkrɪmɪnl]	kriminell	having to do with crime
fantasy [ˈfæntəsi]	Fantasie	Harry Potter lives in a fantasy world.
unlimited [ʌnˈlɪmɪtɪd]	unbegrenzt, unbeschränkt	unlimited ↔ limited
fraudster [ˈfrɔːdstə]	Betrüger(in)	fraudsters usually try to get people's money in a criminal way
to target [ˈtɑːɡɪt]	zielen (auf)	to aim at
deposit [dɪˈpɒzɪt]	Anzahlung, Einlage, Ablagerung	money given in part payment
phishing [ˈfɪʃɪŋ]	Phishing (betrügerisches „Fischen" von Daten)	the stealing of data on the Internet
account [əˈkaʊnt]	Konto	Where do you have your bank account?
to provide sb. with [prəˈvaɪd]	jmdn. versorgen mit	We'll provide you with money.
access [ˈækses]	Zugang	If you have access to sth., it is possible for you to use it or see it.
to participate (in) [pɑːˈtɪsɪpeɪt]	teilnehmen (an)	to take an active part
essay [ˈeseɪ]	Aufsatz	composition
calculation [ˌkælkjʊˈleɪʃn]	Berechnung, Kalkulation	e. g. adding figures
presentation [ˌprezn̩ˈteɪʃn]	Präsentation	We've got lots of information for our presentation to the class.
interactive [ˌɪntərˈæktɪv]	interaktiv	acting in a two-way system
to support [səˈpɔːt]	unterstützen	If you support people, you agree with them and help them.
workplace [ˈwɜːkpleɪs]	Arbeitsplatz	workplace → work → worker → to work
to link [lɪŋk]	verbinden	to connect, to join
leaver [ˈliːvə]	(Schul-)Abgänger(in)	person who leaves school
to decrease [dɪˈkriːs]	abnehmen	to decrease ↔ to increase
dramatic [drəˈmætɪk]	dramatisch	A dramatic film is a very exciting film.
WI-FI [ˈwaɪfaɪ]	W-LAN	wireless Internet connection in your home
flexible [ˈfleksəbl]	flexibel	I can cope with different people. I am very flexible.

Unit vocabulary

portable ['pɔ:təbl]	tragbar	it can be carried
device [dɪ'vaɪs]	Gerät	object used for a certain purpose
ground [graʊnd]	Boden	When you go camping, you usually sleep on the ground.
to record [rɪ'kɔ:d]	aufnehmen	to record → a record
illegal [ɪ'li:gl]	illegal	illegal ↔ legal
provider [prə'vaɪdə]	Anbieter(in)	provider → to provide → provision
measure ['meʒə]	Maßnahme	measure → to measure
piracy ['paɪrəsɪ]	Piraterie, Raubkopieren	piracy → pirate
to keep an eye on [ˌki:p ən 'aɪ ɒn]	im Auge behalten	Please keep an eye on the children while I am doing the shopping.
court [kɔ:t]	Gericht, Hof, Spielfeld	Before people can be sent to prison, they have to appear in court.
prison ['prɪzn]	Gefängnis	Many criminals have to go to prison.
responsible (for) [rɪ'spɒnsəbl]	verantwortlich (für), haftbar	responsible → responsibility

D 1 CD

aircraft ['eəkrɑ:ft]	Flugzeug	plane
youngster ['jʌŋkstə]	Jugendliche(r)	young person
skiing ['ski:ɪŋ]	Skifahren	You can go skiing in Scotland in the winter.
witness ['wɪtnəs]	Zeugin, Zeuge	witness → to witness
truck [trʌk]	Lastwagen	truck (AE) = lorry (BE)
to do poorly [du: 'pɔ:lɪ]	schlecht abschneiden	If you do not work hard at school, you will do poorly.
to pay attention [ˌpeɪ ə'tenʃn]	Aufmerksamkeit schenken	to pay attention at school to what the teacher says
westerly ['westəlɪ]	aus westlicher Richtung	coming from the west
southbound ['saʊθbaʊnd]	in Richtung Süden	southbound ↔ northbound
junction ['dʒʌŋkʃn]	Kreuzung	a place where roads meet
keypad ['ki:pæd]	Tastatur	keyboard
report [rɪ'pɔ:t]	Bericht	report → reporter → to report
to crash [kræʃ]	abstürzen	The plane crashed in the Rocky Mountains.
flame [fleɪm]	Flamme	When you make a fire, the flames go up and turn into smoke.
crash [kræʃ]	Absturz, Unfall	crash → to crash
killing ['kɪlɪŋ]	Tötung	killing → to kill → killer
murder ['mɜ:də]	Mord	murder → to murder → murderer
shower ['ʃaʊə]	Schauer, Dusche	The rain soon stopped – it was only a shower.
thunderstorm ['θʌndəstɔ:m]	Gewitter	What was the weather like? – Not so good. There were some very bad thunderstorms.
temperature ['temprətʃə]	Temperatur	the amount of heat in a place
degree [dɪ'gri:]	Grad	On a hot summer's day the temperature can rise to 30 degrees.
Celsius ['selsɪəs]	Celsius	centigrade = C
bright [braɪt]	hell	In the summer the sun is very bright.
sunny ['sʌnɪ]	sonnig	sunny → sun
motorway ['məʊtəweɪ]	Autobahn	a wide road where you can drive faster than on other roads
lane [leɪn]	Fahrspur	The road around the city has four lanes.
closed [kləʊzd]	gesperrt, geschlossen	closed ↔ open
radio station ['reɪdɪəʊ ˌsteɪʃn]	Radiosender	The DJ works for a radio station.
to come on air [ˌkʌm ɒn 'eə]	auf Sendung sein	to broadcast

D 2

analysis [ə'næləsɪs]	Analyse	analysis → to analyze
cartoonist [kɑ:'tu:nɪst]	Karikaturist(in)	cartoonist → cartoon
to point out [ˌpɔɪnt 'aʊt]	hinweisen auf	If you point out a fact, you tell someone about it.
to observe [əb'zɜ:v]	beobachten	to watch carefully

D 3

yard [jɑ:d]	Hof	Between lessons students often meet in the schoolyard.
corridor ['kɒrɪdɔ:]	Gang, Flur, Korridor	The students walked down the corridor to their classroom.
CCTV (closed circuit television) [ˌsi:si:ti:'vi:]	Videoüberwachungsanlage	In dangerous areas of the town the police has installed CCTV cameras.

Unit vocabulary

head teacher [ˌhedˈtiːtʃə]	Schulleiter(in)	If pupils behave badly, the teacher can send them to the head teacher.
officer [ˈɒfɪsə]	Beamter, Beamtin	A police officer is a man or woman in the police.
pros and cons [ˌprəʊzˌən ˈkɒnz]	Argumente für und gegen etwas	advantages and disadvantages
to suggest [səˈdʒest]	vorschlagen	to suggest → suggestion
in favour of [ɪn ˈfeɪvər əv]	für, zugunsten	to support
to reduce [rɪˈdjuːs]	reduzieren, vermindern	to increase ↔ to reduce

5 Social and economic changes

A

economic [ˌiːkəˈnɒmɪk]	ökonomisch, wirtschaftlich	economic → economy
society [səˈsaɪətɪ]	Gesellschaft	society → social
western [ˈwestən]	westlich	western → west
past [pɑːst]	letzte(r, s), vergangen	past 100 years ↔ next 100 years
to refer (to) [rɪˈfɜː]	sich beziehen auf	refer → reference
lifestyle [ˈlaɪfstaɪl]	Lebensstil	the way you live your life
section [ˈsekʃn]	Abschnitt, Abteilung	department
bookshop [ˈbʊkʃɒp]	Buchhandlung	The bookshop has got books and CDs, but they haven't got magazines.
Indian [ˈɪndɪən]	indisch	Mrs Brooks comes from India, so she cooks Indian food.
origin [ˈɒrɪdʒɪn]	Herkunft, Ursprung	An immigrant who comes from India is of Indian origin.
conventional [kənˈvenʃənl]	konventionell, normal	normal, typical
idyll [ˈɪdəl]	Idylle	a romantic scene
countryside [ˈkʌntrɪsaɪd]	Landschaft, Land	Some people like living in the city, others prefer the countryside.
strawberry [ˈstrɔːbrɪ]	Erdbeere	sweet, red fruit
wage [weɪdʒ]	Lohn	money that is paid for work
proper [ˈprɒpə]	angemessen, passend, richtig	An Englishman's idea of a proper breakfast is eggs with bacon, tomatoes and sausages, and tea to drink.
salary [ˈsælərɪ]	Gehalt	money that is paid every month for work
deduction [dɪˈdʌkʃn]	Abzug, Nachlass	We can offer you a price deduction of 20%.
accommodation [əˌkɒməˈdeɪʃn]	Unterbringung	a place where you can stay, e.g. for a holiday
fee [fiː]	Gebühr	payment for services
left [left]	übrig	If you spend all your money, nothing will be left.
picker [ˈpɪkə]	Pflücker(in)	picker → to pick
meanness [ˈmiːnnəs]	Gemeinheit, Knauserigkeit	meanness → mean
chemist's [ˈkemɪsts]	Apotheke, Drogerie	chemist's (BE) = drugstore (AE)
condom [ˈkɒndɒm]	Kondom	You can have safer sex if you use a condom.
way beyond [ˌweɪ bɪˈjɒnd]	weit entfernt, weit darüber hinaus	farther than
missus [ˈmɪsɪz]	umgangssprachliche Anrede für eine Frau	missus → Mrs
anyway [ˈenɪweɪ]	jedenfalls, trotzdem	The weather was bad but we went to the football match anyway.
to realize [ˈrɪəlaɪz]	erkennen, bemerken	On the way to the airport I suddenly realized I'd forgotten my passport.
to spot [spɒt]	entdecken	to notice
neither [ˈnaɪðə, ˈniːðə]	keine(-r/-s) (von beiden)	Both my parents have bicycles, but neither of them cycles to work.
pregnancy [ˈpregnənsɪ]	Schwangerschaft	period when a woman expects her baby
embarrassment [ɪmˈbærəsmənt]	Peinlichkeit, Verlegenheit	embarrassment → to embarrass → embarrassed
kit [kɪt]	Ausrüstung	special clothes or equipment
engaged [ɪnˈgeɪdʒd]	verlobt	They are engaged and are going to get married next month.
right now [ˌraɪt ˈnaʊ]	in diesem Augenblick	What is he doing right now?
could do with [ˌkʊdˈduː wɪð]	gebrauchen können, vertragen können (Getränk)	need

Unit vocabulary

	resentful [rɪˈzentfəl]	aufgebracht, grollend	angry
	to snap [snæp]	blaffen (ugs.)	to speak in a sharp, unfriendly way
	to shut someone up [ˌʃʌt ˌsʌmwʌn ˈʌp]	jemanden dazu bringen, den Mund zu halten	to stop someone talking
	to head off [hed ˈɒf]	sich aufmachen	The family headed off early on their holidays.
	colloquial [kəˈləʊkwɪəl]	umgangssprachlich	informal, everyday language
	superdrug [ˈsuːpədrʌg]	Name einer britischen Drogeriekette	You can buy cosmetics at Superdrug.
	drugstore [ˈdrʌgstɔː]	Apotheke, Drogerie	drugstore (AE) = chemist (BE)
	satisfied [ˈsætɪsfaɪd]	zufrieden	You are satisfied because you have received what you wanted.
	treatment [ˈtriːtmənt]	Behandlung	treatment → to treat
	definition [ˌdefɪˈnɪʃn]	Definition, Erklärung	'A subject which teaches you about the past' is a definition of the word 'history'.
	medicine [ˈmedsɪn]	Medizin	what your doctor may give you when you're ill
B 1	feminist [ˈfemɪnɪst]	Feministin, Frauenrechtlerin	Feminists fight for women's rights.
	to accommodate [əˈkɒmədeɪt]	Unterkunft bieten, versorgen	accommodate → accommodation
	to hand out [hænd ˈaʊt]	aushändigen, verteilen	Please hand out the papers to the other students.
	credit card [ˈkredɪt ˌkɑːd]	Kreditkarte	plastic card with which you can pay
	drill [drɪl]	Bohrer	You need a drill to make holes in the wall.
	beauty [ˈbjuːtɪ]	Schönheit	beauty → beautiful
	topic [ˈtɒpɪk]	Thema	subject
	documentary [ˌdɒkjʊˈmentərɪ]	Dokumentarfilm	documentary → document
B 2	non-defining relative clause [ˌnɒndɪfaɪnɪŋ ˈrelətɪv ˌklɔːz]	nicht notwendiger Relativsatz	non-defining ↔ defining
	double [ˈdʌbl]	Doppel-, doppelt	A double-decker has two decks. A double room is a room for two people.
	Europe [ˈjʊərəp]	Europa	Britain is in Europe.
	various [ˈveərɪəs]	verschieden	different
	affair [əˈfeə]	Affäre	She had an affair with a married man.
	social [ˈsəʊʃl]	sozial, gesellschaftlich	Rich people and poor people often come from different social backgrounds.
	norm [nɔːm]	Norm, Regel	a way of behaving that people expect from you
	to force [fɔːs]	zwingen	If you force someone to do something, you make them do it.
	poverty [ˈpɒvətɪ]	Armut	poverty → poor
	freedom [ˈfriːdəm]	Freiheit	freedom → free
	comedian [kəˈmiːdɪən]	Komiker(in)	a person whose job is to make people laugh
	to leave out [liːv ˈaʊt]	auslassen	leave out ↔ fill in
	Muslim [ˈmʊzlɪm]	Moslem(in)	a person who believes in Islam (also Moslem)
	profession [prəˈfeʃn]	Beruf	the profession of teaching
	comprehensive school [ˌkɒmprɪˈhensɪv ˌskuːl]	Gesamtschule	Comprehensive schools are for people from 11 to 16 or 18 years old.
	tradition [trəˈdɪʃn]	Tradition	tradition → traditional
	columnist [ˈkɒləmnɪst]	Schreiber(in), Kolumnist(in)	a journalist who writes regular articles in a newspaper or magazine
	award [əˈwɔːd]	Preis, Auszeichnung	an important prize
	religious [rɪˈlɪdʒəs]	religiös	Our neighbours go to church very often. They are religious people.
B 3	to take on [teɪk ˈɒn]	aufgreifen, übernehmen	to pick, to accept
B 4	modal auxiliary [ˌməʊdl ɔːgˈzɪljərɪ]	Hilfsverb	Must, need and can are modal auxiliaries.
	substitute [ˈsʌbstɪtjuːt]	Ersatz	Can you play tennis for Becky on Saturday? She needs a substitute.
C	to anticipate [ænˈtɪsɪpeɪt]	vorhersehen, erwarten	to expect something before it happens
	to skim [skɪm]	überfliegen	to read very quickly
	to scan [skæn]	scannen, durchsuchen	to look at something (a text etc.) carefully because you are looking for special details

Unit vocabulary

subheading ['sʌbˌhedɪŋ]	Zwischenüberschrift	Subheadings divide a text into shorter parts.
multi-tasking [ˌmʌltɪ'tɑːskɪŋ]	Multitasking (mehrere Aufgaben gleichzeitig)	doing several tasks at the same time
global ['ɡləʊbl]	global, weltweit	A global problem is one that the whole world shares.
citizen ['sɪtɪzn]	Bürger(in), Staatsangehörige(r)	If you have German nationality, you are a German citizen.
attitude (to/towards) ['ætɪtjuːd]	Haltung, Einstellung	Your attitude to/towards life is the way you feel about it.
desperate ['desprət]	verzweifelt	If you are desperate, you don't know what to do and need help.
professional [prə'feʃənl]	Fachmann, Profi	expert
application [ˌæplɪ'keɪʃn]	Bewerbung, Anwendung	application → to apply
dull [dʌl]	langweilig	dull ↔ interesting
to hire [haɪə]	einstellen, mieten	If you hire sb., you give them a job.
spontaneous [spɒn'teɪnɪəs]	spontan, kurz entschlossen	not planned
check [tʃek]	Scheck, Kontrolle	a piece of paper ordering a bank to pay money
so-called [ˌsəʊ'kɔːld]	sogenannte(r,s)	called in this way
to surround [sə'raʊnd]	umgeben	The surrounding area is the area around a place.
to arm [ɑːm]	bewaffnen (mit)	to arm → arms
cell phone ['selfəʊn]	Mobiltelefon	cell phone (AE) = mobile phone (BE)
to rely (on) [rɪ'laɪ ˌɒn]	sich verlassen (auf)	to put trust in
automatic [ˌɔːtə'mætɪk]	automatisch	Automatic cars are easier to drive.
to spell [spel]	buchstabieren	spell → to spell
LOL (Abkürzung) [ˌeləʊ'el]	laut lachend	laughing out loud
to confess [kən'fes]	beichten, bekennen	to confess → confession
ILY (Abkürzung) [ˌaɪel'waɪ]	ich liebe dich	I love you.
nevertheless [ˌnevəðə'les]	dennoch, trotzdem	in spite of all that
self-confident [ˌself'kɒnfɪdənt]	selbstbewusst	confident → confidence
creative [krɪ'eɪtɪv]	kreativ, schöpferisch	In creative writing exercises you can use your own ideas.
optimistic [ˌɒptɪ'mɪstɪk]	optimistisch	optimistic ↔ pessimistic
goal-oriented ['ɡəʊlˌɔːrɪəntɪd]	zielgerichtet, zielorientiert	tending to achieve a goal
to appreciate [ə'priːʃieɪt]	schätzen	to welcome sth.
flipside ['flɪpsaɪd]	Rückseite	opposite side
talent ['tælənt]	Talent	If you have talent, you are – or can become – very good at sth.
to concentrate ['kɒnsəntreɪt]	konzentrieren	If you don't concentrate, you will make mistakes.
single ['sɪŋgl]	einzeln, alleinstehend, alleinerziehend	1. not a single person = kein einziger Mensch; 2. a single room = ein Einzelzimmer; 3. I'm single. = Ich bin alleinstehend.
graduate ['ɡrædʒʊət]	Schulabgänger(in), Hochschulabsolvent(in)	school-leaver
grade [ɡreɪd]	Klasse, Schuljahr, Note	class or year
balance ['bæləns]	Gleichgewicht, Balance	equal distribution of life and work
percentage [pə'sentɪdʒ]	Prozentsatz	percentage → percent
culture ['kʌltʃə]	Kultur	culture → cultural
continent ['kɒntɪnənt]	Kontinent, Erdteil	Australia is the smallest continent in the world.
to demand [dɪ'mɑːnd]	verlangen, fordern	to demand → the demand
to fit (in) [fɪt 'ɪn]	(hinein)passen	The right piece in a puzzle will fit in easily.

D 1   **to balance** ['bæləns]   (aus-)balancieren, ins Gleichgewicht bringen   to balance → the balance

CD

single mum [ˌsɪŋgl 'mʌm]	alleinerziehende Mutter	woman who is a single parent
demanding [dɪ'mɑːndɪŋ]	anspruchsvoll	demanding → to demand → the demand
to experience [ɪk'spɪərɪəns]	erfahren, erleben	to experience → an experience
on one's own [ˌɒn wʌnz ˌ'əʊn]	(ganz) allein(e)	Her friends didn't want to go to the cinema, so she went on her own.
single parent [ˌsɪŋgl 'peərənt]	Alleinerziehende(r)	a person who cares for a child or children without another parent in the home
to combine [kəm'baɪn]	kombinieren	combine → combination

260

routine [ruːˈtiːn]	Tagesablauf, Routine	normal activity
D 2 **impact** [ˈɪmpækt]	Einfluss, Auswirkung	effect
society [səˈsaɪətɪ]	Gesellschaft	society → social
to date back to [ˌdeɪt ˈbæk tuː]	zurückliegen	to date from
steam [stiːm]	Dampf	When water boils, you get steam.
locomotive [ˌləʊkəˈməʊtɪv]	Lokomotive	railroad engine
to refer (to) [rɪˈfɜː]	sich beziehen auf	If you refer to sb. as a fool, you call them a fool.
bulb [bʌlb]	Glühbirne	source of electric lighting
motor car [ˈməʊtə ˌkɑː]	Auto, Kraftfahrzeug	automobile
assembly line [əˈsemblɪ ˌlaɪn]	Fließband, Fertigungsstraße	production line
available [əˈveɪləbl]	verfügbar, erhältlich	If something is available, you can get it or buy it.
individual [ˌɪndɪˈvɪdʒʊəl]	Einzelperson, Individuum	Each individual is a unique person.
process [ˈprəʊsəs]	Prozess	a continuous action
CNC production [ˌsiːenˈsiː prəˌdʌkʃn]	numerisch mit Rechnern gesteuerte Produktion	computer numerically controlled production
automated [ˈɔːtəmeɪtɪd]	automatisch, automatisiert	automated → automation
planning [ˈplænɪŋ]	Planung	planning → to plan → the plan
technological [ˌteknəˈlɒdʒɪkl]	technisch	technological → technology
influence [ˈɪnfluəns]	Einfluss	effect
productivity [ˌprɒdʌkˈtɪvətɪ]	Produktivität	productivity → to produce → production
moreover [mɔːˈrəʊvə]	überdies, außerdem	in addition
condition [kənˈdɪʃn]	Bedingung	People in developing countries suffer from poor living conditions.
aeroplane [ˈeərəpleɪn]	Flugzeug	plane, airplane
combustion [kəmˈbʌstʃn]	Verbrennungs-	the process of burning

6 Ecology and economy

A 1 **to flash** [flæʃ]	blinken, blitzen	to create a sudden light
to breathe [briːð]	atmen	to take air into the lungs
ecology [ɪˈkɒlədʒɪ]	Ökologie	the relation between plants, animals, people and their environment
to recycle [ˌriːˈsaɪkl]	recyceln, wiederverwerten	If you recycle used products, you can save raw materials.
vandalism [ˈvændəlɪzm]	Vandalismus, mutwillige Beschädigung	destruction of useful or beautiful things for fun
global [ˈgləʊbl]	global	A global problem is one that the whole world shares.
warming [ˈwɔːmɪŋ]	Erwärmung	warming → warm
worry [ˈwʌrɪ]	Sorge, Ärger	the worry → to worry
rainfall [ˈreɪnfɔːl]	Niederschlag, Regen	rain + fall = rainfall
use [juːs]	Verwendung, Verwendungsmöglichkeit	the use → to use
concern [kənˈsɜːn]	Bedenken, Sorge, Anliegen	concern → concerning
day by day [ˌdeɪbaɪˈdeɪ]	jeden Tag, täglich	every day
increasing [ɪnˈkriːsɪŋ]	zunehmend, steigend, wachsend	increasing → to increase
worried [ˈwʌrɪd]	beunruhigt	"Are you happy?" – "No, I'm worried."
issue [ˈɪʃuː]	Angelegenheit, Problem, Ausgabe (einer Zeitung)	topic
aspect [ˈæspekt]	Aspekt, Gesichtspunkt	This aspect of the problem is most important.
fossil fuel [ˌfɒsl ˈfjʊəl]	fossiler Brennstoff	Coal and oil are fossil fuels.
to emit [ɪˈmɪt]	emittieren, ausstoßen	to give out or send out
gas [gæs]	Gas, Benzin	Most people in Europe use gas or electricity for cooking.
carbon dioxide [ˌkɑːbndaɪˈɒksaɪd]	Kohlendioxyd, CO_2	You get CO_2 gases when you burn coal or wood.
to contribute [kənˈtrɪbjuːt]	beitragen	to contribute → contribution
complex [ˈkɒmpleks]	komplex, vielfältig, kompliziert	consisting of many parts

Unit vocabulary

	likely [ˈlaɪklɪ]	wahrscheinlich, voraussichtlich	Are you sure you want to spend your holidays in Majorca in August? It's likely to be very crowded.
	resource [rɪˈzɔːs]	Ressource, Bodenschatz, Rohstoff	It is important not to waste the world's natural resources.
	range [reɪndʒ]	Angebot, Produktpalette, Reichweite	The supermarket offers a wide range of sweets.
	relating to [rɪˈleɪtɪŋ tuː]	in Bezug auf	in relation to, concerning
	improvement [ɪmˈpruːvmənt]	Verbesserung	to improve → improvement
	responsibility [rɪˌspɒnsəˈbɪlətɪ]	Verantwortung	responsibility → responsible
	to encourage [ɪnˈkʌrɪdʒ]	unterstützen, fördern, ermutigen	to support
	conservation [ˌkɒnsəˈveɪʃn]	Erhaltung, Schutz	conservation → to conserve
	natural [ˈnætʃərl]	natürlich	natural → nature
	community [kəˈmjuːnətɪ]	Gemeinde, Gemeinschaft	We don't live in a big city, our village is just a small community.
	to identify (with) [aɪˈdentɪfaɪ wɪð]	herausfinden, (sich) identifizieren (mit)	to identify → identification
	to range [reɪndʒ]	sich bewegen, reichen	to range → the range
	control [kənˈtrəʊl]	Kontrolle	the control → to control
	to aim [eɪm]	anstreben, zielen	to aim → the aim
	to provide someone with [prəˈvaɪd ˌsʌmwʌn wɪð]	jmdn. versorgen mit	We'll provide you with money.
	to save [seɪv]	sparen	We can save money by walking instead of driving.
A 2	**to punish** [ˈpʌnɪʃ]	bestrafen	Is it right to punish a child who has done something wrong?
	organic [ɔːˈgænɪk]	biologisch angebaut, organisch	natural
	to survive [səˈvaɪv]	überleben	He survived for days at sea in a small boat.
	concerned [kənˈsɜːnd]	betroffen	concerned → concerning → the concern
B 1	**voluntary** [ˈvɒləntrɪ]	freiwillig	When you do voluntary work, you aren't paid for what you do.
	developing world [dɪˌveləpɪŋ ˈwɜːld]	Entwicklungsländer	Most people in the developing world are poor.
	water-related disease [ˌwɔːtəˌleɪtɪd dɪˈziːz]	Krankheit, die durch (unsauberes) Wasser verursacht wird	In Africa you find many water-related diseases.
	thirst [θɜːst]	Durst	thirst → thirsty, hunger → hungry
	gamble [ˈgæmbl]	Risiko	risk
	heartbreaking [ˈhɑːtˌbreɪkɪŋ]	herzzerreißend	It breaks your heart to see young children dying, it is heartbreaking.
	to benefit (from) [ˈbenəfit frɒm]	Nutzen ziehen (aus), profitieren (von)	Oil-producing countries benefit from the high price of oil.
	to conclude [kənˈkluːd]	schließen, folgern	to say the last thing that you are going to say
B 2	**donation** [dəʊˈneɪʃn]	Spende	money that you give to an organization such as the Red Cross
	to donate [dəʊˈneɪt]	spenden	to donate → donation
	surname [ˈsɜːneɪm]	Nachname	last name
	postcode [ˈpəʊstkəʊd]	Postleitzahl	postcode (BE) = zip code (AE)
B 3	**tuna**, pl. **tuna** [ˈtjuːnə]	Thunfisch	large fish that lives in warm seas and is caught for food
	salmon, pl. **salmon** [ˈsæmən]	Lachs	a tasty kind of fish which looks pink when you cut it open
	menu [ˈmenjuː]	Speisekarte	Waiter, what's on the menu today?
	seafood [ˈsiːfuːd]	Fisch und Meeresfrüchte	Seafood is healthy.
	protein [ˈprəʊtiːn]	Protein, Eiweiß	Protein can be found in meat, eggs and milk.
	apart from [əˈpɑːt frəm]	abgesehen von, außer	I'm going to the supermarket later. What else do we need apart from bread, milk and sugar?
	algae pl. [ˈælgiː]	Algen, Tang	plants that live in the water
	to act [ækt]	handeln, sich verhalten, spielen	to act → active → action

Unit vocabulary

	to avoid [əˈvɔɪd]	(ver)meiden	to keep away (from)
	disaster [dɪˈzɑːstə]	Katastrophe, Desaster	A disaster is a very bad accident.
	catastrophe [kəˈtæstrəfɪ]	Katastrophe	an extremely bad thing that happens to you
B 4	**World Nature Fund** [ˌwɜːld ˈneɪtʃə ˌfʌnd]	Fonds zum Schutz der Natur	an organization that helps to protect nature
	branch [brɑːntʃ]	Zweigstelle, Zweig, Abzweigung, Sektor	part of something
	major [ˈmeɪdʒə]	bedeutend, groß, Haupt-	major → majority
	membership [ˈmembəʃɪp]	Mitgliedschaft	membership → member
B 5	**drop** [drɒp]	Tropfen; Abnahme, Verringerung	Oh, I think that was a drop of rain. Let's go before it really starts.
	meaningful [ˈmiːnɪŋfəl]	sinnvoll, aussagekräftig	meaningful → meaning → to mean
	to run out [rʌn ˈaʊt]	ablaufen, auslaufen, zu Ende gehen	Time or money can run out so that there is no more left.
C	**pie chart** [ˈpaɪ ˌtʃɑːt]	Kreisdiagramm	pie chart → bar chart
	non-food [ˌnɒnˈfuːd]	Nichtlebensmittel, Güter, die nicht zum Verzehr gedacht sind	non-food ↔ food
	home food related [ˌhəʊmˌfuːdrɪˈleɪtɪd]	im Zusammenhang mit der häuslichen Nahrungszubereitung	connected with food preparation at home
	retail [ˈriːteɪl]	Einzelhandel	selling goods to the public in small quantities
	fertiliser [ˈfɜːtɪlaɪzə]	Dünger	It makes plants grow more successfully.
	air mile [ˈeə ˌmaɪl]	Flugmeile	air + mile = air mile
	South African [ˌsaʊθˈæfrɪkən]	südafrikanisch	African → Africa
	Argentinian [ˌɑːdʒənˈtɪnɪən]	argentinisch	Argentinian → Argentina
	beef [biːf]	Rindfleisch	meat that comes from cows
	Spanish [ˈspænɪʃ]	spanisch	Spanish → Spain
	Brazilian [brəˈzɪlɪən]	brasilianisch	Brazilian → Brazil
	pineapple [ˈpaɪnæpl]	Ananas	A pineapple is a fruit.
	Indonesian [ˌɪndəˈniːʒn]	indonesisch	Indonesian → Indonesia
	king prawn [ˌkɪŋ ˈprɔːn]	Königskrabbe	seafood, similar to a shrimp but bigger
	banana [bəˈnɑːnə]	Banane	Apples, oranges, strawberries and bananas are all fruit.
	transportation [ˌtrænspɔːˈteɪʃn]	Transport, Beförderung	transportation → transport
	enormous [ɪˈnɔːməs]	riesig, enorm	very large
	to harm [hɑːm]	schaden, verletzen	to damage
	rail [reɪl]	Bahn, Eisenbahn, Schiene	rail → railway
	shipping [ˈʃɪpɪŋ]	Schifffahrt, Versand	shipping → the ship → to ship
	to label [ˈleɪbl]	beschriften	to put a piece of paper on a bottle, box etc. that tells you what it is and what's in it
	label [ˈleɪbl]	Etikett	the label → to label
	aeroplane [ˈeərəpleɪn]	Flugzeug	plane
	researcher [rɪˈsɜːtʃə]	Forscher(in)	researcher → the research → to research
	agriculture [ˈægrɪkʌltʃə]	Landwirtschaft	farming
	process [ˈprəʊses]	Prozess	methods of producing goods in factories
	negative [ˈnegətɪv]	negativ	bad, harmful
	so-called [ˌsəʊˈkɔːld]	sogenannt	so-called → to call
	citizen [ˈsɪtɪzn]	Bürger(in), Staatsangehörige(r)	London has about 7.2 million citizens.
	eco- [ˈiːkəʊ]	Öko-	Our car is eco-friendly.
	to cut [kʌt]	senken, verringern, kürzen	to reduce
	consumption [kənˈsʌmpʃn]	Verbrauch	consumption → consumer → to consume
	as well as [əz ˈwel əz]	sowohl … als auch	We've got two cats as well as a dog.
	rather than [ˈrɑːðə ðən]	eher … als, besser … als	Rather than sitting on the couch all day they should do some sport.
	calorie [ˈkælərɪ]	Kalorie	If you work hard, you use up more calories.
	impact [ˈɪmpækt]	Wirkung, Aufprall	effect
	vegetable [ˈvedʒtəbl]	Gemüse	The Burtons eat lots of vegetables from their garden.

Unit vocabulary

	season [ˈsiːzn]	Saison, Jahreszeit	Summer is the warmest season.
	advisor [ədˈvaɪzə]	Berater(in), Ratgeber(in)	advisor → advice
	solar [ˈsəʊlə]	Sonnen-, Solar-	solar → sun
	to divide [dɪˈvaɪd]	teilen	to divide → division
	effort [ˈefət]	Mühe, Leistung, Versuch	It will take a lot of effort to win the match.
	to compete [kəmˈpiːt]	konkurrieren, mithalten, teilnehmen	to compete → competition
	to argue [ˈɑːɡjuː]	diskutieren, streiten, argumentieren	Young people sometimes argue with their parents.
	assistance [əˈsɪstəns]	Hilfe	assistance → to assist → assistant
	physical [ˈfɪzɪkl]	körperlich, physisch	connected with a person's body
	pain [peɪn]	Schmerz	the feeling you have when something hurts a lot
	object [ˈɒbdʒekt]	Gegenstand, Objekt	you can see and touch it
	to mark [mɑːk]	markieren, kennzeichnen, korrigieren	to label
	declaration [ˌdekləˈreɪʃn]	Erklärung	the American Declaration of Independence
	definite [ˈdefɪnɪt]	bestimmt, klar, definitiv	definite ↔ indefinite
	context [ˈkɒntekst]	Kontext, Zusammenhang	The words and sentences before and after a word; it helps you to show the meaning of the word.
	strict [strɪkt]	streng	"Have a biscuit." – "No, thanks, I'm on a strict diet."
	the elderly [ðɪ ˈeldəlɪ]	ältere Menschen	elderly → old
	to challenge [ˈtʃælɪndʒ]	herausfordern	to invite sb. to compete in a fight or game
	to beat, beat, beaten [biːt, biːt, biːtn]	besiegen, schlagen	We're winning, come on, we can beat the other team!
D 1	**over-consumer** [ˌəʊvəkənˈsjuːmə]	übermäßige(r) Konsument(in)	person who consumes more than he or she needs
	commentary [ˈkɒməntrɪ]	Kommentar	commentary → to comment
CD	**decade** [ˈdekeɪd]	Dekade, Jahrzehnt	ten years
	opposition [ˌɒpəˈzɪʃn]	Gegensatz, Gegner, Opposition	opposition → opposite
	overconsumption [ˌəʊvəkənˈsʌmpʃn]	übermäßiger Verbrauch	overconsumption → over-consumer
	to reproduce [ˌriːprəˈdjuːs]	wiedererzeugen, abbilden, reproduzieren	to reproduce → to produce
	material [məˈtɪərɪəl]	Material, Stoff	stuff, substance
	domestic [dəˈmestɪk]	Haushalts-, häuslich, inländisch	relating to the household
	oriented [ˈɔːrɪentɪd]	orientiert, bezogen	oriented → orientation
	boomerang [ˈbuːməræŋ]	Bumerang	something that comes back
	identical [aɪˈdentɪkl]	identisch	identical → identity
	to escape [ɪˈskeɪp]	entkommen	The murderer escaped from prison.
	soil [sɔɪl]	Boden, Erde	earth, ground
	erosion [ɪˈrəʊʒn]	Erosion, Auswaschung, Verschleiß	the process by which the surface of the earth is washed away
	lack [læk]	Mangel	something missing
	instability [ˌɪnstəˈbɪlətɪ]	Instabilität, Krisenanfälligkeit	instability → instable → stable
	violence [ˈvaɪələns]	Gewalt, Gewalttätigkeit	violence → violent
	limited [ˈlɪmɪtɪd]	begrenzt, beschränkt	limited ↔ unlimited
	habit [ˈhæbɪt]	Gewohnheit	pattern of behaviour
	action [ˈækʃn]	Aktion, Handlung	action → to act
	to add (up) [æd ˈʌp]	zusammenzählen	to add → addition
	step [step]	Schritt, Stufe	a movement by lifting a foot and setting it down again
	sustainable [səˈsteɪnəbl]	nachhaltig, umweltverträglich	capable of being continued with minimum effect on the environment
	to celebrate [ˈseləbreɪt]	feiern	to celebrate → celebration
	commentator [ˈkɒmənteɪtə]	Kommentator(in)	person who discusses news on the radio or on TV
	nature [ˈneɪtʃə]	Natur	nature → natural
	household [ˈhaʊshəʊld]	Haushalt	group of people living together in a flat or house

Unit vocabulary

appliance [ə'plaɪəns]	Gerät, Anwendung	appliance → to apply
conflict ['kɒnflɪkt]	Konflikt, Auseinandersetzung	fight, battle
demand [dɪ'mɑ:nd]	Nachfrage, Bedarf	the demand → to demand
relationship [rɪ'leɪʃnʃɪp]	Beziehung	relationship → relation

D 2 **sustainable** [sə'steɪnəbl] — nachhaltig, kontinuierlich — Only sustainable development can save the environment for our children.

flag [flæg]	Fahne, Flagge	The colours of the American flag are red, white and blue.
non-profit [ˌnɒn'prɒfɪt]	gemeinnützig, keinen Gewinn anstrebend	making no profit
foundation [faʊn'deɪʃn]	Stiftung, Gründung, Fundament	foundation → to found
to concentrate ['kɒnsəntreɪt]	konzentrieren	If you don't concentrate on the traffic while you're driving, you might have an accident.
workshop ['wɜ:kʃɒp]	Werkstatt	workshop → work → to work
concept ['kɒnsept]	Entwurf, Konzept	plan, idea
it's your turn [ɪts jɔ: 'tɜ:n]	du bist an der Reihe	It's your turn now to buy a round of drinks for everyone.
involved (in) [ɪn'vɒlvd]	beteiligt (an)	take part in
to structure ['strʌktʃə]	strukturieren, gliedern	to structure → the structure
suggestion [sə'dʒestʃn]	Vorschlag	suggestion → to suggest
collage [kɒ'lɑ:ʒ]	Collage	Let's put lots of different pictures together and make a collage.
stall [stɔ:l]	Stand, Box, Parkett	On market day, people sell different things at different stalls.
phase [feɪz]	Phase, (Zeit-)Abschnitt	Parents and their teenage children often go through a difficult phase of life.
critique [krɪ'ti:k]	Kritik	examination of a situation or idea
positive ['pɒzətɪv]	positiv	positive ↔ negative
vision ['vɪʒn]	Vorstellung, (Zukunfts-)Vision	A good politician must have visions of the future.
realisation [ˌrɪəlaɪ'zeɪʃn]	Verwirklichung, Realisierung, Erkenntnis	realisation → real → to realise
regarding [rɪ'gɑ:dɪŋ]	in Bezug auf	with regard to
practicability [ˌpræktɪkə'bɪləti]	Durchführbarkeit, Praktikabilität	practicability → practical → practice

7 Man and technology

A

turbine ['tɜ:baɪn]	Turbine	You can use a turbine to produce electricity.
installation [ˌɪnstə'leɪʃn]	Installation, Anlage, Einrichtung	installation → to install
favourable ['feɪvrəbl]	günstig, vorteilhaft	favourable → favour
to blow, blew, blown [bləʊ, blu:, bləʊn]	wehen, blasen	The wind is blowing.
annual ['ænjʊəl]	jährlich	every year
official [ə'fɪʃl]	Beamter, Beamtin	a person in an official position
Nebraska Public Power District [nɪˌbræskə ˌpʌblɪk 'paʊə ˌdɪstrɪkt]	verantwortliche Stelle für die Stromversorgung in Nebraska	Nebraska Public Power District is responsible for wind farms and power stations.
to flow [fləʊ]	fließen, strömen	The Rhine flows into the North Sea.
right [raɪt]	richtig	right ↔ wrong
thief, pl. **thieves** [θi:f, θi:vz]	Dieb(in)	a person who has stolen sth.
to generate ['dʒenəreɪt]	erzeugen, entwickeln, schaffen	to generate → generator
power [paʊə]	Energie, Strom	Electricity is a form of power.
dozen ['dʌzn]	Dutzend	twelve
beside [bɪ'saɪd]	neben	next to
to graze [greɪz]	grasen	to eat grass
cattle (pl. only) ['kætl]	Vieh	The cattle (cows and bulls) are in the field.
beneath [bɪ'ni:θ]	unterhalb, unter	under, below

265

Unit vocabulary

	ton [tʌn]	Tonne (Gewicht)	A metric ton is 1,000 kg, but an American ton only weighs 907 kg.
	blade [bleɪd]	Flügel, Klinge, Blatt	A modern wind turbine usually has two or three blades.
	wind farm ['wɪnd ˌfɑːm]	Windpark	You can find many wind farms near the coast.
	mayor [meə]	Bürgermeister(in)	the head of a town or city
	to view [vjuː]	besichtigen, betrachten, sehen	to look at sth. with great interest
	impressive [ɪm'presɪv]	beeindruckend	impressive → impression
	view [vjuː]	Aussicht, Sicht	You get a nice view of the city from the top of the church.
	steel [stiːl]	Stahl	Steel is used to make things like bridges, cars, knives and forks.
	to complain [kəm'pleɪn]	sich beschweren, klagen	My coffee was cold, so I complained to the waiter.
	trend [trend]	Trend, Mode, Richtung, Tendenz	If you follow the newest trends, you are trendy.
	demand [dɪ'mɑːnd]	Bedarf, Nachfrage, Forderung	the demand → to demand
	wonder ['wʌndə]	Wunder	You say "no wonder" when you are not surprised by sth.
	biofuel ['baɪəʊˌfjʊəl]	Biotreibstoff	bio(logical) + fuel = biofuel
	nuclear ['njuːklɪə]	nuklear	atomic
	hydro power ['haɪdrəʊ ˌpaʊə]	Wasserkraft	Hydro power is used to make electricity in a power station.
	renewable [rɪ'njuːəbl]	erneuerbar	renewable → new
	exhaustible [ɪg'zɔːstəbl]	begrenzt, sich erschöpfend	limited
	dependent (on) [dɪ'pendənt ɒn]	abhängig	dependent ↔ independent
B 1	passive voice [ˌpæsɪv 'vɔɪs]	Passiv (Grammatik)	passive voice ↔ active voice
	to promote [prə'məʊt]	(be-)fördern, veranstalten, werben für	to support
	efficient [ɪ'fɪʃnt]	leistungsfähig, wirksam, effizient	An efficient person or machine works quickly and well.
	deposit [dɪ'pɒzɪt]	Lagerstätte, Guthaben, Anzahlung	You can find deposits of coal or oil in the ground.
B 2	coal-fired [ˌkəʊl'faɪəd]	mit Kohle betrieben, Kohle-	A coal-fired power station uses coal to produce electricity.
	power plant ['paʊə ˌplɑːnt]	Kraftwerk	power station
	steam [stiːm]	Dampf	When water boils, you get steam.
	magnet ['mægnət]	Magnet	a piece of iron which attracts iron
	power line ['paʊə ˌlaɪn]	Starkstromleitung, Überlandleitung	Power lines provide big cities with electricity.
	to cool (down) [kuːl 'daʊn]	(ab-)kühlen	to cool down ↔ to heat up
	finally ['faɪnəlɪ]	schließlich	in the end, at last
B 3	sweater ['swetə]	Pullover	The boy was wearing blue jeans and a sweater.
	cap [kæp]	Kappe, Mütze	Boys often wear baseball caps.
	earring ['ɪərɪŋ]	Ohrring	The girl was wearing big earrings at the party.
B 5	steam engine ['stiːm ˌendʒɪn]	Dampfmaschine, Dampflokomotive	The modern steam engine was designed by James Watt.
	hybrid ['haɪbrɪd]	Hybrid-	A hybrid car usually has a petrol engine and an electric motor.
	hydrogen ['haɪdrədʒən]	Wasserstoff	We can produce hydrogen from water.
C	green-tech ['griːntek]	grüne (umweltfreundliche) Technologie (Abkürzung)	green technology
	revolutionary [ˌrevə'luːʃənrɪ]	revolutionär	revolutionary → revolution
	moral ['mɒrl]	moralisch	Moral issues are about what we believe is right or wrong.
	to turn (into) ['tɜːn ˌɪntə]	werden, sich verwandeln in	to become
	low-carbon [ˌləʊ'kɑːbn]	CO_2-arm	low degrees of CO_2
	offshore [ˌɒf'ʃɔː]	vor der Küste	located at a distance from the shore
	to erect [ɪ'rekt]	errichten, aufstellen	to build, to establish
	insulation [ˌɪnsjʊ'leɪʃn]	Isolierung	This room is very warm. You must have good insulation.
	nationwide [ˌneɪʃn'waɪd]	landesweit	throughout the whole nation

broadband ['brɔːdbænd]	Breitband(-)	capable of a high-speed download
infrastructure ['ɪnfrəˌstrʌktʃə]	Infrastruktur	infrastructure → structure → to construct
biotechnology [ˌbaɪəʊtekˈnɒlədʒɪ]	Biotechnologie	the use of microorganisms in production processes
onshore [ˌɒnˈʃɔː]	auf dem Festland, an der Küste	on land
wave [weɪv]	Welle	In a storm at sea there are big waves.
tidal ['taɪdl]	Gezeiten-	rising and falling of the sea
renewable [rɪˈnjuːəbl]	erneuerbar	which can be replaced
source [sɔːs]	Quelle	a thing or a place from which something comes
environmentally-friendly [ɪnˌvaɪərənˌmentəlɪ ˈfrendlɪ]	umweltfreundlich	friendly to nature
worthwhile [ˌwɜːθˈwaɪl]	lohnend, wertvoll	Helping people in need is worthwhile.
to raise [reɪz]	(hoch)heben, erheben, großziehen	to lift (up)
competitive [kəmˈpetɪtɪv]	wettbewerbsfähig	competitive → to compete → competition
range [reɪndʒ]	Angebot, Auswahl, Reichweite	This shop has a wide range of soft drinks.
rate [reɪt]	Rate	the level of sth. (e.g. of unemployment in a certain area)
view [vjuː]	Ansicht, Aussicht	opinion
related to [rɪˈleɪtɪdˌtuː]	in Beziehung stehend, verwandt mit	related → relation
composition [ˌkɒmpəˈzɪʃn]	Aufsatz, Komposition	a piece of written work especially one that you do at school
connective [kəˈnektɪv]	Bindewort	word or words that connect clauses, e.g. and, or, but
contrast ['kɒntrɑːst]	Gegensatz, Kontrast	There is a sharp contrast between life in the country and in a big city.
point of view [ˌpɔɪntˌəvˈvjuː]	Standpunkt, Ansicht	Your point of view is your way of seeing things.
in short [ɪnˈʃɔːt]	kurz gesagt, kurzum	in a few words
on the whole [ˌɒn ðə ˈhəʊl]	im Großen und Ganzen, alles in allem	all in all

not even [nɒtˌˈiːvn]	nicht einmal	Nobody can do that, not even Superman!
application [ˌæplɪˈkeɪʃn]	Anwendung, Bewerbung	application → to apply
client ['klaɪənt]	Kunde/Kundin, Klient(in)	customer
specialist ['speʃəlɪst]	Spezialist(in)	specialist → special
smart phone ['smɑːtˌfəʊn]	Smartphone	mobile phone which works like a little computer
wherever [weəˈrevə]	wo(hin) auch immer	Wherever you go, I'll come with you.
otherwise ['ʌðəwaɪz]	sonst	Let's buy that music magazine. We can't get the special CD otherwise.
fixed [fɪkst]	fest	fixed → to fix
whenever [wenˈevə]	wann immer	whenever → wherever → whatever
in-box ['ɪnˌbɒks]	Posteingang	box for holding incoming letters
effective [ɪˈfektɪv]	effektiv, wirkungsvoll	effective → effect
enthusiastic [ɪnˌθjuːzɪˈæstɪk]	enthusiastisch	enthusiastic → enthusiasm
to afford [əˈfɔːd]	sich leisten	That's too expensive. I can't afford it.
in the long run [ɪn ðə ˈlɒŋ ˌrʌn]	auf lange Sicht	in the end
D 2 **paperless** ['peɪpələs]	papierlos	without paper
cashier [kæˈʃɪə]	Kassierer(in)	The person who you give your money to in shops.
D 3 **projector** [prəˈdʒektə]	Projektor, Beamer	projector → to project → projection
transcript ['trænskrɪpt]	schriftliche Fassung	written version
to plug in [ˌplʌgˈɪn]	einstecken	to connect to an electrical power source
D 4 **labour** ['leɪbə]	Arbeit	work

8 The tourist industry

A **tourism** ['tʊərɪzm]	Tourismus	tourism → tourist
series, pl. **series** ['sɪəriːz]	Serie	A TV series is a number of programmes with the same title.
sporting ['spɔːtɪŋ]	sportlich, Sport-	sporting → sport

Unit vocabulary

	day off [deɪ ˈɒf]	arbeitsfreier Tag	day without work
	inexpensive [ˌɪnɪkˈspensɪv]	preiswert, billig	cheap
	catalogue [ˈkætəlɒg]	Katalog	In a catalogue you find illustrations, descriptions of products and their prices.
	travel [ˈtrævl]	das Reisen	travel → to travel
	attractive [əˈtræktɪv]	attraktiv	attractive → to attract → attraction
	infrastructure [ˈɪnfrəˌstrʌktʃə]	Infrastruktur	the system of a country with regard to transport, communication, education, energy supply etc.
	consequent [ˈkɒnsɪkwənt]	folgend, folgerichtig	consequent → consequence
	destination [ˌdestɪˈneɪʃn]	Ziel, Reiseziel	What's your destination?
	accessible [əkˈsesəbl]	zugänglich, befahrbar	accessible → access
	faraway [ˌfɑːrəˈweɪ]	fern, weit entfernt	When you are in Germany Australia is a faraway continent.
	booking [ˈbʊkɪŋ]	Buchung, Reservierung	booking → to book
	Spain [speɪn]	Spanien	the country between Portugal and France
	Far East [ˌfɑːrˈiːst]	Ferner Osten	China and Japan belong to the Far East (East Asia).
	adventure [ədˈventʃə]	Abenteuer	I like reading stories about adventures in foreign countries.
	cultural [ˈkʌltʃərl]	kulturell	There are cultural differences between people who come from different countries.
	airline [ˈeəlaɪn]	Fluggesellschaft	a company that owns planes and organises air travel
	sector [ˈsektə]	Sektor	part
	primary [ˈpraɪmərɪ]	primär, hauptsächlich, Erst-	first
	extraction [ɪkˈstrækʃn]	Gewinnung, Förderung, Entnahme	taking raw materials out of the ground
	mining [ˈmaɪnɪŋ]	Bergbau	mining → (coal) mine → miner
	secondary [ˈsekəndrɪ]	sekundär, Zweit-	secondary → second
	tertiary [ˈtɜːʃərɪ]	tertiär	third
B 1	**sightseeing** [ˈsaɪtˌsiːɪŋ]	Besichtigungstour	looking at tourist attractions
	square [skweə]	Platz, Quadrat	Trafalgar Square is in the centre of London.
	opera [ˈɒprə]	Oper	All of the parts in an opera are sung.
	France [frɑːns]	Frankreich	France → French
	Russia [ˈrʌʃə]	Russland	Russia is in the east of Europe.
	Moscow [ˈmɒskəʊ]	Moskau	the capital of Russia
B 2	**Australian** [ɒsˈtreɪlɪən]	Australier(in)	Australian → Australia
	to depart [dɪˈpɑːt]	abfliegen, abfahren	to leave
	departure [dɪˈpɑːtʃə]	Abflug, Abfahrt	the time when a flight or train leaves
	conditional [kənˈdɪʃənl]	Konditional	conditional → condition
	Statue of Liberty [ˌstætʃuː əv ˈlɪbətɪ]	Freiheitsstatue	You can see the Statue of Liberty in New York.
B 3	**fuel** [fjʊəl]	Brennstoff, Treibstoff, Benzin	The cost of fuel is high.
	to hire [haɪə]	mieten	You can hire a car at the airport.
	bin [bɪn]	Mülleimer, Mülltonne	Put your rubbish in the bin, please.
	litter [ˈlɪtə]	Abfall	rubbish
B 4	**imagination** [ɪˌmædʒɪˈneɪʃn]	Vorstellungskraft, Phantasie	the ability to form pictures and ideas in your mind
	lottery [ˈlɒtərɪ]	Lotterie	If you buy a lottery ticket and the numbers you have chosen come up, you may win a lot of money.
B 5	**honeymoon** [ˈhʌnɪmuːn]	Hochzeitsreise	journey after one's wedding
	Ireland [ˈaɪələnd]	Irland	Dublin is the capital of Ireland.
	argument [ˈɑːgjəmənt]	Streit, Argument	Tom had an argument with his girlfriend.
	otherwise [ˈʌðəwaɪz]	sonst	Let's buy that music magazine. Otherwise we can't get the special CD.
	trendy [ˈtrendɪ]	modisch, trendig	trendy → trend
	jealous (of) [ˈdʒeləs]	eifersüchtig	If you are jealous of sb., you feel angry with them because they have sth. you would like to have.
	perfect [ˈpɜːfekt]	vollkommen, perfekt	ideal
	to go wrong [gəʊ ˈrɒŋ]	schiefgehen	to turn out badly

Unit vocabulary

	Majorca [mə'jɔ:kə]	Mallorca	island that belongs to Spain
	never mind! [ˌnevə 'maɪnd]	macht nichts! schon gut! bitte!	= Forget it! It doesn't matter.
C	**initiative** [ɪ'nɪʃətɪv]	Initiative, Entschlusskraft	action you take to solve a problem
	support [sə'pɔ:t]	Unterstützung	support → to support
	nature ['neɪtʃə]	Natur	all of the animals and plants in the world
	to preserve [prɪ'zɜ:v]	bewahren, erhalten, schonen	to keep in the original state
	priority [praɪ'ɒrətɪ]	Vorrang, Dringlichkeit, Priorität	Something that is a priority must be done as soon as possible.
	to establish [ɪ'stæblɪʃ]	aufbauen, (be-)gründen	to establish → establishment
	backup ['bækʌp]	Unterstützung, Sicherung	support
	central ['sentrl]	zentral	central → centre
	barrier reef [ˌbærɪə 'ri:f]	der Küste vorgelagertes Riff	The Great Barrier Reef is near the coast of Australia.
	to be located [bɪ ləʊ'keɪtɪd]	sich befinden, gelegen sein	to be situated
	southern ['sʌðən]	südlich	southern → south
	native ['neɪtɪv]	eingeboren, einheimisch	People who were born in a country are its native people.
	guide [gaɪd]	Führer(in)	a person or a book that gives you information (for example about a city or a museum)
	fascinating ['fæsɪneɪtɪŋ]	faszinierend	very, very interesting
	legend ['ledʒənd]	Legende	an old story which may be true in parts
	Caribbean [ˌkærɪ'bi:ən, kə'rɪbɪən]	Karibik, karibisch	The Caribbean islands are between North and South America.
	condor ['kɒndɔ:]	Kondor	a big bird
	bioreserve ['baɪəʊrɪˌzɜ:v]	(Bio-)Reservat	an area where nature is protected
	variety [və'raɪətɪ]	Vielfalt, Auswahl	a number of different types
	attraction [ə'trækʃn]	Attraktion, Anziehungspunkt, Anziehungskraft	attraction → to attract → attractive
	thermal ['θɜ:ml]	Thermal-, Wärme-	producing heat or caused by heat
	spring [sprɪŋ]	Quelle, Brunnen	water coming from the earth
	forest ['fɒrɪst]	Wald	an area covered with trees
	carving ['kɑ:vɪŋ]	Schnitzarbeit	cutting wood in order to form sth.
	alive [ə'laɪv]	lebendig	alive → to live → life
	to exploit [ɪk'splɔɪt]	ausbeuten	to take unfair advantage of sb., e.g. by not paying them enough
	surroundings [sə'raʊndɪŋz]	Umgebung	the world around us
	ecological [ˌi:kə'lɒdʒɪkl]	ökologisch	ecological → ecology
	sensitive ['sensətɪv]	einfühlsam, sensibel	sensitive → sense
	untouched [ʌn'tʌtʃt]	unberührt, unversehrt	untouched → touch
	function ['fʌŋkʃn]	Funktion, Aufgabe(nbereich)	role, purpose, task
	unknown [ʌn'nəʊn]	unbekannt	unknown → to know
	race [reɪs]	Rasse	group of people who have the same history, language, nationality etc.
	to rephrase [ˌri:'freɪz]	umformulieren	to say in different words
D 1	**to associate** [ə'səʊʃɪeɪt]	verbinden, assoziieren	to connect, to bring into relation with sth. else
CD	**once in a while** [ˌwʌns ɪnˌə 'waɪl]	ab und zu, gelegentlich	from time to time
	to cool off [ku:l 'ɒf]	(sich) abkühlen	to become cooler
	jet-skiing ['dʒetˌski:ɪŋ]	Wassermotorrad fahren	going by jet-ski
	paragliding ['pærəˌglaɪdɪŋ]	Gleitschirm fliegen	a special way of flying
	motorboat ['məʊtəbəʊt]	Motorboot	a boat with an engine or a motor
	alright [ɔ:l'raɪt]	in Ordnung	OK, fine
	resort [rɪ'zɔ:t]	Ferienort, Badeort	We're going to a beautiful resort in the Rocky Mountains for our holidays.
	peaceful ['pi:sfəl]	friedlich	peaceful → peace
	wild [waɪld]	wild	These ponies don't live on a farm. They're wild.
	monkey ['mʌŋkɪ]	Affe	Monkeys are always children's favourite animals at the zoo.

269

Unit vocabulary

	volcano, pl. volcanoes [vɒl'keɪnəʊ]	Vulkan	a mountain out of which material sometimes comes from inside the earth
	to hike [haɪk]	wandern	to go for a long walk in the country
	to float [fləʊt]	treiben, gleiten, mit dem Floß fahren	to move on a river
	overnight [ˌəʊvə'naɪt]	über Nacht	during the night
	medical ['medɪkl]	medizinisch	If a doctor treats you, you get medical attention or treatment.
D 4	investor [ɪn'vestə]	Kapitalanleger, Investor	investor → to invest → investment
	to mine [maɪn]	abbauen, fördern	You can mine coal or gold.

9 Globalisation and multiculturalism

A	globalisation [ˌgləʊblaɪ'zeɪʃn]	Globalisierung	Companies, labour, products, transport become more and more international.
	chance [tʃɑːns]	Chance	She lost the race because the others were too fast. She did not have a chance.
	risk [rɪsk]	Risiko	I used the traffic lights because there was a risk of being hit by a car if I didn't.
	labour ['leɪbə]	Arbeits-	work
	Austrian ['ɒstrɪən]	österreichisch	The Austrian mountains are a great place to go skiing.
	unfashionable [ʌn'fæʃnəbl]	unmodisch, unmodern	The clothes from last year are already unfashionable this year.
	sneaker ['sniːkə]	Turnschuh	I always wear sneakers when I have to walk a lot.
	MP3 player [ˌempiː'θriː ˌpleɪə]	MP3-Spieler	MP3 is the abbreviation for Moving Picture Experts Group (MPEG) Audio Layer 3.
	India ['ɪndɪə]	Indien	India is a country in the east.
	textile ['tekstaɪl]	textil	A textile factory is a place where cloth is manufactured.
	to dye [daɪ]	färben	I would like to have blue hair. I think I will dye it.
	dyer [daɪə]	Färber(in)	A dyer is someone whose job is to change the colour of things.
	chemical ['kemɪkl]	Chemikalie	A chemical is material which is used in industry to change the appearance of a product.
	to risk [rɪsk]	riskieren	I do my job as well as I can because I don't want to risk losing it.
	to make money [meɪk 'mʌnɪ]	Geld verdienen	The top football players make a lot of money.
	whatever [wɒt'evə]	was auch immer	Take whatever you want out of the fridge if you are hungry!
	accessory [ək'sesərɪ]	Zubehör, Accessoire	A handbag or a scarf are nice accessories for women.
	stuff [stʌf]	Zeug	things; We've had that old stuff in the garage for years!
	standard ['stændəd]	Standard, Norm, Maßstab	You can't judge an amateur's work by professional standards.
	apprenticeship [ə'prentɪʃɪp]	Ausbildung	If you want to do a job like working in a bank, you can do an apprenticeship. In Germany this takes between 2 and 3 1/2 years.
	manufacturer [ˌmænjə'fæktʃərə]	Hersteller	manufacturer → manufacturing → to manufacture
	Czech Republic [ˌtʃek rɪ'pʌblɪk]	Tschechische Republik	The Czech Republic is to the east of Germany.
	either way [ˌaɪðə'weɪ, ˌiːðə'weɪ]	so oder so	It does not matter what you do, either way you end up the loser.
B	New Zealand [ˌnjuː 'ziːlənd]	Neuseeland	New Zealand is a country that is close to Australia.
	tutor ['tjuːtə]	Klassenlehrer(in), Betreuer(in)	My tutor tells where I need to go to get my papers done.
	host [həʊst]	Gastgeber(in)	The host at a party is the person who has invited the people.
	regards [rɪ'gɑːdz]	Grüße	Give my kind regards to your mother.
	novel ['nɒvl]	Roman	There are seven 'Harry Potter' novels.
	ice hockey ['aɪs ˌhɒkɪ]	Eishockey	Ice hockey is a popular sport in Canada.
	preposition [ˌprepə'zɪʃn]	Präposition	Examples: of, in, at, on, beneath, under, above
	to apologize [ə'pɒlədʒaɪz]	sich entschuldigen	to say "I'm sorry"

Unit vocabulary

	logistics [lə'dʒɪstɪks]	Logistik, Versorgungs-	Logistics deals with the transportation of goods.
	guideline ['gaɪdlaɪn]	Richtlinie	If you follow the guidelines, you will not have any problems.
	busy ['bɪzi]	besetzt, belegt	Please call another time, the line is busy right now.
	caller ['kɔːlə]	Anrufer(in)	caller → to call
C	**habit** ['hæbɪt]	Gewohnheit, Angewohnheit	Tracy always uses her mobile in restaurants. That's an annoying habit.
	authentic [ɔː'θentɪk]	authentisch	real
	takeaway ['teɪkəweɪ]	Restaurant, das Speisen zum Mitnehmen verkauft	a place where you can buy dishes and take them home to eat
	industrialized [ɪn'dʌstrɪəlaɪzd]	industrialisiert	industrialized countries ↔ developing countries
	radical ['rædɪkl]	radikal, drastisch, durchgreifend	Radical changes are needed to solve the problem of pollution.
	textiles ['tekstaɪlz]	Textilien	cloth
	merchant ['mɜːtʃənt]	Händler, Kaufmann, Handelsmann	salesperson
	original [ə'rɪdʒənl]	original, ursprünglich, unbearbeitet	original → origin
	generation [ˌdʒenə'reɪʃn]	Generation	You think of your parents as the older generation.
	ironical [aɪ'rɒnɪkl]	ironisch	I didn't really mean what I said. It was meant ironically.
	nevertheless [ˌnevəðə'les]	dennoch, trotzdem, nichtsdestotrotz	There is no solution. Nevertheless we still hope that things will get better.
	to carry on [ˌkæri 'ɒn]	weiterführen	I want to carry on playing the guitar.
	racial ['reɪʃl]	Rassen-	racial → race
	diverse [daɪ'vɜːs]	unterschiedlich, vielfältig, verschieden	different
	to escape (from) [ɪ'skeɪp]	flüchten (vor)	The sheriff didn't catch Robin Hood because he escaped at the last minute.
	Latvian ['lætvɪən]	lettisch	People from Latvia are called Latvians.
	Russian ['rʌʃn]	russisch	Russian → Russia
	Asian ['eɪʒən]	asiatisch	Chinese people and people from India are Asians.
	option ['ɒpʃn]	Alternative, Möglichkeit	possibility
	ethnic ['eθnɪk]	ethnisch	an ethnic group shares the same culture, religion, language etc.
	to eliminate [ɪ'lɪmɪneɪt]	beseitigen, entfernen, eliminieren	to cancel
	credit ['kredɪt]	Guthaben, Punkte, Vertrauen, Anerkennung	I can't phone Emily because I've got no credit on my mobile.
	mixture ['mɪkstʃə]	Mischung, Vermischung, Gemenge	A fruit salad is a mixture of different fruits.
D 2	**podcast** ['pɒdkɑːst]	Podcast, aus dem Internet herunterladbare Film- bzw. Hörsequenz	You can download the latest news podcasts from the Internet.
CD	**cocoa** ['kəʊkəʊ]	Kakao	Chocolate is made from cocoa.
	hut [hʌt]	Hütte	a little house made out of wood and/or metal
	listener ['lɪsnə]	Zuhörer(in)	listener → to listen
	aid [eɪd]	Hilfe	help
	to sum up [sʌm 'ʌp]	zusammenfassen	If you sum up what happens in a story, you explain it in a few sentences.

10 International politics

A	**united** [jʊ'naɪtɪd]	vereint(e)	United Nations = Vereinte Nationen
	humanitarian [hjuːˌmænɪ'teərɪən]	humanitär, menschenfreundlich	humanitarian → humanity → human
	peacekeeping ['piːsˌkiːpɪŋ]	Friedenserhaltung, Friedensbewahrung	making sure that a war does not break out
	human ['hjuːmən]	menschlich	It's only human to make mistakes, we all do.
	operation [ˌɒpər'eɪʃn]	Operation, Handlung, Verfahren, Arbeitsgang	act, action, activity

271

Unit vocabulary

	budget ['bʌdʒɪt]	Haushalt, Etat	for example, the amount of money a company has to spend on its advertising
	Zimbabwe [zɪmˈbɑːbweɪ]	Simbabwe	Zimbabwe is a country in southeast Africa.
	TLD (top-level domain) [ˌtiːelˈdiː, ˌtɒplevl dəˈmeɪn]	Bereich oberster Ebene	The last letters of an internet address show its top-level domain. The TLD for Germany is 'de'.
	maize [meɪz]	Mais	a tall plant that produces sweetcorn
	pill [pɪl]	Pille, Tablette	one form of medicine
	to prevent sth. from happening/sb. from doing sth. [prɪˈvent]	verhindern	The rain prevented us from finishing the match.
	stomach ['stʌmək]	Magen	You shouldn't go swimming on a full stomach.
	non-governmental [ˌnɒngʌvənˈmentl]	nichtregierungs-, nichtstaatlich(e)	non-governmental organization = NGO
	two-thirds [ˌtuːˈθɜːdz]	zwei Drittel	Two-thirds plus one-third equals one.
	ration [ˈræʃn]	Zuteilung, Ration	The man has to survive on a ration of a piece of bread and a cup of water a day.
	Zimbabwean [zɪmˈbɑːbwɪən]	simbabwisch, Simbabwer/in	People living in Zimbabwe are called Zimbabweans.
	to flee, fled, fled [fliː, fled, fled]	fliehen	The animals fled from the fire.
	inflation [ɪnˈfleɪʃn]	Inflation, Geldentwertung	If a country introduces too much money, inflation may rise.
	harvest [ˈhɑːvɪst]	Ernte	In the autumn the farmers usually bring in the harvest.
	seed [siːd]	Saat, Samen	A lot of plants can be grown from seed.
	fertilizer [ˈfɜːtɪlaɪzə]	Dünger, Düngemittel	If a farmer uses fertilizer, the harvest will be better than if he does not.
	cholera [ˈkɒlərə]	Cholera	Cholera is a disease which can result from drinking unclean water.
	infection [ɪnˈfekʃn]	Infektion, Ansteckung	infection → to infect → infectious
	to infect [ɪnˈfekt]	infizieren, anstecken	to infect → infection
	care [keə]	Pflege, Sorge	Nurses and doctors work in health care.
	grandchild [ˈgrændtʃaɪld]	Enkelkind, Enkel(in)	grandchild → grandson → granddaughter
	furthermore [ˌfɜːðəˈmɔː]	überdies, außerdem	moreover, additionally
	condition [kənˈdɪʃn]	Kondition, Zustand, Situation	on one condition = unter einer Bedingung
	illiterate [ɪˈlɪtərət]	nicht lesen oder schreiben könnend	John never went to school. He is illiterate.
	desperate [ˈdespərət]	verzweifelt, aussichtslos	If you are desperate, you don't know what to do and you need help.
	barefoot [ˈbeəfʊt]	barfuß	not wearing shoes or socks
	to persecute [ˈpɜːsɪkjuːt]	verfolgen	to persecute → persecution → persecutor
	refuge [ˈrefjuːdʒ]	Asyl, Zufluchtsstätte	a place you can go to if you are in danger
	abbreviation [əˌbriːvɪˈeɪʃn]	Abkürzung	the short form of a term or of a name, for example asap, USA
	cross [krɒs]	Kreuz	cross → to cross → crossing
B 1	eastern [ˈiːstən]	östlich, ost-	The sun rises in the eastern part of the world.
	to fail [feɪl]	versagen	to fail → failure
	rice [raɪs]	Reis	Risotto is made with rice.
	slave [sleɪv]	Sklave/Sklavin	Slaves are not paid for their work and they must do what their owners tell them.
	Senegalese [ˌsenɪgəˈliːz]	senegalesisch, Senegalese/Senegalesin	A person from Senegal is a Senegalese.
	industrial [ɪnˈdʌstrɪəl]	industriell	industrial → industry
B 2	to rewrite [ˌriːˈraɪt]	umschreiben	to rewrite → to write
	to carry out [ˌkærɪ ˈaʊt]	ausführen	If you carry sth. out, you do or complete it.
	short-term [ˌʃɔːtˈtɜːm]	kurzfristig, befristet, kurzzeitig	short-term ↔ long-term
	committee [kəˈmɪtiː]	Komitee, Ausschuss, Gremium	The committee decided to help poor children in Africa.
	zone [zəʊn]	Zone, Gebiet, Bereich	area

Unit vocabulary

B 3	**presenter** [prɪ'zentə]	Präsentator(in), Moderator(in)	presenter → to present → presentation
	thanks [θæŋks]	danke	'Thanks' is short for 'thank you'.
	to arrange [ə'reɪndʒ]	organisieren, ausmachen	I've arranged to meet Rob at seven o'clock.
C	**presidential** [ˌprezɪ'denʃl]	Präsidentschaft-, präsidial	presidential → president
	federal ['fedərəl]	Bundes-	belonging to the central government of a country and not just to a region or state
	parliament ['pɑːləmənt]	Parlament	The people vote for the members of parliament.
	president ['prezɪdənt]	Präsident(in)	the person who has the highest political position in a country
	parliamentary [ˌpɑːlə'mentərɪ]	parlamentarisch	parliamentary → parliament
	majority [mə'dʒɒrətɪ]	Mehrheit	the majority of us = most of us
	to make up (sth.) [meɪk 'ʌp]	etwas bilden, zusammenstellen, erfinden	The party makes up over fifty percent of the parliament.
	separation of powers [sepəˌreɪʃn əv 'paʊəz]	Gewaltenteilung	The separation of powers is one of the main principles of German politics.
	legislative ['ledʒɪslətɪv]	legislativ, gesetzgebend	Parliament belongs to the legislative branch.
	executive [ɪg'zekjətɪv]	exekutiv, ausführend, leitend	When we talk about the executive branch in politics we usually mean the government.
	judicial [dʒuː'dɪʃl]	gerichtlich, rechtsprechend	Judges belong to the judicial branch.
	checks and balances [ˌtʃeks ən 'bælənsɪz]	gegenseitige Kontrolle, Gewaltenteilung	Checks and balances is an important part of the American system of government.
	concentration [ˌkɒnsən'treɪʃn]	Ansammlung, Verdichtung, Konzentration	concentration → to concentrate
	to represent [ˌreprɪ'zent]	repräsentieren, vertreten	to stand for, to act in the place of
	Congress ['kɒŋgres]	Kongress (Parlament in den USA)	Congress makes the laws in the United States.
	to pass [pɑːs]	(ein Gesetz) verabschieden, bestehen, weitergeben	to agree on a law
	bill [bɪl]	Gesetzesvorlage, Banknote, Entwurf, Rechnung	We would like to pay. Can you bring us the bill, please?
	congressional [kən'greʃnl]	Kongress-, den Kongress betreffend	congressional → Congress
	to control [kən'trəʊl]	kontrollieren	to control → the control
	judiciary [dʒuː'dɪʃərɪ]	Judikative, Justizgewalt, Gerichtswesen	judiciary → judicial
	to impeach [ɪm'piːtʃ]	anklagen	to impeach the president = to say that the president has done something illegal
	to reverse [rɪ'vɜːs]	umkehren	to change back
	veto ['viːtəʊ]	Veto, Einspruchsrecht, Einspruch	veto ↔ approval
	to approve [ə'pruːv]	anerkennen, bestätigen, zustimmen, akzeptieren	to approve → approval
	appointment [ə'pɔɪntmənt]	Berufung, Termin	I have an appointment at the bank at 9 am tomorrow morning.
	judge [dʒʌdʒ]	Richter(in), Wettkampfrichter(in)	The judge decides in court and competitions.
	Commander-in-Chief [kəˌmɑːndər ɪn 'tʃiːf]	Oberbefehlshaber	The Commander-in-Chief is the top leader of the military.
	armed forces [ˌɑːmd 'fɔːsɪz]	Militär, Streitkräfte	The airforce, the army and the navy are all part of a country's armed forces.
	leader ['liːdə]	Führer(in)	The group has to follow the leader.
	treaty ['triːtɪ]	Vertrag	When two countries or nations agree on sth., there is an official treaty between them.
	to permit [pə'mɪt]	erlauben, zulassen, genehmigen	to permit → permission
	to declare [dɪ'kleə]	erklären	declaration → to declare
	permission [pə'mɪʃn]	Erlaubnis	My mom gave me permission to stay overnight.
	to limit ['lɪmɪt]	begrenzen	to limit → limit
	to nominate ['nɒmɪneɪt]	ernennen, nominieren, aufstellen	Bruce Willis was nominated for an Oscar.

Unit vocabulary

	Supreme Court [su:ˌpri:m ˈkɔ:t]	Oberstes Bundesgericht	The Supreme Court is the highest court in the United States of America.
	constitution [ˌkɒnstɪˈtju:ʃn]	Verfassung	The constitution is a set of rules for the government.
	unconstitutional [ˌʌnˌkɒnstɪˈtju:ʃənl]	verfassungswidrig	It is unconstitutional to treat men and women differently.
	indirect [ˌɪndaɪˈrekt]	indirekt, mittelbar	indirect ↔ direct
	delegate [ˈdelɪgət]	Delegierte(r), Abgeordnete(r), Bevollmächtigte(r)	People vote for the delegates who then represent the people's interests.
	voter [ˈvəʊtə]	Wähler(in)	The voters elect the people who form the parliament.
	citizenship [ˈsɪtɪzənʃɪp]	Staatsangehörigkeit, Nationalität, Bürgerrecht	Most of the people living in Germany have German citizenship.
	to register [ˈredʒɪstə]	registrieren, einschreiben, anmelden	Students who want to study at the university need to register for their courses first.
	residence [ˈrezɪdns]	Wohnsitz, Wohnhaus	His main residence is in Switzerland.
	mediation [ˌmi:dɪˈeɪʃn]	Sprachmittlung, Vermittlung, Schlichtungswesen	repeating the main ideas of a text in another language
	to paraphrase [ˈpærəfreɪz]	paraphrasieren, mit anderen Worten ausdrücken, umschreiben	to express in a different way but the meaning stays the same
D 1	**Italy** [ˈɪtəlɪ]	Italien	Italy → Italian
	Slovenia [sləˈviː.nɪə]	Slowenien	Slovenia → Slovenian
	Norway [ˈnɔːweɪ]	Norwegen	Norway → Norwegian
	Latvia [ˈlætvɪə]	Lettland	Latvia is located in the north-west of Europe.
	Netherlands [ˈneðələndz]	Niederlande	The Netherlands is on the western border of Germany.
	Bulgaria [bʌlˈgeərɪə]	Bulgarien	Bulgaria is the third-largest country in south-east Europe.
	Turkey [ˈtɜːkɪ]	Türkei	Turkey → Turkish; turkey = Truthahn
	Greece [griːs]	Griechenland	Greece → Greek
	Switzerland [ˈswɪtsələnd]	Schweiz	the country between France, Germany and Italy
CD	**Italian** [ɪˈtælɪən]	italienisch	In Italy people speak Italian.
	Rome [rəʊm]	Rom	Rome is the capital of Italy.
	hometown [ˈhəʊmtaʊn]	Heimatstadt	the town that you come from
	decisive [dɪˈsaɪsɪv]	entscheidend, bestimmend, endscheidungsfreudig	decisive → decision → to decide
	to respect [rɪˈspekt]	respektieren	If you respect sb.'s rights, you accept them.
	democracy [dɪˈmɒkrəsɪ]	Demokratie	One major feature of a democracy is its free elections.
	to function [ˈfʌŋkʃn]	funktionieren	to work
	to define [dɪˈfaɪn]	definieren	When you define something, you explain what it is.
	ally [ˈælaɪ]	Alliierte(r), Verbündete(r)	partner, friend
	thankful [ˈθæŋkfəl]	dankbar	thankful → to thank → thanks
	to foresee [fəˈsiː]	vorhersehen, absehen	to expect something to happen and then it does
	to by-pass [ˈbaɪpɑːs]	überbrücken, umgehen	You by-pass a law when you break it.
	to disappear [ˌdɪsəˈpɪə]	verschwinden	I can't find my MP3 player. It has disappeared.
	to afford [əˈfɔːd]	sich leisten	That's too expensive. I can't afford to buy it.
	bureaucracy [bjʊəˈrɒkrəsɪ]	Bürokratie	Bureaucracy usually means a lot of rules and paperwork.
	to orientate [ˈɔːrɪənteɪt]	orientieren, ausrichten	to orientate → orientation
	international [ˌɪntəˈnæʃənl]	international	interaction between two or more countries
	Irish [ˈaɪrɪʃ]	irisch	of Ireland; There are lots of nice Irish songs.
	enlargement [ɪnˈlɑːdʒmənt]	Vergrößerung, Erweiterung, Erhöhung	enlargement → to enlarge
	continent [ˈkɒntɪnənt]	Kontinent, Erdteil	Europe is a continent.
	stable [ˈsteɪbl]	stabil	stable ↔ unstable
	countryman [ˈkʌntrɪmən]	Landsmann	someone who comes from your country
	corruption [kəˈrʌpʃn]	Korruption, Bestechlichkeit	People use their power to make themselves rich.
	bankrupt [ˈbæŋkrʌpt]	bankrott, insolvent	When a company can no longer pay its production costs or its workers, it is bankrupt.
	potential [pəˈtentʃl]	potenziell, eventuell	possible
	accession [ækˈseʃn]	Beitritt, Einwilligung, Zuwachs	the point at which a country becomes a member of an organization

Unit vocabulary

	criterion, pl. **criteria** [kraɪˈtɪərɪən, kraɪˈtɪərɪə]	Kriterium, Kriterien	standard
D 2	**hostile** [ˈhɒstaɪl]	feindlich	People who are hostile like to fight.
	European Monetary Union [ˌjʊərəˈpiːən ˌmʌnətrɪ ˈjuːnɪən]	Europäische Wirtschafts- und Währungsunion	(short form:) EMS
	referendum [ˌrefəˈrendəm]	Referendum, Abstimmung, Volksbefragung	a direct vote in which citizens can say "yes" or "no" to a special issue
	opponent [əˈpəʊnənt]	Gegner(in)	supporter ↔ opponent
	supporter [səˈpɔːtə]	Anhänger(in), Befürworter(in)	A supporter agrees with you and helps you.
	institution [ˌɪnstɪˈtjuːʃn]	Institution, Einrichtung, Anstalt	Hospitals and schools are examples of institutions.
	commission [kəˈmɪʃn]	Kommission, Provision	The European Commission has one member from each of state of the European Union.
	commissioner [kəˈmɪʃənə]	Beauftragte(r), Bevollmächtigte(r), Auftraggeber(in)	a person who acts officially for his/her government
	to implement [ˈɪmplɪment]	ausführen, verwirklichen, realisieren	to carry out, to fulfill
	council [ˈkaʊnsl]	Gremium, Rat	committee
	intergovernmental [ˌɪntəˌgʌvənˈmentl]	zwischenstaatlich, international	international
	official [əˈfɪʃl]	offiziell	Where can I get information about McFly? – Try their official website.
	to vary [ˈveərɪ]	variieren	If your feelings vary a lot, they change a lot.
	European Court of Justice [ˌjʊərəpiːən ˌkɔːt əv ˈdʒʌstɪs]	Europäischer Gerichtshof	The European Court of Justice is the highest court in the European Union.
	stability [stəˈbɪlətɪ]	Stabilität, Beständigkeit	stability → stable

11 Living and working in Britain

1	**trainee** [ˌtreɪˈniː]	Praktikant(in), Auszubildende(r)	trainee → to train → training
	partnership [ˈpɑːtnəʃɪp]	Partnerschaft	Dortmund has a partnership with the city of Leeds.
	to be delighted [bɪ dɪˈlaɪtɪd]	glücklich sein, sehr zufrieden sein	to be delighted = to be very happy
	Scottish [ˈskɒtɪʃ]	schottisch	Scottish weather is colder than English weather.
	Scotland [ˈskɒtlənd]	Schottland	Scotland is to the north of England.
	opportunity [ˌɒpəˈtjuːnətɪ]	Gelegenheit	chance
	ourselves [ˌaʊəˈselvz]	uns, selbst	We made all the food for the party ourselves.
	wholesaler [ˈhəʊlˌseɪlə]	Großhändler	company which sells goods to retailers
	distributor [dɪˈstrɪbjətə]	Verteiler, Lieferant, Vertrieb	distributor → to distribute → distribution
	front office [ˌfrʌnt ˈɒfɪs]	Empfang	office which has contact to customers
	general office [ˌdʒenrəl ˈɒfɪs]	Büro, Sekretariat	place where normal office work is done
	to recommend [ˌrekəˈmend]	empfehlen	I really liked that movie. I recommended it to all my friends.
	complimentary close [ˌkɒmplɪmentərɪ ˈkləʊz]	Grußformel	Yours …; Yours sincerely …; Sincerely …; Kind regards … are examples of complimentary closes.
	to thank [θæŋk]	danken, (sich) bedanken	I would like to thank you for inviting me.
	to appreciate [əˈpriːʃieɪt]	schätzen	If you appreciate sth., you notice its positive characteristics.
	sincerely [sɪnˈsɪəlɪ]	Mit freundlichen Grüßen	Yours sincerely = Yours faithfully
	salutation [ˌsæljəˈteɪʃn]	Begrüßung, Anrede	You always start a letter with a salutation.
2 CD	**to come over** [kʌm ˈəʊvə]	herüberkommen	Can you come over this afternoon?
	vacancy [ˈveɪkənsɪ]	Stellenangebot, Leere, Lücke	The hotel does not have any vacancies, it's full up.
	bed and breakfast [ˌbed n ˈbrekfəst]	Pension	A bed and breakfast is cheaper than a hotel.
	to charge [tʃɑːdʒ]	in Rechnung stellen, berechnen	Although they charged us a large sum of money for the tickets, the show was very poor.

Unit vocabulary

reduction [rɪ'dʌkʃn]	Reduzierung	to reduce → reduction
dot [dɒt]	Punkt	A sentence ends with a dot.
availability [əˌveɪlə'bɪlətɪ]	Verfügbarkeit, Verwendbarkeit	availability → available → to avail
rate [reɪt]	Rate, Preis	the level of sth., e.g. of unemployment, in a certain area
to catch sth. [kætʃ]	etwas akustisch verstehen	to hear and understand something
to be in touch [bɪ ˌɪn 'tʌtʃ]	mit jemandem in Verbindung stehen, mit jemandem in Kontakt bleiben	I'd like to meet you again. Let's keep in touch.
3 to cut a long story short [tə kʌt ə ˌlɒŋ ˌstɔːrɪ 'ʃɔːt]	langer Rede kurzer Sinn	
to give someone a buzz [gɪv ˌsʌmwʌn ə 'bʌz]	jemanden anrufen	colloquial way of saying 'to call sb.'
New Year's Eve [ˌnjuːˌjɪəz'iːv]	Silvesterabend	the night before the first of January
informal [ɪn'fɔːml]	informell	formal ↔ informal

12 Meeting people

1 colleague ['kɒliːg]	Kollege/Kollegin	a person who works with you in a company
to shake [ʃeɪk]	schütteln; zittern	1. shake + object (= schütteln); 2. shake (without object) (= zittern)
pleased [pliːzd]	erfreut	happy = glad = pleased
to experience [ɪk'spɪərɪəns]	erfahren, erleben	to experience → an experience
to cover for sb. ['kʌvə]	jemanden vertreten	There is no one to cover for me, everyone is sick.
response [rɪ'spɒns]	Reaktion, Antwort	He's still waiting for your response.
2 conversation [ˌkɒnvə'seɪʃn]	Gespräch, Unterhaltung, Konversation	When people talk to each other, they have a conversation.
CD ought to [ɔːt]	sollte, müsste	ought to = must, should
foyer ['fɔɪeɪ]	Vorhalle, Foyer	foyer = entrance
general office [ˌdʒenrəl 'ɒfɪs]	Zentrale, Allgemeine Verwaltung	All of the information relating to this project must go to the general office.
paperwork ['peɪpəwɜːk]	Schreibarbeit, Büroarbeit	She likes working in an office. She is good at paperwork.
general manager [ˌdʒenrəl 'mænɪdʒə]	Generaldirektor(in), Geschäftsführer(in)	The general manager is the head of a company.
onto ['ɒntə]	auf … hinauf	on + to = onto
executive suite [ɪgˌzekjətɪv 'swiːt]	Führungsloge, Vorstandsetage	The executive suite is usually on the top floor of the building.
on duty [ɒn 'djuːtɪ]	im Dienst	The policeman on duty gave me a ticket.
3 straight [streɪt]	gerade, direkt	We're late. Let's go straight to our class.
4 chicken ['tʃɪkɪn]	Hühnerfleisch	I'll have the chicken salad, please.
rainbow ['reɪnbəʊ]	Regenbogen	rain → rainbow
trout, pl. trout [traʊt]	Forelle	one trout – lots of trout
haggis ['hægɪs]	Haggis (traditionelles schottisches Gericht)	
shrimp [ʃrɪmp]	Krabbe, Schrimp	A shrimp is a smaller form of a prawn.
prawn [prɔːn]	Garnele	Prawns are very delicious seafood.
beer [bɪə]	Bier	
dish [dɪʃ]	Gericht	There are many vegetarian dishes on the menu in this café.
spicy ['spaɪsɪ]	würzig, pikant, scharf	spicy = hot
lager beer ['lɑːgə ˌbɪə]	helles Bier, Lagerbier	lager beer ↔ dark beer
starter ['stɑːtə]	Vorspeise	to start → starter
soup [suːp]	Suppe	A bowl of hot soup on a cold day does you good.
cocktail ['kɒkteɪl]	Cocktail	A lot of young people like beer and cocktails.
mussel ['mʌsl]	Muschel	You must open its hard shell before you can eat it.
main course [ˌmeɪn 'kɔːs]	Hauptgericht	I'd like lamb curry for my main course, please.
pea [piː]	Erbse	Peas and carrots are two very common vegetables.
fried [fraɪd]	in der Pfanne gebraten	Fried food is delicious but you mustn't eat too much of it.

	dessert [dɪˈzɜːt]	Dessert, Nachtisch	Children often like the dessert more than the main course.
	pie [paɪ]	gedeckter Obstkuchen	In England you often get apple pie with ice-cream for dessert.
	custard [ˈkʌstəd]	Vanillesauce	Custard is a sweet yellow sauce.
	cream [kriːm]	Sahne, Creme	You can buy cream at the supermarket.
	spirit [ˈspɪrɪt]	Spirituose	a drink with a lot of alcohol in it
	soft drink [ˌsɒft ˈdrɪŋk]	alkoholfreies Getränk	Children are not allowed to drink alcohol in restaurants, therefore they have to order soft drinks instead.
CD	**to fancy** [ˈfænsɪ]	angetan sein von	She fancies him. = She likes him and would like him to be her boyfriend.
	to impress [ɪmˈpres]	beeindrucken	I hoped to impress my new boss by working really hard.
	Roman [ˈrəʊmən]	Römer(in)	The Romans were really good soldiers.
	sparkling water [ˌspɑːklɪŋ ˈwɔːtə]	Mineralwasser mit Kohlensäure	Many people prefer drinking sparkling water to plain water.
5	**orange** [ˈɒrɪndʒ]	Orange	Oranges are usually orange in colour.
	pint [paɪnt]	Pinte (englisches Hohlmaß: 0,57 l)	In England you drink beer in pints instead of litres.
	emotional [ɪˈməʊʃnl]	emotional, gefühlvoll, gerührt	He gets emotional when he hears sad songs on the radio.
	intense [ɪnˈtens]	angestrengt, intensiv, gefühlstief	His reaction was very intense. It really hurt him.
	trainee [ˌtreɪˈniː]	Praktikant(in), Auszubildende(r)	trainee → to train → training
	to circulate [ˈsɜːkjəleɪt]	zirkulieren, herumgehen	to circulate → circle → circulation
	marital status [ˌmærɪtl ˈsteɪtəs]	Ehestand, Familienstand	He has just got married so his marital status has changed.

13 Working in an office

1	**tourist office** [ˈtʊərɪst ˌɒfɪs]	Fremdenverkehrsbüro	place where tourists can receive information
	guide book [ˈgaɪd ˌbʊk]	Reiseführer	book which informs tourists about a country or a city
	to put through [pʊt ˈθruː]	durchstellen, verbinden mit	Can you put me through to Mr Williams, please?
	to hold the line [ˌhəʊld ðə ˈlaɪn]	am Apparat bleiben	to stay on the phone
2	**bookstore** [ˈbʊkstɔː]	Buchladen	shop where you can buy books
	memo [ˈmeməʊ]	Notiz, Kurznachricht	Have you read the memo from the boss?
3	**diary** [ˈdaɪərɪ]	Tagebuch, Terminbuch	Some people write what they have done during the day in a diary. A small diary is just for things you plan to do.
	businessman [ˈbɪznɪsmən]	Geschäftsmann	I could have got more money when I sold my car, but I'm not a very good businessman.
CD	**fairly** [ˈfeəlɪ]	relativ	The test was fairly difficult but I think that I passed.
	flexible [ˈfleksɪbl]	flexibel, biegsam, anpassungsfähig	I can cope with very different people. I'm really flexible.
	What a pity! [ˌwɒt ə ˈpɪtɪ]	Wie schade!	"I can't come to your party." – "Oh, what a pity!"
	available [əˈveɪləbl]	frei, erhältlich	If sth. is available, you can get it or buy it.
	midday [ˌmɪdˈdeɪ]	Mittag	noon
	to be on business [bɪ ˌɒn ˈbɪznɪs]	auf Geschäftsreise sein	I'm sorry the manager can't speak with you. He is away on business.
	to confirm [kənˈfɜːm]	bestätigen	Can you confirm my appointment at 10?
4	**yours sincerely** [ˌjɔːz sɪnˈsɪəlɪ]	Mit freundlichen Grüßen	'Yours sincerely' is used at the end of a formal letter when you know the name of the person you are writing to.
	letterhead [ˈletəhed]	Briefkopf	sender's address in a letter
	attention line [əˈtenʃn ˌlaɪn]	Zeile in der Adresse mit Angabe des Empfängers (zu Händen)	line in the address directing the letter to a certain person
	signature [ˈsɪgnətʃə]	Unterschrift	signature → to sign
	subject line [ˈsʌbdʒekt ˌlaɪn]	Betreffzeile	the subject line lets the reader know immediately what the letter is about
	supplier [səˈplaɪə]	Zulieferer, Lieferant	sb. who provides things that people want or need

Unit vocabulary

	purchase ['pɜːtʃəs]	Einkauf	sth. you buy
	postal code ['pəʊstl ˌkəʊd]	Postleitzahl	number or letters within the address which make it easier to deliver a letter

14 Different countries, different cultures

	culture ['kʌltʃə]	Kultur	culture → cultural
1	**monster** ['mɒnstə]	Monster, Ungetüm	What colour is the monster? – It's blue.
	distillery [dɪ'stɪləri]	Brennerei	Spirits are produced in a distillery.
	North Sea [ˌnɔːθ 'siː]	Nordsee	The North Sea is off the north coast of Germany.
2 CD	**to inquire** [ɪn'kwaɪə]	sich erkundigen, fragen	to inquire → inquiry
	rental ['rentl]	Miete, Verleih	rental → to rent → rent
	saloon [sə'luːn]	Limousine, Salon, Saal	It is more expensive to rent a saloon car than a Mini.
	shoulder bag ['ʃəʊldə ˌbæg]	Umhängetasche	
	toll [təʊl]	Maut	If you want to drive through the tunnel, you must pay a toll.
	to suggest [sə'dʒest]	vorschlagen	to suggest → suggestion
	the Tube [tjuːb]	U-Bahn	Another name for the London Underground is the Tube.
3	**overseas** [ˌəʊvə'siːz]	Übersee-, in Übersee	If you go to the USA, you travel overseas.
CD	**to settle up** [ˌsetl 'ʌp]	bezahlen, Rechnung begleichen	to settle up = to pay
	account [ə'kaʊnt]	Konto, Abrechnung, Berechnung, Wert	Where do you have your bank account?
	wanna (= informal form of 'want to') ['wɒnə]	will/wollen	I really wanna go to that party tomorrow.
	pretty ['prɪti]	ziemlich	sth. that is pretty good is quite good
	stairs [steəz]	Treppe	stairs → upstairs → downstairs
	maintenance ['meɪntənəns]	Wartung, Pflege, Instandhaltung, Unterhalt, Verwaltung	maintenance → to maintain
	inconvenience [ˌɪnkən'viːniəns]	Unannehmlichkeit, Belästigung, Unbequemlichkeit	inconvenience → inconvenient
	pleasant ['pleznt]	angenehm	I like having him around. He is a very pleasant person.
	French fries ['frentʃ ˌfraɪz]	Pommes frites	(AE) French fries = (BE) chips
	to accommodate [ə'kɒmədeɪt]	unterbringen, anpassen, aushelfen	accommodate → accommodation
	gas station (AE) ['gæs ˌsteɪʃn]	Tankstelle	petrol station (BE)
	floor [flɔː]	Stock, Etage	This building has lots of floors.
	cell phone ['sel ˌfəʊn]	Handy, Mobiltelefon	(AE) cell phone = (BE) mobile phone
	check [tʃek]	Rechnung (im Restaurant) (AE), Scheck (AE), Prüfung	check → to check
	bill [bɪl]	Rechnung, Banknote	a piece of paper that shows how much you must pay for sth.
	out of order [ˌaʊt əv 'ɔːdə]	außer Betrieb, gestört	The lift doesn't work anymore. It is out of order.
	closet ['klɒzɪt]	Wandschrank, Kammer	I put all of my clothes into the bedroom closet.
	elevator ['eləveɪtə]	Aufzug	(AE) elevator = (BE) lift
	wedding ['wedɪŋ]	Hochzeit	Paul and Jane really love each other. Their wedding is on Friday.
	anniversary [ˌænɪ'vɜːsəri]	Jubiläum, Hochzeitstag	a day when you remember sth. that happened on the same date one or more years ago
	restroom ['restrʊm]	Toilette	(AE) restroom = (BE) toilet(s)
	gas [gæs]	Benzin	(AE) gas = (BE) petrol
	Mountie ['maʊnti]	kanadische berittene Polizei	a Canadian policeman on horseback
	billboard ['bɪlbɔːd]	Plakatwand	outdoor board on which posters and adverts are displayed
	Aussie (informal) ['ɒzi]	Australier(in)	Aussie = Australian
	Gaelic football [ˌgeɪlɪk 'fʊtbɔːl]	eine Sportart, die vorwiegend in Irland gespielt wird	a type of football played in Ireland

dingo [ˈdɪŋgəʊ]	Dingo (australischer Wildhund)	Dingoes look like pet dogs, but they are wild animals which kill other animals for food.
All Blacks [ˌɔːl ˈblæks]	die neuseeländische Rugby-Union-Nationalmannschaft	the New Zealand national union rugby team
leprechaun [ˈleprəkɔːn]	ein kleiner Kobold aus der irischen Mythologie	a type of fairy said to be found in Ireland
kiwi [ˈkiːwiː]	ein flugunfähiger Vogel, eine Fruchtsorte, eine Eigenbezeichnung der Bewohner Neuseelands	A kiwi can be a bird, a type of fruit, or an informal name for a person from New Zealand.
4 **handout** [ˈhændaʊt]	Informationsblatt, Handout	hand → handout; a piece of paper that gives important information (e. g. from a talk)
impolite [ˌɪmpəˈlaɪt]	unhöflich	impolite ↔ polite
to swear, swore, sworn [sweə, swɔː, swɔːn]	fluchen; schwören	It's not very polite to swear at people.
unnatural [ʌnˈnætʃərəl]	unnatürlich	unnatural ↔ natural
foreigner [ˈfɒrənə]	Ausländer(in)	foreign → foreigner
in general [ɪn ˈdʒenrəl]	im Allgemeinen, generell	In general I am interested in all sports.
stranger [ˈstreɪndʒə]	Fremde(r)	I don't know that man – he's a stranger.
rank [ræŋk]	Rang, Stellung, Rangordnung	A general is the highest rank in the military.
standing [ˈstændɪŋ]	Ansehen, Stellung	Paul is the best student in his class. He has a very good standing with the other students.
queue [kjuː]	Warteschlange	a line of people who are waiting, e.g. in a shop or at a bus stop
Brit [brɪt]	umgangssprachlicher Ausdruck für einen Engländer	a person who lives in Britain
dress code [ˈdres ˌkəʊd]	Kleiderordnung	The dress code tells you what you have to wear.
tie [taɪ]	Krawatte, (Spiel) unentschieden enden	The game ended in a tie: 58-58.
showy [ˈʃəʊɪ]	auffallend, prächtig, protzig	Everybody looked at her because she was wearing a very showy skirt.
pedestrian [pəˈdestrɪən]	Fußgänger(in)	When you walk down the street, you are a pedestrian.
disciplined [ˈdɪsɪplɪnd]	diszipliniert	If you do what you should do all of the time, then you are very disciplined.
tactic [ˈtæktɪk]	Taktik	a plan how to do sth.
5 **quiz** [kwɪz]	Quiz, Ratespiel	quiz = a game to see what you know
incoming [ˈɪnˌkʌmɪŋ]	eingehend, ankommend	We couldn't receive any incoming calls because the phone lines were down.
chief [tʃiːf]	Häuptling	the leader of a group (especially of Native Americans)

15 Enquiries

1 **to run a business** [ˌrʌn ə ˈbɪznɪs]	ein Unternehmen führen	to organize
to supply [səˈplaɪ]	(be)liefern	to provide with
non-food [ˌnɒnˈfuːd]	Non-Food (Gebrauchsgüter)	food ↔ non-food
specification [ˌspesɪfɪˈkeɪʃn]	Anforderung, Beschreibung, Maßangabe	detailed description
outdoor [ˌaʊtˈdɔː]	Freiluft-, im Freien, draußen	Hiking, skateboarding, camping are outdoor activities.
unbeatable [ʌnˈbiːtəbl]	unschlagbar	unbeatable → to beat
importer [ɪmˈpɔːtə]	Importeur	importer → to import → the import
outlet [ˈaʊtlet]	Verkaufsstelle, Absatz, Abfluss	You can buy things more cheaply at a factory outlet.
term [tɜːm]	Bedingung, Begriff, Trimester an der Schule	condition
to place an order [ˌpleɪs ən ˈɔːdə]	einen Auftrag erteilen, eine Bestellung aufgeben	to order
to quote [kwəʊt]	nennen, zitieren	to quote → quotation

Unit vocabulary

2	substitution table [ˌsʌbstɪˈtjuːʃn ˌteɪbl]	Substitutionstabelle, Ersetzungstabelle	substitution → substitute
	sales literature [ˈseɪlz ˌlɪtrətʃə]	Werbematerial	leaflets, brochures
	to obtain [əbˈteɪn]	erhalten, erlangen	to receive
	leading [ˈliːdɪŋ]	führend	leading → to lead → the leader
	rapidly [ˈræpɪdlɪ]	schnell	fast
	to extend [ɪkˈstend]	(sich) ausdehnen	to expand
	supplier [səˈplaɪə]	Zulieferer	somebody who provides things that people want or need
	quotation [kwəʊˈteɪʃn]	(Preis-)Angebot, Belegstelle im Text	quotation → to quote
	sample [ˈsɑːmpl]	Muster, Probe	Sometimes they give you samples of perfume.
	demonstration [ˌdemənˈstreɪʃn]	Demonstration, Vorführung	demonstration → to demonstrate
	prepared [prɪˈpeəd]	bereit, vorbereitet	willing, ready
	expectation [ˌekspekˈteɪʃn]	Erwartung	expectation → to expect
	substantial [səbˈstænʃl]	umfangreich, beträchtlich	large
	to come up to [kʌm ˈʌp tə]	entsprechen, erfüllen, zukommen auf	to match, to equal
	trial [traɪəl]	Probe, Test, Gerichtsverfahren	test
	shortly [ˈʃɔːtlɪ]	in Kürze	He's coming soon, so we will see him shortly.
3	to manufacture [ˌmænjəˈfæktʃə]	fertigen, herstellen	to make in a factory, to produce
	Yours faithfully [jɔːz ˈfeɪθfəlɪ]	Hochachtungsvoll, Mit freundlichen Grüßen	This can be used at the end of a formal letter (Yours sincerely = less formal).
4	value [ˈvæljuː]	Wert	value → valuable
	all over [ˌɔːl ˈəʊvə]	überall	You can meet nice people all over the world.
	stock [stɒk]	Bestand, Vorrat, Aktie	Do you have a good stock of plants in the garden centre?
	freight [freɪt]	Fracht	transport, goods transported
	Indonesia [ˌɪndəʊˈniːʒə]	Indonesien	country in Asia
	to cover [ˈkʌvə]	umfassen, (be)decken	to include
	to delay [dɪˈleɪ]	aufschieben, (ver)zögern	My brother was sick so we delayed going on vacation.
	sari [ˈsɑːrɪ]	Sari	clothes worn by Hindu women
	fabric [ˈfæbrɪk]	Stoff, Gewebe	material of clothes
	seating furniture [ˈsiːtɪŋ ˌfɜːnɪtʃə]	Sitzmöbel	sofas and armchairs
5 CD	model [ˈmɒdl]	Modell, Baureihe, Model	type of product
	particularly [pəˈtɪkjələlɪ]	besonders	especially
6	fork-lift truck [fɔːklɪft ˈtrʌk]	Gabelstapler	small vehicle which transports goods in a warehouse
	Swedish [ˈswiːdɪʃ]	schwedisch	from Sweden
	shelving system [ˈʃelvɪŋ ˌsɪstəm]	Regalsystem	a system consisting of several shelves

16 Offers

1	to grant [grɑːnt]	gewähren	to give
	introductory [ˌɪntrəˈdʌktərɪ]	Einführungs-	introductory → to introduce → introduction
	ex works [ˌeksˈwɜːks]	ab Werk	delivery costs are not included
	receipt [rɪˈsiːt]	Erhalt, Empfang, Beleg	receipt → to receive
	letter of credit [ˌletər əv ˈkredɪt]	Akkreditiv	instrument which helps the supplier to receive the money for the goods delivered
	open account [ˌəʊpn əˈkaʊnt]	Kontokorrent, Zahlung gegen Rechnung	credit granted by a business to the customer
	selection [səˈlekʃn]	Auswahl, Sortiment	range
	to assure [əˈʃʊə]	etw. zusichern	They assured payment within a week.
	sale [seɪl]	Verkauf	Steve sells cars. He gets extra money when he makes a sale.

2	**Incoterms (international commercial terms)** [ˈɪnkəʊtɜːmz (ˌɪntəˌnæʃənl kəˌmɜːʃl ˈtɜːmz)]	Incoterms (internationale Regelungen der Lieferbedingungen für Käufer/Verkäufer bei Auslandsgeschäften)	Incoterms make international trade easier.
	quay [kiː]	Kai, Dock, Anlegestelle	
3	**dated** [ˈdeɪtɪd]	datiert, mit Datum vom	having or showing a date
	to submit [səbˈmɪt]	unterbreiten	to present, to state, to give
	net [net]	netto, ohne Abzug, Netz	The price is net – there are no more deductions.
	EXW [ˌeksˈwɜːks]	ab Werk	ex works
	willing [ˈwɪlɪŋ]	bereit	willing → will
	shipment [ˈʃɪpmənt]	Lieferung, Versendung, Ladung	an act of shipping, sth. that is shipped
	valid [ˈvælɪd]	gültig	My passport is valid until 2015.
	to request [rɪˈkwest]	beantragen, erbitten	to request → the request
	to require [rɪˈkwaɪə]	benötigen	If you require sth., it's necessary for you to have it.
	to get in touch (with) [ˌget ɪn ˈtʌtʃ]	in Verbindung treten (mit)	to make contact (with)
	to execute [ˈeksɪkjuːt]	durchführen	to make, to arrange
	prompt [prɒmpt]	prompt, sofort	immediate
	to deal (with) [diəl]	bearbeiten, handeln (mit, von)	to take action, to handle
5	**on condition (that)** [ɒn kənˈdɪʃn]	unter der Bedingung, dass	if
	moreover [mɔːˈrəʊvə]	überdies, außerdem	in addition, furthermore
	to attach [əˈtætʃ]	anhängen, anbringen	She attached a card to the present.
	heavy duty [ˌhevɪˈdjuːtɪ]	Schwerlast, hohe Beanspruchung	You need heavy duty machines for this hard work.
	desert [ˈdezət]	Wüste	It doesn't rain very often in the desert.
	mechanical engineering [məˌkænɪkl endʒɪˈnɪərɪŋ]	Maschinenbau	the branch dealing with the design and production of machines
	under separate cover [ˌʌndə ˌsepərət ˈkʌvə]	mit getrennter Post	sent separately
6 CD	**storage container** [ˈstɔːrɪdʒ kənˌteɪnə]	Vorratsbehälter, Lagerbehälter	large box which is used to store things
	to tailor (to) [ˈteɪlə]	zuschneiden (auf), maßschneidern	to adapt
7	**speciality** [ˌspeʃɪˈælətɪ]	Spezialität, Spezialartikel	speciality → special

17 Orders

1	**trampoline** [ˈtræmpəliːn]	Trampolin	You can jump up and down on it for exercise or as a sport.
	croquet [ˈkrəʊkeɪ]	Krocket	a game played on grass with balls and long wooden hammers
	irrevocable [ˌɪrɪˈvəʊkəbl]	unwiderruflich	impossible to change or stop
2	**at the latest** [ət ˌðə ˈleɪtɪst]	spätestens	no later than
	in advance [ɪn ədˈvɑːns]	im Voraus	If you want to be sure you'll get a ticket, book one in advance.
	transfer [ˈtrænsfɜː]	Überweisung, Übertragung	passing money from one account to another
	by return [baɪ rɪˈtɜːn]	postwendend, umgehend	by the next mail in the opposite direction
	to acknowledge [əkˈnɒlɪdʒ]	bestätigen, anerkennen	to acknowledge → acknowledgement
	delay [dɪˈleɪ]	Verzögerung	The train is half an hour late. We apologize for the delay.
4	**margin** [ˈmɑːdʒɪn]	Rand	the space around a text on a page
	free [friː]	kostenlos, frei	It's free! You needn't pay for it.
	to dispatch [dɪˈspætʃ]	abschicken, abfertigen	to send
	three-piece suite [ˌθriːpiːs ˈswiːt]	Polstergarnitur	a set of matching pieces of furniture

Unit vocabulary

	trade discount [ˌtreɪd ˈdɪskaʊnt]	Händlerrabatt	a discount from the list price granted by the manufacturer or wholesaler
	hairdryer [ˈheəˌdraɪə]	Haartrockner, Föhn	drier → to dry → dry
5 CD	fortnight [ˈfɔːtnaɪt]	vierzehn Tage, zwei Wochen	two weeks
6	do-it-yourself (DIY) [ˌduːɪtjɔːˈself (ˌdiːaɪˈwaɪ)]	Heimwerker-	doing or making sth. without professional training

18 Complaints

	complaint [kəmˈpleɪnt]	Beschwerde, Mängelrüge	complaint → to complain
1	punctual [ˈpʌŋktʃʊəl]	pünktlich	Emma always arrives late. She's never punctual.
	consignment [kənˈsaɪnmənt]	Warensendung, Lieferung	delivery, cargo
	on schedule [ɒn ˈʃedjuːl]	termingerecht, pünktlich	on time
	carton [ˈkɑːtn]	Karton, Schachtel	a container for goods
	replacement [rɪˈpleɪsmənt]	Ersatz	sth. that takes the place of another
	urgent [ˈɜːdʒənt]	dringend	It must be done immediately – it is urgent.
	campaign [kæmˈpeɪn]	Kampagne	series of advertisements or commercials that try to persuade people to buy a product
	dispatch [dɪˈspætʃ]	Auslieferung, Abfertigung	dispatch → to dispatch
	liable [ˈlaɪəbl]	haftbar, verantwortlich	If sth. goes wrong, you will be liable!
	to entail [ɪnˈteɪl]	verursachen, mit sich bringen	to cause
2	to turn out [tɜːn ˈaʊt]	ausfallen, sich herausstellen als	I was lucky that things did not turn out worse.
	satisfaction [ˌsætɪsˈfækʃn]	Zufriedenheit	satisfaction → satisfied → to satisfy
	considerable [kənˈsɪdrəbl]	beträchtlich	a considerable time = quite a long time
	overdue [ˌəʊvəˈdjuː]	überfällig	Payment should have arrived last month, it is long overdue.
	crate [kreɪt]	Kiste	large wooden box
	defective [dɪˈfektɪv]	fehlerhaft, schadhaft, defekt	not made correctly, not working correctly
	content [ˈkɒntent]	Inhalt	sth. that is inside a box, for example
	to be up to [bɪ ˈʌp tuː]	entsprechen	to come up to
	to look into [ˌlʊk ˈɪntuː]	prüfen, auf den Grund gehen	to check, to examine
	to settle [ˈsetl]	regeln, erledigen	to arrange matters
	position [pəˈzɪʃn]	Position, Haltung, Meinung	opinion, point of view
3	to guarantee [ˌgærənˈtiː]	garantieren, gewährleisten	to make it certain that sth. will happen
	inconvenient [ˌɪnkənˈviːnɪənt]	ungelegen, lästig, unangenehm	causing difficulties
4	to fade [feɪd]	ausbleichen, verblassen	to lose intensity in colour
5 CD	canoe [kəˈnuː]	Kanu	a light boat that you push through the water using a paddle
	to wonder [ˈwʌndə]	sich fragen, sich Gedanken machen	I wonder what it was like to live in the 16th century.
	logistics [ləˈdʒɪstɪks]	Logistik	organisation of transport
	regatta [rɪˈgætə]	Regatta, Bootsrennen	boat race

19 Reminders

	reminder [rɪˈmaɪndə]	Mahnung, (Zahlungs-) Erinnerung	reminder → to remind sb.
1	record [ˈrekɔːd]	Aufzeichnung	record → to record
	oversight [ˈəʊvəsaɪt]	Versehen, Übersehen	error, mistake
	on your part [ɒn ˈjɔː ˌpɑːt]	von Ihrer Seite, Ihrerseits	at your responsibility
	to disregard [ˌdɪsrɪˈgɑːd]	ignorieren, unbeachtet lassen	I wanted to help her but she disregarded my advice.
2	to draw sb.'s attention to [ˌdrɔː əˈtenʃn tuː]	jmds. Aufmerksamkeit lenken auf	to point to
	mistakenly [mɪˈsteɪkənlɪ]	irrtümlicherweise, versehentlich	mistakenly → mistake
	to overlook [ˌəʊvəˈlʊk]	übersehen, überblicken	to fail to notice or to do sth.
	deadline [ˈdedlaɪn]	Termin, Frist	a date or time by which sth. must be done or finished

	legal ['li:gl]	legal, gesetzlich	legal ↔ illegal
	settlement ['setlmənt]	Begleichung, Abwicklung, Siedlung	settlement → to settle
4	mug [mʌg]	Becher	A mug is like a big cup.
	unusual [ʌn'ju:ʒʊəl]	ungewöhnlich	He's got red hair – that's unusual.
	tactful ['tæktfəl]	taktvoll	When you're tactful, it means you try not to hurt other people's feelings.
	with regard to [wɪð rɪ'gɑːd tə]	bezüglich, im Hinblick auf	regarding
5 CD	laboratory [lə'bɒrətəri]	Labor	a large room where people do experiments and research
	to sort out [sɔːt 'aʊt]	klären	I've got a problem with Susan. – Then sort it out with her!

20 Youth unemployment

	nowhere land ['nəʊweəlænd]	Niemandsland	a land that does not exist
	figure ['fɪgə]	Zahl, Ziffer	figure = number
	rejection [rɪ'dʒekʃn]	Ablehnung, Absage	I wasn't qualified for the job so I got a rejection in the post.
	to get used to (+ gerund) [get 'ju:st tə]	sich gewöhnen (an)	It takes time to get used to living in a new place.
	to gain [geɪn]	gewinnen	to get sth. positive (or an advantage) from doing sth.
	failure ['feɪljə]	Versagen	failure → to fail
	homelessness ['həʊmləsnəs]	Obdachlosigkeit	not having a home
	factor ['fæktə]	Faktor, Einfluss	Those factors influenced my decision.
	unhelpful [ʌn'helpfəl]	nutzlos, nicht hilfreich	unhelpful ↔ helpful
	lack of ['læk əv]	Mangel an, mangelnd, fehlend	His lack of experience was the reason why he was fired.
	GCSE [,dʒi:si:es'i:]	Prüfung zum Abschluss der Sekundarstufe I	General Certificate of Secondary Education
	BTec [,bi:ti:i:'si:, 'bi:,tek]	Abschluss an einer Berufs(fach)schule	Business and Technology Education Council
	qualified ['kwɒlɪfaɪd]	qualifiziert	A qualified teacher has learnt how to teach at a special college.
	coaching ['kəʊtʃɪŋ]	Übungsleitung (beim Sport), Nachhilfe	training of a player or a team
	sufficient [sə'fɪʃənt]	ausreichend, genügend	sufficient = enough
	eager ['i:gə]	eifrig	She's always so eager to be the best at everything she does; it really drives me crazy sometimes.
	to fall ill [fɔːl 'ɪl]	krank werden	to become ill
	downhill [,daʊn'hɪl]	abwärts, bergab	He climbed the mountain and then went downhill on his bike.
	assistant [ə'sɪstənt]	Assistent(in), Mitarbeiter(in)	assistant → to assist
	childcare ['tʃaɪldkeə]	Kinderbetreuung	She really likes children so she wants to go into childcare.
	appealing [ə'pi:lɪŋ]	ansprechend, reizvoll	The girl is very good-looking. She is very appealing to the boys.
	critic ['krɪtɪk]	Kritiker(in)	critic → to criticise → criticism → critical
	to hang around [,hæŋ ə'raʊnd]	herumhängen	If you hang around, you stay in one place and don't really do anything.
	to suffer ['sʌfə]	leiden	to experience pain
1	lifelong ['laɪflɒŋ]	lebenslang, lebenslänglich	People have to learn all of the time. Learning is a lifelong task.
	facility [fə'sɪləti]	Einrichtung, Gelegenheit	equipment, opportunity
	search [sɜːtʃ]	Suche	trying to find sth. or sb.
	based on ['beɪst ɒn]	basierend auf	This adventure story is based on the life of a real person.

21 New jobs

	rundown [,rʌn'daʊn]	abgewirtschaftet, verwahrlost	The building was broken. It was a rundown building.
	district ['dɪstrɪkt]	Distrikt, Bezirk, Stadtteil	Harlem is a district in New York City.

Unit vocabulary

	regeneration [rɪˌdʒenəˈreɪʃn]	Erneuerung, Wiederherstellung, Regeneration	If you bring new strength and life to sth., this is called regeneration.
	deprived [dɪˈpraɪvd]	sozial benachteiligt	not having the things that are essential for a comfortable life
	investment [ɪnˈvestmənt]	Investition	investment → to invest
	disabled [dɪˈseɪbld]	behindert	disabled → able
	benefit [ˈbenɪfɪt]	Sozialhilfe, Nutzen	His parents don't have a job. They get benefits from the state.
	activist [ˈæktɪvɪst]	Aktivist(in), jemand, der sich für etwas engagiert	active → activity → activist
	to transform [trænsˈfɔːm]	verwandeln	to transform → transformation → transformer
	forum [ˈfɔːrəm]	Forum, öffentliche Diskussion	I'm sorry, but this is the wrong forum for that kind of discussion. Can we talk about it another time?
	spending power [ˈspendɪŋ ˌpaʊə]	Kaufkraft	the amount of money consumers can spend on goods
	in turn [ɪn ˈtɜːn]	wiederum, abwechselnd	again
	convenience store [kənˈviːnɪənsˌstɔː]	Nachbarschaftsladen, Lebensmittelgeschäft	a retail store with a limited range of goods which is open long hours
	to dismiss [dɪˈsmɪs]	entlassen, freistellen, ablehnen	to dismiss = to fire
	retail [ˈriːteɪl]	Einzelhandel(s-)	retail → to retail
	fear [fɪə]	Angst	the feeling you have when you are scared
	to claim [kleɪm]	behaupten, beanspruchen	to say that sth. is true although it isn't proved
	turnover [ˈtɜːnˌəʊvə]	Absatz, Umsatz	Just because the company has a big turnover it doesn't mean that you earn a lot.
1	basic [ˈbeɪsɪk]	grundlegend	In the first two years of English you learn a lot of basic words and phrases.
	fear [fɪə]	Angst	fear → to fear
4	to chat [tʃæt]	chatten, sich (online) unterhalten	to chat → a chat

22 Modern technology

	fairy tale [ˈfeərɪ ˌteɪl]	Märchen	In fairy tales the youngest of the three sons is often the hero.
	billion [ˈbɪljən]	Milliarde	a billion = a thousand millions (1,000,000,000)
	powerful [ˈpaʊəfəl]	stark	powerful → power
	search engine [ˈsɜːtʃ ˌendʒɪn]	Suchmaschine	A search engine helps you to find information on the Internet.
	domain [dəʊˈmeɪn]	Domain	part of a website address
	misspelling [mɪsˈspelɪŋ]	falsche Schreibweise, Rechtschreibfehler	misspelling → to spell
	googol [ˈguːgɒl, ˈguːgəl]	Googol	1×10^{100}
	zero [ˈzɪərəʊ]	Null	the figure 0
	to google [ˈguːgəl]	googeln	to search for information on the Internet using the Google search engine
	pop-up advertising [ˌpɒpʌp ˈædvətaɪzɪŋ]	Werbung in einem Pop-up-Fenster (auf einem Monitor)	an online advertisement that is shown in a new window
	user [ˈjuːzə]	Benutzer(in)	user → to use
	design [dɪˈzaɪn]	Design, Entwurf, Gestaltung	to design → designer → design
	to be related to [bɪ rɪˈleɪtɪd ˌtuː]	sich beziehen auf, betreffen	related → relation → to relate
	to enter [ˈentə]	eingeben	enter → entrance → entry
	click [klɪk]	Klick(en)	the click → to click
	link [lɪŋk]	Verbindung, Link	connection
	ingenious [ɪnˈdʒiːnɪəs]	genial, raffiniert	very clever

earnings ['ɜːnɪŋz]	Einnahmen, Erträge	earnings → to earn
criticism ['krɪtɪsɪzm]	Kritik	criticism → to criticize
privacy ['prɪvəsɪ; 'praɪvəsɪ]	Privatsphäre	privacy → private
image ['ɪmɪdʒ]	Bild, Image	picture
doubt [daʊt]	Zweifel	without doubt = certainly
security [sɪ'kjʊərətɪ]	Sicherheit	security → secure
theoretical [θɪə'retɪkl]	theoretisch	theoretical ↔ practical
to assign [ə'saɪn]	zuordnen	to relate
data ['deɪtə]	Daten	facts, items of information
third party [ˌθɜːd 'pɑːtɪ]	Dritte	other people

2	**religion** [rɪ'lɪdʒn]	Religion	religion → religious → R.E. (Religious Education)
4	**cleanliness** ['klenlɪnəs]	Reinheit, Sauberkeit	cleanliness → clean
	compromise ['kɒmprəmaɪz]	Kompromiss	This deal is the ideal compromise between our needs.
6	**nanorobot** ['nænəʊˌrəʊbɒt]	Nanoroboter	very small automatic device

23 Plastic money for young people

	cool [kuːl]	cool, kühl	School is cool!
	pre-paid [ˌpriː'peɪd]	vorausbezahlt	You must pay for it before you can use it.
	must-have ['mʌsthæv]	etwas Unentbehrliches	something that people think is very important and fashionable
	massive ['mæsɪv]	massiv, umfangreich	very large
	campaign [kæm'peɪn]	Kampagne	planned activity carried out over a period of time
	logical ['lɒdʒɪkl]	logisch	Mathematics is a logical science.
	to withdraw (withdrew, withdrawn) [wɪð'drɔː, wɪð'druː, wɪð'drɔːn]	abheben, (sich) entfernen	If you need cash, you can withdraw money from your bank account.
	cash machine ['kæʃ məˌʃiːn]	Bankautomat	an appliance that lets you get money from your account
	to top up [tɒp 'ʌp]	füllen, aufladen	to make something full again
	personal identification number [ˌpɜːsənl aɪˌdentɪfɪ'keɪʃn ˌnʌmbə]	persönliche Identifikationsnummer	secret number that you use with a bank card, for example
	transaction [træn'zækʃn]	Übertragung, Transaktion, Geschäft	a piece of business
	debt [det]	Schulden	a sum of money that you owe somebody
	to consider [kən'sɪdə]	nachdenken über, überlegen, betrachten	to think about
	to cancel ['kænsl]	stornieren, sperren, absagen	One of the singers was ill, so the concert was cancelled.
	to issue ['ɪʃuː]	herausgeben	to give out, to come out
	monthly ['mʌnθlɪ]	monatlich	every month
	to reload [ˌriː'ləʊd]	wieder aufladen	to load again, to top up
	to discover [dɪ'skʌvə]	entdecken	to find sth. for the first time; to find sth. out
	notification [ˌnəʊtɪfɪ'keɪʃn]	Benachrichtigung, Meldung	information
	database ['deɪtəbeɪs]	Datenbank	collection of data stored in a computer
	sensible ['sensɪbl]	vernünftig	based on reason and not on feelings
	to handle ['hændl]	umgehen mit, handhaben	to deal with
	virtual ['vɜːtʃʊəl]	virtuell	In a computer game, everything you do is virtual, it's not real.
5	**picnic** ['pɪknɪk]	Picknick	outdoor meal
	hamper ['hæmpə]	Korb, Deckelkorb	basket
	soda bread ['səʊdəbred]	Brot (mit Backsoda gebacken)	special kind of bread baked with baking soda

24 Business, transport and ecology

	to revolutionize [ˌrevə'luːʃənaɪz]	revolutionieren	to revolutionize → revolution
	to shop [ʃɒp]	einkaufen	to go shopping

Unit vocabulary

	founder member [ˌfaʊndə ˈmembə]	Gründungsmitglied	person who helped to establish a company
	to reveal [rɪˈviːl]	enthüllen, preisgeben, verraten	to inform the public
	weekly [ˈwiːklɪ]	wöchentlich	every week
	groceries [ˈgrəʊsərɪz]	Lebensmittel	usually plural: groceries – food and other things for the home that are bought regularly
	evolution [ˌiːvəˈluːʃn]	Evolution, Entwicklung	development
	drastic [ˈdræstɪk]	drastisch	If prices rise drastically, they suddenly go up a lot.
	behaviour [bɪˈheɪvjə]	Verhalten, Benehmen	behaviour → to behave
	shopper [ˈʃɒpə]	Käufer(in)	shopper → shopping
	horrified [ˈhɒrɪfaɪd]	entsetzt	horrified → horror
	to select [sɪˈlekt]	auswählen	to choose
	out-of-town [ˌaʊt ̩əv ˈtaʊn]	außerstädtisch	built in the countryside outside a town
	hypermarket [ˈhaɪpəˌmɑːkɪt]	Hypermarkt, Einkaufszentrum, großer Einkaufsmarkt	very large supermarket, usually built outside a town
	to emerge [ɪˈmɜːdʒ]	aufkommen, sich entwickeln	to appear
	via [vaɪə]	via, über	Please contact me via e-mail.
	to focus (on) [ˈfəʊkəs]	sich konzentrieren (auf)	to concentrate on
	to maintain [meɪnˈteɪn]	behaupten, aufrechterhalten	to point to
	vast [vɑːst]	riesig	huge, very large
	to promote [prəˈməʊt]	fördern, unterstützen	to support
	carbon footprint [ˌkɑːbn ˈfʊtprɪnt]	CO$_2$-Bilanz	emission of carbon dioxide
	efficient [ɪˈfɪʃnt]	effizient, leistungsfähig, ertragreich	An efficient person or machine works quickly and well.
1	**progressive** [prəˈgresɪv]	fortschrittlich, progressiv	interested in new ideas
	to found [faʊnd]	gründen	to establish
2	**to make sense** [meɪk ˈsens]	Sinn machen	If sth. makes sense, you can understand it.
5	**convenient** [kənˈviːnɪənt]	bequem, günstig	If sth. is convenient, it is easy and quick to use.
	luxurious [lʌgˈʒʊərɪəs]	luxuriös	exclusive, comfortable, expensive
	suite [swiːt]	Suite, Zimmerflucht, Appartement	set of rooms
	air conditioning [ˈeəkənˌdɪʃənɪŋ]	Klimaanlage	device for controlling the temperature of rooms
	Cantonese [ˌkæntəˈniːz]	kantonesisch	connected with an area in southern China
	recommendation [ˌrekəmenˈdeɪʃn]	Empfehlung	recommendation → to recommend
	classic [ˈklæsɪk]	klassisch	typical
	refined [rɪˈfaɪnd]	raffiniert, verfeinert, fein	brought to a finer state
	Premier League [ˌpremɪə ˈliːg]	höchste englische Spielklasse im Fußball	Chelsea, Arsenal and Manchester United are Premier League clubs.
	quay [kiː]	Kai	where boats can stop
	waterfront [ˈwɔːtəfrʌnt]	nahe am Wasser	situated near the water
	entertainment [ˌentəˈteɪnmənt]	Unterhaltung	Movies, songs and plays are all kinds of entertainment.

25 Globalisation and fair trade

ethics [ˈeθɪks]	Gesinnung, Ethik, Moral	principles, belief
rebel [ˈrebəl]	Rebell(in)	sb. who is against traditional ways of doing things
capitalist [ˈkæpɪtəlɪst]	Kapitalist	In a capitalist society, industry is owned privately, and not by the state.
hippy [ˈhɪpɪ]	Hippie	person, especially of the late 1960s, who was against established institutions and values
boost [buːst]	Aufschwung, Anstieg	increase
overall [ˌəʊvəˈrɔːl]	insgesamt, global, allgemein	as a whole
statistics [stəˈtɪstɪks]	Statistik	Statistics show facts in the form of figures.

Unit vocabulary

	mainstreamed ['meɪnstriːmd]	akzeptiert, etabliert	mainstream → stream
	to urge [ɜːdʒ]	drängen	to try to persuade
	throughout [θruːˈaʊt]	während der/des ganzen …	from beginning to end
	supply [səˈplaɪ]	Lieferung, Beschaffung	supply → to supply
	livelihood ['laɪvlɪhʊd]	Existenz, Lebensgrundlage	livelihood → to live → life
	ethical ['eθɪkl]	ethisch, moralisch	ethical → ethics
	acceptable [əkˈseptəbl]	akzeptabel, annehmbar	acceptable → to acecpt
	hype [haɪp]	Rummel, Medienrummel	exaggerated publicity
	to greenwash ['griːnwɒʃ]	ein grünes Mäntelchen umhängen, schönfärben mit Umweltphrasen	to whitewash – to make sth. look better than it really is
	PR (Public Relations) [piːˈɑː]	Öffentlichkeitsarbeit	actions of a company to promote relations to the public
	to boast [bəʊst]	angeben, prahlen	This is what show-offs often do.
	to amount (to) [əˈmaʊnt̮ tə]	ausmachen, sich belaufen (auf)	to amount → the amount
	bean [biːn]	Bohne	This vegetable is often green, but it can also be red, white or even black.
	to call on ['kɔːl ɒn]	appellieren an, besuchen	to ask, to appeal to
	to come clean [kʌm ˈkliːn]	reinen Wein einschenken, die Wahrheit sagen	to tell the truth
	to react [rɪˈækt]	reagieren	What did he say? How did he react?
	not before time [ˌnɒt̮ bɪˌfɔː ˈtaɪm]	keine Minute zu früh	a little late
5	**to certify** ['sɜːtɪfaɪ]	zertifizieren, bescheinigen	to certify → certificate
	honey ['hʌnɪ]	Honig	sweet yellow or brown food made by bees

Video lounge

Video lounge 1
Applying for a job placement

1	**to take a seat** [ˌteɪk ə ˈsiːt]	Platz nehmen, hinsetzen	You don't need to stand. You can take a seat.
	self-confidence [ˌselfˈkɒnfɪdəns]	Selbstbewusstsein	Debbie has got a lot of self-confidence. She believes that she can do anything.
	exhausting [ɪgˈzɔːstɪŋ]	anstrengend, erschöpfend	The meeting lasted for four hours. It was exhausting for everyone.
	coordination [kəʊˌɔːdɪˈneɪʃn]	Koordination, Abstimmung	To be good at sport your hand-eye coordination must be good.
	faux pas [ˌfəʊˈpɑː]	Fehlgriff, Fehltritt, Entgleisung, Fauxpas	doing sth. that is impolite
	to embarrass [ɪmˈbærəs]	verlegen machen, verwirren, blamieren	While I was kissing my boyfriend my mum came in. That was really embarrassing.
	uncomfortable [ʌnˈkʌmftəbl]	unbequem	uncomfortable ↔ comfortable
	Japanese [ˌdʒæpəˈniːz]	japanisch	Japanese → Japan
	to bow [baʊ]	sich verbeugen	When sb. bows they show respect.
	no matter [ˌnəʊ ˈmætə]	egal	I will stay with you no matter what happens.
	calm [kɑːm]	ruhig	calm ↔ nervous
	providing [prəˈvaɪdɪŋ]	vorausgesetzt	providing → to provide

Video lounge 2
Manufacturing

transformation [ˌtrænsfəˈmeɪʃn]	Verwandlung, Umgestaltung	transformation → to transform
to boast (sth.) [bəʊst]	angeben, sich einer Sache rühmen	This is what show-offs often do.
symbol ['sɪmbl]	Symbol	A heart can be used as a symbol of love.
presence ['prezəns]	Gegenwart, Präsenz	presence → present tense
humpback whale [ˌhʌmpbæk ˈweɪl]	Buckelwal	very large animal living in the oceans

287

Unit vocabulary

giant ['dʒaɪənt]	riesig	very big
under wraps [ˌʌndə 'ræps]	heimlich, geheim	wrap → to wrap
Working Lunch [ˌwɜːkɪŋ 'lʌntʃ]	Arbeitsessen	title of a BBC series
shot [ʃɒt]	Aufnahme, Schuss	shot → to shoot
Danish ['deɪnɪʃ]	dänisch	If you go north through Germany, you'll come to the Danish border.
incredible [ɪn'kredəbl]	unglaublich	That's an incredible story.
expansion [ɪk'spænʃn]	Ausdehnung, Expansion	expansion → to expand
involved [ɪn'vɒlvd]	beteiligt, involviert	If you are involved, you take part in sth.
fantastic [fæn'tæstɪk]	fantastisch	Surfing is fantastic.
to presume [prɪ'zjuːm]	annehmen, vermuten	to suppose
to lobby ['lɒbɪ]	sich einsetzen für	to try to influence politicians
viable ['vaɪəbl]	brauchbar, praktikabel	practicable, workable
in charge of [ɪn 'tʃɑːdʒ ɒv]	verantwortlich für	responsible for
confidence ['kɒnfɪdəns]	Vertrauen	confidence → confident
undeveloped [ˌʌndɪ'veləpt]	nicht entwickelt	undeveloped → developed → to develop
reflection [rɪ'flekʃn]	Spiegelbild, Reflektierung	reflection → to reflect
approach [ə'prəʊtʃ]	Einstellung, Annäherung	approach → to approach
vibrant ['vaɪbrənt]	dynamisch	dynamic
obvious ['ɒbvɪəs]	offensichtlich	easy to see or understand
business park ['bɪznɪs ˌpɑːk]	Gewerbegebiet	area where a lot of companies are situated
coastal ['kəʊstl]	Küsten-	belonging to the coast
strip [strɪp]	Streifen	a long, narrow piece of sth., for example cloth, metal, land
torrid ['tɒrɪd]	glühend heiß, hier eher: mühselig, schwierig	very hot
scenery ['siːnərɪ]	Landschaft	what you see around you when you're out in the country
to thrive [θraɪv]	gut gehen, prosperieren	to do well, to grow strongly
recession [rɪ'seʃn]	Rezession, Konjunkturschwäche	a serious slowdown in economic activity
to boom [buːm]	einen Aufschwung nehmen	to boom → the boom
proximity [prɒk'sɪmətɪ]	Nähe, Nachbarschaft	proximity ↔ distance
package ['pækɪdʒ]	Paket	a package → to pack

Video lounge 3

Ecology and/or economy?

to drill [drɪl]	bohren	to make a hole
unspoiled [ʌn'spɔɪlt]	unberührt, unbeschädigt	undamaged, intact
wilderness ['wɪldənəs]	Wildnis	wilderness → wild → wildlife
fragile ['frædʒaɪl]	zerbrechlich	Glass is very fragile. You need to take care.
undeveloped [ˌʌndɪ'veləpt]	nicht entwickelt	undeveloped ↔ developed
wildlife ['waɪldlaɪf]	Tierwelt (in freier Wildbahn)	all animals that don't live in zoos, people's homes or on farms
circle ['sɜːkl]	Kreis	Please put the chairs into a circle.
coastal ['kəʊstl]	Küsten-	coastal → coast
plain [pleɪn]	Ebene, Fläche	a wide, open space
corporation [ˌkɔːpə'reɪʃn]	Aktiengesellschaft	The corporation employs some 60,000 people worldwide.
to lobby for sth. ['lɒbɪ]	sich für etwas einsetzen	to lobby → lobbyist
to exploit [ɪk'splɔɪt]	verwerten, ausbeuten	to use sth. in order to make money
pristine ['prɪstiːn]	makellos	completely clean
haven ['heɪvən]	Zufluchtsort, Hafen	a place that is safe
musk ox ['mʌsk ˌɒks]	Moschusochse	a mammal that lives in the Arctic
wolf, pl. wolves [wʊlf; wʊlvz]	Wolf	Wolves belong to the dog family.
caribou ['kærɪbuː]	Rentier, Karibu	A caribou is a North American reindeer.
to keep out [kiːp 'aʊt]	abhalten, fernhalten	Keep out of my room! I want to be alone!

Unit vocabulary

calving grounds [ˈkɑːvɪŋ ˌɡraʊndz]	Gebiet, in dem Säugetiere ihre Jungen bekommen (gebären)	a place where wild animals give birth
hunt [hʌnt]	Jagd	hunt → to hunt → hunter
underway [ˌʌndəˈweɪ]	unterwegs, im Gange	on the move
herd [hɜːd]	Herde	many animals of one kind living together
to suspect [səˈspekt]	vermuten, misstrauen	to believe, to mistrust
migration [maɪˈɡreɪʃn]	Migration, Abwanderung, Umzug	migration ↔ immigration
sprawl [sprɔːl]	Ausbreitung	expansion, spread
to stretch [stretʃ]	dehnen, strecken	Before you do any sport you should do some stretching exercises.
to extract [ɪkˈstrækt]	gewinnen, herausziehen, entnehmen	to take sth. out (of the ground)
survival [səˈvaɪvl]	Überleben	to survive → survival → survivor

Video lounge 4
Travel and tourism

guess [ɡes]	Vermutung	guess → to guess
degree [dɪˈɡriː]	Hochschulabschluss	title given by a university or college when a student successfully completes a course
move [muːv]	Schritt, Bewegung, Zug	move → to move
tour operator [ˈtʊərˌɒpəreɪtə]	Reiseveranstalter(in)	operator → to operate
to happen to do sth. [ˌhæpn tə ˈduː ˌsʌmθɪŋ]	zufällig etwas tun	to do sth. by chance
Egypt [ˈiːdʒɪpt]	Ägypten	country in the north east of Africa
to get hooked on [ɡet ˈhʊkt ɒn]	süchtig werden nach	hooked → hook
obvious [ˈɒbvɪəs]	offensichtlich	easy to see or understand
lifestyle [ˈlaɪfstaɪl]	Lebensstil, Lebensart	the way you live your life
cause [kɒz]	weil	(short form of) because
sort (of) [sɔːt]	Art, Sorte	kind (of)
preferable [ˈprefrəbl]	wünschenswert	preferable → to prefer
to get on with [ˌɡet ˈɒn wɪð]	mit jmdm. auskommen	to have good relations
beneficial [ˌbenəˈfɪʃl]	nützlich, vorteilhaft	helpful
to put sb. off [pʊt ˌsʌmbədɪˈɒf]	jmdm. die Lust nehmen, jmdn. ablenken	to make sb. lose interest in
in essence [ɪn ˈesəns]	in der Hauptsache, im Wesentlichen	mainly
to get sth. under sb.'s belt [ɡet ˌsʌmθɪŋ ˌʌndə ˌsʌmbədɪz ˈbelt]	hier etwa: Erfahrung bekommen	to make sb. have some experience
prior to [ˈpraɪə tuː]	bevor	before
guidebook [ˈɡaɪdbʊk]	Reiseführer	Tourists often take a guidebook when they visit new places.
library [ˈlaɪbrərɪ]	Bibliothek, Bücherei	There are many interesting books in our library.
logistics [ləˈdʒɪstɪks]	Logistik(leistung), Unterbringungs- und Verpflegungswesen	logistics → logical
to pick up [pɪkˈʌp]	abholen	to take a person into a car
spot on [ˌspɒtˈɒn]	genau richtig	right
smooth [smuːθ]	glatt	free from difficulties
minor [ˈmaɪnə]	klein, gering(fügig)	not important
hiccup [ˈhɪkʌp]	Problemchen, Schluckauf	not very important problem
itinerary [aɪˈtɪnərərɪ]	Programmablauf, Reiseroute	a detailed plan of a journey
self-centred [ˌselfˈsentəd]	ichbezogen, egozentrisch	A person whose interests always come first is self-centred.
to get along with [ˌɡet əˈlɒŋ wɪð]	mit jmdm. auskommen, sich verstehen mit	to have good relations
walk of life [ˌwɔːk əv ˈlaɪf]	Gesellschaftsschicht, soziale Schicht	social background

Unit vocabulary

throughout [θruː'aʊt]	während des/der ganzen ...	from the beginning to the end
guy [gaɪ]	Typ, Mann	Our new classmate is a really cool guy.
to grab [græb]	greifen, (sich) schnappen	I was late so I just grabbed my school bag and left.
package tour ['pækɪdʒ ˌtʊə]	Pauschalreise	a planned tour in which one fee is charged for all expenses
rep [rep]	Vertreter(in), Beauftragte(r), Agent(in)	(short form of) representative
to run [rʌn]	durchführen, führen, laufen	to organize (a company, business etc.)
off the beaten track [ˌɒf ðə ˌbiːtn 'træk]	abseits der ausgetretenen Pfade	out of the ordinary
inevitable [ɪn'evɪtəbl]	unvermeidlich	sure to happen, certain
at ease with [ət 'iːz wɪð]	behaglich bei, wohl bei	carefree, not worried
backpack ['bækpæk]	Rucksack	back + pack = backpack; a bag that you carry on your back
tedious ['tiːdɪəs]	ermüdend, langweilig, nervtötend	tiring, boring
to block [blɒk]	abblocken, absperren	to keep out
campsite ['kæmpsaɪt]	Campingplatz	On a camping trip you stay on a campsite.
tent [tent]	Zelt	The campsite was so full that there was almost no space between the tents.
distinct [dɪ'stɪŋkt]	eindeutig, unterschieden	clear, separate, different
downside ['daʊnsaɪd]	Nachteil, Kehrseite	disadvantage
to bottle sth. up [ˌbɒtl ˌsʌmθɪŋ 'ʌp]	in sich hineinfressen	to keep things to oneself
to absorb [əb'zɔːb]	absorbieren, schlucken	to take up
track [træk]	Spur, Fährte, Weg	Some animals leave tracks in the forest.
to alleviate [ə'liːvɪeɪt]	erleichtern, verringern	to make easier
boredom ['bɔːdəm]	Langeweile	boredom ↔ amusement
to crop up [krɒp 'ʌp]	auftreten, sich zeigen	to appear suddenly

Video lounge 5
American immigration

Mexican ['meksɪkn]	mexikanisch	a Mexican town = a town in Mexico
to thrive [θraɪv]	Erfolg haben, gedeihen, blühen	A thriving business can bring a lot of money into a town.
dusty ['dʌstɪ]	staubig	If you don't clean your room, everything starts to get dusty.
anticipation [ænˌtɪsɪ'peɪʃn]	Vorahnung, Erwartung	speculation, expectation
shadow ['ʃædəʊ]	Schatten	Shadows are longer in the evening than in the middle of the day.
to gather ['gæðə]	(sich) sammeln	to collect, to get together, to understand
brick [brɪk]	Ziegelstein	Nearly all of the houses in Germany are made of brick.
equipped [ɪ'kwɪpt]	ausgestattet, ausgerüstet	equipped → to equip → equipment
desert ['dezət]	Wüste	It doesn't rain very often in the desert.
exhaustion [ɪg'zɔːstʃn]	Erschöpfung, Überanstrengung	I couldn't run anymore. I was crying from exhaustion.
urban ['ɜːbn]	städtisch	Towns and cities are urban areas.
undergrowth ['ʌndəgrəʊθ]	Gestrüpp, Unterholz	We were not able to go through the undergrowth because it was too thick.
trick [trɪk]	Trick	an illusion is a kind of trick played on sb.
to dig, dug, dug [dɪg, dʌg, dʌg]	graben	They dug a big hole in our garden for the new swimming pool.
border patrol ['bɔːdə pəˌtrəʊl]	Grenzschutz	The border patrol checks the borders day and night.
giant ['dʒaɪənt]	riesig	huge, big
fan [fæn]	Ventilator	It is very hot in this room. Could you please turn on the fan?
to give chase to sb. [gɪv 'tʃeɪs]	jemanden verfolgen	to run after sb. in order to catch them
tally ['tælɪ]	Summe, Anzahl	a number of things

Unit vocabulary

on the lookout [ɒn ðə ˈlʊkaʊt]	Ausschau halten	watching for sth.
terrorist [ˈterərɪst]	Terrorist(in)	terrorist → terrible → terrified
to be deported [bɪ dɪˈpɔːtɪd]	abgeschoben werden	to make an immigrant leave a country he or she has entered illegally
to light up [laɪt ˈʌp]	beleuchten	to light up → light
flashlight [ˈflæʃlaɪt]	Taschenlampe	an electric light that you can hold in your hand
deer, pl. deer [dɪə]	Hirsch	If you are lucky, you may see a deer in the woods.
Minuteman, pl. Minutemen [ˈmɪnɪtmæn]	Freiwilliger, der auf Abruf bereit steht	We need the Minutemen to stop people crossing the border illegally.
determination [dɪˌtɜːmɪˈneɪʃn]	Entschlossenheit	determination → to determine
night vision goggles [ˌnaɪtvɪʒn ˈgɒglz]	Nachtsichtgerät	I need my night vision goggles to see in the dark.
migrant [ˈmaɪgrənt]	Migrant(in), Übersiedler(in)	migrant → to migrate → migration
gun [gʌn]	Schusswaffe	A man with a gun went into a shop and said, "Give me the money!"
Dad's Army [ˌdædzˈɑːmɪ]	englische Fernsehkomödie	
self-defence [ˌselfɪˈfens]	Selbstverteidigung, Notwehr	The man attacked me so I hit him in self-defence.
to commit [kəˈmɪt]	begehen, verüben	He committed suicide.
bitter [ˈbɪtə]	bitter, verärgert	When my friend lied to me I was very bitter.
battle [ˈbætl]	Schlacht	Armies fight in battles.
migration [maɪˈgreɪʃn]	Migration, Wanderung, Umzug	migration → to migrate → migrant
flimsy [ˈflɪmzɪ]	schwach, dünn, fadenscheinig	The walls are very flimsy. The next strong wind will blow them away.
fence [fens]	Zaun	With a fence around the field, the cattle can't get out.
economics [ˌiːkəˈnɒmɪks]	Volkswirtschaftslehre, Wirtschaftswissenschaften	economics → economy → economist
leaf, pl. leaves [liːf; liːvz]	Blatt	leaf → to leaf (e.g. through a book)

Video lounge 6
A job placement at reception

absolutely [ˌæbsəˈluːtlɪ]	absolut	completely
valid [ˈvælɪd]	gültig	The credit card isn't valid anymore, it expired last month.

Role cards

Unit 6

B5	overfishing [ˌəʊvəˈfɪʃɪŋ]	Überfischung	overfishing → fishing → fish
	exotic [ɪgˈzɒtɪk]	exotisch	I love exotic dishes, but I don't always want to know exactly what I'm eating.
	economic [ˌiːkəˈnɒmɪk]	ökonomisch, wirtschaftlich	economic → economy
	fisherman, pl. fishermen [ˈfɪʃəmən]	Fischer	fisherman → fishing → fish

Unit 8

D4	economical [ˌiːkəˈnɒmɪkl]	wirtschaftlich, sparsam	economically → economic → economical → economy

Unit 11

2	full board [ˌfʊlˈbɔːd]	Vollpension, Vollverpflegung	full board ↔ half board
	half board [ˌhɑːfˈbɔːd]	Halbpension	half board ↔ full board

Unit 12

5	ferry [ˈferɪ]	Fähre	a boat that takes passengers and cars across a river or a narrow bit of sea
	ballroom dancing [ˌbɔːlrʊm ˈdɑːnsɪŋ]	Gesellschaftstanz	a formal kind of dancing

291

Alphabetical vocabulary

A

abbreviation Abkürzung 81
above oben 8
absolutely absolut 171
to absorb absorbieren, schlucken 170
acceptable akzeptabel, annehmbar 164
access Zugang 37
accessible zugänglich, befahrbar 65
accession Beitritt, Einwilligung, Zuwachs 86
accessory Zubehör, Accessoire 73
to accommodate unterbringen, anpassen, aushelfen 102
accommodation Unterbringung 41
according to laut, entsprechend 36
account Konto, Abrechnung, Berechnung, Wert 102
accountancy Rechnungswesen, Buchführung 20
to acknowledge bestätigen, anerkennen 122
to act handeln, sich verhalten, spielen 51
action Aktion, Handlung 54
active aktiv 21
activist Aktivist(in), jemand, der sich für etwas engagiert 148
to act out aufführen 27
additional zusätzlich 28
to add (up) zusammenzählen 54
adjective Adjektiv 35
administration Verwaltung, Regierung, Behörde 23
adult Erwachsene(r) 10
adventure Abenteuer 65
advert Anzeige 21
advertiser Inserent(in), Werbefachmann/-frau 28
advertising agency Werbeagentur 9
to advise (sb. to do sth.) (jmdm.) raten (etwas zu tun) 13
advisor Berater(in), Ratgeber(in) 52
aeroplane Flugzeug 52
affair Affäre 42
to affect auswirken, beeinflussen 33
to afford sich leisten 86
aged im Alter von 33
agency Agentur 30
agriculture Landwirtschaft 52
aid Hilfe 79
to aim anstreben, zielen 49
air conditioning Klimaanlage 163
aircraft Flugzeug 38
airline Fluggesellschaft 65
air mile Flugmeile 52
alert Alarm 28
algae pl. Algen, Tang 51
alive lebendig 68

All Blacks die neuseeländische Rugby-Union-Nationalmannschaft 102
to alleviate erleichtern, verringern 170
all over überall 108
ally Alliierte(r), Verbündete(r) 86
alright in Ordnung 70
to amount (to) ausmachen, sich belaufen (auf) 164
analysis Analyse 39
to analyze analysieren 31
anniversary Jubiläum, Hochzeitstag 102
annual jährlich 57
to anticipate vorhersehen, erwarten 44
anticipation Vorahnung, Erwartung 171
anyway jedenfalls, trotzdem 41
apart from abgesehen von, außer 51
to apologize sich entschuldigen 75
appealing ansprechend, reizvoll 144
appliance Gerät, Anwendung 54
applicant Bewerber(in) 22
application Anwendung, Bewerbung 62
appointment Berufung, Termin 84
to appreciate schätzen 89
apprenticeship Ausbildung 73
approach Einstellung, Annäherung 168
to approve anerkennen, bestätigen, zustimmen, akzeptieren 84
Argentinian argentinisch 52
to argue diskutieren, streiten, argumentieren 53
argument Streit, Argument 67
to arm bewaffnen (mit) 45
armed forces Militär, Streitkräfte 84
to arrange organisieren, ausmachen 83
art Kunst 26
Asian asiatisch 76
aspect Aspekt, Gesichtspunkt 49
assembly line Fließband, Fertigungsstraße 47
to assign zuordnen 152
to assist assistieren, helfen 13
assistance Hilfe 53
assistant Assistent(in), Mitarbeiter(in) 144
assistant tax consultant Steuerfachangestellte(r) 13
to associate verbinden, assoziieren 70
to assure etw. zusichern 113
as well as sowohl … als auch 52
at ease with behaglich bei, wohl bei 170
at risk gefährdet 28
to attach anhängen, anbringen 116
attention line Zeile in der Adresse mit Angabe des Empfängers (zu Händen) 99
at the latest spätestens 122
attitude (to/towards) Haltung, Einstellung 44

to attract anziehen 31
attraction Attraktion, Anziehungspunkt, Anziehungskraft 68
attractive attraktiv 65
auction Versteigerung 28
Aussie (informal) Australier(in) 102
Australian Australier(in) 66
Austrian österreichisch 72
authentic authentisch 76
automated automatisch, automatisiert 47
automatic automatisch 45
availability Verfügbarkeit, Verwendbarkeit 90
available frei, erhältlich 97
average Durchschnitt 33
to avoid (ver)meiden 51
award Preis, Auszeichnung 43

B

background Hintergrund 14
backpack Rucksack 170
backup Unterstützung, Sicherung 68
balance Gleichgewicht, Balance 45
to balance (aus-)balancieren, ins Gleichgewicht bringen 46
ballroom dancing Gesellschaftstanz 174
ban Verbot 31
to ban verbieten 31
banana Banane 52
bank clerk Bankkaufmann/-frau 22
bank employee Bankkaufmann, Bankkauffrau 22
bankrupt bankrott, insolvent 86
bar chart Säulendiagramm, Balkendiagramm 32
barefoot barfuß 81
based on basierend auf 145
basic grundlegend 149
battle Schlacht 171
bean Bohne 164
to beat, beat, beaten besiegen, schlagen 53
beauty Schönheit 42
to be based Geschäftssitz haben 28
bed and breakfast Pension 90
to be delighted glücklich sein, sehr zufrieden sein 88
to be deported abgeschoben werden 171
beef Rindfleisch 52
beer Bier 94
to behave sich benehmen 28
behaviour Verhalten, Benehmen 160
to be in touch mit jemandem in Verbindung stehen, mit jemandem in Kontakt bleiben 90
to be located sich befinden, gelegen sein 68

292

Alphabetical vocabulary

below unten 8
beneath unterhalb, unter 57
beneficial nützlich, vorteilhaft 170
benefit Sozialhilfe, Nutzen 148
to benefit (from) Nutzen ziehen (aus), profitieren (von) 50
to be on zu sehen sein (Sendung) 30
to be on business auf Geschäftsreise sein 97
to be related to sich beziehen auf, betreffen 152
beside neben 57
to be up to entsprechen 130
bid Gebot 28
bill Rechnung, Banknote 102
billboard Plakatwand 102
billion Milliarde 152
bin Mülleimer, Mülltonne 67
biofuel Biotreibstoff 57
Biology Biologie 10
bioreserve (Bio-)Reservat 68
biotechnology Biotechnologie 60
bitter bitter, verärgert 171
blade Flügel, Klinge, Blatt 57
to block abblocken, absperren 170
blog Internet-Tagebuch 8
to blow, blew, blown wehen, blasen 57
to boast (sth.) angeben, sich einer Sache rühmen 168
to boast angeben, prahlen 164
booking Buchung, Reservierung 65
bookshop Buchhandlung 40
bookstore Buchladen 97
boomerang Bumerang 54
to boom einen Aufschwung nehmen 168
boost Aufschwung, Anstieg 164
border patrol Grenzschutz 171
boredom Langeweile 170
to bottle sth. up in sich hineinfressen 170
to bow sich verbeugen 168
bracket Klammer 19
brain Gehirn 33
branch Zweigstelle, Zweig, Abzweigung, Sektor 51
brand Marke 17
Brazilian brasilianisch 52
to breathe atmen 48
brick Ziegelstein 171
bright hell 38
Brit umgangssprachlicher Ausdruck für einen Engländer 103
broadband Breitband(-) 60
browser Browser 34
BTec Abschluss an einer Berufs(fach)schule 144
budget Haushalt, Etat 80
bulb Glühbirne 47
Bulgaria Bulgarien 86
bureaucracy Bürokratie 86
business field Geschäftsbereich 17
businessman Geschäftsmann 97
business park Gewerbegebiet 168
business studies Betriebswirtschaftslehre 9

busy besetzt, belegt 75
button Knopf, Taste 35
to by-pass überbrücken, umgehen 86
by return postwendend, umgehend 122

C

cafeteria Kantine, Cafeteria 25
calculation Berechnung, Kalkulation 37
caller Anrufer(in) 75
to call on appellieren an, besuchen 164
calm ruhig 168
calorie Kalorie 52
calving grounds Gebiet, in dem Säugetiere ihre Jungen bekommen (gebären) 169
campaign Kampagne 156
campsite Campingplatz 170
to cancel stornieren, sperren, absagen 28
candidate Bewerber(in) 22
canoe Kanu 134
Cantonese kantonesisch 163
cap Kappe, Mütze 59
capitalist Kapitalist 164
carbon dioxide Kohlendioxyd, CO_2 49
carbon footprint CO_2-Bilanz 160
care Pflege, Sorge 81
Caribbean Karibik, karibisch 68
caribou Rentier, Karibu 169
to carry on weiterführen 76
to carry out ausführen 82
carton Karton, Schachtel 129
cartoonist Karikaturist(in) 39
carving Schnitzarbeit 68
cash desk Kasse 15
cashier Kassierer(in) 62
cash machine Bankautomat 156
catalogue Katalog 64
catastrophe Katastrophe 51
catastrophic katastrophal 30
to catch sth. etwas akustisch verstehen 90
cattle (pl. only) Vieh 57
cause weil 170
CCTV (closed circuit television) Video-überwachungsanlage 39
to celebrate feiern 54
cell phone Handy, Mobiltelefon 45
Celsius Celsius 38
central zentral 68
certain bestimmt, gewiss 29
to certify zertifizieren, bescheinigen 166
chain Kette 19
challenge Herausforderung 21
to challenge herausfordern 53
chance Chance 72
to change one's mind seine Meinung ändern 29
character Charakter, (Roman-)Figur 22
to charge in Rechnung stellen, berechnen 90
to chat chatten, sich (online) unterhalten 150
check Rechnung (im Restaurant) *(AE)*, Scheck *(AE)*, Prüfung 102

checkout Kasse, Abschlusskontrolle, Auschecken 21
checks and balances gegenseitige Kontrolle, Gewaltenteilung 84
chef Koch, Köchin 12
chemical Chemikalie 73
chemist's Apotheke, Drogerie 41
chicken Hühnerfleisch 94
chief Häuptling 103
childcare Kinderbetreuung 144
cholera Cholera 81
circle Kreis 169
to circulate zirkulieren, herumgehen 95
citizen Bürger(in), Staatsangehörige(r) 52
citizenship Staatsangehörigkeit, Nationalität, Bürgerrecht 84
to claim behaupten, beanspruchen 148
classic klassisch 163
cleanliness Reinheit, Sauberkeit 154
click Klick(en) 152
to click klicken 34
client Kunde/Kundin, Klient(in) 62
climate Klima 30
closed gesperrt, geschlossen 38
closet Wandschrank, Kammer 102
CNC production numerisch mit Rechnern gesteuerte Produktion 47
coaching Übungsleitung (beim Sport), Nachhilfe 144
coal-fired mit Kohle betrieben, Kohle- 58
coastal Küsten- 169
cocktail Cocktail 94
cocoa Kakao 79
collage Collage 55
colleague Kollege/Kollegin 92
colloquial umgangssprachlich 41
columnist Schreiber(in), Kolumnist(in) 43
to combine kombinieren 46
combustion Verbrennungs- 47
to come clean reinen Wein einschenken, die Wahrheit sagen 164
comedian Komiker(in) 43
to come on air zu Sendung sein 38
to come over herüberkommen 90
to come up to entsprechen, erfüllen, zukommen auf 106
Commander-in-Chief Oberbefehlshaber 84
comment Kommentar, Stellungnahme 36
to comment kommentieren, Stellung nehmen 36
commentary Kommentar 54
commentator Kommentator(in) 54
commercial Werbespot 27
commission Kommission, Provision 87
commissioner Beauftragte(r), Bevollmächtigte(r), Auftraggeber(in) 87
to commit begehen, verüben 171
committee Komitee, Ausschuss, Gremium 82
common gemeinsam, gebräuchlich 25
community Gemeinde, Gemeinschaft 49

293

Alphabetical vocabulary

to compete konkurrieren, mithalten, teilnehmen 53
competitive wettbewerbsfähig 60
to complain sich beschweren, klagen 57
complaint Beschwerde, Mängelrüge 128
complex komplex, vielfältig, kompliziert 49
complicated kompliziert 35
complimentary close Grußformel 89
composition Aufsatz, Komposition 61
comprehensive school Gesamtschule 43
compromise Kompromiss 154
to concentrate konzentrieren 45
concentration Ansammlung, Verdichtung, Konzentration 84
concept Entwurf, Konzept 55
concern Bedenken, Sorge, Anliegen 49
concerned betroffen 49
to conclude schließen, folgern 50
conclusion Schlussfolgerung 33
condition Kondition, Zustand, Situation 81
conditional Konditional 66
condom Kondom 41
condor Kondor 68
confectionery Süßwaren 17
to confess beichten, bekennen 45
confidence Vertrauen 168
to confirm bestätigen 97
confirmation Bestätigung 28
conflict Konflikt, Auseinandersetzung 54
to confuse verwirren 33
confused verwirrt 25
Congress Kongress (Parlament in den USA) 84
congressional Kongress-, den Kongress betreffend 84
connective Bindewort 61
consequence Konsequenz, Folge 33
consequent folgend, folgerichtig 65
conservation Erhaltung, Schutz 49
to consider nachdenken über, überlegen, betrachten 156
considerable beträchtlich 130
consignment Warensendung, Lieferung 128
to consist of bestehen aus 14
constant beständig, andauernd, konstant 33
constitution Verfassung 84
consumer Konsument(in), Verbraucher(in) 25
consumption Verbrauch 52
content Inhalt 130
context Kontext, Zusammenhang 53
continent Kontinent, Erdteil 86
contract Vertrag 29
contrast Gegensatz, Kontrast 61
to contribute beitragen 49
control Kontrolle 21
to control kontrollieren 84
convenience food Fertiggericht 17
convenience store Nachbarschaftsladen, Lebensmittelgeschäft 148
convenient bequem, günstig 163

conventional konventionell, normal 40
conversation Gespräch, Unterhaltung, Konversation 93
convinced überzeugt 22
cooking Kochen 30
cool cool, kühl 156
to cool (down) (ab-)kühlen 58
cooling-off period Widerspruchsfrist 28
to cool off (sich) abkühlen 70
coordination Koordination, Abstimmung 168
corporation Aktiengesellschaft 169
corridor Gang, Flur, Korridor 39
corruption Korruption, Bestechlichkeit 86
cosmetics Kosmetik 25
cosmopolitan atmosphere weltoffene Atmosphäre 12
could do with gebrauchen können, vertragen können (Getränk) 41
council Gremium, Rat 87
countryman Landsmann 86
country of origin Herkunftsland 13
countryside Landschaft, Land 40
County Council etwa: Kreisverwaltung 28
court Gericht, Hof, Spielfeld 37
to cover umfassen, (be)decken 108
to cover for sb. jemanden vertreten 93
crash Absturz, Unfall 38
to crash abstürzen 38
crate Kiste 130
cream Sahne, Creme 94
to create schaffen 30
creative kreativ, schöpferisch 45
credit Guthaben, Punkte, Vertrauen, Anerkennung 77
credit card Kreditkarte 42
crime Verbrechen 37
criminal kriminell 37
criterion, pl. **criteria** Kriterium, Kriterien 86
critic Kritiker(in) 144
criticism Kritik 152
critique Kritik 55
to crop up auftreten, sich zeigen 170
croquet Krocket 121
cross Kreuz 81
cultural kulturell 65
culture Kultur 100
curriculum vitae Lebenslauf 20
custard Vanillesauce 94
to cut senken, verringern, kürzen 52
to cut a long story short langer Rede kurzer Sinn 91
Czech Republic Tschechische Republik 73

D

Dad's Army englische Fernsehkomödie 171
Danish dänisch 168
data Daten 152
database Datenbank 156
to date back to zurückliegen 47
dated datiert, mit Datum vom 114

day by day jeden Tag, täglich 49
day off arbeitsfreier Tag 64
deadline Termin, Frist 138
to deal (with) bearbeiten, handeln (mit, von) 114
dealer Händler(in) 18
debt Schulden 156
decade Dekade, Jahrzehnt 54
decisive entscheidend, bestimmend, endscheidungsfreudig 86
declaration Erklärung 53
to declare erklären 84
to decrease abnehmen 37
deduction Abzug, Nachlass 41
deer, pl. **deer** Hirsch 171
defective fehlerhaft, schadhaft, defekt 130
to define definieren 86
definite bestimmt, klar, definitiv 53
definition Definition, Erklärung 41
degree Hochschulabschluss 170
delay Verzögerung 122
to delay aufschieben, (ver)zögern 108
delegate Delegierte(r), Abgeordnete(r), Bevollmächtigte(r) 84
to delete löschen 28
demand Bedarf, Nachfrage, Forderung 54
to demand verlangen, fordern 45
demanding anspruchsvoll 46
democracy Demokratie 86
demonstration Demonstration, Vorführung 106
dental assistant zahnmedizinische(r) Fachangestellte(r) 13
to depart abfliegen, abfahren 66
departure Abflug, Abfahrt 66
dependent (on) abhängig 57
deposit Lagerstätte, Guthaben, Anzahlung 58
deprived sozial benachteiligt 148
desert Wüste 171
design Design, Entwurf, Gestaltung 152
desktop Desktop, Benutzeroberfläche 34
desperate verzweifelt, aussichtslos 45
dessert Dessert, Nachtisch 94
destination Ziel, Reiseziel 65
detailed detailliert 29
determination Entschlossenheit 171
device Gerät 37
dialogue Dialog, Gespräch 27
diary Tagebuch, Terminbuch 97
to dig, dug, dug graben 171
dingo Dingo (australischer Wildhund) 102
disabled behindert 148
to disappear verschwinden 86
disaster Katastrophe, Desaster 51
disciplined diszipliniert 103
discount Rabatt, Nachlass 30
to discover entdecken 156
dish Gericht 94
dislike Abneigung 9
to dismiss entlassen, freistellen, ablehnen 148

294

Alphabetical vocabulary

dispatch Auslieferung, Abfertigung 129
to dispatch abschicken, abfertigen 124
to disregard ignorieren, unbeachtet lassen 137
distillery Brennerei 100
distinct eindeutig, unterschieden 170
distribution Vertrieb, Verteilung 30
distributor Verteiler, Lieferant, Vertrieb 88
district Distrikt, Bezirk, Stadtteil 148
diverse unterschiedlich, vielfältig, verschieden 76
to divide teilen 53
doctor's assistant medizinische(r) Fachangestellte(r) 13
documentary Dokumentarfilm 42
do-it-yourself (DIY) Heimwerker- 126
domain Domain 152
domestic Haushalts-, häuslich, inländisch 54
to donate spenden 50
donation Spende 50
to do poorly schlecht abschneiden 38
dot Punkt 90
double Doppel-, doppelt 42
doubt Zweifel 152
downhill abwärts, bergab 144
to download herunterladen 35
downside Nachteil, Kehrseite 170
dozen Dutzend 57
dramatic dramatisch 37
drastic drastisch 160
to draw sb.'s attention to jmds. Aufmerksamkeit lenken auf 138
dress code Kleiderordnung 103
drill Bohrer 42
to drill bohren 169
driving licence Führerschein 21
drop Tropfen; Abnahme, Verringerung 51
to drop (herunter)fallen, fallen lassen 27
drugstore Apotheke, Drogerie 41
dull langweilig 45
dusty staubig 171
to dye färben 73
dyer Färber(in) 73

E

eager eifrig 144
earnings Einnahmen, Erträge 152
earring Ohrring 59
eastern östlich, ost- 82
eco- Öko- 52
ecological ökologisch 68
ecology Ökologie 48
economic ökonomisch, wirtschaftlich 40
economical wirtschaftlich, sparsam 173
economics Volkswirtschaftslehre, Wirtschaftswissenschaften 171
educational lehrreich, bildend 33
effective effektiv, wirkungsvoll 62
efficient effizient, leistungsfähig, ertragreich 160
effort Mühe, Leistung, Versuch 53
Egypt Ägypten 170

either way so oder so 73
the elderly ältere Menschen 53
electrician Elektriker(in) 22
electricity Elektrizität 35
electronic elektronisch 33
elevator Aufzug 102
to eliminate beseitigen, entfernen, eliminieren 77
to embarrass verlegen machen, verwirren, blamieren 168
embarrassment Peinlichkeit, Verlegenheit 41
to emerge aufkommen, sich entwickeln 160
to emit emittieren, ausstoßen 49
emotional emotional, gefühlvoll, gerührt 95
to enclose beifügen 21
to encourage unterstützen, fördern, ermutigen 49
ending Ende 24
engaged verlobt 41
enlargement Vergrößerung, Erweiterung, Erhöhung 86
enormous riesig, enorm 52
to entail verursachen, mit sich bringen 129
to enter eingeben 152
entertainment Unterhaltung 163
enthusiastic enthusiastisch 62
environment Umwelt, Umgebung, Umfeld 35
environmentally-friendly umweltfreundlich 60
equipped ausgestattet, ausgerüstet 171
to erect errichten, aufstellen 60
erosion Erosion, Auswaschung, Verschleiß 54
to escape (from) flüchten (vor), entkommen 54
essay Aufsatz 10
essential wichtig 20
to establish aufbauen, (be-)gründen 68
ethical ethisch, moralisch 164
ethics Gesinnung, Ethik, Moral 164
ethnic ethnisch 77
Europe Europa 42
European Europäer(in); europäisch 13
European Court of Justice Europäischer Gerichtshof 87
European Monetary Union Europäische Wirtschafts- und Währungsunion 87
ever since seitdem 17
evolution Evolution, Entwicklung 160
to exchange umtauschen, austauschen 26
to execute durchführen 114
executive exekutiv, ausführend, leitend 84
executive suite Führungsloge, Vorstandsetage 93
exhaustible begrenzt, sich erschöpfend 57
exhausting anstrengend, erschöpfend 168

exhaustion Erschöpfung, Überanstrengung 171
exotic exotisch 173
to expand (sich) ausdehnen, expandieren 18
expansion Ausdehnung, Expansion 168
expectation Erwartung 106
to experience erfahren, erleben 93
expert Experte/Expertin 30
to exploit verwerten, ausbeuten 169
to extend (sich) ausdehnen 106
extract Auszug 28
to extract gewinnen, herausziehen, entnehmen 169
extraction Gewinnung, Förderung, Entnahme 65
extreme extrem 30
EXW ab Werk 114
ex works ab Werk 112

F

fabric Stoff, Gewebe 108
facility Einrichtung, Gelegenheit 145
factor Faktor, Einfluss 144
to fade ausbleichen, verblassen 133
to fail versagen 82
failure Versagen 144
fairly relativ 97
fairy tale Märchen 152
to fall ill krank werden 144
fan Ventilator 171
to fancy angetan sein von 95
fantastic fantastisch 168
fantasy Fantasie 37
faraway fern, weit entfernt 65
Far East Ferner Osten 65
fascinated fasziniert 30
fascinating faszinierend 68
faux pas Fehlgriff, Fehltritt, Entgleisung, Fauxpas 168
favourable günstig, vorteilhaft 56
fear Angst 149
federal Bundes- 84
fee Gebühr 41
feedback Rückmeldung, Feedback 28
feminist Feministin, Frauenrechtlerin 42
fence Zaun 171
ferry Fähre 174
fertiliser Dünger 52
fertilizer Dünger, Düngemittel 81
figure Zahl, Ziffer 144
file Datei 35
finally schließlich 58
fisherman, pl. fishermen Fischer 173
to fit (in) (hinein)passen 45
fixed fest 62
flag Fahne, Flagge 55
flame Flamme 38
to flash blinken, blitzen 48
flashlight Taschenlampe 171
to flee, fled, fled fliehen 81
flexible flexibel 37
flimsy schwach, dünn, fadenscheinig 171
flipside Rückseite 45

295

Alphabetical vocabulary

to float treiben, gleiten, mit dem Floß fahren 70
floor Stock, Etage 102
to flow fließen, strömen 57
fluency Sprachbeherrschung, Sprachgewandtheit 19
fluent flüssig 20
flyer Flugblatt 30
to focus (on) sich konzentrieren (auf) 160
to force zwingen 42
foreground Vordergrund 14
foreigner Ausländer(in) 103
to foresee vorhersehen, absehen 86
forest Wald 68
fork-lift truck Gabelstapler 110
formula Formel 31
fortnight vierzehn Tage, zwei Wochen 126
forum Forum, öffentliche Diskussion 148
fossil fuel fossiler Brennstoff 49
to found gründen 161
foundation Stiftung, Gründung, Fundament 55
founder member Gründungsmitglied 160
foyer Vorhalle, Foyer 93
fragile zerbrechlich 169
France Frankreich 66
fraudster Betrüger(in) 37
free kostenlos, frei 124
freedom Freiheit 42
freight Fracht 108
French fries Pommes frites 102
fried in der Pfanne gebraten 94
front office Empfang 89
frozen gefroren 17
fuel Brennstoff, Treibstoff, Benzin 67
full board Vollpension, Vollverpflegung 174
full-time (F/T) Vollzeit-, ganztags 9
function Funktion, Aufgabe(nbereich) 69
to function funktionieren 86
further education höhere Schulbildung, Aus- und Weiterbildung 21
furthermore überdies, außerdem 81

G

Gaelic football eine Sportart, die vorwiegend in Irland gespielt wird 102
to gain gewinnen 144
gamble Risiko 50
gas Gas, Benzin 49
gas station *(AE)* Tankstelle 102
to gather (sich) sammeln 171
GCSE Prüfung zum Abschluss der Sekundarstufe I 144
Geneva Genf 9
gender Geschlecht 30
general manager Generaldirektor(in), Geschäftsführer(in) 93
general office Zentrale, Allgemeine Verwaltung 93
to generate erzeugen, entwickeln, schaffen 57
generation Generation 76

Geography Geographie 10
to get along with mit jmdm. auskommen, sich verstehen mit 170
to get an insight einen Einblick bekommen 22
to get changed sich umziehen 14
to get dressed sich anziehen 27
to get hooked on süchtig werden nach 170
to get in touch (with) in Verbindung treten (mit) 114
to get on with mit jmdm. auskommen 170
to get sth. under sb.'s belt hier etwa: Erfahrung bekommen 170
to get used to (+ gerund) sich gewöhnen (an) 144
giant riesig 171
to give chase to sb. jemanden verfolgen 171
to give someone a buzz jemanden anrufen 91
global global 48
globalisation Globalisierung 72
to go ahead fortfahren 35
goal-oriented zielgerichtet, zielorientiert 45
to google googeln 152
googol Googol 152
to go wrong schiefgehen 67
to grab greifen, (sich) schnappen 170
grade Klasse, Schuljahr, Note 45
graduate Schulabgänger(in), Hochschulabsolvent(in) 45
grandchild Enkelkind, Enkel(in) 81
to grant gewähren 112
to graze grasen 57
Greece Griechenland 86
green-tech grüne (umweltfreundliche) Technologie (Abkürzung) 60
to greenwash ein grünes Mäntelchen umhängen, schönfärben mit Umweltphrasen 164
groceries Lebensmittel 160
ground Boden 37
to guarantee garantieren, gewährleisten 131
guess Vermutung 170
guide Führer(in) 68
guide book Reiseführer 96
guideline Richtlinie 75
gun Schusswaffe 171
guy Typ, Mann 170

H

habit Gewohnheit, Angewohnheit 76
haggis Haggis (traditionelles schottisches Gericht) 94
hairdryer Haartrockner, Föhn 125
half board Halbpension 174
hamper Korb, Deckelkorb 159
to handle umgehen mit, handhaben 156
handout Informationsblatt, Handout 103
to hand out aushändigen, verteilen 42
to hang around herumhängen 144

to happen to do sth. zufällig etwas tun 170
to harm schaden, verletzen 52
harmful schädlich, nachteilig 35
harvest Ernte 81
haven Zufluchtsort, Hafen 169
heading Überschrift 24
to head off sich aufmachen 41
headquarters Zentrale, Stammsitz 17
head teacher Schulleiter(in) 39
heartbreaking herzzerreißend 50
heavy duty Schwerlast, hohe Beanspruchung 117
herd Herde 169
hiccup Problemchen, Schluckauf 170
to hike wandern 70
hippy Hippie 164
to hire mieten 67
to hold the line am Apparat bleiben 96
home food related im Zusammenhang mit der häuslichen Nahrungs-zubereitung 52
homelessness Obdachlosigkeit 144
home-made hausgemacht 17
hometown Heimatstadt 86
honey Honig 166
honeymoon Hochzeitsreise 67
horrified entsetzt 160
host Gastgeber(in) 74
hostile feindlich 87
household Haushalt 54
HTML eine Programmiersprache für das World Wide Web 37
huge riesig 17
human menschlich 80
humanitarian humanitär, menschenfreundlich 80
humpback whale Buckelwal 168
hunt Jagd 169
hurricane Wirbelsturm, Hurrikan 30
hut Hütte 79
hybrid Hybrid- 59
hydrogen Wasserstoff 59
hydro power Wasserkraft 57
hype Rummel, Medienrummel 164
hypermarket Hypermarkt, Einkaufszentrum, großer Einkaufsmarkt 160

I

ice hockey Eishockey 75
icon Icon, Symbol, Bildschirmsymbol 34
ICT Informations- und Kommunikationstechnologie (Kurzform) 9
identical identisch 54
to identify (with) herausfinden, (sich) identifizieren (mit) 49
idyll Idylle 40
ignorant ignorant 20
illegal illegal 37
illiterate nicht lesen oder schreiben könnend 81
ILY (Abkürzung) ich liebe dich 45
image Bild, Image 152

Alphabetical vocabulary

imagination Vorstellungskraft, Phantasie 67
impact Wirkung, Aufprall 52
to impeach anklagen 84
to implement ausführen, verwirklichen, realisieren 87
impolite unhöflich 103
importer Importeur 105
to impress beeindrucken 95
impression Eindruck 8
impressive beeindruckend 57
improvement Verbesserung 49
in addition zusätzlich, außerdem 35
in advance im Voraus 122
in-box Posteingang 62
in charge of verantwortlich für 168
incoming eingehend, ankommend 103
incoming goods department Wareneingang 15
inconvenience Unannehmlichkeit, Belästigung, Unbequemlichkeit 102
inconvenient ungelegen, lästig, unangenehm 131
Incoterms (international commercial terms) Incoterms (internationale Regelungen der Lieferbedingungen für Käufer/Verkäufer bei Auslandsgeschäften) 113
increasing zunehmend, steigend, wachsend 49
incredible unglaublich 168
independent unabhängig 18
India Indien 73
Indian indisch 40
indirect indirekt, mittelbar 84
individual Einzelperson, Individuum 47
Indonesia Indonesien 108
Indonesian indonesisch 52
industrial industriell, Industrie- 13
industrialized industrialisiert 76
in essence in der Hauptsache, im Wesentlichen 170
inevitable unvermeidlich 170
inexpensive preiswert, billig 64
in favour of für, zugunsten 39
to infect infizieren, anstecken 81
infection Infektion, Ansteckung 81
inflation Inflation, Geldentwertung 81
influence Einfluss 47
to influence beeinflussen 34
informal informell 91
infrastructure Infrastruktur 65
in general im Allgemeinen, generell 103
ingenious genial, raffiniert 152
initiative Initiative, Entschlusskraft 68
innovation Neuerung 35
in particular im Besonderen 28
to inquire sich erkundigen, fragen 101
in short kurz gesagt, kurzum 61
instability Instabilität, Krisenanfälligkeit 54
installation Installation, Anlage, Einrichtung 56
institution Institution, Einrichtung, Anstalt 87

insulation Isolierung 60
to intend beabsichtigen 22
intense angestrengt, intensiv, gefühlstief 95
interactive interaktiv 37
intergovernmental zwischenstaatlich, international 87
intermediate Zwischen-, dazwischen liegend 21
international international 86
to interview befragen 13
in the long run auf lange Sicht 62
introductory Einführungs- 112
in turn wiederum, abwechselnd 148
investment Investition 148
investor Kapitalanleger, Investor 71
involved (in) beteiligt (an), involviert 55
Ireland Irland 67
Irish irisch 86
ironical ironisch 76
irrevocable unwiderruflich 121
issue Angelegenheit, Problem, Ausgabe (einer Zeitung) 49
to issue herausgeben 156
Italian italienisch 86
Italy Italien 86
item Punkt, Gegenstand 25
itinerary Programmablauf, Reiseroute 170
it's your turn du bist an der Reihe 55

J

Japanese japanisch 168
jealous (of) eifersüchtig 67
jet-skiing Wassermotorrad fahren 70
jingle Jingle, kurze Tonfolge in der Werbung 30
journalist Journalist(in) 13
judge Richter(in), Wettkampfrichter(in) 84
judicial gerichtlich, rechtsprechend 84
judiciary Judikative, Justizgewalt, Gerichtswesen 84
junction Kreuzung 38

K

to keep an eye on im Auge behalten 37
to keep out abhalten, fernhalten 169
keypad Tastatur 38
killing Tötung 38
king prawn Königskrabbe 52
kit Ausrüstung 41
kiwi ein flugunfähiger Vogel, eine Fruchtsorte, eine Eigenbezeichnung der Bewohner Neuseelands 102

L

label Etikett 52
to label beschriften 52
laboratory Labor 142
labour Arbeits- 72
lack of Mangel an, mangelnd, fehlend 54
lager beer helles Bier, Lagerbier 94
lane Fahrspur 38
Latvia Lettland 86

Latvian lettisch 76
leader Führer(in) 84
leading führend 106
leaf, pl. leaves Blatt 171
to leave out auslassen 43
leaver (Schul-)Abgänger(in) 37
left übrig 41
left-hand linksseitig, links stehend 14
legal legal, gesetzlich 138
legend Legende 68
legislative legislativ, gesetzgebend 84
leprechaun ein kleiner Kobold aus der irischen Mythologie 102
letter Buchstabe 18
letterhead Briefkopf 99
letter of credit Akkreditiv 112
level Niveau, Pegelstand 30
liable haftbar, verantwortlich 129
library Bibliothek, Bücherei 170
lifelong lebenslang, lebenslänglich 145
lifestyle Lebensstil, Lebensart 170
lifetime Lebensdauer, Lebenszeit, Lebzeiten 30
to light up beleuchten 171
likely wahrscheinlich, voraussichtlich 49
to limit begrenzen 84
limited begrenzt, beschränkt 54
link Verbindung, Link 152
to link verbinden 37
listener Zuhörer(in) 79
litter Abfall 67
livelihood Existenz, Lebensgrundlage 164
loaf of bread Brotlaib 19
to lobby for sth. sich für etwas einsetzen 168
local council etwa: Gemeinderat 29
location Einrichtung, Standort, Lage 14
locomotive Lokomotive 47
logical logisch 156
logistics Logistik(leistung), Unterbringungs- und Verpflegungswesen 170
logo Firmenemblem 25
LOL (Abkürzung) laut lachend 45
lonely einsam 25
to look into prüfen, auf den Grund gehen 130
lottery Lotterie 67
low-carbon CO_2-arm 60
lunchtime Mittagszeit 11
luxurious luxuriös 163

M

magnet Magnet 58
main course Hauptgericht 94
mainstreamed akzeptiert, etabliert 164
to maintain behaupten, aufrechterhalten 160
maintenance Wartung, Pflege, Instandhaltung, Unterhalt, Verwaltung 102
maize Mais 81
major bedeutend, groß, Haupt- 51
Majorca Mallorca 67

297

Alphabetical vocabulary

majority Mehrheit 84
to make money Geld verdienen 73
to make sense Sinn machen 161
to make up (sth.) etwas bilden, zusammenstellen, erfinden 84
managing director Geschäftsführer(in), Mitglied der Geschäftsführung 35
to manufacture fertigen, herstellen 107
manufacturer Hersteller 73
manufacturing Herstellung 16
margin Rand 124
marital status Ehestand, Familienstand 95
to mark markieren, kennzeichnen, korrigieren 53
to market vermarkten, verkaufen 30
marketing Marketing 31
market research department Marktforschungsabteilung 9
massive massiv, umfangreich 156
material Material 35
mayor Bürgermeister(in) 57
meaningful sinnvoll, aussagekräftig 51
meanness Gemeinheit, Knauserigkeit 41
measure Maßnahme 37
mechanical engineering Maschinenbau 117
mediation Sprachmittlung, Vermittlung, Schlichtungswesen 85
medical medizinisch 70
medicine Medizin 41
membership Mitgliedschaft 51
memo Notiz, Kurznachricht 97
menu Speisekarte 51
merchandising Verkaufsförderung, Merchandising, Vermarktung 30
merchant Händler, Kaufmann, Handelsmann 76
messaging service Dienst zur Versendung von (Sofort-)Nachrichten 34
Mexican mexikanisch 171
midday Mittag 97
migrant Migrant(in), Übersiedler(in) 171
migration Migration, (Ab-)Wanderung, Umzug 169
to mine abbauen, fördern 71
mining Bergbau 65
minor klein, gering(fügig) 170
Minuteman, pl. Minutemen Freiwilliger, der auf Abruf bereit steht 171
missing fehlend, vermisst 30
misspelling falsche Schreibweise, Rechtschreibfehler 152
missus umgangssprachliche Anrede für eine Frau 41
mistakenly irrtümlicherweise, versehentlich 138
mixture Mischung, Vermischung, Gemenge 77
mobile mobil, beweglich 35
mobile phone Mobiltelefon, Handy 25
modal auxiliary Hilfsverb 43
model Modell, Baureihe, Model 110
monitor Monitor, Bildschirm 33

monkey Affe 70
monster Monster, Ungetüm 100
monthly monatlich 156
moral moralisch 60
moreover überdies, außerdem 47
Moscow Moskau 66
motorboat Motorboot 70
motor car Auto, Kraftfahrzeug 47
motor mechanic Kfz-Mechaniker(in) 22
motorway Autobahn 38
Mountie kanadische berittene Polizei 102
move Schritt, Bewegung, Zug 170
MP3 player MP3-Spieler 72
mug Becher 140
multicultural multikulturell 12
multi-tasking Multitasking (mehrere Aufgaben gleichzeitig) 44
murder Mord 38
musk ox Moschusochse 169
Muslim Moslem(in) 43
mussel Muschel 94
must-have etwas Unentbehrliches 156

N

nanorobot Nanoroboter 155
nationality Nationalität 12
nationwide landesweit 60
native eingeboren, einheimisch 68
natural natürlich 49
nature Natur 68
Nebraska Public Power District verantwortliche Stelle für die Stromversorgung in Nebraska 57
negative negativ 52
neither keine(-r/-s) (von beiden) 41
net netto, ohne Abzug, Netz 114
Netherlands Niederlande 86
network Netz, Netzwerk 37
never mind macht nichts, schon gut, bitte 67
nevertheless dennoch, trotzdem, nichtsdestotrotz 76
New Year's Eve Silvesterabend 91
New Zealand Neuseeland 74
night vision goggles Nachtsichtgerät 171
no matter egal 168
to nominate ernennen, nominieren, aufstellen 84
no-name product Billigprodukt, ohne Markenname 25
non-defining relative clause nicht notwendiger Relativsatz 42
non-food Nichtlebensmittel, Güter, die nicht zum Verzehr gedacht sind 52
non-governmental nichtregierungs-, nichtstaatlich(e) 81
non-profit gemeinnützig, keinen Gewinn anstrebend 55
norm Norm, Regel 42
normally normalerweise 11
North Sea Nordsee 100
Norway Norwegen 86
not before time keine Minute zu früh 164

not even nicht einmal 62
notification Benachrichtigung, Meldung 156
novel Roman 75
nowhere land Niemandsland 144
nuclear nuklear 57
nursery school Vorschule 22

O

object Gegenstand, Objekt 53
to observe beobachten 39
to obtain erhalten, erlangen 106
obvious offensichtlich 170
officer Beamter, Beamtin 39
official Beamter, Beamtin 57
offshore vor der Küste 60
off the beaten track abseits der ausgetretenen Pfade 170
once in a while ab und zu, gelegentlich 70
on condition (that) unter der Bedingung, dass 116
on duty im Dienst 93
on offer im Angebot 22
on one's own (ganz) allein(e) 46
on schedule termingerecht, pünktlich 129
onshore auf dem Festland, an der Küste 60
on the lookout Ausschau halten 171
on the whole im Großen und Ganzen, alles in allem 61
onto auf … hinauf 93
on your part von Ihrer Seite, Ihrerseits 137
open account Kontokorrent, Zahlung gegen Rechnung 113
open-minded aufgeschlossen, unvoreingenommen 21
opera Oper 66
to operate bedienen 16
operation Operation, Handlung, Verfahren, Arbeitsgang 80
opponent Gegner(in) 87
opportunity Gelegenheit 88
opposition Gegensatz, Gegner, Opposition 54
optimistic optimistisch 45
option Alternative, Möglichkeit 77
orange Orange 95
organic biologisch angebaut, organisch 49
to orientate orientieren, ausrichten 86
oriented orientiert, bezogen 54
origin Herkunft, Ursprung 40
original original, ursprünglich, unbearbeitet 76
otherwise sonst 67
ought to sollte, müsste 93
ourselves uns, selbst 88
outdoor Freiluft-, im Freien, draußen 105
outlet Verkaufsstelle, Absatz, Abfluss 105
out of order außer Betrieb, gestört 102

298

Alphabetical vocabulary

out-of-town außerstädtisch 160
overall insgesamt, global, allgemein 164
over-consumer übermäßige(r)
  Konsument(in) 54
overconsumption übermäßiger
  Verbrauch 54
overdue überfällig 130
overfishing Überfischung 173
to overlook übersehen, überblicken 138
overnight über Nacht 70
overseas Übersee-, in Übersee 102
oversight Versehen, Übersehen 137
overweight übergewichtig 33

P

package Paket 168
package tour Pauschalreise 170
packaging Verpackungsmaterial 25
pain Schmerz 53
paperboy Zeitungsausträger 12
paperless papierlos 62
paperwork Schreibarbeit, Büroarbeit 93
paragliding Gleitschirm fliegen 70
to paraphrase paraphrasieren, mit
  anderen Worten ausdrücken,
  umschreiben 85
parliament Parlament 84
parliamentary parlamentarisch 84
to participate (in) teilnehmen (an) 37
particularly besonders 110
partnership Partnerschaft 88
to pass (ein Gesetz) verabschieden,
  bestehen, weitergeben 84
passive voice Passiv (Grammatik) 58
past letzte(r, s), vergangen 40
to pay attention Aufmerksamkeit
  schenken 38
payment Bezahlung 28
pea Erbse 94
peaceful friedlich 70
peacekeeping Friedenserhaltung,
  Friedensbewahrung 80
pedestrian Fußgänger(in) 103
percentage Prozentsatz 45
perfect vollkommen, perfekt 67
permanent dauerhaft 20
permission Erlaubnis 84
to permit erlauben, zulassen,
  genehmigen 84
to persecute verfolgen 81
personal identification
  number persönliche
  Identifikationsnummer 156
personality Persönlichkeit 9
personnel Personal 16
to persuade überreden 29
phase Phase, (Zeit-)Abschnitt 55
phishing Phishing (betrügerisches
  „Fischen" von Daten) 37
phrase Ausdruck 16
physical körperlich, physisch 53
Physics Physik 10
picker Pflücker(in) 41
to pick up abholen 170
picnic Picknick 159

pie gedeckter Obstkuchen 94
pie chart Kreisdiagramm 52
pill Pille, Tablette 81
pineapple Ananas 52
pint Pinte (englisches Hohlmaß:
  0,57 l) 95
piracy Piraterie, Raubkopieren 37
to place an order einen Auftrag erteilen,
  eine Bestellung aufgeben 105
placement Praktikum, Platzierung,
  Vertriebspolitik 10
plain Ebene, Fläche 169
planet Planet 30
planning Planung 47
plant Fabrikanlage 23
platform Plattform 28
pleasant angenehm 102
pleased erfreut 93
to plug in einstecken 63
podcast Podcast, aus dem Internet
  herunterladbare Film- bzw.
  Hörsequenz 79
point of view Standpunkt, Ansicht 61
to point out hinweisen auf 39
pop-up advertising Werbung in einem
  Pop-up-Fenster (auf einem Monitor) 152
portable tragbar 37
portrait Portrait, Konterfei 26
position Position, Haltung, Meinung 130
positive positiv 55
postage Porto, Postgebühr 28
postal code Postleitzahl 99
postcode Postleitzahl 50
potential potenziell, eventuell 86
poverty Armut 42
power Energie, Strom 57
powerful stark 152
power line Starkstromleitung,
  Überlandleitung 58
power plant Kraftwerk 58
PR (Public Relations)
  Öffentlichkeitsarbeit 164
practicability Durchführbarkeit,
  Praktikabilität 55
practice Praxis, Übung 13
prawn Garnele 94
preferable wünschenswert 170
pregnancy Schwangerschaft 41
Premier League höchste englische
  Spielklasse im Fußball 163
premium rate
  number Sonderrufnummer 28
pre-paid vorausbezahlt 156
prepared bereit, vorbereitet 106
preposition Präposition 75
presence Gegenwart, Präsenz 168
presentation Präsentation 37
presenter Präsentator(in),
  Moderator(in) 83
to preserve bewahren, erhalten,
  schonen 68
president Präsident(in) 84
presidential Präsidentschaft-,
  präsidial 84
to presume annehmen, vermuten 168

pretty ziemlich 102
**to prevent sth. from happening/sb. from
  doing sth.** verhindern 81
primary primär, hauptsächlich, Erst- 65
to print drucken 35
priority Vorrang, Dringlichkeit,
  Priorität 68
prior to bevor 170
prison Gefängnis 37
pristine makellos 169
privacy Privatsphäre 152
process Prozess 52
productivity Produktivität 47
profession Beruf 43
professional Fachmann, Profi 45
programming
  language Programmiersprache 37
progressive fortschrittlich,
  progressiv 161
project Projekt 10
projector Projektor, Beamer 63
to promote fördern, unterstützen 160
promotion Werbung, Promotion 30
prompt Stichwort 10
prompt prompt, sofort 114
proper angemessen, passend, richtig 41
pros and cons Argumente für und gegen
  etwas 39
protein Protein, Eiweiß 51
to provide sb. with jmdn. versorgen
  mit 37
provider Anbieter(in) 37
providing vorausgesetzt 168
proximity Nähe, Nachbarschaft 168
publishing date
  Veröffentlichungsdatum 35
punctual pünktlich 128
to punish bestrafen 49
purchase Einkauf 99
to purchase kaufen 29
purchasing Einkauf 23
to put sb. off jmdm. die Lust nehmen,
  jmdn. ablenken 170
to put through durchstellen, verbinden
  mit 96

Q

qualification Qualifikation 20
qualified qualifiziert 144
quay Kai 163
queue Warteschlange 103
quiet Ruhe 30
quiz Quiz, Ratespiel 103
quotation (Preis-)Angebot, Belegstelle im
  Text 106
to quote nennen, zitieren 105

R

race Rasse 69
racial Rassen- 76
radical radikal, drastisch,
  durchgreifend 76
radio station Radiosender 38
rail Bahn, Eisenbahn, Schiene 52
rainbow Regenbogen 94
rainfall Niederschlag, Regen 48

299

Alphabetical vocabulary

to raise (hoch)heben, erheben, großziehen 60
range Angebot, Auswahl, Reichweite 60
to range sich bewegen, reichen 49
rank Rang, Stellung, Rangordnung 103
rapidly schnell 106
rate Rate, Preis 90
rather than eher … als, besser … als 52
ration Zuteilung, Ration 81
raw material Rohstoff 16
to react reagieren 164
realisation Verwirklichung, Realisierung, Erkenntnis 55
to realize erkennen, bemerken 41
rebel Rebell(in) 164
receipt Erhalt, Empfang, Beleg 112
recession Rezession, Konjunkturschwäche 168
recipe Rezept 16
to recommend empfehlen 89
recommendation Empfehlung 163
record Aufzeichnung 137
to record aufnehmen 37
recyclable wiederverwertbar, wiederverwendbar 35
to recycle recyceln, wiederverwerten 48
to reduce reduzieren, vermindern 39
reduction Reduzierung 90
to refer (to) sich beziehen auf 47
referendum Referendum, Abstimmung, Volksbefragung 87
refined raffiniert, verfeinert, fein 163
reflection Spiegelbild, Reflektierung 168
refuge Asyl, Zufluchtsstätte 81
regarding in Bezug auf 55
regards Grüße 74
regatta Regatta, Bootsrennen 134
regeneration Erneuerung, Wiederherstellung, Regeneration 148
to register registrieren, einschreiben, anmelden 84
regulation Regelung, Vorschrift 28
rejection Ablehnung, Absage 144
related to in Beziehung stehend, verwandt mit 61
relating to in Bezug auf 49
relationship Beziehung 54
relevant relevant, bedeutend 29
reliable zuverlässig 22
religion Religion 154
religious religiös 43
to reload wieder aufladen 156
to rely (on) sich verlassen (auf) 45
reminder Mahnung, (Zahlungs-)Erinnerung 136
renewable erneuerbar 60
rental Miete, Verleih 101
rep Vertreter(in), Beauftragte(r), Agent(in) 170
to rephrase umformulieren 69
replacement Ersatz 129
report Bericht 38
to represent repräsentieren, vertreten 84

representative Vertreter(in) 31
to reproduce wiedererzeugen, abbilden, reproduzieren 54
reputation Ansehen, Ruf 21
to request beantragen, erbitten 114
to require benötigen 114
requirement Anforderung 20
research Forschung 16
researcher Forscher(in) 52
resentful aufgebracht, grollend 41
residence Wohnsitz, Wohnhaus 84
resort Ferienort, Badeort 70
resource Ressource, Bodenschatz, Rohstoff 49
to respect respektieren 86
response Reaktion, Antwort 93
responsibility Verantwortung 49
responsible (for) verantwortlich (für), haftbar 37
restroom Toilette 102
retail Einzelhandel(s-) 148
retailer Einzelhändler(in) 18
retailing Einzelhandel 30
retail trade Einzelhandel 21
to reveal enthüllen, preisgeben, verraten 160
to reverse umkehren 84
revolutionary revolutionär 60
to revolutionize revolutionieren 160
rewarding lohnend 21
to rewrite umschreiben 82
rice Reis 82
right Recht 28
right richtig 57
right-hand rechtsseitig, rechts stehend 14
right now in diesem Augenblick 41
ringtone Klingelton 28
risk Risiko 72
to risk riskieren 73
role Rolle 13
Roman Römer(in) 95
Rome Rom 86
routine Tagesablauf, Routine 46
to run durchführen, führen, laufen 170
to run a business ein Unternehmen führen 104
rundown abgewirtschaftet, verwahrlost 148
to run out ablaufen, auslaufen, zu Ende gehen 51
Russia Russland 66
Russian russisch 76

S

salad Salat 14
salary Gehalt 41
sale Verkauf 113
sales literature Werbematerial 106
salesperson Verkäufer(in) 13
sales talk Verkaufsgespräch 14
salmon, pl. **salmon** Lachs 51
saloon Limousine, Salon, Saal 101
salutation Begrüßung, Anrede 89
sample Muster, Probe 106

sari Sari 108
satisfaction Zufriedenheit 130
satisfied zufrieden 41
to save sparen, retten 13
scam Betrug 28
to scan scannen, durchsuchen 44
scenery Landschaft 168
Science Wissenschaft 10
scientist Wissenschaftler(in) 33
Scotland Schottland 88
Scottish schottisch 88
to scream schreien 14
screen Bildschirm 33
script Drehbuch 30
seafood Fisch und Meeresfrüchte 51
search Suche 145
search engine Suchmaschine 152
season Saison, Jahreszeit 52
seating furniture Sitzmöbel 109
secondary sekundär, Zweit- 65
secondary school weiterführende Schule 21
section Abschnitt, Abteilung 40
sector Sektor 65
to secure absichern, bewirken, schützen 35
security Sicherheit 152
seed Saat, Samen 81
to select auswählen 160
selection Auswahl, Sortiment 113
self-centred ichbezogen, egozentrisch 170
self-confidence Selbstbewusstsein 168
self-confident selbstbewusst 45
self-defence Selbstverteidigung, Notwehr 171
Senegalese senegalesisch, Senegalese/Senegalesin 82
sensible vernünftig 156
sensitive einfühlsam, sensibel 68
separation of powers Gewaltenteilung 84
series, pl. **series** Serie 64
server Server, zentrale Einheit im Netzwerk 35
to settle regeln, erledigen 130
settlement Begleichung, Abwicklung, Siedlung 138
to settle up bezahlen, Rechnung begleichen 102
shadow Schatten 171
to shake schütteln, zittern 92
sharp steil, stark, scharf 17
shelf, pl. **shelves** Regal 21
shelving system Regalsystem 110
shipment Lieferung, Versendung, Ladung 114
shipping Schifffahrt, Versand 52
to shop einkaufen 160
shopper Käufer(in) 160
short code Kurzwahlnummer 28
shortly in Kürze 106
short-term kurzfristig, befristet, kurzzeitig 82

Alphabetical vocabulary

shot Aufnahme, Schuss 168
shoulder bag Umhängetasche 101
shower Schauer, Dusche 38
showy auffallend, prächtig, protzig 103
shrimp Krabbe, Schrimp 94
to shut someone up jemanden dazu bringen, den Mund zu halten 41
sightseeing Besichtigungstour 66
signature Unterschrift 99
silver Silber 25
similar ähnlich 25
sincerely Mit freundlichen Grüßen 89
single einzeln, alleinstehend, alleinerziehend 45
single mum alleinerziehende Mutter 46
single parent Alleinerziehende(r) 46
situation Situation 14
skiing Skifahren 38
to skim überfliegen 44
slave Sklave/Sklavin 82
slogan Slogan, Werbespruch 30
Slovenia Slowenien 86
smart phone Smartphone 62
smooth glatt 170
to snap blaffen (ugs.) 41
sneaker Turnschuh 72
so-called sogenannt 52
social sozial, gesellschaftlich 42
to socialize ausgehen 12
society Gesellschaft 47
soda bread Brot (mit Backsoda gebacken) 159
soft drink alkoholfreies Getränk 94
software Software (Computerprogramme) 37
soil Boden, Erde 54
solar Sonnen-, Solar- 52
sort (of) Art, Sorte 170
to sort out klären 142
soup Suppe 94
source Quelle 60
South African südafrikanisch 52
southbound in Richtung Süden 38
southern südlich 68
Spain Spanien 65
Spanish spanisch 52
sparkling water Mineralwasser mit Kohlensäure 95
specialist Spezialist(in) 62
speciality Spezialität, Spezialartikel 118
specification Anforderung, Beschreibung, Maßangabe 105
to spell buchstabieren 45
spending power Kaufkraft 148
spicy würzig, pikant, scharf 94
spirit Spirituose 94
sponsoring Sponsoring, Förderung, finanzielle Unterstützung 30
spontaneous spontan, kurz entschlossen 45
sporting sportlich, Sport- 64
to spot entdecken 41
spot on genau richtig 170
sprawl Ausbreitung 169

spring Quelle, Brunnen 68
square Platz, Quadrat 66
stability Stabilität, Beständigkeit 87
stable stabil 86
stairs Treppe 102
stall Stand, Box, Parkett 55
standard Standard, Norm, Maßstab 73
standing Ansehen, Stellung 103
starter Vorspeise 94
statistics Statistik 164
Statue of Liberty Freiheitsstatue 66
stay Aufenthalt 12
steady stetig 17
to steal stehlen 35
steam Dampf 58
steam engine Dampfmaschine, Dampflokomotive 59
steel Stahl 57
step Schritt, Stufe 54
stock Bestand, Vorrat, Aktie 15
stomach Magen 81
storage container Vorratsbehälter, Lagerbehälter 118
storage room Lagerraum 15
storyline Handlung 30
straight gerade, direkt 94
stranger Fremde(r) 103
strawberry Erdbeere 40
to stretch dehnen, strecken 169
strict streng 53
strip Streifen 168
stripe Streifen 25
to structure strukturieren, gliedern 55
stuff Zeug 73
subheading Zwischenüberschrift 44
subject line Betreffzeile 99
to submit unterbreiten 114
substantial umfangreich, beträchtlich 106
substitute Ersatz 43
substitution table Substitutionstabelle, Ersetzungstabelle 106
to suffer leiden 144
sufficient ausreichend, genügend 144
to suggest vorschlagen 101
suggestion Vorschlag 55
suitable geeignet 13
suite Suite, Zimmerflucht, Appartement 163
to summarize zusammenfassen 33
summary Zusammenfassung 29
to sum up zusammenfassen 79
sunny sonnig 38
superstore großer Supermarkt 18
supplier Zulieferer 106
supply Lieferung, Beschaffung 164
to supply (be)liefern 104
support Unterstützung 68
to support unterstützen 37
supporter Anhänger(in), Befürworter(in) 87
Supreme Court Oberstes Bundesgericht 84
surname Nachname 50

surprising überraschend 33
to surround umgeben 45
surroundings Umgebung 68
survival Überleben 169
to survive überleben 49
to suspect vermuten, misstrauen 169
sustainable nachhaltig, kontinuierlich 55
to swear, swore, sworn fluchen; schwören 103
sweater Pullover 59
Swedish schwedisch 110
Switzerland Schweiz 9
sweet Süßigkeit 16
symbol Symbol 168

T

tactful taktvoll 140
tactic Taktik 103
to tailor (to) zuschneiden (auf), maßschneidern 118
to take a seat Platz nehmen, hinsetzen 168
takeaway Restaurant, das Speisen zum Mitnehmen verkauft 76
to take on aufgreifen, übernehmen 43
to take orders Bestellungen entgegennehmen 14
talent Talent 45
tally Summe, Anzahl 171
target Ziel 24
to target zielen (auf) 37
task Aufgabe 29
technological technisch 47
tedious ermüdend, langweilig, nervtötend 170
telecommunications Tele-kommunikation 35
temperature Temperatur 38
to tend (to) zu etwas neigen 33
tent Zelt 170
term Bedingung, Begriff, Trimester an der Schule 105
terrorist Terrorist(in) 171
tertiary tertiär 65
textile textil 73
textiles Textilien 76
text message Textmitteilung, SMS 28
to thank danken, (sich) bedanken 89
thankful dankbar 86
thanks danke 83
theoretical theoretisch 152
theory Theorie 31
thermal Thermal-, Wärme- 68
thief, pl. **thieves** Dieb(in) 57
third party Dritte 152
thirst Durst 50
three-piece suite Polstergarnitur 125
to thrive Erfolg haben, gedeihen, blühen 171
throughout während des/der ganzen … 170
thunderstorm Gewitter 38
tick Häkchen 25
tidal Gezeiten- 60

301

Alphabetical vocabulary

tie Krawatte, (Spiel) unentschieden enden 103
tip Tipp, Hinweis 28
TLD (top-level domain) Bereich oberster Ebene 81
toll Maut 101
ton Tonne (Gewicht) 57
top Top, Oberteil 14
topic Thema 42
to top up füllen, aufladen 156
torrid glühend heiß, hier eher: mühselig, schwierig 168
tourism Tourismus 64
tourist office Fremdenverkehrsbüro 96
tour operator Reiseveranstalter(in) 170
toxic giftig 35
track Spur, Fährte, Weg 170
trade discount Händlerrabatt 125
trader Händler(in) 28
tradition Tradition 43
trainee Praktikant(in), Auszubildende(r) 95
trainer Turnschuh 25
trampoline Trampolin 121
transaction Übertragung, Transaktion, Geschäft 156
transcript schriftliche Fassung 63
transfer Überweisung, Übertragung 122
to transform verwandeln 148
transformation Verwandlung, Umgestaltung 168
transportation Transport, Beförderung 52
travel das Reisen 64
treatment Behandlung 41
treaty Vertrag 84
trend Trend, Mode, Richtung, Tendenz 57
trendy modisch, trendig 67
trial Probe, Test, Gerichtsverfahren 106
trick Trick 171
trout, pl. trout Forelle 94
truck Lastwagen 38
to trust vertrauen 28
truthful ehrlich 25
to try on anprobieren 26
the Tube U-Bahn 101
tuna, pl. tuna Thunfisch 51
turbine Turbine 56
Turkey Türkei 86
to turn (into) werden, sich verwandeln in 60
to turn out ausfallen, sich herausstellen als 130
turnover Absatz, Umsatz 148
tutor Klassenlehrer(in), Betreuer(in) 74
two-thirds zwei Drittel 81
to type tippen 19

U

unbeatable unschlagbar 105
uncomfortable unbequem 168
unconstitutional verfassungswidrig 84
undergrowth Gestrüpp, Unterholz 171
underlined unterstrichen 27

under separate cover mit getrennter Post 117
underway unterwegs, im Gange 169
under wraps heimlich, geheim 168
undeveloped nicht entwickelt 169
unfashionable unmodisch, unmodern 72
unhelpful nutzlos, nicht hilfreich 144
uniqueness Einzigartigkeit 30
united vereint(e) 80
unknown unbekannt 69
unlimited grenzenlos, unbegrenzt, unbeschränkt 26
unnatural unnatürlich 103
to unpack auspacken 27
unspoiled unberührt, unbeschädigt 169
untouched unberührt, unversehrt 68
unusual ungewöhnlich 140
to update aktualisieren 35
urban städtisch 171
to urge drängen 164
urgent dringend 129
use Verwendung, Verwendungsmöglichkeit 48
user Benutzer(in) 152

V

vacancy Stellenangebot, Leere, Lücke 90
valid gültig 171
value Wert 108
vandalism Vandalismus, mutwillige Beschädigung 48
variety Vielfalt, Auswahl 68
various verschieden 42
to vary variieren 87
vast riesig 160
vegetable Gemüse 52
veto Veto, Einspruchsrecht, Einspruch 84
via via, über 160
viable brauchbar, praktikabel 168
vibrant dynamisch 168
view Ansicht, Aussicht 61
to view besichtigen, betrachten, sehen 57
violence Gewalt, Gewalttätigkeit 54
virtual virtuell 156
vision Vorstellung, (Zukunfts-)Vision 55
volcano, pl. volcanoes Vulkan 70
voluntary freiwillig 50
voter Wähler(in) 84

W

wage Lohn 41
walk of life Gesellschaftsschicht, soziale Schicht 170
wallpaper Hintergrundbild, Tapete 28
wanna (= informal form of ‚want to') will/wollen 102
warming Erwärmung 48
waterfront nahe am Wasser 163
water-related disease Krankheit, die durch (unsauberes) Wasser verursacht wird 50
wave Welle 60

way beyond weit entfernt, weit darüber hinaus 41
web Netz 35
website Website, Internetseite 10
wedding Hochzeit 102
weekly wöchentlich 160
westerly aus westlicher Richtung 38
western westlich 40
What a pity! Wie schade! 97
whatever was auch immer 73
whenever wann immer 62
whereas während 35
wherever wo(hin) auch immer 62
wholesaler Großhändler 88
WI-FI W-LAN 37
wild wild 70
wilderness Wildnis 169
wildlife Tierwelt (in freier Wildbahn) 169
willing bereit 114
wind farm Windpark 57
wireless drahtlos 35
to withdraw (withdrew, withdrawn) abheben, (sich) entfernen 156
with reference to betreffend, bezüglich 21
with regard to bezüglich, im Hinblick auf 140
witness Zeugin, Zeuge 38
wolf, pl. wolves Wolf 169
wonder Wunder 57
to wonder sich fragen, sich Gedanken machen 134
word web Wortnetz 22
Working Lunch Arbeitsessen 168
workplace Arbeitsplatz 37
workshop Werkstatt 55
World Nature Fund Fonds zum Schutz der Natur 51
worldwide weltweit 37
World Wide Web weltweites Netz innerhalb des Internets 37
worried beunruhigt 49
worry Sorge, Ärger 48
worthwhile lohnend, wertvoll 60

Y

yard Hof 39
youngster Jugendliche(r) 38
yourself selbst 19
Yours faithfully Hochachtungsvoll, Mit freundlichen Grüßen 107
Yours sincerely Mit freundlichen Grüßen 98

Z

zero Null 152
Zimbabwe Simbabwe 80
Zimbabwean simbabwisch, Simbabwer/in 81
zone Zone, Gebiet, Bereich 82

Basic vocabulary

Abkürzung

AE = Gebrauch im amerikanischen Englisch

A

a couple of ein paar
a little etwas, ein bisschen
a lot of viel(e)
a number of einige
ability Fähigkeit
abroad im/ins Ausland
to accept annehmen, akzeptieren
accident Unfall
accurate genau
to achieve erreichen
active aktiv
activity Aktivität
to add hinzufügen, addieren
additional zusätzlich
address Adresse
advantage Vorteil
advert(isement) Werbeanzeige, Anzeige
to advertise werben, inserieren
advertiser Inserent, Werbefachmann
advertising Werbung
advice Rat, Ratschlag
to advise (be)raten
afternoon Nachmittag
afterwards danach
again wieder
against gegen
age Alter, Zeitalter
ago vor
to agree einverstanden sein, zustimmen
agreement Übereinstimmung, Übereinkunft
aim Ziel
air Luft
airport Flughafen
alert Alarm
all alle(s), ganz
to allow erlauben
almost fast, beinahe
alone allein
along entlang
already schon, bereits
also auch
alternative Alternative, Wahl; alternativ
although obwohl
always immer
among zwischen, unter
amount Betrag, Summe
to analyze analysieren
angry wütend
animal Tier
to announce bekannt geben, ansagen
announcement Bekanntgabe, Durchsage
another noch eine(r, s), ein(e) andere(r, s)

to answer; answer (be)antworten; Antwort
any irgendeine(r, s)
any time jederzeit
anybody irgendjemand
anyone irgendjemand
anything irgendetwas
to appear (er)scheinen
apple Apfel
applicant Bewerber(in)
application Bewerbung
to apply (for) sich bewerben (um)
area Gebiet
around um (herum), ungefähr
arrival Ankunft
to arrive ankommen
article Artikel
as wie, da, als
as well auch, ebenso gut
to ask (for) fragen, bitten (um)
at first anfangs
at home zu Hause
at last schließlich, endlich
at least wenigstens
at once sofort
at present im Augenblick, jetzt
at risk gefährdet
at the moment im Moment, jetzt
at work bei der Arbeit
atmosphere Atmosphäre
to attend (school) (Schule) besuchen
attention Aufmerksamkeit
attitude Haltung, Einstellung
to attract anziehen
aunt Tante
autumn Herbst
away weg
awful furchtbar, schrecklich

B

back Rücken; zurück
background Hintergrund
bad schlecht, schlimm, böse
bag Tasche, Tüte
baggage Gepäck
to bake backen
baker Bäcker(in)
balcony Balkon
to ban; ban verbieten, Verbot
bank Bank (Geldinstitut)
basket Korb
bathroom Badezimmer
to be able können
to be afraid (of) Angst haben (vor)
beach Strand
beard Bart
beautiful schön
because weil
because of wegen

to become, (became, become) werden
bed Bett
bedroom Schlafzimmer
before vor, bevor
to begin, (began, begun) anfangen, beginnen
beginning Anfang, Beginn
to behave sich benehmen, sich verhalten
behaviour Verhalten, Benehmen
behind hinter
to believe glauben
to belong to gehören zu
best beste(r, s), am besten
best wishes alles Gute
better besser
between zwischen
bicycle Fahrrad
big groß
bike Fahrrad (Kurzform)
bill Rechnung, Gesetzesvorlage, Banknote, Entwurf, Schnabel
bird Vogel
birth Geburt
birthday Geburtstag
bit Stückchen
to bite, (bit, bitten) beißen
black schwarz
blackboard (Wand-)Tafel
to blame (for) verantwortlich machen (für)
block of flats Wohnblock
blog Internet-Tagebuch
blood Blut
blue blau
board Brett, Verpflegung
boat Boot
body Körper
to boil kochen
to book; book buchen; Buch
boot Stiefel
border Grenze
bored gelangweilt
boring langweilig
to borrow sich ausleihen
both beide
bottle Flasche
bottom Boden
box Schachtel, Kiste, Karton
boy Junge
boyfriend Freund
bread Brot
break Pause
to break, (broke, broken); break (zer)brechen, kaputt machen; Pause
to break down zusammenbrechen
breakfast Frühstück
bridge Brücke
to bring, (brought, brought) bringen

303

to broadcast, (broadcast, broadcast) übertragen, senden
brochure Broschüre, Prospekt
brother Bruder
brown braun
to brush; brush bürsten; Bürste
to build, (built, built) bauen
building Gebäude
to burn, (burnt, burnt) brennen
business Geschäft
busy beschäftigt, besetzt, belegt
but aber
butcher Metzger(in)
to buy, (bought, bought) kaufen
buyer Käufer(in)
by durch, mit, bei, neben, bis, um
by the way übrigens

C

cake Kuchen
to calculate (be)rechnen
to call; call (an)rufen, nennen, heißen; Anruf
camera Kamera, Fotoapparat
to camp; camp zelten, lagern; Lager
to campaign; campaign Wahlkampf führen; Kampagne, Wahlkampf
can können; Büchse, Dose
capital Großbuchstabe, Hauptstadt
car Auto
card Karte
to care; care sorgen; Sorge
career Beruf, Laufbahn, Karriere
careful vorsichtig, sorgfältig
careless sorglos
cargo Fracht, Ladung
to carry tragen
case Fall, Koffer, Kiste
cash Bargeld
cat Katze
to catch, (caught, caught) fangen
to cause; cause verursachen; Ursache
ceiling Zimmerdecke
centre Zentrum, Mittelpunkt
century Jahrhundert
certain sicher, bestimmt, gewisse
chair Stuhl
chalk Kreide
to change; change wechseln, (sich) (ver)ändern; Änderung, Wechsel(geld)
channel Kanal
chart Schaubild, Tabelle, Karte
cheap billig
to check; check (über)prüfen, kontrollieren; Kontrolle, Rechnung (im Restaurant), *(AE)* Scheck, Prüfung
cheers Tschüs, zum Wohl
cheese Käse
child(ren) Kind(er)
chips Pommes Frites, Kartoffelchips
chocolate Schokolade, Praline
choice Wahl
to choose, (chose, chosen) (aus)wählen
Christmas Weihnachten
church Kirche

cigarette Zigarette
cinema Kino
city Stadt
class (Schul-)Klasse
classmate Klassenkamerad(in)
classroom Klassenzimmer
to clean; clean reinigen, putzen; sauber
to clear; clear säubern, räumen; klar
clever klug, schlau, clever
to climb klettern
clock (Wand-)Uhr
to close; close schließen; dicht, nahe
clothes Kleidung
cloud Wolke
coal Kohle
coast Küste
coat Mantel
coffee Kaffee
coin Münze
cold kalt
to collect sammeln, abholen
collection Sammlung
college (Fach-)Hochschule, College
colour Farbe
to comb; comb kämmen; Kamm
to come, (came, come) kommen
comfortable bequem
to communicate kommunizieren, übermitteln
communication Kommunikation, Übermittlung
company Gesellschaft, Firma
to compare vergleichen
competition Wettbewerb, Konkurrenz
competitor Konkurrent(in), Wettbewerbsteilnehmer(in)
to complete; complete fertigstellen, vervollständigen; vollständig
to connect verbinden
connection Verbindung, Zusammenhang
to contact; contact sich in Verbindung setzen mit; Verbindung, Kontakt
to contain enthalten
container Behälter
to continue fortsetzen, weitermachen, weitergehen
to cook; cook kochen; Koch, Köchin
cooker Herd
to cooperate zusammenarbeiten
cooperation Zusammenarbeit
to copy; copy kopieren, abschreiben; Kopie, Exemplar
corner Ecke
to correct; correct korrigieren, verbessern; korrekt, richtig
correction Verbesserung, Korrektur
to cost, (cost, cost); cost kosten; Kosten
cotton Baumwolle
to count zählen, ins Gewicht fallen
counter Ladentisch, Schalter
country Land
couple Ehepaar, Paar
course Kurs, Lauf, Gang, Strecke
to cover; cover (be)decken, besetzen; Abdeckung, Umschlag

cow Kuh
to cross überqueren
crossing Kreuzung
crowd (Menschen-)Menge
crowded dicht gedrängt, voll
to cry; cry schreien, weinen; Schrei
cup Tasse
curious neugierig, seltsam
curtain Vorhang
customer Kunde, Kundin
customs Zoll, Zoll-
to cut, (cut, cut); cut schneiden; Schnitt
to cycle Fahrrad fahren

D

daily täglich
to damage; damage beschädigen; Schaden
to dance; dance tanzen; Tanz
danger Gefahr
dangerous gefährlich
dark dunkel
darkness Dunkelheit
date Datum, Zeitpunkt, Verabredung
date of birth Geburtsdatum
daughter Tochter
day Tag
dead tot
to deal, (dealt, dealt) (in, with); deal handeln (mit, von); Geschäft
dear lieb
death Tod
to decide (sich) entscheiden
decision Entscheidung
deep tief
to deliver liefern, (Rede) halten
delivery Lieferung
department Abteilung
department store Kaufhaus
to depend (on) abhängen (von)
to describe beschreiben
description Beschreibung
to design; design entwerfen, konstruieren; Entwurf, Muster
desk Schreibtisch
to destroy zerstören
destruction Zerstörung
detail Einzelheit, Detail
to develop entwickeln
development Entwicklung
to dial (Telefon) wählen
to dictate diktieren
dictation Diktat
dictionary Wörterbuch
to die sterben
to differ (from) sich unterscheiden (von)
difference Unterschied
different verschieden, unterschiedlich
difficult schwierig, schwer
difficulty Schwierigkeit
dining room Esszimmer
dinner (Mittag-, Abend-)Essen
to direct (to); direct richten, lenken (auf); direkt
direction Richtung

Basic vocabulary

dirty dreckig, schmutzig
disadvantage Nachteil
to disagree (with) anderer Meinung sein, nicht übereinstimmen (mit)
to discuss besprechen, diskutieren
discussion Gespräch, Diskussion
to dislike nicht mögen
distance Entfernung, Strecke, Abstand
doctor Arzt, Ärztin
dog Hund
door Tür
down hinunter, unten
downstairs die Treppe hinunter, unten, im Erdgeschoss
to draw, (drew, drawn) zeichnen, ziehen
drawing Zeichnung
to dream; dream träumen; Traum
to dress; dress (sich) anziehen; Kleid, Kleidung
to drink, (drank, drunk); drink trinken; Getränk
to drive, (drove, driven); drive fahren; Fahrt
driver Fahrer(in)
to dry; dry trocknen; trocken
during während
dustbin Mülltonne
duty Pflicht, Zoll

E

each jede(r, s)
each other einander, sich
ear Ohr
early früh
to earn verdienen
earth Erde
east Osten; östlich, Ost-, ostwärts
easy leicht
to eat, (ate, eaten) essen
economy Wirtschaft
edge Kante, Rand, Schneide
to educate erziehen
education Erziehung
to effect; effect durchführen, erzielen, leisten; Wirkung
egg Ei
either ... or entweder ... oder
to elect wählen
election Wahl
electric elektrisch
electricity Elektrizität
electronics Elektronik
else sonst
emergency Notfall
to employ beschäftigen, einstellen
employed beschäftigt
employee Angestellte(r), Arbeitnehmer(in)
employer Arbeitgeber(in)
employment Beschäftigung, Anstellung, Arbeit
empty leer
to end; end (be)enden; Ende, Schluss
energy Energie, Kraft
engine Motor, Triebwerk, Lokomotive

engineer Ingenieur(in), Techniker(in)
engineering Technik; technisch
to enjoy genießen, sich freuen an
enjoyable schön, angenehm, unterhaltsam
enough genug
to enquire (about) sich erkundigen (nach), fragen (nach)
enquiry Anfrage, Erkundigung, Untersuchung
to enter eintreten, eingeben
entrance Eintritt, Eingang
envelope Umschlag
environment Umwelt, Umgebung, Umfeld
equal gleich
equipment Ausrüstung, Ausstattung
especial besondere(r, s)
even eben, gleich; sogar, selbst
evening Abend
event Ereignis
ever je, jemals
every jede(r, s)
everybody jeder
everyone jeder
everything alles
everywhere überall
exact genau
exam(ination) Prüfung
example Beispiel
excellent ausgezeichnet, hervorragend
exciting aufregend
to excuse; excuse (sich) entschuldigen; Entschuldigung
exercise Übung
to exist existieren, bestehen
exit Ausgang, Ausfahrt
to expect erwarten
expensive teuer
experience Erfahrung
to explain erklären
explanation Erklärung
to export; export exportieren, ausführen; Ausfuhr, Export
to express; express ausdrücken, äußern; Schnellzug, als Eilsache
expression Ausdruck
extra besonders
eye Auge

F

to face; face (einer Sache) ins Auge sehen, gegenübertreten; Gesicht
fact Tatsache
factory Fabrik
fair Messe, Markt; gerecht, fair
to fall, (fell, fallen); fall fallen; Fallen, Sturz; (AE) Herbst
false falsch
family Familie
famous berühmt
far weit
fare Fahrpreis, Fahrgeld
farm Bauernhof, Farm
farmer Landwirt

farming Landwirtschaft
fast schnell
fat dick, fett
father Vater
favourite Lieblings-
to feed, (fed, fed) füttern
to feel, (felt, felt) fühlen
feeling Gefühl
few wenige
field Feld
to fight, (fought, fought); fight kämpfen; Kampf
to fill füllen
final Finale, Endrunde; letzte(r, s), endgültig
to find, (found, found) finden
fine Strafe; fein, schön, gut
to finish; finish beenden, abschließen, aufhören; Ziel, Vollendung
to fire; fire feuern; Feuer
firm Firma; fest, verbindlich
first erste(r, s), zuerst
first of all zuerst, vor allem
to fish; fish fischen; Fisch
to fit; fit (zusammen)passen, einbauen; gesund, in Form
to fix befestigen, reparieren, besorgen
flat Wohnung; flach
flight Flug
floor Boden, Stock, Etage
flower Blume
to fly, (flew, flown); fly fliegen; Fliege
to follow folgen
food Essen, Nahrung, Lebensmittel
foot, feet Fuß, Füße
football Fußball
for example zum Beispiel
foreign ausländisch, fremd
forever für immer
to forget, (forgot, forgotten) vergessen
fork Gabel
to form; form formen, gestalten; Form, Formular, Klasse
fortunate glücklich
forward(s) vorwärts
to free; free befreien; frei, kostenlos
freeway (AE) Autobahn
frequent häufig
fresh frisch
fridge Kühlschrank
friend Freund(in)
friendly freundlich
front Vorderseite
fruit Obst, Frucht, Früchte
full (of) voll (von, mit)
fun Spaß
furniture Möbel
further weiter
future Zukunft

G

game Spiel
garage Autowerkstatt, Garage
garden Garten
gate Tor

305

Basic vocabulary

gentleman Herr
to get, (got, got) bekommen, erhalten, werden
to get married heiraten
to get up aufstehen
girl Mädchen
girlfriend Freundin
to give, (gave, given) geben
to give up aufgeben
glad froh
glass Glas
glasses Brille
glove Handschuh
to go, (went, gone) gehen, fahren
to go down untergehen, sinken, fallen
to go on weitergehen, weitermachen
to go shopping einkaufen gehen
to go up hinaufgehen, wachsen, steigen
good gut
goodbye auf Wiedersehen
goods Güter, Waren
to govern regieren
government Regierung
grandfather Großvater
grandmother Großmutter
grandparents Großeltern
grateful dankbar
great groß, großartig
green grün
to greet grüßen
grey grau
grocer Lebensmittelhändler(in)
ground Boden
group Gruppe
to grow, (grew, grown) wachsen
grown-up Erwachsene(r)
growth Wachstum
to guess (er)raten
guest Gast

H

hair Haar
half Hälfte; halb
hall Flur, Saal
ham Schinken
handbag Handtasche
handkerchief Taschentuch
to hang, (hung, hung) (auf)hängen
to happen geschehen, passieren
happy glücklich, heiter
harbour Hafen
hard hart, schwierig, anstrengend
hardly kaum
hat Hut
to hate; hate hassen; Hass
to have (got), (had, had) haben
to have to müssen
to head; head anführen, fahren nach; Kopf, Leiter
headache Kopfschmerz
headline Überschrift
health Gesundheit
healthy gesund
to hear, (heard, heard) hören
heart Herz

to heat; heat heizen; Hitze
heating Heizung
heavy schwer
height Höhe
hello hallo
to help; help helfen; Hilfe
helpful hilfreich
here hier
here you are bitte(schön)!
to hesitate zögern
to hide, (hid, hidden) (sich) verstecken
high hoch
high tech (high technology) Hochtechnologie
hill Hügel
history Geschichte
to hit, (hit, hit); hit schlagen; Schlag, Treffer, Erfolg
to hold, (held, held) halten
hole Loch
holiday Urlaub, Ferien, freier Tag, Feiertag
home Zuhause
homework Hausaufgaben
honest ehrlich
to hope; hope hoffen; Hoffnung
horse Pferd
hospital Krankenhaus
hot heiß, scharf
hour Stunde
house Haus
housewife Hausfrau
housework Hausarbeit
how wie
how are you? wie geht es Dir/Ihnen?
however jedoch
hundred Hundert
hungry hungrig
to hurry; hurry sich beeilen; Eile
to hurt, (hurt, hurt) verletzen
husband Ehemann

I

ice cream Eiskrem
idea Idee, Vorstellung
if wenn, falls, ob
ill krank
illness Krankheit
to imagine sich vorstellen
immediate unmittelbar, unverzüglich
immigrant Einwanderer, Einwanderin
to immigrate einwandern
to import; import einführen, importieren; Einfuhr, Import
importance Wichtigkeit
important wichtig
impossible unmöglich
to improve (sich) verbessern
in fact tatsächlich
in front of vor
in italics kursiv
in my opinion meiner Meinung nach
in time rechtzeitig
inch Zoll (Maßeinheit)

to include einschließen
income Einkommen
to increase zunehmen, steigen, erhöhen
indeed tatsächlich
industry Industrie
to inform informieren
inside in, innerhalb
instead (of) anstatt
to instruct unterrichten, anweisen
instruction Unterricht, Anweisung, (Gebrauchs-)Anleitung
insurance Versicherung
to intend beabsichtigen
interest Interesse, (Plural) Zinsen
interesting interessant
to introduce einführen, vorstellen
introduction Einführung, Vorstellung
to invent erfinden
invention Erfindung
to invest investieren
invitation Einladung
to invite einladen
island Insel
IT Informationstechnik

J

jacket Jacke
jam Marmelade
job Arbeit, Beruf, Job
to join (sich) anschließen, beitreten
journey Reise
juice Saft
to jump; jump springen; Sprung
just genau, soeben, nur
to keep, (kept, kept) (be)halten, aufbewahren
key Schlüssel
to kill töten
kilo(gram) Kilo(gramm)
kind Art, Sorte; freundlich
king König
to kiss; kiss küssen; Kuss
kitchen Küche
knee Knie
knife Messer
to knock klopfen
to know, (knew, known) wissen, kennen
knowledge Wissen

L

ladder Leiter
lady Dame
lake See
lamp Lampe
land Land
landlady Vermieterin, Wirtin
landlord Vermieter, Wirt
language Sprache
large weit, groß
to last; last dauern; letzte(r, s)
late spät
later on später
latest neueste(r, s)
to laugh lachen
laughter Gelächter

Basic vocabulary

law Gesetz
to lay, (laid, laid) legen
lazy faul
to lead, (led, led) führen, leiten
leaflet (Hand-)Zettel, Flugblatt
to learn, (learnt, learnt) lernen
learner Lernende(r), Anfänger(in)
least wenigste(r, s), geringste(r, s)
to leave, (left, left) (ver)lassen, abfahren
left links; übrig
leg Bein
leisure Freizeit
lemon Zitrone
to lend, (lent, lent) verleihen
length Länge
less weniger
lesson Unterrichtsstunde
to let, (let, let) lassen
letter Brief, Buchstabe
to lie, (lied, lied) lügen
to lie, (lay, lain) liegen
life (lives) Leben
to lift; lift anheben, aufheben; Aufzug, Mitfahrgelegenheit
light Licht, Lampe; hell, leicht
to like; like mögen; wie
to limit; limit beschränken, begrenzen; Grenze, Beschränkung
line Linie, Zeile
lip Lippe
to list; list aufführen, auflisten; Liste
to listen (to) (zu)hören
little klein, wenig
to live; live leben, wohnen; direkt, live
living room Wohnzimmer
to load; load laden; Ladung
local lokal, ortsansässig, örtlich
long lang
to look schauen, (aus)sehen
to look after sich kümmern um
to look for suchen
to look forward to sich freuen auf
to look out aufpassen, hinaussehen
to look up nachschlagen, heraussuchen, aufblicken
lorry Lastwagen
to lose, (lost, lost) verlieren
loss Verlust
lot Menge, Los
lots of viel(e)
loud laut
to love; love lieben; Liebe
lovely hübsch
low niedrig
luck Glück, Schicksal
lucky glücklich (im Sinne von: Glück haben)
luggage Gepäck
lunch Mittagessen

M

machine Maschine, Gerät, Automat
mad verrückt
madam gnädige Frau
magazine Zeitschrift

mail Post
main Haupt-
mainly hauptsächlich
to make, (made, made) machen, herstellen
man (men) Mann (Männer), Mensch
to manage zu Stande bringen, schaffen, leiten, verwalten
management (Geschäfts-)Leitung, Verwaltung, Durchführung
many viele
map (Land-)Karte
market Markt
marmalade (Orangen-)Marmelade
married verheiratet
to marry heiraten
mass Masse
to match; match passen, zuordnen; Wettkampf, Streichholz
mathematics Mathematik
to matter; matter etwas ausmachen; Angelegenheit
may dürfen
maybe vielleicht
meal Mahlzeit
to mean, (meant, meant) bedeuten, meinen
meaning Bedeutung
(in the) meantime inzwischen
meanwhile inzwischen
meat Fleisch
mechanic Mechaniker(in)
media Medien
to meet, (met, met) (sich) treffen, kennenlernen
meeting Treffen
member Mitglied
to mend reparieren
to mention erwähnen
message Mitteilung, Nachricht
method Methode
metre Meter
microwave Mikrowelle
middle Mitte; mittlere(r, s)
midnight Mitternacht
might könnte(n); Gewalt, Macht
mile Meile
milk Milch
to mind; mind etwas ausmachen; Meinung, Gedanken, Verstand
mine Bergwerk
minute Minute
mirror Spiegel
Miss Fräulein
to miss vermissen, verfehlen, verpassen
mistake Fehler
to mix; mix mischen; Mischung
moment Augenblick
money Geld
month Monat
moon Mond
more mehr
morning Morgen
most meiste(r, s), die meisten

mother Mutter
mountain Berg
mouth Mund
to move bewegen, umziehen
movement Bewegung
Mr Herr (Anrede)
Mrs Frau (Anrede für eine verheiratete Frau)
Ms Frau (Anrede)
much viel
mum Mutter, Mama
music Musik
must müssen
must not nicht dürfen

N

to name; name benennen; Name
narrow eng
near nahe
nearby nahe gelegen
nearly fast, beinahe
necessary notwendig
to need; need brauchen, benötigen; Notwendigkeit
neighbour Nachbar(in)
neither … nor weder … noch
never nie(mals)
new neu
news Nachrichten, Neuigkeit
newspaper Zeitung
next nächste(r, s)
nice nett, schön, hübsch, gut
night Nacht
no kein(e); nein
no longer nicht mehr
no one niemand
nobody niemand
noise Lärm, Geräusch
noisy laut
noon Mittag
north Norden; nördlich, Nord-, nordwärts
nose Nase
not nicht
not either auch nicht
not even nicht einmal
not yet noch nicht
note Notiz
to note notieren
nothing nichts
to notice; notice bemerken; Aushang, Kenntnis, Beachtung
now jetzt
nowadays heutzutage
nowhere nirgendwo
number Zahl, Nummer, Anzahl
nurse Krankenschwester
nursery school teacher Erzieher(in)

O

o'clock Uhr (Zeitangabe)
ocean Meer, Ozean
of course natürlich
off von … weg, aus, weg
to offer; offer anbieten; Angebot
office Büro, Amt

307

Basic vocabulary

often oft, häufig
oil Öl
old alt
on time pünktlich
once einmal, einst
only nur, erst
to open; open öffnen; offen, geöffnet
opinion Meinung
opposite Gegensatz
or oder
to order; order bestellen, befehlen; Bestellung, Befehl, Reihenfolge
organization Organisation
to organize organisieren
other andere(r, s)
out of work arbeitslos
outside Außenseite; draußen, außerhalb
to own; own besitzen; eigene(r, s)
owner Eigentümer(in)

P

to pack; pack packen; Packung
packet Paket
page Seite
to paint; paint malen; Farbe
pair Paar
paper Papier
parent Elternteil
to park; park parken; Park
part Teil
to pass vorbeigehen, (Prüfung) bestehen, (ein Gesetz) verabschieden, zupassen
passenger Passagier(in), Fahrgast
passport Pass
past Vergangenheit
to pay, (paid, paid); pay (be)zahlen; Lohn, Bezahlung
peace Friede
pen Stift, Füller
pence Plural von Penny
pencil Bleistift
penny Penny (engl. Münze)
people Leute, Volk
per cent Prozent
perfect vollkommen, perfekt
perhaps vielleicht
period Periode, Zeitraum, Schulstunde
personal persönlich
petrol Benzin
to phone; phone anrufen, telefonieren; Telefon
photograph Foto
to pick pflücken, wählen
to pick up nehmen, aufheben
picture Bild
piece Stück
pipe Pfeife, Röhre
to place; place stellen, legen; Platz, Ort, Stelle
to plan; plan planen; Plan
plane Flugzeug
to plant; plant pflanzen; Pflanze, Fabrikanlage
plate Teller, Platte, Schild
platform Bahnsteig, Plattform

to play; play spielen; (Schau-)Spiel
player Spieler(in)
playground Spielplatz
please bitte
pleasure Vergnügen
pocket Tasche
to point; point zeigen; Punkt
police Polizei
policeman Polizist
policewoman Polizistin
political politisch
politician Politiker(in)
politics Politik
to pollute verschmutzen
polluted verschmutzt
pollution Umweltverschmutzung
poor arm
popular beliebt, populär
population Bevölkerung
port Hafen
possibility Möglichkeit
possible möglich
post office Post
postcard Postkarte
postman Briefträger, Postbote
pot Topf
potato Kartoffel
pound Pfund
power Kraft, Energie, Strom
power station Kraftwerk
practice Übung
to practise üben
to prefer vorziehen
to prepare vorbereiten
to present; present vorstellen; Geschenk, Gegenwart; anwesend, gegenwärtig
to press; press drücken, pressen; Presse
pretty hübsch, ziemlich
price Preis
pride Stolz
prize Preis, Gewinn
probable wahrscheinlich
to produce produzieren, herstellen
producer Hersteller(in), Produzent(in)
product Produkt
production Herstellung, Produktion
to profit; profit profitieren; Gewinn
profitable rentabel, einträglich, lohnend
programme Programm, Sendung
to promise; promise versprechen; Versprechen
to pronounce aussprechen
pronunciation Aussprache
to protect schützen
protection Schutz
proud stolz
pub Kneipe
public Öffentlichkeit; öffentlich
to pull ziehen
pupil Schüler(in)
purpose Zweck, Absicht
to push; push schieben, stoßen; Stoß
to put, (put, put) setzen, stellen, legen
to put on anziehen, auftragen, aufsetzen

to put up (Hand) heben, bauen, aufstellen

Q

quality Qualität
quantity Menge
quarter Viertel
queen Königin
question Frage
quick schnell
quiet ruhig
quite ganz, ziemlich

R

railway Eisenbahn
to rain; rain regnen; Regen
to raise (hoch)heben, erheben, großziehen
rather ziemlich
to reach erreichen
to read, (read, read) lesen
reader Leser(in)
ready fertig, bereit
real wirklich
reality Wirklichkeit
reason Grund
reasonable vernünftig, günstig
to receive erhalten, bekommen
recent jüngst, kürzlich
reception Empfang
receptionist im Empfang arbeitende Person
to record; record aufnehmen; Rekord, Aufnahme, Schallplatte
red rot
regular regelmäßig
relative Verwandte(r); relativ
to relax entspannen, sich erholen
to remain bleiben
to remember sich erinnern an, daran denken
to remind (of) erinnern an
to rent; rent mieten, vermieten; Miete
to repair; repair reparieren; Reparatur
to repeat; repeat wiederholen; Wiederholung
to replace ersetzen
to reply; reply antworten; Antwort
to report; report berichten; Bericht
reputation Ansehen, Ruf
to rescue; rescue retten; Rettung
to rest; rest ruhen; Rest, Ruhe
to result; result resultieren; Ergebnis
to return; return zurückkommen; Rückkehr, Rückgabe
rich reich
to ride, (rode, ridden); ride reiten, fahren; Ritt, Fahrt
right richtig, rechts
to ring, (rang, rung); ring klingeln, anrufen; Ring, Anruf
to rise, (rose, risen); rise (auf)steigen, zunehmen; Aufstieg, Zunahme
river Fluss
road Straße
roof Dach

Basic vocabulary

room Zimmer, Raum, Platz
round rund, herum
rubber (Radier-)Gummi
rubbish Abfall, Müll
to rule; rule herrschen; Regel
to run, (ran, run) laufen, rennen

S

sad traurig
safe sicher
safety Sicherheit
sale (Schluss-)Verkauf
salesman/woman Verkäufer(in)
salt Salz
same der-/die-/dasselbe, gleiche(r, s)
to save retten, sparen
to say, (said, said) sagen
school Schule
sea Meer
seat Sitz
second Sekunde; zweite(r, s)
secret Geheimnis; geheim
secretary Sekretär(in)
to see, (saw, seen) sehen, verstehen
to seem (er)scheinen
to sell, (sold, sold) verkaufen
seller Verkäufer(in)
to send, (sent, sent) schicken, senden
to sentence; sentence verurteilen; Satz, Urteil
serious ernst
to serve (be)dienen, servieren
to service; service (Auto) warten; Dienst, Betrieb
to set, (set, set) setzen, stellen, legen
several mehrere
shall sollen
to share; share teilen; Anteil
sheet Blatt, Bogen
shelf Regal
to shine, (shone, shone) scheinen, leuchten
to ship; ship verschicken; Schiff
shirt Hemd
shoe Schuh
shop Geschäft, Laden
shop assistant Verkäufer(in)
short kurz
should sollte(n)
shoulder Schulter
to shout rufen
to show, (showed, shown); show zeigen; Ausstellung, Vorstellung, Show
to shut, (shut, shut) schließen
sick krank
side Seite
sight Sicht, Anblick, Sehenswürdigkeit
to sign; sign unterschreiben; Zeichen
simple einfach
since seit
since then seitdem
to sing, (sang, sung) singen
sir Herr (Anrede)
sister Schwester
to sit, (sat, sat) sitzen

to sit down sich hinsetzen
size Größe
skill Fertigkeit, Fähigkeit, Können
skirt Rock
sky Himmel
to sleep, (slept, slept); sleep schlafen; Schlaf
slim schlank
slow langsam
to slow down verlangsamen
small klein
to smell, (smelt, smelt); smell riechen; Geruch
to smile; smile lächeln; Lächeln
to smoke; smoke rauchen; Rauch
to snow; snow schneien; Schnee
so far bisher, bis jetzt
soap Seife
soccer Fußball
sock Socke
soft weich
solution Lösung
to solve lösen
some einige, etwas
somebody jemand
someone jemand
something etwas
sometimes manchmal
son Sohn
song Lied
soon bald
sorry betrübt, tut mir Leid!, Entschuldigung!
to sound; sound klingen; Geräusch, Klang
south Süden; südlich, Süd-, südwärts
space Raum, Platz, Weltraum
spare time Freizeit
to speak, (spoke, spoken) sprechen
speaker Sprecher(in)
special besondere(r, s), spezielle(r, s)
speech Rede
speech bubble Sprechblase
to speed; speed schnell fahren; Geschwindigkeit
to speed up beschleunigen
to spell, (spelt, spelt); spell buchstabieren; Zauber(spruch)
to spend, (spent, spent) ausgeben, verbringen
spoon Löffel
spring Frühling, Quelle, Brunnen
staff Belegschaft, Kollegium
stamp Briefmarke
to stand, (stood, stood) stehen
to start; start anfangen, beginnen; Anfang
to state; state erklären, darlegen; Staat, Zustand
station Bahnhof
to stay bleiben
still dennoch, noch
stone Stein
to stop; stop beenden, anhalten, aufhören; Halt

to store; store lagern, speichern; (AE) Laden, Kaufhaus, Lager
storm Sturm
story Geschichte
strange merkwürdig
street Straße
to strike; strike streiken, schlagen; Streik, Treffer, Schlag
strong stark
to study; study studieren; Studium, Studie
subject Fach, Thema
suburb Vorort
to succeed (in) Erfolg haben (in, bei)
success Erfolg
successful erfolgreich
such solche(r, s)
sudden plötzliche(r, s)
sugar Zucker
to suit; suit passen; Anzug
suitcase Koffer
sum Summe
summer Sommer
sun Sonne
sunshine Sonnenschein
supermarket Supermarkt
supper Abendessen
to suppose annehmen, vermuten
sure sicher
to surprise; surprise überraschen; Überraschung
surprised überrascht
survey Überblick, Umfrage
sweet süß
to swim, (swam, swum) schwimmen
to switch; switch schalten, wechseln; Schalter

T

table Tisch, Tabelle
to take, (took, taken) nehmen
to take part in teilnehmen an
to take place stattfinden
to talk; talk reden, sprechen; Gespräch, Unterhaltung, Vortrag
tall hoch(gewachsen), groß
to taste; taste schmecken, probieren; Geschmack
tasty lecker
tax Steuer
tea Tee
to teach, (taught, taught) lehren, unterrichten
teacher Lehrer(in)
team Team, Mannschaft
technical technisch
technology Technik, Technologie
(tele)phone Telefon
television (TV) Fernsehen
to tell, (told, told) erzählen
terrible schrecklich, furchtbar
to test; test testen, überprüfen, untersuchen; Klassenarbeit, Versuch
than als
to thank danken, sich bedanken

309

Basic vocabulary

that dass; jene(r, s), welche(r, s)
then dann, damals
there dort, da
there is/are es gibt
therefore deshalb
these diese
these days heutzutage
thick dick
thin dünn
thing Ding, Sache
to think, (thought, thought) denken, glauben, meinen
thirsty durstig
this diese(r, s)
those diese, jene
though obwohl, trotzdem
thousand Tausend
through durch
to throw, (threw, thrown) werfen
thus so
ticket Fahr-, Eintrittskarte
tidy ordentlich, aufgeräumt
till bis
time Zeit, Zeitdauer, Uhrzeit
times Mal(e)
tired müde
tobacco Tabak
today heute
toe Zeh
together zusammen
toilet Toilette
tomato Tomate
tomorrow morgen
tongue Zunge
tonight heute Abend
too auch
tool Werkzeug
tooth, teeth Zahn, Zähne
top Spitze, Top, Oberteil
tour (Rund-)Reise, Tour
toward(s) in Richtung
tower Turm
town Stadt
toy Spielzeug
to trade (in); trade handeln (mit); Gewerbe, Handwerk, Handel
traditional traditionell, herkömmlich
traffic Verkehr
traffic light(s) Ampel
to train; train ausbilden, trainieren, eine Ausbildung machen; Zug
training Ausbildung, Training
to translate übersetzen
translation Übersetzung
to transport; transport transportieren; Transport
to travel reisen, fahren
tree Baum
trip (Kurz-)Reise
trouble Schwierigkeit(en)
trousers Hose
true wahr, richtig
truth Wahrheit
to try; try versuchen; Versuch

to turn (sich) drehen, wenden
to turn left/right links/rechts abbiegen
to turn on/off ein-/ausschalten
to turn over umdrehen, überschlagen
twice zweimal
type Art, Typ
typewriter Schreibmaschine
typical typisch
typist Schreibkraft

U

umbrella Schirm
uncle Onkel
to understand, (understood, understood) verstehen
unemployed arbeitslos
unemployment Arbeitslosigkeit
unfortunate unglücklich
unfortunately leider
unfriendly unfreundlich
unhappy unglücklich
university Universität
until (till) bis
upon auf
upstairs (nach) oben, im Obergeschoss
to use gebrauchen
used gebraucht, gewohnt
useful nützlich
useless nutzlos
usual gewöhnlich

V

vacation (AE) Ferien
van Lieferwagen
vegetable(s) Gemüse
vehicle Fahrzeug
very sehr
village Dorf
to visit; visit besuchen; Besuch
visitor Besucher(in)
vocabulary Wortschatz, Vokabelverzeichnis
voice Stimme
to vote; vote abstimmen, wählen; Abstimmung, Stimme

W

to wait warten
waiter Kellner
waitress Kellnerin
to wake, (woke, woken) (up) wecken, aufwachen
to walk; walk gehen; Spaziergang
wall Wand, Mauer
to want wollen
war Krieg
warehouse Lager
to warm; warm wärmen; warm
to warn warnen
to wash waschen
washing machine Waschmaschine
to waste; waste verschwenden; Abfall, Verschwendung
to watch; watch beobachten, sehen; Uhr
water Wasser

way Weg, Art und Weise
weak schwach
to wear, (wore, worn) (Kleidung) tragen
weather Wetter
week Woche
weekend Wochenende
weight Gewicht
to welcome; welcome willkommen heißen, begrüßen; Willkommen, Empfang
well gut, gesund; na ja …
well-known bekannt
west Westen, westlich, West-, westwärts
wet nass, feucht
what was
what about … was ist mit …
what else was noch
what … for wofür, wozu
wheel Rad
when wann
where wo
whether ob
which welche(r, s)
while während
white weiß
who wer
whole ganz
whom wem, wen
whose wessen
why warum
wide weit
wife (wives) Ehefrau(en)
will werden; Wille
to win, (won, won) gewinnen
window Fenster
wine Wein
to wish; wish wünschen; Wunsch
within innerhalb
without ohne
woman (women) Frau (Frauen)
wonderful wunderbar
wood Holz, Wald
wool Wolle
word Wort
to work; work arbeiten; Arbeit
worker Arbeiter(in)
world Welt
worse schlechter
worst am schlechtesten
worth wert
to write, (wrote, written) schreiben
writer Verfasser(in), Schriftsteller(in)
wrong falsch

Y

year Jahr
yellow gelb
yesterday gestern
yet jedoch, schon
you're welcome gern geschehen!
young jung
youth Jugend

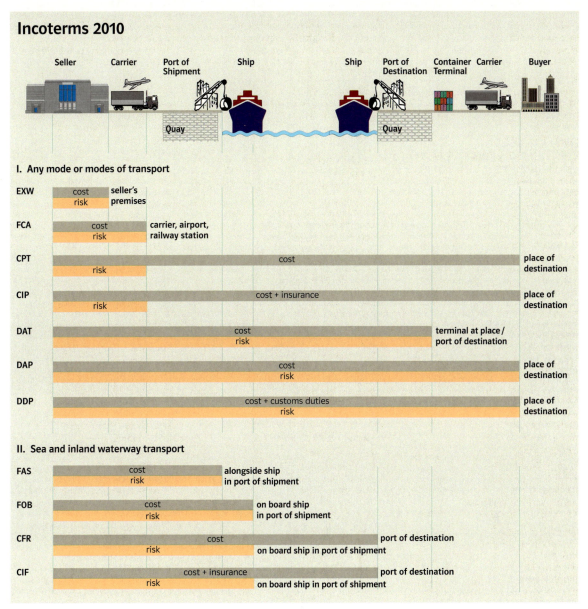

Bildquellennachweis

4 iStockphoto (Andrey Tsidvintsev), Calgary, Alberta; **4** Klett-Archiv, Stuttgart; **4** Avenue Images GmbH (stock disc), Hamburg; **5** Fotolia LLC (Olga Khoroshunova), New York; **5** Thinkstock (iStockphoto), München; **5** Thinkstock (Ryan McVay), München; **6** Thinkstock (Hemera), München; **6** Thinkstock (Digital Vision), München; **8** Thinkstock (Creatas Images), München; **8** Klett-Archiv (Alexandr Maximov), Stuttgart; **8** Avenue Images GmbH (Fancy), Hamburg; **8** laif (Ian Hanning/REA), Köln; **8** Dream Maker Software (RF), Colorado; **10** iStockphoto (René Mansi), Calgary, Alberta; **10** iStockphoto (Anastasia Pelikh), Calgary, Alberta; **10** JupiterImages photos.com (photos.com), Tucson, AZ; **10** iStockphoto (Anton Gvozdikov), Calgary, Alberta; **10** iStockphoto (Chris Bernard), Calgary, Alberta; **10** shutterstock (Lorraine Swanson), New York, NY; **11** iStockphoto (VMJones), Calgary, Alberta; **12** iStockphoto (Mehmet Salih), Calgary, Alberta; **12** Thinkstock (Digital Vision/Jack Hollingsworth), München; **14** iStockphoto (Sean Locke), Calgary, Alberta; **14** iStockphoto (Oleg Prikhodko), Calgary, Alberta; **15** Thinkstock (iStockphoto), München; **15** shutterstock (Baloncici), New York, NY; **15** Thinkstock (Photodisc), München; **15** Thinkstock (Polka Dot), München; **15** Getty Images RF (Digital Vision/Jochen Sand), München; **15** Fotolia LLC (CandyBoxPhoto), New York; **16** iStockphoto (Joris van Caspel), Calgary, Alberta; **16** shutterstock (Andy Lim), New York, NY; **16** Fotolia LLC (richard villalon), New York; **16** Fotolia LLC (endostock), New York; **16** shutterstock (Jason Stitt), New York, NY; **17** iStockphoto (Duncan Walker), Calgary, Alberta; **18** BigStockPhoto.com (starfotograf), Davis, CA; **20** iStockphoto (Adam Gregor), Calgary, Alberta; **21** shutterstock (Andresr), New York, NY; **22** iStockphoto (Jacob Wackerhausen), Calgary, Alberta; **22** Dreamstime LLC (Koh Sze Kiat), Brentwood, TN; **22** Fotolia LLC (AVAVA), New York; **22** shutterstock (Losevsky Pavel), New York, NY; **23** iStockphoto (nullplus), Calgary, Alberta; **23** iStockphoto (Neustockimages), Calgary, Alberta; **23** Thinkstock (Stockbyte), München; **24** Fotolia LLC (Yuri Arcurs), New York; **24** Fotolia LLC (Sandor Jackal), New York; **24** iStockphoto (Zsolt Nyulaszi), Calgary, Alberta; **25** Avenue Images GmbH (Image Source), Hamburg; **27** iStockphoto (VanDenEsker), Calgary, Alberta; **28** Fotolia LLC (mangostock), New York; **29** iStockphoto (RF/Alex Brosa), Calgary, Alberta; **30** iStockphoto (Olivier Blondeau), Calgary, Alberta; **30** iStockphoto (Can Balcioglu), Calgary, Alberta; **30** iStockphoto (Oks_Mit), Calgary, Alberta; **30** shutterstock (Maksim Shmeljov), New York, NY; **30** shutterstock (JustASC), New York, NY; **31** GREENPEACE, Hamburg; **33** Fotolia LLC (Joanna Zielinska), New York; **34** Thinkstock (iStockphoto), München; **35** Dreamstime LLC (Monkey Business Images), Brentwood, TN; **37** iStockphoto (Jorge Delgado), Calgary, Alberta; **37** iStockphoto (IndigoBetta), Calgary, Alberta; **37** iStockphoto (deanm1974), Calgary, Alberta; **38** iStockphoto (Andrey Tsidvintsev), Calgary, Alberta; **39** www.cartoonstock.com (ahun20), Bath; **39** www.cartoonstock.com (Slane, Chris), Bath; **39** BigStockPhoto.com (PCUMMINGS), Davis, CA; **39** www.cartoonstock.com (RUDI TAPPER), Bath; **40** Fotolia LLC (NMSI/Science Museum), Berlin; **40** iStockphoto (ricardoazoury), Calgary, Alberta; **40** shutterstock (Khafizov Ivan Harisovich), New York, NY; **40** Interfoto (Archiv Friedrich), München; **42** Wikimedia Foundation Inc. (PD), St. Petersburg FL; **43** Corbis (Eric Robert/Sygma), Düsseldorf; **44** iStockphoto (Morgan Lane Studios), Calgary, Alberta; **44** Fotolia LLC (nyul), New York; **45** iStockphoto (Robert Simon), Calgary, Alberta; **45** Fotolia LLC (kentoh), New York; **45** Thinkstock (Goodshoot/Jupiterimages), München; **46** Cagle Cartoons (Dave Granlund), Santa Barbara, CA; **46** shutterstock (Monkey Business Images), New York, NY; **47** iStockphoto (Sharon Meredith), Calgary, Alberta; **47** JupiterImages photos.com, Tucson, AZ; **47** Thinkstock (iStockphoto), München; **48** www.cartoonstock.com (Hawkins, Len), Bath; **48** www.cartoonstock.com (Eales, Stan), Bath; **48** www.cartoonstock.com (Baldwin, Mike), Bath; **50** iStockphoto (JasonRWarren), Calgary, Alberta; **51** Fotolia LLC (Michal Adamczyk), New York; **52** iStockphoto (Dan Barnes), Calgary, Alberta; **52** iStockphoto (Joanna Pecha), Calgary, Alberta; **54** Buy Nothing Day (www.buynothingday.co.uk), Yapton - Arundel - West Sussex; **54** Thinkstock (Hemera), München; **54** shutterstock (Losevsky Pavel), New York, NY; **55** iStockphoto (Sean Locke), Calgary, Alberta; **55** Fotolia LLC (Olga Khoroshunova), New York; **55** Klett-Archiv (Renate Weber), Stuttgart; **55** Fotolia LLC (BVDC), New York; **55** iStockphoto (Dan Chippendale), Calgary, Alberta; **56** iStockphoto (Hans F. Meier), Calgary, Alberta; **56** shutterstock (Colin Stitt), New York, NY; **56** shutterstock (ND Johnston), New York, NY; **56** Fotolia LLC (Otmar Smit), New York; **57** shutterstock (yvon52), New York, NY; **59** iStockphoto (Mostafa Hefni), Calgary, Alberta; **59** iStockphoto (Christopher O Driscoll), Calgary, Alberta; **60** iStockphoto (yvon52), Calgary, Alberta; **62** Thinkstock (Pixland/Jupiterimages), München; **63** www.cartoonstock.com (Love, Jason), Bath; **64** iStockphoto (John Hoffman), New York, NY; **64** laif (Sasse), Köln; **64** shutterstock (Fernando Rodrigues), New York, NY; **65** Fotolia LLC (pressmaster), New York; **66** Kessler-Medien, Saarbrücken; **66** Dreamstime LLC (Debra James), Brentwood, TN; **67** Fotolia LLC (Franz Pfluegl), New York; **68** shutterstock (Sharon K. Andrews), New York, NY; **68** Corbis (Pablo Corral V), Düsseldorf; **70** Fotolia LLC (Monkey Business), New York; **70** iStockphoto (RF/Celso Pupo Rodrigues), Calgary, Alberta; **72** shutterstock (Rafael Ramirez Lee), New York, NY; **72** iStockphoto (René Mansi), Calgary, Alberta; **72** shutterstock (Kevin Britland), New York, NY; **72** iStockphoto (Ana Abejon), Calgary, Alberta; **72** Dreamstime LLC (Nikhil Gangavane), Brentwood, TN; **73** iStockphoto (Miodrag Gajic), Calgary, Alberta; **73** Fotolia LLC (pressmaster), New York; **73** Fotolia LLC (kristian sekulic), New York; **74** iStockphoto (Andrew Rich), Calgary, Alberta; **75** shutterstock (Blazej Maksym), New York, NY; **75** iStockphoto (Jacom Stephens), Calgary, Alberta; **76** Dreamstime LLC (Zdravko Bajazek), Brentwood, TN; **76** Fotolia LLC (CROSS DESIGN), New York; **78** shutterstock (photo25th), New York, NY; **78** iStockphoto (Jessica Liu), Calgary, Alberta; **78** Picture-Alliance (dpa), Frankfurt; **78** TransFair e.V., Köln; **78** www.cartoonstock.com (Lynch, Mark), Bath; **79** Fotolia LLC (Andre Bonn), New York; **79** shutterstock (Olga Lyubkina), New York, NY; **79** iStockphoto (Dužan Zidar), Calgary, Alberta; **80** United Nations Photo Library, New York; **81** Geoatlas, Hendaye; **82** iStockphoto (Duncan Walker), Calgary, Alberta; **82** Fotolia LLC (Loic LE BRUSQ), New York; **83** Dreamstime LLC (Darren Robertson), Brentwood, TN; **83** shutterstock (Estelle), New York, NY; **84** iStockphoto (Joseph C. Justice Jr.), Calgary, Alberta; **84** Corbis (Patsy Lynch/Retna Ltd.), Düsseldorf; **84** iStockphoto (Lisa F. Young), Calgary, Alberta; **86** www.cartoonstock.com (RGJ -Richard Jolley), Bath; **87** Photographic service of the Council of the EU © European Communities; **88** Thinkstock (Creatas Images), München; **88** iStockphoto (Rich Legg), Calgary, Alberta; **88** iStockphoto (Martin McCarthy), Calgary, Alberta; **88** iStockphoto (Kimberly Cubero), Calgary, Alberta; **90** iStockphoto (Charlotte Allen), Calgary, Alberta; **90** iStockphoto (Dori OConnell), Calgary, Alberta; **90** iStockphoto (MARIA TOUTOUDAKI), Calgary, Alberta; **90** iStockphoto (Adam Kazmierski), Calgary, Alberta; **91** iStockphoto (Dmitriy Shironosov), Calgary, Alberta; **92** iStockphoto (Jeffrey Smith), Calgary, Alberta; **92** Thinkstock (Comstock), München; **92** shutterstock (Diego Cervo), New York, NY; **95** shutterstock (Keith Murphy), New York, NY; **96** Thinkstock (Digital Vision/Christopher Robbins), München; **96** Thinkstock (Stockbyte/George Doyle), München; **96** Fotolia LLC (nyul), New York; **100** Fotolia LLC (Jan Rose), New York; **100** iStockphoto (Angus Forbes), Calgary, Alberta; **100** iStockphoto (Marcus Lindström), Calgary, Alberta; **100** iStockphoto (Jan Rose), Calgary, Alberta; **101** iStockphoto (Timothy Large), Calgary, Alberta; **101** shutterstock (Vibrant Image Studio), New York, NY; **101** Dreamstime LLC (Kasiden), Brentwood, TN; **101** Fotosearch Stock Photography (Banana Stock), Waukesha, WI; **101** Thinkstock (Rayes), München; **102** Thinkstock (Goodshoot), München; **104** Thinkstock (Comstock), München; **104** Thinkstock (iStockphoto), München; **104** Imago (Niehoff), Berlin; **105** Thinkstock (iStockphoto), München; **108** Thinkstock (iStockphoto), München; **108** Thinkstock (Jupiterimages), München; **109** Thinkstock (Photos.com/Jupiterimages), München; **109** Thinkstock (AbleStock.com/Hemera Technologies), München; **109** Thinkstock (iStockphoto), München; **110** shutterstock (R-photos), New York, NY; **112** Thinkstock (Photodisc), München; **112** Fotolia LLC (WK), New York; **112** Thinkstock (BananaStock), München; **112** Thinkstock (Jupiterimages), München; **113** Thinkstock (William Bacon), Calgary, Alberta; **116** Thinkstock (Erik Snyder), München; **117** iStockphoto (vm), Calgary, Alberta; **117** Thinkstock (David De Lossy), München; **118** shutterstock (iofoto), New York, NY; **118** BigStockPhoto.com (Baloncici), Davis, CA; **120** Thinkstock (iStockphoto), München; **120** shutterstock (Sibear), New York, NY; **125** Thinkstock (Hemera), München; **125** Thinkstock (iStockphoto), München; **125** Thinkstock (Jupiterimages), München; **125** Thinkstock (BananaStock), München; **128** iStockphoto (runamock), Calgary, Alberta; **128** iStockphoto (kutay tanir), Calgary, Alberta; **128** shutterstock (JohnKwan), New York, NY; **128** Klett-Archiv, Stuttgart; **129** BBC Information and archives, London; **131** BBC Information and archives, London; **132** iStockphoto (Steve Debenport), Calgary, Alberta; **132** iStockphoto (Lisa Fletcher), Calgary, Alberta; **132** iStockphoto (Brasil2), Calgary, Alberta; **133** iStockphoto (davide chiarito), Calgary, Alberta; **133** Corbis (Paul A. Souder), Düsseldorf; **134** iStockphoto (Sebastian Santa), Calgary, Alberta; **134** iStockphoto (blackred), Calgary, Alberta; **136** Thinkstock (Hemera), München; **136** iStockphoto (NuStock), Calgary, Alberta; **136** iStockphoto (Sharon Meredith), Calgary, Alberta; **140** iStockphoto (Anna Milkova), Calgary, Alberta; **140** Thinkstock (Jupiterimages), München; **141** Thinkstock (Ryan McVay), München; **142** iStockphoto (Paulo Resende), Calgary, Alberta; **142** Fotolia LLC (Mat Hayward), New York; **144** BigStockPhoto.com (stvan4245), Davis, CA; **146** www.cartoonstock.com (Lynch, Mark), Bath; **146** Thinkstock (iStockphoto), München; **147** iStockphoto (Joshua Hodge Photography), Calgary, Alberta; **148** shutterstock (Mikhail Olykainen), New York, NY; **149** www.cartoonstock.com (Mosedale, Mike), Bath; **151** shutterstock (Phil Emmerson), New York, NY; **152** Corbis (James Leynse), Düsseldorf; **154** iStockphoto (Jerry McElroy), Calgary, Alberta; **154** www.cartoonstock.com (Fran), Bath; **154** www.cartoonstock.com (Lynch, Mark), Bath; **155** iStockphoto (gerenme), Calgary, Alberta; **155** shutterstock (Christian Darkin), New York, NY; **156** Fotolia LLC (Rob), New York; **158** www.cartoonstock.com (Bacall, Aaron), Bath; **158** Thinkstock (Digital Vision), München; **159** shutterstock (Ingrid Petitjean), New York, NY; **160** Getty Images (The Image Bank/Alan Thornton), München; **162** www.cartoonstock.com (Cordell, Tim), Bath; **162** www.cartoonstock.com (Martin, John), Bath; **162** www.flaggen-server.de; **163** Picture-Alliance (Photopqr/Ouest France/JM Niester), Frankfurt; **163** Thinkstock (Stockbyte), München; **164** TransFair e.V., Köln; **164** www.cartoonstock.com (Fran), Bath; **166** Ullstein Bild GmbH (Lineair/Ron Giling), Berlin; **167** Thinkstock (AbleStock.com/Hemera Technologies), München; **168** BBC Information and archives, London; **170** BBC Information and archives, London; **177** Avenue Images GmbH (Fancy), Hamburg; **177** Thinkstock (James Woodson), München; **177** Thinkstock (George Doyle), München; **178** Dreamstime LLC (Jeremyrichards), Brentwood, TN; **178** Thinkstock (Digital Vision), München; **180** iStockphoto (René Mansi), Calgary, Alberta; **182** iStockphoto (kzenon), Calgary, Alberta; **182** Thinkstock (Digital Vision), München; **184** iStockphoto (Justin Horrocks), Calgary, Alberta; **184** Thinkstock (Jupiterimages, Brand X Pictures), München; **188** Thinkstock (Jupiterimages), München; **188** Avenue Images GmbH (Fancy), Hamburg; **191** iStockphoto (Nigel Carse), Calgary, Alberta; **193** Thinkstock (iStockphoto), München; **195** iStockphoto (Aleksandar Nakic), Calgary, Alberta; **199** BigStockPhoto.com (Yuri_Arcurs), Davis, CA; **202** iStockphoto (blackred), Calgary, Alberta; **211** shutterstock (Jason Stitt), New York, NY; **213** iStockphoto (Rich Legg), Calgary, Alberta; **215** iStockphoto (lana13r), Calgary, Alberta; **217** Fotolia LLC (Robert Cocquyt), New York; **220** iStockphoto (Chris Schmidt), Calgary, Alberta; **222** Avenue Images GmbH (Fancy), Hamburg; **224** iStockphoto (Chris Schmidt), Calgary, Alberta; **226** Thinkstock (iStockphoto), München; **248** Klett-Archiv, Stuttgart; **311** iStockphoto (William Bacon), Calgary, Alberta; **COVER** Corbis RF (ImageShop), Düsseldorf; **COVER** Avenue Images GmbH (Jupiter Images), Hamburg

Sollte es in einem Einzelfall nicht gelungen sein, den korrekten Rechteinhaber ausfindig zu machen, so werden berechtigte Ansprüche selbstverständlich im Rahmen der üblichen Regelungen abgegolten.